Essay on the Origins
of the Technical Language
of Islamic Mysticism

Essay on the Origins of the Technical Language of Islamic Mysticism

BY

LOUIS MASSIGNON

TRANSLATED FROM THE FRENCH WITH AN INTRODUCTION BY

Benjamin Clark

FOREWORD BY

Herbert Mason

University of Notre Dame Press
Notre Dame, Indiana

Manufactured in the United States
Composition by Kelby and Teresa Bowers

Library of Congress Cataloging-in-Publication Data

Massignon, Louis, 1883–1962.
[Essai sur les origines du lexique technique de la mystique musulmane. English]
Essay on the origins of the technical language of Islamic mysticism / by Louis Massignon; translated by Benjamin Clark.
p. cm.
Includes bibliographical references and indexes.
ISBN 0-268-00928-7 (alk. paper)
1. Sufism. 2. Sufism — Terminology. 3. Arabic language — Terms and phrases. I. Title.
BP189.M3413 1997
297'.4'014 — dc20 93–40284
CIP

The paper used in this publication meets the minimum requirements of the American National Standard for Information Sciences — Permanence of Paper for Printed Library Materials, ANSI Z39.48-1984.

CONTENTS

TRANSLATOR'S NOTE ON TRANSLITERATION AND CONVENTIONS

Between the introductory pages (numbered with small Roman numerals) and the appendix (beginning on page 215), the translator and editor's voice does not intrude, except: (1) in footnotes marked by an asterisk rather than a number (e.g. p. 5, p. 19, p. 29); (2) within the author's footnotes (these being numbered consecutively within each of the five chapters), in square brackets (e.g. p. 13, note 1, p. 53 n 141); (3) occasionally, in the body of the text, when the comment is obviously editorial and the section of text is particularly footnote-like, in square brackets (e.g. p. 13, p. 33). In addition to the asterisks that mark the translator's notes, there are others in the main text of the book. These are Massignon's own indications, which have various purposes: e.g., to refer to the sections of the author's *Akhbār al-Ḥallāj* that are numbered *1, *2, *3, etc., as the bottom of p. 13, or to emphasize certain letters to the *jafr*, as on pp. 69–71. Where there is no footnote, the asterisk is Massignon's. The 1922 edition of the *Essai* also has starred pages, *1–*104, to which I refer on p. 215. The use of asterisks, square brackets and curly braces in the editorial sections at the end is explained under the appropriate section headings in the appendix and at the beginning of the bibliography.

A few Arabic words frequently used in English are given in their ordinary forms—Arab, emir, Mecca, Shiite, Sunni, and others—except, of course, in titles and transliterated Arabic phrases. The Arabic alphabet is represented according to the list below. I have not added final hamza where Massignon omits it, and I hope that most of the possible confusions on this account will be resolved by the distinction between ā and ä.

alif: hamza: a, i, u
    long: ā
    maqṣūra: ä
b, t, th, j, ch, ḥ, kh, d, dh, r, z, s, sh, ṣ, ḍ, ṭ, ẓ, ᶜ, gh, f, q, k (g), l, m, n, h, w (ū), y (ī)
hamza: ͻ
tanwīn: an, in, un

For those who do not understand the curious symbols: In Arabic, ʾ is a glottal stop, like a strong version of the beginning of "utterly," and ʿ is glottal fricative, hard to explain. The words in which these consonants occur may be expediently said to oneself in the modern Persian manner, in which both of the letters often simply mark either a change from one vowel to the next, with little besides the change itself to indicate that the consonant is there, or a slight lengthening of a syllable. Also, the "ś" in *iśvara* is pronounced like the English "sh."

The bibliography contains inconsistencies relative to this system, because of the desirability of exact transcription of the titles of certain books and articles published in Europe and India, when these titles were originally printed in Roman transliteration. In particular, ' and ' are sometimes substitutes for ʾ and ʿ.

ABBREVIATIONS

In this list, the abbreviation "s.n." refers the reader to the Bibliography, under the name given here. All references to the *Passion* cite the second edition and the English translation, unless otherwise indicated. These references usually take the form "*Passion*, Fr 3:218/Eng 3:206," meaning *Passion*, 2nd ed. (Paris, 1975), vol. 3, p. 218, corresponding to *Passion*, trans. Herbert Mason (Princeton, 1982), vol. 3, p. 206.

A = Aḥmad (in a name)
A, a = Abū (in a name)
A, Akhb, or Akhbar, s.n. Massignon
^{c}A = ^{c}Abd
^{c}AA = ^{c}Abdallah
AB = Abū Bakr
Aflākī = *Les Saints . . .*, s.n., Huart
afp = ancien fonds persan, Persian ms. Paris, Bibliothèque Nationale (v. Blochet's *Catalogue*)
Aghānī, s.n., Iṣbahānī, Abū'l-Faraj
ap. = *apud*, quoted from, as appearing in
^{c}AR = ^{c}Abd al-Rahmān
^{c}Atf, s.n., Daylamī
^{c}Aṭṭār (followed by a roman numeral), s.n., ^{c}Aṭṭār, *Tadhkira*, ed. Nicholson
^{c}Awārif, s.n., Suhrawardī
^{c}Ayn, s.n., al-Khalīl b. Aḥmad

b = ibn
Bahja, s.n., Shaṭṭanawfī
Baqli (followed by a roman numeral) = *Tafsīr*, Cawnpore lithograph
Bayan, s.n., Jāḥiẓ
bib. = bibliography
BIFAO = *Bulletin de l'Institut Français d'Archéologie Orientale*, Cairo
Book of the Dove, s.n., Bar Hebraeus
G. Budé = *Lettres d'humanité* of the Association Guillaume Budé

c. = *circa*, approximately
cf. = *confer*, compare
ch. = chapter
Chr. = Christian

D = *Dīwān al-Ḥallāj*, s.n., Ḥallāj
DI = *Der Islam*
Dove, s.n., Bar Hebraeus

E = *Essay* (*Essai*), s.n., Massignon
ed. = editor, edited, edition
e.g. = *exempli gratia*, for example
EI = *Encyclopaedia of Islam*
EI2 = *Encyclopaedia of Islam*, 2nd ed.
Eng = English, especially in references to the *Passion*

Farq, s.n., Baghdādī
fihr = *Fihrist*, s.n., Ibn al-Nadīm
Firaq, s.n., Nawbakhtī
firdaws, s.n., Wahrānī
Fr = French, especially in notes to the *Passion*
Fut, *Futūḥāt*, s.n., Ibn ^{c}Arabī

G.A.L., s.n., Brockelmann
gr. = grammar

Ḥanbal, s.n., Ibn Ḥanbal, *Musnad*
Ḥazm, s.n., Ibn Ḥazm, *Fiṣal*
Hebr. = Hebrew
Hujwīrī, *kashf*, s.n., Hujwīrī, trans. Nicholson

Ibid. = *ibidem*, in the same place
Ibn al-Athīr = *Kāmil fi'l-ta$^{\supset}$rikh*
Ibn al-Fāriḍ = *tā$^{\supset}$iyya* (= *Naẓm al-sulūk*)
IFAO = Institut Français d'Archéologie Orientale
ikmāl, s.n., Ibn Bābūya
in = concerning, in
^{c}*Iqd*, s.n., Ibn ^{c}Abd Rabbihi
iṣāba, some clues suggest Sakhāwī or Suyūṭī rather than Ibn Ḥajar
I^{c}tidāl, s.n., Dhahabī

Jamhara, s.n., Ibn Durayd
Jāmī = *Nafaḥāt al-uns*
JAOS = *Journal of the American Oriental Society*
JAP = *Journal Asiatique* (Paris)
JRAS(B) = *Journal of the Royal Asiatic Society* (Bombay)

k. = *kitāb*
Ka^{c}bī, see ch. I n I
Kal. = Kalābādhī, *Ta^{c}arruf*
Kashf, s.n., Hujwīrī, trans. Nicholson
Khaṭīb = *Ta$^{\supset}$rīkh Baghdād*

l. = line
Lisān = *Lisān al-^{c}arab*, s.n., Ibn Manẓūr
LM = Louis Massignon
Luma^{c}, s.n., Sarrāj

M = Muḥammad
Madārij, s.n., Ibn Qayyim
majm = *majmū^{c}*
ms., mss. = manuscript(s)
Mukhaṣṣaṣ, s.n., Ibn Sīda
Murūj, s.n., Mas^{c}ūdī

MW = *Moslem World* (later, *Muslim World*)

n = note
no., nos. = number(s)

OLZ = *Orientalistische Literaturzeitung*
OM = *Opera Minora*, s.n., Massignon
opp. = "as opposed to," "in a doublet with," or "in some way comparable to"

P. = Paris
P = *Passion*, s.n., Massignon (see also above, explanation of references to the *Passion*)
p, pp = page(s)
Passion, s.n., Massignon

QA = Qāḍī^{c}askar Mulla Murad ms.
Qāmūs, s.n., Fīrūzābādī
Quatre textes, s.n., Massignon
Qush = Qushayrī, *Risāla*
Quṣṣaṣ, s.n., Ibn al-Jawzī
Qut. = Ibn Qutayba

Recueil = *Recueil de textes inédits*, s.n., Massignon
REI, *Rev. Et. Isl.* = *Revue des études islamiques*
rem = reminder
RHR = *Revue de l'histoire des religions*
RMM = *Revue du monde musulman*

s.a. = *sub anno* (*annis*), under the year(s)
S.A. = Shahīd ^{c}Alī mss., Istanbul
Sh. Ṭab = Sha^{c}rāwī, *Ṭabaqāt*
Siḥāḥ, s.n., Jawharī
Sīra Ḥalabiyya, s.n., Ḥalabī
s.n. = *sub nomine*, under the name (in this list, see bib., under the name given here)
Stb, s.n., Sulamī, *Ṭabaqāt*
Stf, s.n., Sulamī, *Tafsir*
Sulamī = *Ḥaqā$^{\supset}$iq al-tafsīr*
s.v. = *sub verbo*, under the word

Tagr, Tagrib = s.n., Ibn Taghrībirdī, *Nujūm*
Tanbīh, s.n., Mas^{c}ūdī
Ṭarā$^{\supset}$iq, s.n., Ma^{c}ṣūm ^{c}Alī Shāh
Ṭaw = *Ṭawāsīn,* s.n., Hallāj (1913)
trans. = translator, translated, translation
Tusy's List = *List of Shia Books,* s.n. Ṭūsī

v. = *vide,* see
var. = variant
v.i. = *vide infra,* see below
v.s. = *vide supra,* see above

Wüst. = Wüstenfeld
WZKM = *Wiener Zeitschrift für die Kunde des Morgenlandes*

Yāq., Yāqūt, = Yāqūt's *Mu^{c}jam al-udabā*
Yoga, s.n., Patañjali
Yq. = Ya^{c}ūb
Yq. = Yāqūt's *Mu^{c}jam al-buldān*

Zak. = Zakariyā
ZDMG = *Zeitschrift der deutschen morgenländischen Gesellschaft*

FOREWORD TO THE ENGLISH TRANSLATION

In 1991 *Les Amis de Louis Massignon,* a group constituted informally in Paris following the distinguished orientalist's death in 1962, and including members of his family, scholars, writers, and diplomats, established the *Institut de Recherches Louis Massignon* in association with the Musée des Sciences de l'Homme. French and foreign scholars were appointed as *directeurs d'Etudes* and the process of identifying qualified researchers and raising money for fellowships and publishing subventions was begun. The intent of the Institut was and is to continue and extend the research of Louis Massignon along the lines of his various scholarly and spiritual interests and beyond to a further assessment of the primary sources that formed the basis of his investigations begun with intensity in 1907 into the civilization, religion, and particularly the mystical tradition of Islam. As Louis Massignon was also a Catholic thinker and close friend and correspondent of Jacques Maritain, Teilhard de Chardin, Paul Claudel, François Mauriac, and others of his faith and time, his special significance as an ecumenicist places him apart from his distinguished contemporaries and is a major line of inquiry supported by the Institut.

The pattern of forming a group of "Friends" of a famous scholar or author following his or her death is a familiar one in France. It is a somber assemblage that usually performs a rite of cultural embalming whose fluid is nostalgia and whose monument to the newly deceased "immortal" erodes away over time with the deaths of the devoted. The psychology of this impulse to bury and preserve intact is a recurring theme in French and in particular Parisian history, a kind of underground Gallic necrological manifest destiny, but one that Louis Massignon himself described and would have summarily dismissed for himself. For though thoroughly French, he was also paradoxically a completely expatriated mind. It must be said to their credit, however, that these "Friends" felt duty-bound to adhere to their friend's unconventional wishes, even if such ran counter to their own thematic impulse. Their sense of duty and their grasp of the thought and drive of Louis Massignon led them to the establishment of an institute that would inevitably wrest the future from their hands.

Louis Massignon (1883–1962) was a combination of a brilliant linguist, prolific author, man of action, ambassador-at-large, adventurer, scientist, poet, mystic, and radical humanitarian. He was both deeply French and deeply any thing other than French. To many Muslims he was a profound Muslim, to his Catholic co-religionists he was a devout revert to the faith of his origins (he was in fact a Franciscan tertiary and in 1950, at age 67, he became a Melkite priest, though he was married with grown children). He was a man of dramatic contrasts and apparent contradictions who some who knew him partially believed never reconciled his parts. But those who knew him well recognized in him a mystery resolved interiorly by his sense of transcendent unity that is, however, inadequately understood by either personal memoirs or so-called objective studies.

Several attempts at capturing his life and thought have appeared in recent years, some in the form of doctoral theses, some as heavily documented biographies, some as impressionistic novels, some as brief evocative homages, and these in several languages, including Arabic, Persian, German, French, Italian, and English. More are announced as forthcoming and eventually a provisional portrait of merit will appear — this of a man who did not like to have his photograph taken but who also never concealed anything about his life from anyone. The Western impulse to arrive at a definitive study will always be delusional and erroneous.

It is not the intent of the Institut, in any case, to focus on Massignon himself but on those sources he helped discover and make known; and further, on a critical assessment of his work that may even contradict some of his conclusions. And finally, the intent is to extend the bridge between civilizations he strengthened by his remarkable spirit and scholarship.

The present volume is the first in a series of envisioned updatings, translations, and editions. It is his seminal *thèse supplémentaire, Essai sur les origines du lexique technique de la mystique musulmane,* presented along with his magnum opus, *La Passion d'al-Hallaj,*[1] for his Doctorat d'Etat at the Sorbonne, defended after World War I and first published in complete form in 1922. These two works were the basis for his appointment to the chair in Muslim sociology at the Collège de France and established his international reputation as a pioneering scholar of the first magnitude. It was his choice to approach something far larger but less known to his countrymen than French literature and to penetrate beyond the European literary concept of "the orient." However, his passion to understand the world of Islam at its source in the Qurʾān and through the direct experiences and testimonials of those pious traditionalist, yet radical ascetic and mystic,

1. *The Passion of al-Hallaj,* Bollingen Series XCVIII, 4 vols., (Princeton, Princeton University Press, 1982).

practitioners of the faith also came to refresh his knowledge and appreciation of his own kindred tradition and faith. From this passionately made choice he bequeathed twelve books and four large volumes of shorter studies on numerous cross-cultural subjects based meticulously on devotion to primary sources.

It is fortunate for the English-speaking world that America and Britain have produced in recent years a crop of gifted young scholars and translators with similar passions to understand Islamic civilization, religion, and particularly mysticism through its sources and firsthand accounts, in the Massignon spirit if not in the direct line of his own variety of interests and methodological approach. Benjamin Clark is one such scholar-translator who is a serious student of Arabic, fluent in French, and skilled in Persian, learned beyond his years in both literatures, and has found in Massignon's lexical approach to Islamic thought and tradition a guide pointing him in further directions of research he had already chosen and for which he is exceptionally well prepared. He has done an excellent job, not only of translating Massignon's often difficult prose style, but also in editing the text in light of Massignon's own and of other scholars' subsequent additions and corrections, while remaining true to his author's scholarly intent, form, and values.

The reader will be reminded by chapter 1 that Massignon's *Essay* was written originally as a doctoral thesis, not as a book for the educated but general reader. Subsequent chapters, resting necessarily on the methodology of chapter 1, will however prove both philosophically and lyrically rewarding to the general reader who persists and finds his or her own growing passion to understand.

Herbert Mason

TRANSLATOR'S ACKNOWLEDGMENTS

For support of this translation I am grateful to Daniel Massignon and the Institut de Recherches Louis Massignon; to Jon Westling, Executive Vice-President and Provost, Boston University; and to the University Professors of Boston University. Too many to thank have read sections of the manuscript and saved me from errors: I owe the most to Laura Hayes, David Reisman, Merlin Swartz, Rosanna Warren, and Jeannette Morgenroth. The staff of the Interlibrary Loan Service of Mugar Memorial Library made the bibliography and corrections possible. Herbert Mason encouraged and oversaw the whole project. He has been Louis Massignon's *rāwī* and my *shaykh*.

TRANSLATOR'S INTRODUCTION

Louis Massignon's *Essay on the Origins of the Technical Language of Islamic Mysticism* is the classic survey of the first three centuries of Islamic mysticism, or Sufism. It is also a treatise shaped to make two major points, both of them radical in their day: first, that Sufism is based on the Qurʾān and innate to Islam, not imported from outside; and, second, that Ḥallāj (d. 922) was the culmination of the mystical movement up to his time, not a break with the past and a foreshadowing of what Massignon and others saw as the later decline of integrity and humility among the Sufis. The *Essay* achieves, by its focus on the formation of the language of one figure, a remarkable mix of concentration and breadth.

The first of the arguments, for Sufism as a natural development of Islam, is made mostly in the first third of the book, through chapter three. This section is elliptical and full of lists of words. To read it without consulting the library of primary texts to which it refers is to skim it. The author attempts to provide the record of the sources for his claims, and he consequently gives a good sense of the difficulties in verifying them. It may be tempting to skip to the beginning of the fourth chapter, which summarizes what goes before. In that place, Massignon's discussion of the Qurʾān,[1] recapitulated and augmented, comes at the beginning of a story with more immediate rewards for the reader. The fourth and fifth chapters, the latter two-thirds of the book, benefit from the movement of history, through the mystics' lives in Kūfa, Baṣra, Syria, Khurāsān, and Baghdād. Large extracts from their writings are the substance of a compelling narrative.

I recommend against moving too hastily through the first part of the *Essay*. While it is possible to go lightly over the lists of words and names, it is extremely desirable to get at least a glimpse of the argument, as it treats possible and actual influence on Sufism from other Semitic cultures, Greece, Iran, and India. The comparison to Hinduism is still provocative. The general conclusions in chapter three — on ceremony, dogma, *ḥadīth*, Khiḍr, and the *abdāl*, among other things — are important.

1. Which "Muḥammad *did not make*" (herein, ch. 4 n 28); i.e., it is the word of God. Massignon was the first of the Western orientalists to treat the Qurʾān with reverence in this manner.

For those who are already, or will now become, convinced that it is worthwhile to read the original texts, I have the following advice. The short list of books to assemble in order to follow the material includes, first and foremost, a Qurʾān,[2] and, then, Massignon's editions of Ḥallāj's *Akhbār* (3rd ed., 1957), *Ṭawāsīn* (1913), and *Dīwān* (1931 or 1955).[3]

A copy of the *Essai* in French would be valuable for its supplement of Ḥallājian texts, especially the excerpts from Sulamī's *Ḥaqāʾiq al-tafsīr*. These are not reprinted here, and, while I have given some indications of where the texts may be found in new editions, many are still available only in manuscript (see below, Appendix). Even those that now exist in printed versions, which are easier to read than Massignon's handwriting, are useful because they are together in one place. The index that constitutes chapter 1 is limited without this supplement, its usable references then being only to the published works or the French editions of the *Essai*.

For the history of Sufism beyond Ḥallāj, Massignon's *Recueil de textes inédits* (1929) supplies the originals (mostly Arabic) of the excerpts translated in chapters 4 and 5. His *Muḥaḍarāt*, or lectures on philosophical language, outline some of the intellectual context of Ḥallāj's thought.[4] European-Islamic equivalents are particularly useful or suggestive and will clarify many difficult points in the *Essay*.

Notes referring to the *Akhbār* have had to be updated to correspond to the 3rd edition of 1957;[5] those referring to the *Passion d'al-Ḥallāj*, to both the 2nd edition and the English translation. These appear in the form, "*Passion*, Fr 3:218/Eng 3:206," which would mean *Passion*, 2nd ed. (Paris, 1975), vol. 3, p. 218, corresponding to *Passion* (Princeton, 1982), vol. 3, p. 206. When variants relative to the first edition are significant, they are noted. References to manuscripts have been left as they were, and those to other printed works as well, except where a page number or other such indication was corrected. The one exception is Goldziher's *Vorlesungen*: because Massignon already refers to the French translation rather than to the original, the notes here are to the recent English version. In a further effort

2. Most readers will need the table of conversion from Flügel's edition to the Egyptian text, in *Bell's Introduction* (see Bibliography, s.n., Watt).

3. The text refers to Massignon's editions, for the sake of homogeneity. There have been others of the *Ṭawāsīn* and *Dīwān* (see Bibliography, s.n., Nwyia and Ḥallāj, for details), which are of course to be consulted. The *Dīwāns* of 1931 and 1955 are identical, except that the later one contains a useful supplement.

4. These were given in Arabic, in Cairo, in 1912–13, and edited recently. They have not yet received much attention because they were unpublished for so long. Massignon wrote that they were the first of the three parts (the other two being the *Passion* and the *Essay*) of his investigation into Ḥallāj's mystical language (*Passion* Fr 1:16–17/Eng 1:lii—see the next paragraph for the form of notes like this). A fourth part now available is the collection of Ḥallājian articles in Massignon's *Opera Minora*, II, 9–342.

5. The second edition (1936) will suffice if absolutely necessary for most of the Arabic, insofar as the numbering system is identical.

to make the *Essay* more usable, each chapter's *addenda* from the 1954 edition, as well as all *corrigenda,* have been incorporated into the text and notes. Most references to time (e.g. "in the past seventy years") are relative to 1922, and any apparent anachronisms are in the later material. A bibliography has been added.

The difficulties with the text are only the beginning. The humblest teachings can be the hardest to put into practice, and Massignon demands of his readers not only careful study but that, at least in the mind, to whatever extent possible, they try the experiments of the mystics on themselves. If a reader wants to take the *Essay* provisionally as his guide, this experience begins with meditation upon the words marking the history of Sufism. Whether he was reading Arabic or writing French, Massignon kept in mind the *istinbāṭ* of difficult words, the "chewing" and "swallowing" that the mystics practiced in order to assimilate Qurʾānic terms into their lives.[6] The index at the end of this volume, and in the *Passion* and *Muḥāḍarāt,* will locate his own relevant remarks on Arabic technical terms. A brief discussion is required here, about both Arabic and French words, and about the English approximations that have been found for them.

Shaṭḥ[7] (lit., "overflowing": "ecstatic" or "enigmatic" language, "inspired paradox") is the first and most significant of these terms. The *Passion* and *Essai* of 1922 treat it differently as the sense changes in context. In the second editions of the two works, all new mentions of *shaṭḥ* are accompanied by the translation, *locution théopathique.*[8] This expression, rendered as "theopathic locution" in English, is often used by others with little sense of its meaning as an equivalent of *shaṭḥ.*

Théopathique is not in the French dictionaries of Robert or Littré. Carl Ernst discusses Massignon's treatment of *shaṭḥ* and gives references, for the English "theopathetic" and "theopathic," to Evelyn Underhill's *Mysticism* (1911) and William James's *Varieties of Religious Experience* (1902).[9] The *Oxford English Dictionary* cites the "creedless theopathy" of the "Sufi school, the 'Methodists of the East'" (1881), and "the theopathic and contemplative quietism of the East" (1899).[10] These quotations are crucial clues to the doctrine contained in *locution théopathique.* It seems reasonable to suppose that

6. The word *istinbāṭ* means literally "finding the source of running water." Nicholson translates it, in a manner typically divergent from Massignon's, as "intuitive deduction."

7. For Massignon the defining characteristic and "crucial symptom" of Islamic mysticism.

8. In the *Essay,* the mentions of *locution théopathique* from the *addenda* of 1954 are incorporated as ch. 3, notes 69 and 81.

9. *Words,* p. 134 (and *passim* for *shaṭḥ* in general). Note that James's use is eccentric in the English history of the word. Ernst also mentions the use of *locución* by St. John of the Cross, of whom Massignon was no doubt thinking is some way when he wrote *locution.*

10. Both from the same periodical. Henry Martyn is the orientalist authority given for the first quotation.

Massignon was aware of writers of English in the nineteenth century who were using "theopathy" and "theopathic" in discussions of Sufism. He was against assuming any necessary link between theopathy (suffering the influence of God) and quietism. In the English language, since the eighteenth century, there had been mentions of "theopathetic" affections or emotion. Underhill's "theopathetic mystics," who, he says, are often inarticulate,[11] are those passive with respect to God, active with respect to men.[12]

Islamic mystics in the highest form of *shaṭḥ* were given not inarticulate feeling but speech, which they often used in their public teachings and sermons. They received true *shaṭḥ*, as Massignon saw it, sometimes in ecstasy, always in a "theopathetic" state. This word has a more appropriate history in English than "theopathic," but the latter is to be preferred because of Massignon's emphasis on mysticism's medicinal worth in society. He intends to make a comparison to "homeopathic," with attention to the difference between events caused naturally and those caused by God's intervention. Perhaps he was expecting an informed reader to be aware that *théopathique* usually referred to a theopathetic state, not to speech. "Speech" or "sayings" is better than the stilted "locution." Not all of the theopathetic states of mystics have led to *shaṭḥ*, nor are all attested phenomena called *shaṭḥ* true theopathic speech. Massignon naturally concentrated on instances he supposed to be authentic. For cases of "*shaṭḥ*" in general, the works of other historians are to be consulted.

Another difficult French word is *apotropéen*. It had existed previously, but Massignon practically recoined it, developing a theme from Huysmans, the decadent writer turned Catholic. The "apotropaic saints" are defenders from harm, protectors ready to be substituted for others and suffer in their place. The doctrine of mystical substitution is at the heart of Massignon's work. His discussion of Islam always returns to the voluntaristic mystics who put the possibility of providential benefit for the community and direct experience of God's love before their own safety and personality.

The French words, *dogme, doctrine, grâce, expérience,* and *conscience* are noteworthy. Massignon's refusal to use the first two in a pejorative sense challenges a prejudice held as much among scholars of mysticism as in Republican France and modern Protestant countries. Dogmas have sometimes been founded on or influenced by the experience of the mystics. A softer but etymologically sound translation, such as "teaching," would have been untrue to the original.

11. *Mysticism* (London: Methuen, 1977), 514.

12. Ruysbroeck is particularly significant to both Massignon and Underhill (*Mysticism*, 210). Underhill's first use of "theopathetic" is in reference to ʿAṭṭār (ibid., 157) and is relevant, but the full discussion of theopathy is on the medieval Christian mystics (514 ff.).

Massignon uses *grâce* as the translation of several Arabic words,[13] in contexts where other French expressions are possible. In only some of these instances is the English "grace" correct. In the French, the "grace" of doctrine seems less removed from ordinary life and writing, because *grâce* also means "thanks," "charm," and "favor."

Expérimental becomes "experimental" rather than "experiential," which would connote too much passivity. The experience of the mystics, as Massignon describes it, was passive only at its highest point, after many difficult, voluntary preparations.[14] "Mystical experimentation" was an active trial upon the self, preceding ministry to others. Massignon's vocabulary is intentionally medical and scientific, in accord with many of the Arabic authors.

Conscience is inevitably divided into "conscience" and either "consciousness" or "awareness." The distinction in English specifies something tactfully veiled in the French word, though rarely softened in Massignon's argument: consciousness is common to pagans and Muslims, but it is the monotheists who examine their conscience. He was as hostile as the Qurʾān itself to *shirk*, polytheism,[15] and though possessing a flexible, ecumenical mind, he was free of anachronistic relativism.

Massignon's own personal proclivities defined an area of study for him, as they do for any scholar, and, with a frankness always rare in academics, he did not attempt to hide them. He had a decided interest in schools of Islamic thought that made mystical experience a support of Qurʾānic orthodoxy.[16] As his secretary and bibliographer Youakim Moubarac wrote, ". . . we have opted for the narrow but orthodox way of Islamic mysticism, as much against the dominant legalism of Islam as against esoterism."[17] Massignon was full of Christian feeling, but he did much to discredit the assertions of other Christian scholars of Islam who had read influence into every apparent likeness between mystics in the two traditions. The *Essay* emphasizes Sufism's originality.[18] Massignon thought that the similarities between the careers of Ḥallāj and Jesus, upon which many Muslims have commented, were not an imitation but a real parallel, a conformity effected by God. Readers stirred or disturbed by the vigor of his history of the polemic about Qurʾān 57:27 and the Prophetic tradition *lā rahbāniyya* (herein, ch. 4, sec. 1. B.), concerning the ascetic and eremetic life in Islam, should notice that his argument is in its substance no more than a report

13. *Niʿma, luṭf, shukr,* and others.

14. In one place (*Passion,* Fr 1:29 / Eng 1:lxv) Massignon translates *théopathie* into Arabic as *ikhlāṣ.*

15. See especially ch. 2, sec. 3. E., herein.

16. See herein, ch. 4, sec. 5. A.

17. *L'Islam et le dialogue Islamo-chrétien.* Pentalogie, 3, p. 132.

18. E.g., ch. 4 n 201.

of some early exegetes' opinions. His interpretations of scripture are based on Islamic tradition.

No reader can escape the signs tht Massignon had a vibrant inner life, and numerous disciples have tried to elucidate it.[19] Its relationship to his research is complex, and it will be useful to describe some aspects of the context, which has grown very distant, in which the *Essay* was written.

In the France of the first and second decades of this century, rhetoric about religion was in a high temper. Massignon, after an overwhelming religious experience in 1908, developed a fervent and eccentric Catholicism. The *bien-pensant* Christianity of the day is part of the unfriendly background of all of his work on Ḥallāj's death. In 1903 Léon Bloy described the milieu in this way: "Among those in appearance least foreign to the divine, among the most pious Catholics, ignorance is now so complete, and hearts so abased, that Sanctity seems a superlative of Virtue.... No one seems to remember that sanctity is the supernatural Favor that so separates one man from all other men that it seems to alter his nature."[20]

Massignon wished to convince readers of the efficacy of the suffering of the martyrs. One of the principles of the *Passion,* he would state looking back, was that true sanctity was "necessarily excessive, excentric, abnormal and shocking."[21] Many years before, he concluded his first article on Ḥallāj in a different, but not dissonant tone: "The idea of sacrifice is eternally beautiful. The example of a heroic sacrifice never loses its force; its memory does not die."[22] Only in appearance is this ideal of heroic suffering difficult to reconcile with the *Essay's* traditionalism. The author's investigations of the earlier, more conservative mystics are rings around the "flaming target" of Ḥallāj's death.

Massignon's sources convinced him that Ḥallāj was one of the "real elite" of history, a saint who had become in the Islamic Community, like Joan of Arc in France, "a factor in the survival of society and a leaven of immortality."[23] Massignon was not the only Frenchman of the period during and after the Dreyfus Affair (1894–1906 and beyond) to write on martyrs who had precipitated crises of conscience. Saint Joan was a favorite. Contemporary works on her are in a range from Anatole France's skeptical

19. Most systematically, Jacques Waardenburg, in *L'Islam dans le miroir de l'occident,* where Massignon is treated with all the thoroughness of phenomenology, along with four other orientalists: Goldziher, Snouck-Hurgronje, Becker, and Macdonald. The best account of Massignon's significance among some Christians is the life by Giulio Bassetti-Sani, *Louis Massignon: Christian Ecumenist.*

20. From *Les Dernières colonnes de l'église.* Reproduced in *Oeuvres de Léon Bloy,* vol. 4 (Paris: Mercure de France, 1965), 263. See *Passion,* Fr 1:27/ Eng 1:1xiii, on Bloy.

21. In the preface to the new edition, *Passion,* Fr 1:31/Eng 1:Lxvi.

22. *OM,* II, p. 17. The article is "La Passion d'al-Halladj et l'ordre des Halladjiyyah," in *Mélanges Hartwig Derenbourg* (Paris, 1909).

23. *Passion,* Fr 1:44/Eng 1:3.

biography, a handbook of anticlericalism,[24] to the Catholic mystery plays of the Dreyfusard Charles Péguy.[25] To take Dreyfus's side was often in part—not as often as one would like—to take a stand against antisemitism. The *Essay* and *Passion* defend, with a forcefulness verging on polemic, a point of view both semitic and profoundly Catholic: their decisive argument against the theory that Islamic mysticism was of Iranian, that is, Aryan, origin, is the part that stands out as a particularly just and admirable product of its time.[26]

The theory can be, and was, embraced for reasons that do not necessarily make an antisemite. It seemed at least plausible to those for whom Persian mystical lyric and didactic verse were the primary means of understanding Sufism. Lovely as some of these later poems are, they contain unreliable accounts of the mystics' lives in the tenth century and before. The theory did not withstand the exegesis of the early mystics' Arabic writings. Massignon was an exegete, an establisher and interpreter of old, inspired texts, though he lived in a time when even the word *exégèse* ("exegesis") was frequently applied to any sort of commentary on religious or general culture. Péguy wrote in 1911, against this considerable trend in contemporary usage, that exegesis was or was supposed to be only scientific.[27] It had simply not been performed on these texts, at least not by Westerners. Presenters of pseudo-evidence, abetted by an impressionistic response to poetry that had seemed to favor their views, had been allowed to rule the minds of the orientalists.

For many people, Massignon removed a critical blind spot towards an aspect of the semitic tradition. On the other hand, it was perhaps out of a blindness in himself that, in spite of his great affection for Aṭṭār and certain other poets, he dismissed Persian poetry in general as the fabrication of excessive sensualists. He thought that Persian, like all of its Indo-European cousins, including French, was an idolatrous language, friendlier than Hebrew, Aramaic, and Arabic to paganism and the vanity of esthetes. The *Essay* is not a treatise on literature, and Massignon's opinion will not necessarily prejudice lovers of Persian poetry against him. A reader's enjoyment may even be enhanced by the information provided here about the early figures to whom the poets allude and who first developed Sufism's universal allegories. Individual witness always interested Massignon more than any system of thought. He deplores certain tendencies in mysticism that he as-

24. *Vie de Jeanne d'Arc* (Paris, 1908).

25. Like Massignon, Péguy turned to Christianity in 1908. He had also written on her before that year.

26. V.i., ch. 2, sec. 3. A.

27. He was responding to a reviewer who had called Anatole France's work "pious and secular exegeses": "On avait cru jusqu'ici qu'il n'y avait qu'une exégèse, et qu'elle était, ou qu'elle prétendait être *scientifique*." In Péguy, *Oeuvres en prose, 1909–1914* (Paris, 1961), 898.

sociates with poetry and the arts, but the achievements of some artists moved him. Though the Arabic poet Ibn al-Fāriḍ uses commonplaces associated with Ibn ᶜArabī, Massignon could distinguish the poet's "burning lyric" from the gnostic's "calculated, icy symbolism."[28] Massignon was undeniably more sensitive to Arabic than to Persian. Is it not possible that Jalāl al-Dīn Rūmī is more like Ibn al-Fāriḍ than like the members of the Bektashi order with whom the *Essay* unflatteringly lumps him?

The question of how to build on Massignon's work and diverge from it has been very fruitful for scholars over the years. He himself, at the same time that he was breaking with nineteenth-century notions about Sufism, kept continuity with the earlier works that would endure, the critical editions of Arabic texts.

His own students have been able to build on both his editions and his insights. He was a discoverer in a large field of inquiry, and they have worked to correct omissions and mistakes. Fathers Gardet and Anawati, following Joseph Maréchal and Jacques Maritain, have systematized his general view of Islamic mysticism, from the viewpoint of Catholic theology. Paul Nwyia has sought to find mystics before Ḥallāj who were bolder than Massignon thought, or later figures, dismissed with their contemporaries as decadent, who ought to be valued highly by Massignon's own standard. Nwyia especially has continued the work of hunting through old manuscripts for a mystical language at grips with the real, with life itself. In a different direction, Henri Laoust and George Makdisi have taken Massignon's remarks on Ḥanbalism as the indication of a rich area in which to do original research. Another student, Henry Corbin, pursued the neognostic branch of Sufism and has had a great influence on the study of the mystics in France, America, and elsewhere.

It was Massignon who put the old edition of Suhrawardī's *Ḥikmat al-ishrāq* in Corbin's hands,[29] setting him on a track that would lead to Ibn ᶜArabī. Corbin tried to respect his teacher's ideas on early mysticism while simultaneously casting a favorable light upon the later period. This shift is as fundamental as Massignon's own correction of earlier scholars' views of Sufism as a whole. Corbin saw Ibn ᶜArabī's philosophy as an accurate description of mystical experience like that of Ḥallāj, and as a metaphysical innovation of the highest order.

Scholars of Sufism are often divided by favorable or unfavorable views of Ibn ᶜArabī.[30] The factions tend to pursue their research independently, and the debate between them, in spite of its potential richness, is moribund. In-

28. Following Nallino: *RMM*, vol. 44–45 (Apr.-June 1921): 309.

29. *Présence de Louis Massignon*, ed. D. Massignon, 56–57, article by H. Nasr.

30. There is a balanced summary of both sides of this argument in Annemarie Schimmel's *Mystical Dimensions*, 259–74.

stead of replying to the substance of Massignon's critique,[31] scholars, when disputing his views, often argue only against "existential monism," the expression that he eventually found as a translation of the traditional name of Ibn ᶜArabī's school, *waḥdat al-wujūd.* Like *locution théopathique, monisme existentiel* is inadequate to sum up a number of perceptive descriptions and arguments. As jargon, the term merits criticism, but if one's attack is on a bit of jargon alone, it is wasted effort. Those who treat Massignon like a scholastic manualizer do a disservice to their own arguments, as they fail to engage his. In his early articles he uses the word "monism" more flexibly: in the *Muḥaḍarāt,* it alone is his version of both *waḥdat al-wujūd* and *waḥdat al-adyān* (unity of all systems of ritual practice).[32] Some scholars claim that because Ibn ᶜArabī did not affirm substantial continuity between God and creatures, "existential monism" is a bad translation for *waḥdat al-wujūd.* This conclusion does not follow. In an article of 1912, Massignon describes the *wujūdī* reinterpretation of Ḥallāj's "I am the Truth" as "an abstract modification based on the monist idea of the *a priori* unity of Being"[33] (≠ continuity of substance). A full argument on this point would be welcome. In the end, some will decide, with Annemarie Schimmel and Seyyed Hossein Nasr, that for the chosen saints there must simply be two ways to knowledge of God, the practical and the contemplative. In any case, even if we agree that a systematization of early Sufi doctrine[34] is desirable, Massignon's first writings on the subject present a powerful case that Ibn ᶜArabī did not succeed in making one. Massignon's argument has been ignored by some of those who do not like its conclusions, but it has not yet been refuted.

Ibn ᶜArabī's enthusiasts tend to make the whole debate esoteric. They celebrate the source of the word *wujūd* in the verb *wajada,* "to find," but they tend to write as if the derivation somehow guarantees that Islamic discussions of *wujūd* will have greater vigor than anything about "existence" in the West. If the root sense of *existere,* "to stand forth," is taken into account, as it is by lively philosophers, Western "existence" need be no less satisfying in itself than its Islamic counterpart. The Wujūdīs tend to speak dismissively of Western philosophy, proceeding as if it were coterminous with modern nominalism. They would convince many skeptics if they could reply, for example, to the *Passion*'s chapters on doctrine.

For Massignon, the decline of Sufism is commensurable with neoplatonic encroachment of the life of Islam.[35] He thought that neoplatonism

31. Which is supported by those within the Islamic tradition, like ᶜAlāʾ al-Dawla Simnānī, who have criticized Ibn ᶜArabī. For more critical interpretations of Simnānī, see Bibliography, s.n. Landolt, Molé.

32. See *Muḥaḍarât,* p. 149, on "monism" among Westerners.

33. Fr. *être,* which can also mean "existence": *wujūd* in any case. *OM,* II, p. 37.

34. E.g., the one sketched in the *Passion,* vol. 3.

35. "Qarmathianism" is often used by him to signify Hellenistic syncretism as combined with ᶜAlid loyalties in Islam. See sympathetic researches in his article, "Ḳarmaṭians," in *EI*1, and his

was a sign of decay, not specifically Greek, arising whenever a society had passed its zenith.[36] But although any neoplatonist myths replacing religion are anathema to him, he quotes Plato sympathetically in the *Essay*. There is nothing anti-intellectual in his lament of the rift between the philosophical appreciation of mystical experience and the strenuous efforts of ascetics, after the twelfth century.[37] Like Muḥāsibī, Massignon was not a philosopher but knew enough philosophy to use the arguments of the rationalists against them. His active life of faith has been a touchstone for more systematic intellectuals. In having that kind of influence he has become like Kierkegaard, with whom he shared an intense Christian humility and a knack for public religious protest that critics called histrionic. He wanted to live, like Charles de Foucauld, under the sign and according to the pact of Abraham, the guiding light to the anguished in Kierkegaard's famous eulogy.

The link through Abraham between Christianity and Islam appears in much orientalist writing as a hackneyed commonplace. In Massignon it was not manufactured affinity but living root, manifest in Arabic language and prayer. In the preface to the *Essay*, in order to define an aspect of that common ground, he quotes Christian Snouck-Hurgronje on the "interreligional" quality of Islamic mysticism. This neologism (in French as in English) is used because the attested words of related meaning would have tended toward syncretism, would have hinted at Islam's resemblance to other religions in the realm of ideas, at an indistinct, common search for the One. Snouck and Massignon are describing the example of devotion that gave the Muslim missionaries the power to make Indian and Malaysian converts to Islam.

Massignon held fast to the idea that it was not enough for the religious to savor the sweets of intellectual ecstasy in private, for an elite circle. He maintained that the analysis of mystical texts had to be kept in balance by an examination of the authors' effects upon disciples and society as a whole. A few years before the *Essay* was written, William James had made much the same point by quoting the Sermon on the Mount ("By their fruits ye shall know them") to the effect that mystics could not be judged in isolation.[38] Even Emile Durkheim would have had to agree. But in in-

---

bibliographies collected in *OM* I p. 627–66. Throughout the *Essay*, this loose usage must be kept in mind. Ivanow calls it an erroneous *pars pro toto* (*Guide*, 1), and perhaps "Ismailism" would have been better.

36. There are tantalizingly brief but compelling remarks on this subject in "L'experience mystique et les modes de stylisation littéraire," in *OM*, II, p. 374–75.

37. See Massignon's "Avicenne, philosophe, a-t-il été aussi un mystique?" (1954) *OM*, II, p. 466–69; trans. as "Was Avicenna, the Philosopher, also a Mystic?" in *Testimonies and Reflections*, 111–15.

38. *The Varieties of Religious Experience*, Lecture 1 (Reprint Harmondsworth: Penguin, 1982), 20.

NOTE [1922]

To my comrades of the
56th regiment of colonial infantry
fallen in the Levant
1916–1917

With one hand, take the cane (of exile)
That guides those who weep,
And, with the other, in the hearth of pain
Light your torch

Niyāzī, *Dīwān*, 3rd *qāfiyya*

The manuscript of the first half of this work had just been submitted, in early August, 1914, to the Istas Press at Louvain, when the printing house was burned in the fire set by German troops on the twenty-sixth of that month.

After seven very busy years, I have been able to reconstitute the part that had been destroyed; and to revise it, filling gaps noticed by Mr. Casanova in 1914 and responding to Dr. Snouck-Hurgronje's valuable observations.

The research for this essay was done principally from manuscript sources not used until now, and it is entirely original. Particular emphasis is placed on two psychological biographies, of Ḥasan Baṣrī and Muḥāsibī.

Louis Massignon

NOTICE TO THE SECOND EDITION [1954]

In 1922 this *Essay* presented the public with a French translation of a group of archaic Islamic mystical texts (of the first three centuries) from unpublished manuscripts, most of them not readily available. These documents made it possible to examine how Islam had produced what was later called Sufism.

The Arabic originals, published in 1929 in my *Recueil de textes inédits concernant l'histoire de la mystique en pays d'Islam,* can now be consulted. A concordance between the *Essay* and the *Recueil* is therefore given below.

Readers are still without an edition of Sulamī's *Ṭabaqāt al-Ṣūfiyya* (one by Johs. Pedersen was supposed to follow my *Recueil* in the same series),* but they can now consult the monumental *Finery of the Saints* (*Ḥilyat al-awliyā*) of Abū Nu^caym Isfahānī, published from 1932 to 1938 in ten volumes, in Cairo. A comparison of that work with the criticisms of the behavior of the "saints" in Ibn al-Jawzī's *Talbīs* (Cairo, 1923) will demonstrate the lasting interest of my initial perspectives.

No comprehensive work has yet taken up my program of terminological and psychological inquiry of 1922.

On the other hand, there has been quite a large number of valuable monographs, to be indicated below, on several of the mystical authors remarked upon here.[1]

It seemed worthwhile to rework and complete the text of my *Essay* of 1922, which was long out of print. The new edition includes a recast first chapter on the Ḥallajian lexicon, with an added section on the lexicon's formation; *addenda* to the other chapters (supplementing the *errata* of the first edition); additions to the Arabic supplement; and two updated indexes.

*The *Recueil* was vol. 1 of *Collection de textes inédits relatifs à la mystique musulmane.* Pederson's edition was finally published, in 1960, by another house (Leiden, E. J. Brill). Contrary to what Massignon says, there was a Cairene edition of 1953.

1. I thank the editors of this Collection [Etienne Gilson and Louis Gardet] for planning a third edition of the *Akhbār al-Ḥallāj* [1957], one of the most characteristic, and most difficult to find, of such monographs.

NOTICE TO THE SECOND EDITION

CONCORDANCE [OF TRANSLATED PASSAGES IN THE *Essay* AND THEIR ARABIC ORIGINALS IN THE *Recueil de textes inédits*]

The following is a concordance of translated passages in the *Essay* and their Arabic originals in the *Recueil de textes inédits,* ed. Massignon, 1929. Criticism and corrections of the *Recueil* by August Fischer, Hussein Wahitaki, and Louis Massignon are in *Islamica* V, 1932. Selected texts are translated in Joseph Schacht's *Der Islam** (Tübingen, Mohr, 1931), pp. 87–128. A new Arab printing is cited by Moustaphe Abderraziq in the Cairene periodical *Ma^{c}rifa,* 1931, nos. 1–2.**

Author	*Essay*	*Recueil*
Ḥasan Baṣrī	E 125–135	Rec. 1–5
^{c}Abdalwāḥid ibn Zayd	E 148	Rec. 5
Rābi^{c}a and Rabāḥ	E 149–152	Rec. 6–9
Wakī^{c}	E ch 4 n 490	Rec. 9
Shaqīq	E 173	Rec. 10
Muslim Khawwāṣ	E ch 2 n 1	Rec. 10
^{c}Abdak	E 79, 105	Rec. 11
A. ibn ^{c}Āṣim Anṭaki	E 155–156	Rec. 12–14
Dhū'l-Nūn	E 143–147	Rec. 115–17
Burjulānī	E 52	Rec. 14
Muḥāsibī	E 101, 164ff.	Rec. 17–23
Ibn Karrām	E 174ff.	Rec. 24–25
Yaḥyā Rāzī	E 180–181	Rec. 26–27
A.Y. Bisṭāmī	E 184ff.	Rec. 27–33
Ḥ. Tirmidhī	E 195ff.	Rec. 33–39, 253–254
Sahl Tustarī	E 200–203	Rec. 29–42 and Sālimiyya
A.S. Kharrāz	E 204–205	Rec. 42–43
Junayd	E 208	Rec. 51
Ibn ^{c}Aṭā	E 209	Rec. 54
A.B. Wāsiṭī	E ch 4 n 15	Rec. 73
Naṣrābādhi	E ch 3 n 70	Rec. 84
M. Ghazālī	E ch 2 n 49	Rec. 94
A. Ghazālī	E ch 4 n 132 and n 484	Rec. 97
Ṭ. Maqdisī	E 81	Rec. 225

*The *Essai*, all editions, cites the periodical *Der Islam*, an error repeated in P *1695u*.
**See bib., s.n. ^{c}Abd al-Rāziq.

PREFACE

To Hartwig Derenbourg

The basis of this study is the lexical inventory of one author, Ḥallāj. The main supporting texts are reproduced in an appendix;* they are very brief, condensed fragments, meant to shed light on certain technical terms as used in experimental definitions.

We know that the Arab grammarians (*ᶜAyn, Jamhara, Ṣiḥāḥ*; then *Mukhaṣṣaṣ, Lisān al-ᶜarab, Qāmūs*) made their general catalogue of the classical Arabic language by referring only to pure literature, above all poetry, preferably the earliest poems. The illustrative examples, *shawāhid*, are from the Bedouin poets of the Arabian desert, none later than the third century A.H. All of civilization is therefore excluded from the standard dictionaries: all technical terms or *iṣṭilāḥāt* (grammar, *ḥadīth*, law, sciences) in general, and all mystical terms in particular. The conservative and anti-intellectualist viewpoint of these Near-Eastern philologists[1] survives in Dozy, although he acknowledges its inconveniences. It is appropriate that his *Supplément* to the Arabic dictionaries should be heterogeneous and full of gaps, but it deliberately rules out selected categories of technical terms. "I would fear to become disoriented," he says in his preface,[2] "if I were to plunge into the study of certain classes of words; into the labyrinthine terminology of the Sufis, for example. That is a task I happily leave to others."

At first it is tempting to follow his example: the Arabic vocabulary and style of the Muslim mystics give an impression of paradoxically individual "speaking in tongues." But by closely studying their language, especially by tracing it back towards its origins, we discover unmistakable signs of a fundamental intellectual achievement deserving our full interest. It was the first attempt to interiorize[3] the Qurʾānic vocabulary and to integrate it into

*See *Essai*, 2nd ed., pp. 336–449.

1. Necessarily held also by their Western colleagues. We are told with whom Malherbe studied the French of his time and among which subjects our dialectologists go to make their representative sound recordings. The personal interpolation of the subject is thus reduced to a minimum.

2. P. xi.

3. The word is Goldziher's (*Vorlesungen über den Islam* [Eng. trans., *Introduction to Islamic Theology and Law*, Andras and Ruth Hamori, Princeton, Princeton University Press, 1981, 147, where the reader will find not "interiorization" but "spiritual experience." Massignon refers to F. Arin's French translation of the *Vorlesungen*; the notes here refer to the recent English version]).

ritual practice. The mystics were the first to appropriate the Arabic idiom[4] for a system of psychological introspection, and therefore a moral theology. They made the earliest outline of a critical lexicon for philosophical questions.

By 1745, this achievement had been perceived in part by the Indian Tahānuwī, who put some Islamic "scientific technical terms," including the most important mystical vocabulary, into his admirable *Kashshāf.*[5] by 1845, two of Dozy's contemporaries, Flügel and Sprenger, showed they had understood completely, when they published three lexicons devoted entirely to mysticism, Flügel for Ibn ᶜArabī and Jurjānī, Sprenger for ᶜAbd al-Razzāq Kāshānī.

In the past seventy years, orientalist studies of Islamic mysticism's technical terminology have multiplied.[6] There are three tendencies or methods.

The first method, analytical and paleographic, is to publish the most comprehensive lexicons of Near-Eastern origin that can be found; there are some compilations by early but minor writers, and others by noted syncretists but well after the early period. This method was introduced by Flügel, then borrowed by Nicholson.[7] Its advantage is the immediate "enrichment" of our stock of documents. But richness of lexicography, though it is the great virtue in a general dictionary, is secondary in a particular discipline, where the doctrinal homogeneity of the collected materials comes first. The desired quality cannot be produced by this method. And neither Flügel nor Nicholson edited the essential collection, by far the richest in the genre, Sulamī's *Ḥaqāᵓiq al-tafsīr,* and Baqlī's new edition of it.[8]

The second method, synthetic and biographical, is an "indirect" study of technical terms through a critique of the dogmatic structure of the systems in which they occur. Enormous philosophical erudition is required. Asin Palacios was able to treat Ghazālī's dogma in this way; Carra de Vaux, the *ishrāq* of Suhrawardī Ḥalabī.[9] The method's flaw is an excessive reliance, in the manner of Islam's last great universal historians, on a peremptory classification of doctrines into stereotyped categories defined by biased polemicists. In the last twenty years, we have given too much credit to the heresiographers and critics of a certain school of literalist *ahl al-ḥadīth,* the *a priori* anti-mystic Ḥashwiyya, such as Ibn Saᶜd, Ibn Ḥazm, Ibn

4. There is as yet no comprehensive study of the parallel Western phenomenon, "mystical Latin" (as Huysmans and Rémy de Gourmont prefer to call what should be called "church Latin"); a comparison of these two "consecrated languages" would be fruitful.

5. Ed. Sprenger. Before Tahānuwī other non-Arab Muslims, in this case Persian (Āmulī, for example) and Ottoman encyclopedists and lexicographers, had collected materials.

6. See my own *Bibliographie hallagienne* (*Passion,* ch. 15 nos. 1639, 1665, 1670, 1671, 1685, 1689, 1692, 1708, 1729, 1736, [same numbers in all editions, French and English, of the *Passion*]).

7. Who critically edited or translated Sarrāj and Hujwīrī.

8. *ᶜArāᵓis al-bayān,* lithographed in India.

9. And Nyberg, Ibn ᶜArabī.

al-Jawzī, Ibn Taymiyya, and Dhahabī. They argue with a clarity that can be seductive, but their interpretation of doctrine, and especially of terminology,[10] very often betrays the unthinking haste of polemic.

Thirdly, the scholar may work slowly and patiently to exhaust his sources and build homogeneous lexicons, one for each author. In 1908, August Fischer recommended this method for the preparation of a scientific dictionary of Arabic, with direct quotations from serious editions of texts (*Muᶜallaqāt, Mufaḍḍaliyāt, Ḥamāsatayn,* Ḥarīrī, etc.) to be examined by a team of scholars. The method (which, when applied to poets, has proved fertile by making it easier to distinguish *spuria* from *authentica* in their *dīwāns*) is indispensable for mystic authors. The only way to understand how they formed their vocabulary is to juxtapose the development of their writings and the progessive stages of their careers. I have used this method here. It was necessary to choose a highly developed case, a model author whose originality is clearly demonstrated in history. Early Islam offered Muḥāsibī, Ḥallāj, and Ghazālī (with, to a lesser extent, Ghazālī's model, Abū Ṭālib Makkī). I chose Ḥallāj, because he makes the clearest, most theoretical, and most practical exposition of mysticism's crucial symptom, the experimental phenomenon of *shaṭḥ,* which is the sign of transforming union and the exchange of wills.

It is dangerous to minimize the role of the mystical lexicon in the development of Islamic dogma. The mysticism of Islam is what has made it an international and universal religion. International, through the proselytizing work of mystics visiting infidel countries: the persuasive example of Muslim hermits, as well as that of the Chishtiyya, Shaṭṭāriyya, and Naqshbandiyya sheikhs who learned the local dialects and mingled with the people, did much more than the tyrannical fanaticism of conquerors speaking foreign languages to convert so many Indians and Malays to Islam.[11] Universal, because the mystics were the first to understand the existence and moral efficacy of *al-ḥanīfiyya,* the rational monotheism natural to all men.[12] The result was Muḥāsibī's and Ibn Karrām's apostolic universalism, followed, in a later, degenerate form, by the theosophical syncretism of Ibn ᶜArabī, Jalāl Rūmī, and the Bektāshīs. Snouck-Hurgronje makes the point strongly:[13] "Through its mysticism Islam has found the means to rise to a height from which it can see farther than its own, severely limited horizon . . . in it there is something *interreligional.*"

10. Ibn al-Jawzī on *makr* (*Passion,* Fr. 3:51 n 2/Eng 3:43 n 121); Dhahabī on *fārigh min al-dunyā wa'l-ākhira* (*Passion,* Fr 2:57 n 4/Eng 2:48 n 166).

11. Note the very different percentages of Muslims in Behar and Bengal, both subjugated politically during the same period (Arnold, *Preaching of Islam,* s.v.).

12. *Passion,* Fr 3:116/Eng 3:105.

13. *Politique musulmane de la Hollande,* in *RMM* (1911) 446, 448 (= 70, 72 of the offprint).

On the other hand, we must not reduce mysticism to its formal esthetic. It is not merely an exercise of the speculative imagination, refining on the subtlety of terms. The sonorous chains of rare words in a text such as the "Letter from Junayd to Yaḥyā Rāzī"[14] are nothing but the variations of a virtuoso amusing himself. As for the instances of alliteration in Ḥallāj's *Ṭawāsīn,* I have argued elsewhere that such sequences follow long, fully reasoned passages because of the need to free the mind from the previous discursive effort and to clear the way for meditation.[15] Excessively frequent usage of willfully obscure, esoteric terms[16] is the mark of the decadence heralded by Ibn ᶜArabī's school. Early Islam's great mystics acted otherwise.

Sufism, which "enlivened" Islam (as Ghazālī, the author of the *Iḥyā,* is the last, in his *Munqidh,* to have explained satisfactorily), was a method of thorough introspection, of making use *ab intra* of all of life's events, fortunate or unfortunate. It was ritual experimentation with pain, and it transformed those loyal enough to persevere to the end into physicians, to whom others could then go for treatment. As Muḥāsibī[17] said, "In the light of the divine Wisdom, they cast their eyes toward the lands where remedies[18] grow. After God had taught them how to work the cure by healing their own hearts, He commanded them to comfort those who suffer..." Sufism is more than simple nomenclature or pharmaceutical prescriptions. It is therapy that the attending physician has tried on himself, to allow others to benefit. "Sufism," said Nūrī, "is neither a group of texts nor a system of speculative knowledge, it is customs," i.e., a way of living, a rule. Junayd said to Jurayrī, "We did not learn Sufism by listening to those who say this or that, but by enduring hunger, renouncing the world, severing ourselves from what is familiar and delightful to us."[19]

The social importance of Islamic mysticism comes precisely from this source, from its alleged worth as a medical treatment. Were its masters able, as they claimed, to extract from the wells of their inner lives the means to "heal the pain of men's hearts," to dress the wounds of a community torn by the vices of unworthy members? Our only way to verify the reality that was the goal of the Islamic mystics' experiments is to probe their social consequences, to examine the mystical rules' value and effec-

14. Sarrāj, *Lumaᶜ,* 358. [The "letter" is also available in Ali Hassan Abdel-Kader's *Life, Personality, and Writing of al-Junayd,* E. J. W. Gibb Mem. Series, new series XXII, London, 1962, 2 (Arabic section) and 123 (in translation).] Nor is there any point in wasting time on kabbalism, which is only a degeneration of intelligible symbols (figured phrases, *dawāᵓir*) transformed into objects of superstition "and made a trap for fools" [in English in the original].

15. *Passion,* Fr 3:358–59/Eng 3:340–41.

16. The only tolerable catechistic precaution is the one suggesting silence under deceitful and hypocritical interrogation.

17 *Maḥabba.*

18. He means simple medicinal herbs.

19. [*Recueil,* p. 51]; Hujwīrī, *Kashf,* 42; Qush, 22, Tagrib, II, 178 (cf. John 19:13).

tiveness in curing the body of society. We must not allow our curiosity to become absorbed by those sudden, strange flights of the intelligence into abstract ecstacy, where certain mystics boast, in their solitude, of forgetting in God to have pity for men.

The enduring power of Islamic mysticism is not in the haughty, morose isolation in which Majdhūb proclaims:[20] "Bury your secret in the earth, seventy cubits down./And let all creatures moan until the Last Judgment."

The power is in the superhuman desire for sacrifice for the sake of one's brothers; in the martyr's transcendent ecstasy sung by Ḥallāj:[21] "Forgive them, and do not forgive me ... Since You are consuming my humanity in Your divinity, by what Your divinity owes to my humanity, I ask You to be merciful to these, who have worked to bring about my death."

20. Ap. Ibn ᶜAjība, *Futūḥāt*, I, 46.

21. *Passion*, Fr 1:649–50, 3:231/Eng 1:599–600, 3:219 [book 3, ch. 20 of *Mirṣād al-ᶜibād* of Najm al-Dīn Rāzī (d. 654/1256)].

1

THE LEXICON

1. Alphabetical List of Mystical Technical Terms Taken from the Works of al-Ḥallāj

The terms are given in Arabic alphabetical order, according to their roots. Initials refer to the sources indicated below.[1] The Arabic numerals refer to the numbering systems in texts published either previously (T, A) or, in an appendix, herein [in the *Essay*, 1st and 2nd Fr eds.] (S, B, R, K, C, J, G, Y, H, M, W); a Roman numeral following the letter T indicates the number of the chapter in the *Ṭawāsīn*.

The senses of these terms can be consulted in translation through the indexes of my two works (P, E).[2] It is useful to compare the meanings intended in the uses from the following list to the definitions suggested for 143 terms by Sarrāj (*Lumaᶜ*, 333–74), for 106 terms by Hujwīrī (*Kashf*, 367–

1. A = *Akhbār al-Ḥallāj* (2nd ed., 1936) [references are not always to the 2nd ed; some are to the first *Akhbār*. When the listed number is followed by a number in parentheses, the former is that of the main numbering system in both the 2nd and 3rd (1957) ed. of the *Akhbār*, and the latter is the number LM gives, which usually corresponds to the one in the 1st ed. An asterisk before a number means that it is in the *mulḥaq*, supplement. The *Akhbār's* index of technical terms (3rd ed., 129–37) further specifies the references given here.] B = Baqlī, *tafsīr* (the page numbers refer to the Berlin manuscript, the volume numbers to the Cawnpore lithograph). Bāk = Ibn Bākūya, *Bidāya* (*Quatre textes*, II). C = Baqlī, *Shaṭḥiyāt* (page number alone refers to the Shahīd ᶜAlī manuscript; page number with recto or verso, to the Qāḍīᶜaskar Mullā Murād ms.). D = *Dīwān*, nos., ed. 1931 [in general, in the French, Roman numerals after "D" are for *qaṣīdas*, Arabic numerals for *muqaṭṭaᶜāt*. As there are also some page numbers mixed in, I have added "Q." and "M." and "p." where appropriate. When I could not find the word, I have left Massignon's numbers as they appear in the original]. Fānī = *Sharḥ khuṭba*. G = Sulamī, *Ghalaṭāt*. H = Kirmānī. J = Sulamī, *Jawāmiᶜ*. K = Kalābādhī, *Taᶜarruf*. *Kashf* = Hujwīrī. Kaᶜbī = Kaᶜbī, *Manāqib*. Khark. = Khargūshī, *Tahdhīb*. M = Munāwī. Q = Qushayrī. R = *Riwāyāt al-Ḥallāj*. S = Sulamī, *Tafsīr*. T = *Ṭawāsīn*, ed. 1913. U = list of the works of Ḥallāj (in the *Fihrist*, p. 192). W = ᶜAṭṭār, *Tadhkira*. Yazd = Ibn Yazdānyār, *Rawḍa*. Z = Sulamī, *ṭabaqāt* [trans. herein, ch. 5, sec. 6. Perhaps the numbers LM gives for Z are those of a manuscript he owned. I have placed them in parentheses. The main numbers given here are those of ch. 5, sec. 6. The Arabic word may be found easily through a comparison of the translation with Pedersen's ed., 308–13. The Arabic letters following the main numbers are the *abjad* section indication in the corresponding (almost identical) text in the *Akhbār*, *1. Other indications (e.g., ᶜAṭṭār, ᶜ*Aṭf*) refer to texts added to the Arabic section for the 2nd ed. of the *Essai*, where they are found in the last few pages of that section.]

2. *Passion*, *Essay*.

92), for 102 by Qushayrī (*Risāla*, 36–159, 166–85), for 100 by Harawī (*Manāzil al-sāʾirīn*), and for 143 by Baqlī (*Shaṭḥiyāt*, ff. 114a, 119a [= *Lumaʿ*]).

ʾ*BD*. *abad* (opp. *azal*) A 8, 26; S 200; R 8, 10, 12, 19; C 213; T VI:17, 35; P. *abadī* A 31; P; S 206. *maʾbūd* P; U 7.
ʾ*ThR*. *athar* (opp. *khabar*) P; S 55; Z 7 *ṭāʾ* (16); T VI:23, XI:11; A 2, 10 (15), 47 (52), *1. *maʾthūra* T IV:7. ʾ*ithār* P. *muʾaththira* P.
ʾ*KhDh*. *maʾkhudh* P; C 183.
ʾ*DB*. *adab* A 58. *ādāb* S 117. *taʾdīb* (see *taʾnīb*).
ʾ*DM*. *Adam* S 102, 192. *adamiyya* S 18.
ʾ*DhY*. *yuʾdhī* A 20.
ʾ*ZL*. *azal* (opp. *abad*) A 64; R 19; S 41, 152, 163; P; T VI:11, X:17; U 1; S 68, 71, 108, 161, 172; C 187, 213. *azal(iyya)* S 172; R 8, 9; C 213; A 2, 31.
ʾ*ṢL*. *aṣl* P; U 11, 17; A 29, 34, 45.
ʾ*FQ*. *āfāq* T 17.
ʾ*LF*. (*alif*) *maʾlūf* (opp. *maqṭūʿ*) P; U 26; A 46, 64; D (M. 27).
ʾ*LH*. *ilah al-alihat* P; A 7; (*fī'l-samāʾ wa'l-arḍ*) P; A 2, 9. *ilāhiyya* S 5, 101, 114; A 25. ʾ*ulūhiyya* S 47; T X:26. *lāhūt* (opp. *nāsūt*) D. *lāhūtiyya* C 191. Yazd. 1.
ʾ*MR*. ʾ*amr* (opp. *irāda*) P; B 27; R 19; J 2; T VI:14; U 10. *amīr* R 3. *taʾmūr* A 10.*
ʾ*MM*. *umm* D (Q. X).
ʾ*MN*. ʾ*amān* (opp. *dhikr*) P; R; S. *amāna* P; S 130. ʾ*īmān* (opp. *islām*) P; K 23; (opp. *maʿrifa*) P. *muʾmin* P; S 12.
ʾ*NN*. ʾ*annī* (or *innī*) D (M. 55); A 50; T I:14, II:5, V:8, IX:2; R 19. ʾ*anniyya* (opp. *māhiyya*) P; Q; C 169.
ʾ*NA*. *anā* J 6; T II:8, VIII:7. *anā huwa* A 7(12). *anā anta* A 50. *anā'l-Ḥaqq* T VI:23.
ʾ*NB*. *taʾnīb* S 54.
ʾ*NS*. ʾ*uns* H 5; K 35; D; A 9, 38. *maʾnūs* T V:37. ʾ*inās* T XI:25.
ʾ*H*. T IV:11, IX:2–3.
ʾ*HL*. ʾ*ahl* T III:3, V:34.
ʾ*WL*. ʾ*awwal* (opp. *ākhir*) S 168, 171, 172, R 24. *taʾwīl* Q 9; T I:12.
ʾ*YD*. ʾ*iyād* A 9 (14).
ʾ*YN*. ʾ*ayn* T II:7, V:11, 23, IX:9; A 46, 50, 51 (51, 52, 53); Q1.
ʾ*YY*. ʾ*iyyaʾhu*, *iyyāʾy* K 51; S 74. *āya* T V:35.

*Massignon, perhaps more by oversight than in deference to the early sources (e.g., Jawharī, *Ṣiḥāḥ*, s.v.), given his announced principles in this chapter, puts this word (*taʾmūr*) under the root *TMR*. The right place is here, where I have put it (and where Massignon knew it belonged, v. *Dīwān*, M 31) to avoid confusion. See Lane's brief history of this question, in the *Arabic-English Lexicon*, under ʾMR, book I, p. 98.

BDʾ. badʾ (*al-khalq*) S 113. *bidāya* (opp. *nihāya*) C 177; T III:1, VI:30. *badʾ al-asmā* C 214.
BDʿ. mabdūʿ S 2.
BDL. Budalā (= *Abdāl*) K 54; R 22.
BRʾ. bariyāt R 9.
BRJ. burj T I:1.
BRQ. barq R 11; T I:11; D (M. 39).
BRHN. burhān K 15; A 2; R 12; D (Q. VIII).
BṢR. baṣar (opp. *samʿ*) R 1. *baṣāʾir* W 45.
BSṬ. basṭ (opp. *qabḍ*) A 11. *bisāṭ* S 66, 126; C 163; T VI:21; A 47. *mabsūṭ* S 54. *inbisāṭ* S 66; H 5.
BShR. bashariyya (opp. *ṣamadiyya*) S 5, 191; A 1, 25, 29; Z 28. *mubāshara* (opp. *sabab*) S 187.
BʿTh. mabʿath R 25.
BʿD. buʿd (opp. *qurb*) T VI:12; A 3, 5, 13, 14.
BʿḌ. baʿḍī (opp. *kullī*) C 164; D (M. 33); A 11, 55.
BṬN. bāṭin (opp. *ẓāhir*) A 6; R 24. *bawāṭin* T IV:4.
BQY. baqā (opp. *fanā*) K 47; U 15.
BLGh. iblāgh S 123. *balāgh* S 9.
BLY. balā (opp. *niʿma*) S 97, 138; K 14, 26; B 22; W 47; C 192; R 19. *ibtilā* T VI:14, VII:2; A 1.
BWQ. bawāʾiq T V:32.
BYT. bayt R 10.
BYʿ. bayʿa S 154; B 24.
BYN. bayn P; S 48; A 31, 50; T V:23, VI:10; K 15. *bayān* S 123; A 2, 40, 51; U 9. *tibyān* K 15; D (M. 63, Q. VIII).

TḤF. utḥiftu A 22.
TRQ. tiryāq T V:35.
TMM. itmām G.
TNN. tinnīn A 16; W 46.
TWB. tawba S 3, 156: J 1; R 20; W 49; P.
TYH. tīh T V:35; D (M. 12, 69).

ThBT. ithbāt A 50; C 191.
ThQL. thaqalayn T II:7.
ThNY. ithnayn D; A 50.
ThWB. thawāb (opp. *ʿiqāb*) S 135; D.

JBR. jabrūt S 66; R 20. *tajabbur* T VI:11.
JḤD. juḥūd T VI:10.
JḤM. jaḥīm (*khumūd al*) B 31.

JDhB. majdhūb C 183.
JRD. tajrīd (opp. *tawḥīd*) Z 25; T VI:7; K 51. *mujarrad* T VIII:5.
JFY. jafā al-khalq S 184.
JLS. majlis (*Allah*) R 17. *mujālasa* R 19.
JLY. tajallī K 45, 44; S 130, 136, 187, 198; A 2, 3, 10 (15), 55; C 214. *mutajallī(ya)* A 2, 8 (13), 53; U 18.
JMᶜ. jumᶜa qāʾima R 27. *mujmiᶜ* R 12. *ᶜayn al-jamᶜ* B 27; C 163. Cf. *Mélanges Joseph Maréchal*, 1950, 2:281.
JML. jumlat al-kull C 164; D.
JNN. aṣḥāb al-janna B 30. *jannat al-qalb* C 190.
JNDR. jandarat al-mulk R 26.
JNS. tajānus (opp. *tajāwuz*) K 15; C 178; D (Q. VIII).
JHD. majhūd T XI:1. *mujāhid* A 17. *mujtahid* R 22.
JHL. jahl T XI:5.
JWD. jūd S 180.
JWZ. majāz U 46. *tajāwuz* C 178.
JWL. jawlān T V:18.
JWHR. jawhar S 113; T I:8, IX:11; U 11.
JYʾ. majī S 47, 93.

ḤBB. ḥubb D (M. 24); A *2 (4), 36, 44; P. *muḥibbūn* R 21. *maḥbūb* H 5. *Ḥabīb* R 27. *maḥabba* (= *dhāt al-dhāt*) R 7, 13, 17, 20, 21, 26; K 10, 38; C 190; B 1, 13; J 8; S 14.
ḤJJ. D (M. 51). *ḥajj akbar* P; R 23. *ḥujja* B 6; A 29.
ḤJB. ḥijāb (*al-qalb*) T XI:5, 15; H 4; C 178, 188; Q 3. *maḥjūbūn* H 4; C 184. *iḥtijāb* A 5, 51, 53.
ḤDD. ḥadd (pl. *ḥudūd*) T IX:5, X:9; A 5, 13, 44, 47, 50; R 5, 19. *ḥaddayn* T XI:12; Q 1.
ḤDTh. ḥadath (opp. *qidam*) Q 1; A 1, 13. *ḥādith* T I:8, X:9. *muḥdath* U 2. *muḥādatha* C 213.
ḤRR. ḥurriyya Q 7.
ḤRF ḥurūf, aḥruf S 2, 113; K 8; Q 1; R 19; T V:36; U 2; A 34, 39, 40, 46, 64.
ḤSB. ḥisbān Q 9. *ḥasb* S 148.
ḤSN. iḥsān S 170; R 21.
ḤṢL. ḥuṣūl (*ᶜayn al*) P; S 21. *taḥṣīl* K 17.
ḤḌR. ḥaḍra A 10 (15). *ḥuḍūr* A 5, 10; D.
ḤẒẒ. ḥuẓūẓ S 189, 54.
ḤQQ. (*al*) *Ḥaqq Qur.* 22:6; *al-Ḥaqq* with: *shahāda, ḥaqīqa, istīlā, ilhām, takālum, dalīl* S 32, 36, 61, 194, 83, 84, 117; *al-Ḥaqq* A 26 (33); B 8; R 5; T I:9, IV:5–6, IX:6–7, X:8, 9, XI:26. *ḥaqīqa* (pl. *ḥaqāʾiq*, opp. *wasāʾiṭ*)

D (M. 17, 40); T II:1, 3, 8, IV:1, V:32; S 194; B 24, 30; U 45; D (M. 39); Z 1 *alif* (9); B 15; R. 19. *taḥqīq* C 177. *muḥiqq* A 44 (50); Z; Q. *taḥaqquq* S 1; D. *istiḥqāq* A 50; S 207. Formula: (*asʾaluka*) *biḥaqq* . . . A 1, 44.

ḤKM. *ḥukm* (pl. *aḥkām*) A 2, 10. *ḥikma* T I:17, VII:1; R 24; Ibn Diḥya 100; ʿAṭṭār 13.

ḤLL. *maḥall* S 155. *ḥulūl* D (M. 61); Z 5 bis *zāl* (14); S 172; C 178.

ḤMD. *ḥamd* R 19; 119. *Aḥmad, Muḥammad* T I:15, VI:1; R 18.

ḤML. *ḥaml* (*al-nūr, al-amāna*) S 130, 188; U 4.

ḤNF. *ḥanīf* C 24.

ḤWṬ. *iḥāṭa* U 8. *ḥiyāṭa* T III:1.

ḤWL. *ḥal.* (pl. *aḥwāl*) D; S 81. *ḥāla* (pl. *ḥālāt*) A 1, 13, 36, 67. *ḥawl* T VI:2.

ḤYY. Ḥayy T VII:5; S 147. *ḥayāt* S 35, 76; U 3; R 9. *taḥiyya* C 213, 214. *ḥayā* Z 14 *yaw* (23); A *1 (7).

ḤYR. *ḥāʾir* T X:5, B 28. *taḥayyur* T IV:2, III:1; C 34; A 5. *ḥīra* A 9, 32; T IV: 6.

KhBR. *khabar* (opp. *athar*) T XI:2, 11; A 67 (58); (opp. *naẓar*) T II:4, III:4; A 10, 53, 67.

KhRM. *ikhtirām* T I:10.

KhṢṢ. *khāṣṣ* (pl. *khawāṣṣ*) S 55, 86, 115, 137; C 178; T V:32, XI:25. *khāṣṣiyya* S 30, 55. *takhaṣṣuṣ* A 9; S 120.

KhṬṬ. *khaṭṭ* (cf. *istiwā*) A 32, 34.

KhṬB. *khiṭāb* C 123. *mukhāṭaba* S 93; B 4.

KhṬR. *khāṭir* (pl. *khawāṭir*) D; S 4, 191; Z 11, 12; C 164; A *1 (1), 8, 46; Q 14. *khāṭirān* A 33, 67 (35, 58).

KhṬF. *ikhtiṭāf* A 5, 10.

KhFY. *khafīya* S 98; A 41, 62, 67.

KhLL. *khulla* S 22. *khalal* (pl. of *khalla*) D.

KhLṢ. *khilāṣ* T V:32. *khalīṣ* R 27. *mukhliṣ* T VI;16. *ikhlāṣ* S 199; R 13; U 29. *takhalluṣ* Z 12.

KhLṬ. *takhlīṭ* (ʿ*ilal al*) S 177.

KhLF. *takhāluf* (opp. *tawāfuq*) B 31; S 44.

KhLQ. *khalq* (*badʾal*) T XI:26; S 51, 78, 101, 123, 144; U 9, 22, 28; R 18. *khuluq* S 186, 187; W 41. *khalīqa* (pl. *khalâʾiq*) T II:1, III:8; U 28; D.

KhLY. *khalā* (opp. *malā*) C 185.

KhMR. *takhmīr* (*al-arwāḥ*) R 13.

KhWḌ. *khawḍān* A 53, 32.

KhWF. *khawf* S 127; Q 3.

KhYR. *khayrāt* U 26. *ikhtiyār* S 167; T V:35; VI:11, 28; D.

KhYL. takhyīl A 47.

DBR. tadbīr (opp. *tafwīḍ*) K 19; S 102, 128; J 1; T VI:17. *tadabbur* T III:1; K 55; R 24.
DRR. durra (*bayḍā*) R 22.
DRJ. darajāt S 125; Z 11 *yaj** (20).
DRK. darak 2, S 28. *idrāk* Z 10; T XI:2. *darrāk* S 2.
*D*ᶜ*W. da*ᶜ*wa* (pl. *da*ᶜ*āwä*) S 79, 190; D (Q. I, p. 12, Q. V, p. 22); A 2, 14, 58; S 34, 82; B 29; R 27; T V:36, VI:1, 13, 18, 24. *dā*ᶜ*ī* (pl. *dawā*ᶜ*ī*) J 8; R 3.
DQQ. daqīqa (pl. *daqā*ᵓ*iq*) K 22; T V:32.
DLL. dalīl (opp. *madlūl*) T 19, III:10. *dalāl* A 36; T II:2. *istidlāl* C 169; K 44.
DNW. dunūw T V:31–32. *dunyā* D; A 55; R 6, 11, 14.
DHR. dahr (pl. *duhūr*) C 214; S 40, 180; Q 10; U 5.
*DWR. dā*ᵓ*ira* T IV:1, V:2–5, VII:1–5 (diagrams),** IX:13–14, X:1. *dā*ᵓ*irat al-ḥaram* T IV:10, V:31.
DYJR. dayjūr P.
DYR. dārayn Z 7 *ṭā*ᵓ (16). *diyār* D.

DhRR. dharr S 10. *dharriyya* S 55, 102. *dharra* S 50.
DhKR. dhikr (opp. *madhkūr; fikr*) K 32, 33, 34, 48; J 3; D (M. 18); S 2, 19, 53, 72, 110, 134, 150; H 1; A 12; R 5, 9, 13, 26. T V:18, 19, VI:15.
DhHL. dhuhūl S 21. *idhhāl* C 179.
DhWB. tadhwīb S 188.
DhWY. dhāt (shortened, *dhā*) A 2, 9, 12, 25, 50; S 183; T IX:8, X:9, 13, 18; XI:10; C 213. *dhātī* A 2.

*R*ᵓ*S. ra*ᵓ*siyāt* A 2, 44.
*R*ᵓ*Y. ru*ᵓ*ya* K 37; B 7, 8, 16; Z 5 *wāw* (13); S 68; D.
RBB. rabb al-arbāb A 7 (12). *marbūb* S 206. *rubūbiyya* S 7, 15, 47, 101, 108, 126, 167, 191, 198; B 15; C 163; A 7. *rabbāniyūn* S 161; T V:3; *rabbāniyya* T XI:15.
*RJ*ᶜ. *rujū*ᶜ *ilä'l-aṣl* T VI:11.
RZQ. rizq S 124, 125.
RSM. rasm (opp. *ism*) T II:4; B 32; S 4, 13, 94, 123. *marsūmāt* T IX:13. *tarassum* S 17.
RḌY. riḍā (opp. *irāda, amr*), J 1, A 43; W 46; R 17.
RFY. rafī T I:8 *rafawī* id.
RQB. murāqaba H 7.
RKB. rukūb D.

*Pedersen reads *rāḥāt*; A*1 still reads *darajāt*.

**See also the collected diagrams, in the versions of another manuscript, *Ṭawāsīn*, facing p. 178

RKN. rukn R 5, 19.
RMZ. ramz D.
RMS. rams (opp. *ṭams*, pl. *rawāmis*) *Yazd.*
RWḤ. rūḥ (*nāṭiqa*) S 87, 113; C 184, 188; D (M. 6, 21, 32, 37, 41); R 1, 9, 17, 19, 23, 25; A 2, 9, 10; T IX:11. *rūḥāniyya* C 178. *rīḥ* (pl. *riyaḥ*) S 126; R 187. *rāʾiḥa*, pl. *rawāʾiḥ* Z 11 *yaj* (20); A 44 (50).
RWD. murīd (opp. *murād*) J 6; W 49, 50; Z 6, 7 *ḥāʾ, ṭāʾ* (15, 16); B 21; A 5. *irāda* B 27; S 84, 128, 179, 191; C 214; T V:38, VI:11, IX:11; R 21.

ZKY. zakāt kubrā R 23.
ZLQ. yazliq R 16.
ZNDQ. zanādaqa (opp. *tawḥīd*) T V:2; A 47.
ZNR. zānir al-ʿawra T V:30.*
ZHD. zuhd W 52; *ʿAṭṭār* 26.

SBB. sabab (pl. *asbāb*) S 13, 182; A 53.
SBḤ. subuḥāt S 100; R 15. *tasbīḥ* C 214; R 24, 26.
SBQ. sawābiq S 45, 96; T VI:32.
STR. sitr D (Q. V).
SRJ. sirāj T I:1.
SRR. sirr (opp. *ḍamīr*, pl. *asrār*) C 163, 164; A 33, 36, 44; D (M. 22, 52); Q 8; T III:11, VI:7, IX:1, XI:2. *sirr al-sirr* D 68. *sarīra* (pl. *sarāʾir*) Z 14 bis *yaz* (24); A 36 (13).
SRMD. sarmad S 200.
SQṬ. isqāṭ (*al-wasāʾiṭ*).
SKR. sukr A 43; B 16. *sukrān* Z 15 *yaḥ* (25).
SKN. sakīna K 47.
SLB. salb (*al-ʿaql*) C 179; T IV:6.
SLṬ. taslīṭ (*al-ʿaql*) S 127 (*al-aḥwāl*) Z 8 *yāʾ* (17). *sulṭān* K 15, 39; T X:24.
SLM. taslīm A 44. *silm* A 3.
SMR. samīr D. *masmūr* T X:4.
SMʿ. samāʿ S 68; Yazd. 2. *istimāʿ* S 62; Yazd. 2.
SMY. ism (pl. *asmā*) D (Q. VII, M. 34, 69); S 102, 113; Z 1, 2 *alif, bāʾ* (9, 10); R 15; C 213; T V:28–29; U 2. *ism-aʿẓam* R 13, 15, 17, 25. *musammā* T X:14, XI:6.
SNḤ. sunḥ (pl. *sawāniḥ*) Z 4 *dāl* (12); A 47 (52).
SNY. sanā A 2; D.
SWY. Istiwā (cf. *khaṭṭ*).

*Corrected from the text ("*min zānid al-ʿawra*") of 1913 (v. P Fr 3:321/Eng 3:304), which Massignon had confessed (T p. 168) he did not understand. If Nwyia did not seem to be unaware of this correction (v. his ed. of *Ṭaw.*, bottom of p. 203), I would be readier to accept his modification (with additional mss.: *man zanada'l-ʿurwa*; p. 203, 221) of Massignon's original shot in the dark.

ShʾN. shaʾn A 2, 40; T V:37; R 13.
ShBḤ. shabaḥ S 170.
ShBH. shabh A 8, 25. *tashbīh* T X:9.
ShJR. shajara T III:6–7.
ShKhṢ. shakhṣ C 213, 214; U 16; D; T V:32, VI:14, XI:25.
ShRB. sharāb (al-uns) S 126, 129.
ShRḤ. sharḥ (al-ṣadr) T 12.
ShR^{c}. sharī^{c}a (opp. *ḥaqīqa*) S 21; B 15; A 6, 41, 47, 49.
ShRQ. mushriq R 24. *ishrāq* S 196; T I:2, 9.
ShRK. shirk khafī A 62; S 50, 69.
Sh^{c}Sh^{c}. tasha^{c}shu^{c} D (M. 39). *sha^{c}sha^{c}ānī* P.
ShKR. shukr A 1, 12; J 2; K 28, 29; Z 9 *yā* (18); B 12; S 72; R 26.
ShKK shakk (opp. *yaqīn*) A 46; Q 3; Z 3 *jīm* (11) [see ch. 5 n. 387].
ShKL. shikl (pl. *ashkāl*, opp. *aḥwāt*) C 178; T II:4, IV:4.
ShHD. shāhid (opp. *mithāl*, pl. *shawāhid, shuhūd*) S 159, 164, 181, 183; S 16, 21; A 2, 50. *shāhid al-qidam* D (Q. VI); A 2; S 183; R 18, 27. *shahadāt (al-dharr)*[3] S 9, 10, 12, 32. *mushāhada* B 30; T VI:35; R 4.
ShWR. ishāra S 10, 146, 151; T I:9, X:3; A 29, 2; Q 12.
ShYʾ. shayʾ S 113. *mashīʾa* S 101, 107, 113, 152, 180; B 6; C 213; A 2; T VII:1; R 19, 21.

ṢBB. ṣubb A 43.
ṢBḤ. miṣbāḥ A 10; T II:2.
ṢBR. ṣabr (opp. *shukr*) S 44; W 53; Ka^{c}bī.
ṢḤḤ. ṣiḥḥa T VI:1.
ṢḤW. ṣaḥw (opp. *sukr*) K 41.
ṢDQ. ṣidq A 47, 53; S 29; T III:1; U 29. *ṣādiq* S 128, 129. *ṣiddīq* S 88, 89, 90. T I:4.
ṢRF. taṣārīf S 21, 96. *taṣarruf.*
ṢFY. ṣafā T III:1, V:9, X:19. *ṣafawī* T I:8, III:1. *iṣṭifā* S 13.
ṢLB.[4] S 112.
ṢLD. iṣṭilād T III:1.
ṢLM. iṣṭilām Bāk.
ṢLY. ṣalāt R 23; U 25.
ṢMD. ṣamadiyya S 104. *maṣmūd* S 58; Z 20.
ṢN^{c}. ṣan^{c} R 4; T XI:8; S 100; J 1. *ṣan^{c}a* (pl. *ṣanā'i^{c}*) R 9, 15, 25, 26.
ṢHR. ṣayhūr Q 10; U 5.
ṢWR. ṣūra S 99, 113, 181; C 214; A 1, 2, 8 (13), 52; Q 1; R 13, 15, 26, 27. *taṣwīr* A 13, 25.

3. See *tawḥīd*.
4. Cf. *Rev. Et. Isl.*, 1932, IV ("Le Christ dans les Evangiles selon Ghazali").

ṢWF. *ṣūfiyya* Khark. 2, 3; T V:8. *taṣawwuf* C 191; D.
ṢYR. *taṣyīr* T III:11.
ṢYM. *ṣiyām akbar* R 23. *ṣimṣām(at) al-ṣiyām* T V:21.

ḌDD. *ḍidd* (pl. *aḍḍād*) K 7; T VI:19.
ḌRR. *ḍarūrī* Q 1. *iḍṭirār* K 8, S 116; B 18, 23.
ḌMR. *ḍamīr* (opp. *sirr*) T III:11, IX:2, X:5; A *1 (3), 8, 25, 44, 47; D (M. 11, 25, 38, 61). *iḍmār* D; K 43.
ḌMHL. *iḍmihlāl* T X:23.
ḌYA. *ḍiyā* (*mukhammara*) K 18; A 9; R 13. *istiḍā*$^{\supset}$ (opp. *naẓar*) A 2, 67.
ḌYR. *ḍayr* (*qhayr*) T VI:6.
ḌYF. *ḍayf* D (M. 37).

ṬB^c. *ṭab*^{c} Bāk 19. *ṭabī*^{c}*a* S 109. Cf. Eranos, 1945.
ṬRQ. *ṭarīqa* T V:36. *ṭarq* D.
ṬS. *ṭā sīn* U 1.
ṬL^c. *ṭal*^{c}*a* (pl. *ṭulū*^{c}, *ṭawāli*^{c}) K 15; S 94; A 47, 55. *iṭṭilā*^{c} S 16, 130; R 2; C 183; A 67. *muṭāla*^{c}*a* S 184.
ṬMS. *ṭams* (opp. *rams*) B 31; Yazd (= C 191); T V:37.
ṬWṬ. *ṭawṭ* C 172.
ṬW^c. *ṭā*^{c}*a* S 58, 72; R 26. *muṭā*^{c} P.
ṬWF. *ṭawāf* K 60; D.
ṬWL. *ṭūl* (opp. ^{c}*arḍ*) T XI:16.
ṬYR. *ṭayrān* B 26.

ẒLM. *ẓālim* (*muqtaḍid*) S 133. *ẓulumāt* U 16.
ẒNN. *ẓann* Q 9; A 3, 51 (53). *ẓānn* T II:6.
ẒHR. *ẓāhir* (opp. *bāṭin*, *ishāra*) S 84, 171; T IV:4, X:3. *ẓuhūr* S 162.

^{c}*BD*. *ta*^{c}*abbud* K 53. *ma*^{c}*būd* R 9; T VI:13. ^{c}*ubūdiyya* Q 7; S 75; B 15.
^{c}*BR*. ^{c}*ibāra* K 3; S 42; Z 20; D. *i*^{c}*tibār* U 28. ^{c}*ibra* Yazd.
^{c}*JB*. *i*^{c}*jāb* H 4.
^{c}*DD*. ^{c}*adad* (*nāqiṣ*) A 9; C 173. ^{c}*idd* T X:9, 23 (XI:1).
^{c}*DL*. *i*^{c}*tidāl* (opp. ^{c}*adl*) A 5.
^{c}*DM*. ^{c}*adam* (opp. *wujūd*) S 5, 86, 113.
^{c}*DhR*. ^{c}*adhār* D (M. 26).
^{c}*RJ*. *mi*^{c}*rāj* (pl. *ma*^{c}*ārij*) A 2.
^{c}*RS*. ^{c}*arūs* T V:37.
^{c}*RḌ*. ^{c}*arḍ* (opp. *ṭūl*) T XI:16.
^{c}*RF*. ^{c}*ārif* T I (cf. Qur. 2:141; *Ḥazm* III, 201; IV, 206): 5, 13, VI:24, 34, X:24, XI:1, 20, 24; Q 14; S 112. ^{c}*irfān* C 169; T XI:24. *ma*^{c}*rifa* Z 4 *dāl* (12); W 39, 40; T V:36, XI. *ta*^{c}*arruf* K 13, 49; C 169. *ma*^{c}*rifa* (*aṣliyya*) S

41, 80, 100, 152; R 4; C 184; A 13, 29. *maʿārif* K 15, S 49; R 8. *maʿrūf* T XI:24.

ʿZZL. ʿAzāzil T VI:18, 26, 30.

ʿZL. iʿtizāl A 5, *1 (8).

ʿShQ. ʿishq C 213, 214 (cf. A 49); W 92; *Daylamī* (*ʿAṭf* 21a, 28b–31a, 47b).

ʿṬR. ʿawāṭir al-qurb A 44.

ʿẒM. ʿaẓama R 2, 4; U 24. *ʿaẓamatayn* (= *azal* and *abad*) S 68.

ʿQB. iʿtiqāb K 8.

ʿQL. ʿaql D (M. 22, 66); A 33, 62; S 4; R 9; T I:9, VI:10; K 12, 17; S 4; C 179.

ʿLL. ʿilla A 53; W 44; T X:16; G. *muʿill* S 60, 168, 173.

ʿLQ. ʿalāʾiq K 22; B 20; T II:1. V:32.

ʿLM. ʿilm (opp. *kashf, maʿrifa*) S 30, 122, 152, 172; A 14, 34, 53; J 7; D (Q. II, M. 10, Q. IV p. 20); K 2, 54; T X:19, XI. *ʿilm ladunnī* S 117, 83 (cf. R 6, T IV:9). *maʿlūm* S 168, 155; B 27; T VI:1, XI:10.

ʿML. ʿawāmil C 174. *Maʿmūl lahu* S 85; Z 19.

ʿNY. maʿnä R 17; C 213; T V:36, VI:1, IX:14, X:19, XI:21; D; [A 46].

ʿWḌ. ʿiwaḍ K 53; S 53, 56.

ʿYN. ʿayn S 126; A 47; R 22, 25; D (M. 65). *ʿayn al-ʿayn* S 195; T V:23, VI:1, X:15. *ʿayn al-jamʿ* P. *ʿayān* R 5; S 84; C 169, 193; T V:37.

GhRR. maghrūr T X:4.

GhFR. ghufrān [A 44].

GhFL. ghafla (opp. *dhikr*) S 106, 111; H 1.

GhLB. ghalaba S 84.

GhMḌ. ghāmiḍ S 113; A 31.

GhNY. ghanī (opp. *faqīr*) K 26.

GhYB. al-Ghayb (= *ghayb al-Huwa*) S 41, 84, 108, 152; R 1, 22; A 51. *ghayba* (opp. *ḥuḍūr*) A 10; D.

GhYR. ghayr (pl. *aghiyār*) S 124; B 22; T VI:16; A 1.

GhYY. ghāya T II:8; A 46.

FTR. fitra A 12 (18).

FTN. maftūn A 46.

FTY. fatā A 43. *futuwwa* T VI:20–21. *fitya* D (Q. II).

FDY. fadaytuka D.

FRD. fard (pl. *afrād*) C 181. *tafrīd* (opp. *tawḥīd*) T VI:8; B 14; *Kashf* 36. *ifrād* K 51; S 148. *infirād* K 15; D (Q. VIII); *ʿaṭf* 29b; Z 13; A 5, 12; C 213, 214; T III:1. *tafarrud* A 9, 25, 51. *fardāniyya* T VI:8.

FRS. firāsa A 67; S 74. *tafarrus* Q 9.

FRSh. farāsh T II:2.

FRḌ. farḍ T XI:16; S 112.

FR^c. far^c (opp. *aṣl*) A 34.
FRQ. farq T XI:6–10. *iftirāq* K 37; S 126, 172. *tafarruq* C 181.
FQD. faqd (opp. *wajd*) T III:1, XI:3, 22.
FQR. faqīr A 42; K 21, 25, 26b; W 38; S 132, 179. *iftiqār* K 21; S 132.
FṢL. faṣl (opp. *waṣl*) D; T I:9, XI:1. *infiṣāl* S 17, 42 (opp. *ittiṣāl*).
FḌḌ. iftiḍāḍ S 191; *Luma^c* 231; M.
F^{c}L. fi^{c}l (pl. *af^{c}āl*) Z 27; Q I; C 214. *maf^{c}ūlāt* T IX:13.
FKR. fikr K 48; A 32 (34); T X:12. *fikra* A 12 (18).
FNY. fanā (*bi*) S 165. *fanā* (*^{c}an*) S 165; Yazd. 3.
FHM. fahm T V:11, IX:7, X:19, XI:16; R 14; A 67 (58). *mafhūmāt* T X:17.
FWT. tafāwut S 99, 100.
FWZ. mafāza T II:8, III:1, IV:1.
FY. fī T VIII:3.
FTḌ. fayḍ C 172.

QBḌ. qabḍ A 16; D (M. 30, 33). *qabḍa* S 77 (cf. 29). Cf. Qur. 39:67; *Asˀas* 159.
QTL. qatl D (Q. X, M. 23).
QDR. qadr S 70. *qudra* R 2, 17; T VII:1; Z 9; A 10, 12 (15, 18); C 214; S 39, 145. *taqdīr* S 54, 113; T VI:11–17. *maqādir* S 54, 113; T VI:17.
QDS. quds R 8, 16; D (Q. IV, M. 30); A 9, 38. *taqdīs* D (M. 28); A 12, 46, 51 (53); D (M. 65); T VI:10. *arḍ muqaddasa* R 16.
QDM. qidam (opp. *ḥadath*) A 1, 3, 5, 7, 12, 13, 51, 63; R 5; S 108. *qadīm* T XI:4.
QRB. qurb S 84, 110, 150; A 3, 5, 8, 12–14, 36, 44; Q 1. *qurba* R 2 (S 5, 181); T 187.
QRN. maqrūn (opp. *manūt*) S 69, H 6. *iqtirān* S 72; *^{c}Aṭṭār* 18; *Jurayrī* St No. 42.
QSW. qaswat (*al-qalb*) S 139, 142; D.
QṬ^c. qaṭ^c S 33. *munqaṭi^c* T XI:9.
QLB. qalb A 9, 12, 37, 46, 51, 53; D (M. 23, 62); T VI:5, XI:15; S 130; C 163, 190. *taqlīb* S 110, 111, 150.
QHR. qāhiriyya S 31.
QWS. qaws R 10, 24. *qāb qawsayn* T V:23.
QWL. maqāl (opp. *ḥaqīqa*) T IX:7. *miqwal* A 2.
QWM. qiyām (*biḥaqq*) A 1, 10; S 14, *qiwām Fānī*; A 29; S 114, 175. *maqām* (pl. *maqāmāt*) S 21; B 21; A 5; Q 14; T III:1; S 123.
QWY. quwwa mukhayyama R 11.
QYS. miqyās (*al-^{c}adam*) S 86.

Kˀ. kaˀannī T II:5. *kaˀannahu* T XI:23.
KˀS. kaˀs A 16.

KBR. *kibrīt aḥmar* U 41.
KRR. *karrāt* A 2; OK 466.
KRM. *karam* S 77, 180.
KSB. *kasb* (pl. *aksāb*) S 24.
KSW. *kiswa* S 116, 192.
KShF. *kashf* S 38; A 22, 45, 51, 55; S 34. *kashūf* K 48. *mukāshafa* T VI:16; A 38.
KFR. *kufr* D (M. 20), A 3, 7, 32, 35, 41, 48, 58, 66.
KFḤ. *mukāfaḥat al-khiṭāb* S 77.
KLF. *taklīf* S 17, 49, 204.
KLL. *kullī* (opp. *ba*^{c}*dī*) A 38; D. *jumlat al-kull* D.
KLM. *kalām* T X:10, I:9; D; R 4. *kalima* R 4, 24.
KWN. *kān* T XI:2; S 174. *makān* (^{c}*urf al*) T XI:2; S 174, 155. *kawn* (pl. *akwān*) S 25, 90, 137, 175; T X:26; A 33 (35). *takwīn* S 55, 193, 185. *kun*! S 63, 118, 137.
KYD. *kayd* U 10.
KYF. *kayfiyya* U 45, 46 (cf. U 39, 44; Q 12; R 19).

LA. *lā* T VII:3, X:22. *talāshī* (see LSHY). *lā*^{ʔ}*iya* [*lāyi*^{ʔ}*a*] D (M. 55).
LBB. *lubb* (pl. *albāb*) A 55; C 190.
LBS. *talbīs* S 46; D (M. 66); A 12, 50; T VI:14. *iltibās* T VI:1; A 8, 53; U 1.
LBY. *labbayka* D.
LḤẒ. *laḥẓa* (pl. *luḥūẓ*, *alḥāẓ*) T VI:7.
LḤQ. *mulḥaq* (opp. *mazīd*) T IX:7.
LDhDh. *taladhdhudh* S 116.
LSN. *lisān* (*al-Ḥaqq*, etc.) A 12, 29, 34, 53; R 26.
LShY. *talāshī* A 10; T II:4, XI:20.
LṬF. *laṭīfa* (pl. *laṭā*^{ʔ}*if*) C 190, 213; S 166, 208.
L^{c}*L*. *la*^{c}*all* S 4.
LHM. *ilhām* S 83.
LHW. *lahw* (opp. *sayr*) A 15.
LW. *lawlāka* A 53.
LWḤ. *lā*^{ʔ}*iḥ* D (Q. VII), 21; R 23 (*alūḥā*).
LWN. *talwīn* K 43. *mulawwanāt* T X:26.

M. *mīm* T I:15, V:27, IX:9, X:19; A 46; R 22; D (M. 65).
MA. *mā*^{ʔ}*iyya* T X:19.
MThL. *mathal* K 3; T X:1; A 2; U 20. *mithāl* (opp. *shāhid*) P.
MḤN. *miḥna* S 115, 156; B 23.
MḤW. *maḥw* (opp. *ithbāt*) C 169, 178, 191.
MDD. *madad* (*al-Rūḥ*) K 18.
MZJ. *imtizāj* D.

M^c. *ma^c* A 46; T XI:20.
MKR. *makr* S 45, 46, 71; C 213.
MKN. *tamkīn* (opp. *talwīn*) S 155; T I:1.
MLQ. *tamalluq* C 190.
MLK. *malak* R 7, 11; S 103. *malik* C 214. *mamlūk* C 214.
MWT. *mawt* S 103.
MYDN. *maydān* (pl. *mayādīn*) A 5; T I:17.

NBṬ. *istinbāṭ* S 2; B 5 bis.
NBY. *nabī* (opp. *rasūl*) A 10.
NJY. *munāja* A 9.
NDM. *nadīmī* A 15.
NZL. *nuzūl* (*Kull Layla*) R 22, 23. *manāzil* J 4. *intizāl* A 5.
NZH. *tanzīh* T X:1; A 13, 51; S 7, 108.
NSB. *nasab* S 90.
NṬQ. *nuṭq* S 50, 93; A 7, 12, 14, 37, 53; C 182; D *nāṭiqa* (cf. *rūḥ*).
NẒR. *naẓar* (opp. *khabar*) C 184, 213; R 10, 25; T II:4. *Manẓūr* T II:4. *nāẓir* D (M. 55, Q. III).
N^{c}T. *na^{c}t* (pl. *nu^{c}ūt*, opp. *waṣf*) S 15, 206; C 178.
N^{c}Y. *ni^{c}ā* A 2.
NFKh. *nafkh* A 10; D (M. 21).
NFS. *nafs* (pl. *nufūs*) D p. 127; K 27; S 27, 54 bis, 113, 189, 191, 197; Z 13 *yah* (22); C 175, 178, 184; A 5, 7, 38, 65, 66 (cf. S 163, 176). *nafas* (pl. *anfās*) S 203; C 163; A 44; T V:20.
NQṢ. *manqūṣ* T IX:4.
NQṬ. *nuqṭa aṣliyya* S 41, 45; U 22; A 10, 27, 64; T IV:2, V:1, IX:4.
NKR. *nakira* (opp. *ma^{c}rifa*) T XI:1, X:4; A 7.
NMS. *nāmūsī* D 38 [cf. A 40].
NHY. *nihāya* K 49; T I:9, XI:2.
NWB. *ināba* S 143.
NWR. *Nūr* S 107 (pl. *anwār*) U 1, 17; S 30, 99, 100, 101, 107, 109, 111, 113, 137, 161; A 9, 10, 28, 33, 40; T I:6, I:1; Z 15, 16 *yaḥ* (25, 26); R 8, 18, 26; OK 447.
NWS. *nāsūt* (opp. *lāhūt*) C 178; D (M. 5, 42); T V:37; A 10, 53. *nāsūtiyya* A 1, 10.
NWṬ. *manūṭ* S 69; G.
NWL. *tanāwul* (*nūr al-shams*) A 51; D.

HTF. *hātif* A 8.
HJR. *hajr* D (M. 13, 23).
HJS. *hājis* S 158.
HḌM. *haḍma rūḥāniyya* T IX:11–12.

HLL. hilāl S 6; Z 5 bis *zāl* (14); R 26. *tahlīl* C 214.
HLK. istihlāk A 1, 7, 9, 10, 30; Yazd. 3.
HMM. hamm T VI: 33; D. *himma* T I: 1, 7; D.
HNʾ. tahnīʾa C 214.
HW. huwa huwa U 38; A 20; S 205; C 214; T I: 14, X: 7, 15. *huwī* A 2. *huwiyya* A 7, 32, 50, 53; S 155; D (M. 55); *ʿAṭf* 48a (opp. *āniyya*).
HWS. hawas A 47 (52). *tahwīs* T VI: 10; A 12.
HWY. hawä A 2, 43.
HYKL. haykal (var. *hākūl*, pl. *hayākīl*) C 178; S 13; G; A 2, 8; D (M. 53).

WTR. witr (al-qaws) T V: 29.
WThQ. wathīqa T III: 11, V: 36. *mīthāq* R 12, 19.
WJD. wajd K 24; B 13; C 169, 173. *mawājīd* K 48; Z 14 bis *yaz* (23); U 27; D (M. 19). *tawājud* K 39. *ifrād al-wājid* S 148. *wujūd* K 15; *Fānī* U 40, 43; T XI: 4; R 26; D (Q. VIII, M. 40). *mawjūd* T VI: 34. *ʾījād* Z 17 *kāf* (27).
WJH. wajh (Allah) A 1, *1 (8). *wujūh* S 113. *muwājaha* S 93. *jihāt* T X: 17, 22.
WḤD. wāḥid, aḥad, waḥīd, muwaḥḥad T VIII: 2, 6–10, VI: 6; R 9. *āḥād* Z 12 *yad* (21); B 20; A *1 (7). *tawḥīd* (opp. *tajrīd, tafrīd*) U 32; K 15, 51; S 166, 167, 173, 207; A 47, 39, 57, 62, 63 (52, 39, 42, 43, 48, 59); Q 1, 2; C 163, 185; Z 15 *yaḥ* (25); T VIII: 3, IX: 7, 8, 14, X: 7, 14; B 2. *ittiḥād* B 19. *tawaḥḥud* K 15. *waḥdāniyya* S 10, 108, 90; B 19; C 187; A 53.
WḤSh. waḥsha A 38 (36). *istīḥāsh* T XI: 25.
WḤY. waḥy A 2, 10; Z 4 *dāl* (12); S 159.
WDD. tawaddud A 20; R 13.
WRD. mawārid A 67.
WSṬ. wasāʾiṭ (opp. *ḥaqāʾiq*) S 17, 49, 169; B 24.
WSL. wasīla S 26.
WSM. maysam D (Q. VII).
WSWS. waswās T XI: 25.
WṢF. wāṣif, mawṣūf T III: 9. *waṣf* A 12; Q 1. *ṣifa* C 213; T V: 36, X: 9–10, 18; A 7. *ittiṣāf* S 13.
WṢL. waṣl T XI: 1. *ittiṣāl* K 36; Z 28; T V: 34.
WẒB. muwāẓaba S 112.
WQT. waqt K 52; S 70; T VI: 15; W 36, 51; Q 1; A 51 (53). *mawāqīt* S 47.
WQF. mawāqif S 93.
WQY. taqwä S 149, 156.
WKL. tawakkul K 30, 31; S 73, 67, 182, 24; J 5; R 17.
WLH. walah J 8; R 22. *tawalluh* K 34.
WLY. walī (pl. *awliyā*) K 51; A 3, 14; R 21, 25. *istīlā (al-Ḥaqq)* Q 8. *mawlāya* D.
WHM. wahm (pl. *awhām*) S 72; T V: 11; A 13, 25, 37, 47, 51.

YTM. *yatīm* R 2; D (Q. II). (Cf. the Ismailis; *yatīm* Abī Ṭālib.)
YSR. *maysūr* (opp. *maqdūr*) S 65.
YQT. *yaqūt aḥmar* R 13, 15.
YQN. *yaqīn* (*ᶜilm, ᶜayn, ḥaqq al*) S 120, 201, 202; R 6; A 22 (28); U 31. syn. *tinnīn* W 46.

2. Earlier Terms and Themes "Orchestrated" by Ḥallāj

From the preceding list, I shall now consider several terms that Ḥallāj deepened and orchestrated in his works.

I undertook the same sort of comparative work for his poems, in my edition of the *Dīwān* (1931), pp. 110–30. The information published there should now be augmented as follows:

The metaphor of mixed perfumes (D, M. 41) was taken from Bashshār (Yāqūt, *Udabā*, VI, 67).[5] The Ḥallajian theme of perilous love (D, M. 24) was taken up by Mutanabbī (*fa ʾaḥla'l-hawā . . .*); the theme of the wanderings of the seeker of God (D, M. 12: and *zidnī taḥayyuran*) by Muʾayyad Shīrāzī (*Diw.* ms. SOS, London); of the Guest who takes all (D, M. 23) by Bahāʾuldīn Zuhayr (*Diw.* ed. 1305, p. 55; commentary by K. Yafī); of the fragile temple of the body, by the Nuṣayrī Khaṣībī (D, M. 53; and *Diw.* Khaṣībī, ms. Manchester, 120a). This last poem is also attributed to Suhrawadrī of Aleppo (*Alwāḥ ᶜimādiyya*, ms. Berl. 153a), who took up other Ḥallajian themes (D, M. 22, 52; p. 130: his great *hāʾiyya*).

Note also that Fakhr Rāzī's "great tafsīr" contains a commentary on nos. 68 and 69 [M.] of Ḥallāj's *Dīwān* (*Tafs. kab.*, I, 149).

ʾLF. *alif*, the letter A, and the number 1. *maʾlūf*, "accustomed," as opposed to *maqṭūᶜ*, "left alone, lonely." Ḥallāj applies it to any spiritual monad, while the tradition, as much among mystics as among Shiite extremists, reserves it for Iblīs. The *alif* "has refused the *sujūd*" (Sarī, ap. *Lisān*, III, 14: contradicting *Futūḥāt*, II, 197, where, instead, the *lām-alif*, the *jawzahr*, rebelled). *"Al alif mutaʾakhkhar al-sujūd yantaẓir al-amr al-ilāhi"* (= Iblīs: ms. Nuṣ. 34, f. 124). Ḥallāj sees in it the monad, the ambivalent Ego, the *yaqīn* (= *tinnīn*).
ʾMR. *amr*, the divine Commandment (distinct from *irāda*, the unbreakable decree). Ḥallāj parts company with the Sālimiyya and Sahl (cf. Tawḥīdī, *Baṣāʾir*, 91, 256) by centering mystical union on *Amr*, through the "fiat" (cf. *kun*).

5. By this time Fuḍayl b ᶜIyāḍ had already given a mystical interpretation to a secular verse of Bashshār (Tawḥīdī, *Baṣāʾir*, 108).

ʾ*MN*. ʾ*īmān*, faith. Ḥallāj sees in it "the nocturnal light of the stars" (Stf 19), which does not reveal the divine Sun (cf. Harawi = Wāsiṭī, ap. *Luma*^{c} 314, ^{c}AQ. Hamadhānī, *Shakwā* 39).

ʾ*HL*. *ahl*, cognatic family, as a result of philoxenia (*jiwār*: as opposed to *āl*, agnatic family; cf. *Rev. Et. Isl.* 1946, 151). Ḥallāj (*Ṭaw.* V:34; and Ālūsī, *Tafs.* I, 231) spiritualizes the Shiite idea of the *ahl al-bayt* into the divine hospitality accorded to the *gharīb* (cf. *ghurba*; and divine adoption of the *yatīm*).

BDL. *Abdāl, Budalā* (cf. Suyūṭī, *Khabar dāll*, quoted in *Machriq* 12, see bib., s.n. Anastase), the apotropaic saints, intercessors for humanity since Abraham, according to the *ḥadīth* of ^{c}Abd al-Wāḥid Ibn Zayd (*Ḥilya*, VI, 165; but see herein ch. 5 n. 344). Cf. Jaḥiẓ, *Tarbī*^{c}, 97–98; Tirmidhī, *Nawādir*, 69, 158; Ja^{c}far ibn Manṣūr al-Yaman, *Kashf*, 123; *Ikhw.*, II, 95.

B^{c}*Ḍ*. *ba*^{c}*ḍī*, the share that is mine (= God; as opposed to my all = my created being). Cf. Ibn Sab^{c}īn, *K. ba*^{c}*ḍ al-Wāḥid* (title in Ibn Taymiyya, *Sab.*, 93). *Ḥallāj* "essentializes" this paradoxical Manichaean term: "^{c}*Isā ba*^{c}*ḍ min Allah*" (Ibn Ṭāhir Maqdisī, *Bad*ʾ, III, 122).

ḤJZ. *ḥājiz*, the barrier that separates (from God: role of the Prophet, of the *Mīm*), *Ṭaw.* V:22 — a Shiite idea (Nuṣayri ms. P. 1450, 99a; Muṣṭafā Yūsuf Salām, 129), juxtaposed with *Sīn* or Saint, who by his teaching supplies a conception of God (*Tāwīl al-zakāt*, 409).

ḤQQ. *ḥaqq*, (1) in law, an ambivalent term, "debt" or "claim"; (2) in Hellenistic philosophy, the truth (objective truth, as opposed to *ṣidq*, subjective sincerity); (3) in mysticism, very early, the implied subject of the inspired saying, of the preaching that personalizes and realizes; the (open) Real, Creative Truth in act. Because of the Sufis, this dynamic term, fundamentally Ḥallajian and closely tied to the Qurʾān (50:41: *ṣayḥa bi'l-Ḥaqq*; cf. 42:17) became the common name for God in the Turkish, Persian, and Indian lands. The statement attributed to Ḥallāj, "*Anā al-Ḥaqq*," is well known: "My 'I' is the Creative Truth" (cf. *DI*, 1913; Qush. 161; Stf 168, 173).

The formula "*biḥaqq* . . . ," "by the claim of . . . on . . . ," formula for an oath, of Mu^{c}tazilī and Shiite origin (*Ikmāl* 204; *Bākūrā* 49: "*biḥaqq al-Masīḥ ibn Umm al-Nūr*," ms. Ng. 4), was used in mysticism by Ḥallāj (relying on the doctrine of the two natures, divine and human; cf. *Luma*^{c}, 260).

ḥaqīqa, (1) in grammar, the literal (as opposed to *majāz*, the figurative); (2) in philosophy, the real meaning of a term; (3) in mysticism, *ḥaqīqa* is used in the sense of "closed" or finite reality (as opposed to the "open" or infinite Real; as "deity" is to God), which, through static bad usage, finally came to mean the ultimate (ideal) divine reality of the universe (already in ^{c}Aṭṭār).

ḤLL. ḥulūl, (1) in grammar, the incidence of the accident of inflection (*iʿrāb*); (2) in the law, the application of a statute: substitution of the curator for the testator (Ibn ʿĀbidīn, IV, 597); (3) in Hellenistic philosophy, the (illuminating) information of the passive intellect by the active intellect, and of the body by the immaterial soul; (4) in mysticism (Muḥāsibī), intervention of divine grace in man (*fāʾida*); (5) divine visitation, in the Shiite Imām (= *badā*: *Ghayba,* 41, 63), in the saint (Ḥallāj). A term with Christian resonance, condemned by Muʿtazilite theologians and Bāqillānī (against Fāris the Ḥallajian), for whom speaking of a "place," a point of impact for immaterial realities, was to materialize them. Ḥallāj himself rejected the term (in his prose, C 178).

KhṬṬ. khaṭṭ al-istiwā, equatorial writing (*Akhb.* 32, 34). The 28 Arabic letters were traditionally identified with the 28 astral mansions of the zodiac (and Fāṭima with the western reddening of sunsets when the Moon [= the Imām] appears; this Shiite metaphor (Jaʿfar ibn Manṣūr al-Yaman, *Kashf;* and the Ḥurūfīs) is "sublimated" by Ḥallāj in a *via negativa* (*Lām-Alif*).

KhMD. khumūd . . . taḥt mawārid . . . , "the ember kept hot . . . under the rain of ash . . ." Ḥallajian metaphor taken up by four contemporaries: Ṣubayḥi (*Ḥilya,* X, 354; Stb 60);* Abū ʿUthmān Maghribī (Baqlī, I, 44); Ṣuʿlūkī (Qush. 182); and Wāsiṭī (Baqlī, I, 539; cf. id. on Qur. 12:83).

DHRY. dhāriyāt, the burning simoom of the Judgment (*Akhb.,* no. 2). This Qurʾānic term (Sura 51) is the oldest known example of apocalyptic exegesis in Islam; for spreading word of it, Ṣabīgh ibn ʿIsl, a *sayyid* of the Ḥanẓali clan of the Tamīm, was ordered flagellated by the caliph ʿUmar (add "*Qūt,* II, 116" to the reference given in my "Salmān Pāk," 1933, p. 27). = *ghamāma, ẓullat Madyan.*

RWḤ. Rūḥ Nāṭiqa, the Speaking Spirit (color: white). Term of Ismaili origin (OK, 441, 445; Abū Ḥātim Rāzī, *Aʿlām,* 200), which Ḥallāj was the only Sufi to use. Also *rūḥ qadīma* (eternal spirit), an extremist (cf. R 17) Ḥanbalite term (cf. also Rabāḥ, Kulayb; Nūrī in Qush. 126) connoting the *Rūḥ al-Amr* of the Qurʾān, the Holy Spirit; also connoting the secret guest of the holy soul. Opposed to the *nafs nāṭiqa* (the speaking soul) of the Hellenistic philosophers.

ShʿShʿ. Nūr shaʿshaʿānī, "scintillating light," the first emanation of the *Nūr ʿulwī* (supreme light) according to the Qarmathians (Malaṭi, f. 16). The *nūr shaʿshaʿānī* is a *rūḥ shaʿshaʿānī,* "spirit scintillating (with love)," informing the heart of the believer in the second flash of divine love (ʿAmr Makkī, ap. Daylamī's *ʿAṭf,* no. 39, cf. Ḥallāj, ap. *ʿAṭf,* 48a). It is also the red light (Ibn ʿArabī *Tajalliyāt,* P. 6640, 67a), which will radiate

* The numbering Massignon uses is also that of Pederson's edition.

from the center of the Sun of Judgement (Nuṣayrī theory: Balansi, 84–85; *I*ᶜ*tidāl,* II, 73, article on Fāṭima; OK 460: Fātir; Khaṣībī, *Hidāya,* 263a; ᶜ*Aqīda ḥalabiyya,* 4b; Kīlānī, *Ghunya,* 11, 132).

ShHD. shāhid (pl. *shawāhid,* rather than *shuhūd*), means (1) instrumental ("purified") witness in sacred law; (2) an authoritative grammatical example in verse; (3) a living being (especially a human being) who expresses and bears witness to God (by the beauty of his face, which becomes suspect of idolatry; or by the accent of his speech). The third sense is relevant to the mystic "holders" of this term (*qā*ᵓ*ilūn bi'l-shāhid*: after Abū Ḥamza and Nūrī: Ḥallāj, Fāris, and AB Wāsiṭī; Abū Ḥulmān), which was rejected starting with Ibn Yazdānyār (Sarrāj, fragment of the *Luma*ᶜ, ed. Arberry).

ḌMR. ḍamīr, the conscious self of man (as opposed to *sirr,* his deep unconscious). Taken from the grammatical meaning of "pronoun" (= *muḍmar,* according to the Baṣran school; as opposed to *maknī,* Kūfan school).

ẒLL. ẓill mamdūd, the shade extended (Qur. 77:30) of Paradise, which is ambivalent (Jaᶜfar ibn Manṣūr al-Yaman, *Kashf,* 69, where it is the Sīn).

ᶜ*ShQ.* ᶜ*ishq,* love as desire (as opposed to *maḥabba,* the static idea of love). Audacious term, of Ḥasan Baṣrī's school (cf. herein, ᶜAbd al-Wāḥid ibn Zayd); its theological definition by Ḥallāj is explained at length, as to origins and consequences, in "Interférences philosophiques et percées métaphysiques dans la mystique hallagienne: Notion de 'l'Essentiel Désir'" ["Philosophical Interferences and Metaphysical Breakthroughs in Hallajian Mysticism: The Notion of 'Essential Desire,'"] in *Mélanges Joseph Maréchal,* Brussels and Paris, 1950, 2:263–96).

GhMR. taghmīr al-qalb, the anointing of the heart: Ibn ᶜ*Aṭā* (*Ḥilya,* V, 302; Fāris, on Sura 12).

QWM. maqāmāt, the stages or degrees of mystical union (as opposed to *aḥwāl,* the states of mystical union), from the point of view of the mystic's effort (as opposed to the point of view of the gifts of divine informing grace). The traditional list of *maqāmāt* comprises two parallel series: ten degrees, and nine gifts (the X: *tawba, wara*ᶜ*, zuhd,* [*ṣabr*], *faqr, shukr, khawf,* [*rajā*], *tawakkul, riḍā*; the IX: *maḥabba, shawq,* ᵓ*uns, qurb, ḥayā, ittiṣāl, qabḍ* [*basṭ*], *fanā* [*baqā*], *jam*ᶜ [*tafriqa*]—according to Sarrāj, *Luma*ᶜ, 42, Qush. 38, ᶜ*Awārif,* IV, 232, 276, 290; Kalabādhi gives seventeen; Harawi gives one hundred *manāzil,* in ten groups of ten). Ḥallāj, who goes beyond these, toward the Master of the "XL" degrees and gifts (*Ṭaw.* III:1), once enumerated "twelve *dawā*ᶜ*ī*" corresponding to Jaᶜfar's twelve *burūj* [*Essai,* 1st and 2d French ed., supplement, J 8].

N.B., by the time Dhū'l-Nūn Miṣrī was working out these lists, the profane poets Ibn Dāwūd (*Zahra* 19) and Nifṭawayh (ap. *Mughaltay,* 42) had made lists of the (8, or 5) mental stages of the malady of love, with analogous technical terms (*istiḥsān, mawadda, maḥabba,* ★ *khulla, hawä, ᶜishq, tatyīm, walah; irāda, maḥabba, hawä, ᶜishq, tatayyum*). Cf. also Ibn Ḥazm's list (*Mudāwāt al-nufūs,* 36).

KᶜB. kaᶜba, the Black Stone of the Ḥaram in Mecca, symbol of the primordial Covenant of souls. By extension, Ḥallāj, in his infamous "Letter to Shākir ibn Aḥmad," for which he was condemned, uses the name *kaᶜba* for the human body of a witness for God who offers himself as an Abrahamic victim to the sword of the Law (Ibn Diḥya, *Nibrās,* 103). This sense is taken up by Shushtarī (*Diw. Ḥallāj,* p. 137).

KWN. kun, "be," "fiat," Stf no. 1. Used eight times in the Qur'ān (Muqātil, in *Passion* Fr 3:115 n 4/Eng 3:104 n 32), each time for "ᶜIsä and the Judgment." *Kun* is the word that realizes directly, that creates without a middle term, "without anything else" (*bi-laysa;* which the Ismailis contrast to *bi-aysa*), e.g., the Throne, Ṭūbä, Adam (according to *Tawaddud,* 44). It is Ibn ᶜArabī's *faḥwāniyya* (ms. P. 6640, 72b, 76a; Ism. Ḥaqqī, *Rūḥ,* II, 329; Muṣṭ. Yf. Salām, 249). It is contrasted with creation by the "two hands," *yadayni* (cf. this word), which give life (= ᶜilm + qudra, Akhb. 2).

LBS. talbīs, murky ambiguity. Mukhammisa Shiite term, meaning the god ᶜAlī's illusory plurality, reflected in the other four "people of the mantle" (Bashshār, in Kāshī, 253). Term limited by Ḥallāj to consideration of the *taklīf ᶜan al-wasā'iṭ,* the legal duty concerning mediate causes (which allow access to God only by their disappearance).★★

Lāhūt, divines nature (as opposed to human nature, *nāsūt*). Both are Syriac Christian and Manichaean terms reworked by the Ismailis (Malaṭī, *Tanbīh*) and Nuṣayrīs: Khaṣībī (*Diw.* 22b: *lāhūt* = Ism = Mīm; 34a: *nāsūt* = qudra + ījād = Sīn). Ḥallāj, according to Daylamī (ᶜAṭf 48b) and Ibn ᶜArabī (*Fut.* IV, 367), is the only Sufi to have used these two terms, which Ibn Khafīf would later condemn. Cf. *Ikhw. Ṣafā,* III, 97; OK 472; Ibn al-Fāriḍ, v. 455.

LHM. ilhām (Qur. 91:8), private inspiration (as opposed to *waḥy,* angelic inspiration), accepted as a legal source by the Shafiᶜites alone (Baghdādī, *Uṣūl*). According to Harawī, this was the basic problem, which the judges, by condemning Ḥallāj, rashly decided (Harawī, *Ṭab.* s.v.; cf. *Madārij,* I, 24–27, II, 277; Hujwīrī, 271, 284; Fakhr Razi, *Tafs.* II, 426). Stf 83, 84, 119.

LWḤ. lā'iḥ, the shining appearance of God. Ḥallāj's term (*Diw.,* p. 26, 48; *Riw.* 23: *alūḥā*), daringly taken up by Harawī at the end of his *Manāzil*

★ Left out of the list in *Essai,* by simple oversight; see *Passion* Fr 1:389/Eng 1:341.

★★ V. Stf 49, P Fr 1:589/Eng 1:543. Surely "mediate causes" (*causes médiates*), as a translation of *wasā'iṭ,* is used in the bastard sense. Viz. "secondary causes" or "intermediaries."

al-sā$^{\supset}$irīn (*Madārij*, III, 332), to Ibn Taymiyya's great indignation (*Minhāj*, III, 86, 93).

MWT. law kushifa lamātū$^{\supset}$ (Stb no. 1), death, conceived as the raising of the veil of the Name imposed on us by God. Quotation from a pronouncement by Sahl (*sirr al-rubūbiyya*: cf. herein, ch. 5, sec. 4. Ḥallāj's very phrase is grafted onto the rhyme of a phrase of Sarī Saqaṭī: "*man aḥabba Allah* ^{c}āsha; *wa man māla ilä'l-dunyā* ṭāsha; *wa'l-aḥmaq yaghdū wa-yarūḥ fī* lāshi" (*Kitāb rawḥ al-*^{c}*ārifin*, attributed to Najm Kubrä, printed at Constantinople, 1275 A.H., p. 80).

NẒR. nāẓir al-^{c}*ayn*, the nadir of the eye (inaccessible; as opposed to *bāṭin al-qalb*, the inside of the heart: *Akhb.* 50). Sublimation of a Shiite term (Ja^{c}far ibn Manṣūr al-Yaman, *Ta*$^{\supset}$*wīl al-zakāt*, 98).

YD. yadayni = the two hands of the Creator (*min aysa*) = *qudra* + *baqā* (Ibn Taymiyya, *Fat.* V. 241) or *ni*^{c}*ma* + *iḥsān* (Ibn al-Jawzī) or *Nūr sha*^{c}*sha*^{c}*ānī* + *ḥikma* (mystical Druze manuscript, 29). Mode of creation by the *yadayni mabsūṭatayni* of God (Qur. 5:69; Ibn Taymiyya, 1.c. V, 72) = *du*^{c}*ā* + ^{c}*ibāda* (Ḥallāj, ap. ^{c}Aṭṭār, *Tadhk.*, in supplement). Superior to creation *ex nihilo* by the *kun* according to the Ismailis (*Sab*^{c}*īniyya*, 22); or inferior, according to Ḥasan Baṣrī (*Qūt*, II, 87; Shahrast., II, 124).

Yā Hū = *Qāyim Nāṭiq* (Y. Khachab, *Nasiré Khosrau*, 155), as opposed to *Yā Sīn* = Qiyām Salsal (cf. *Akhb.* 27). Ḥallajian term of Shiite origin (Nuṣayrī: *yā Hū* = ^{c}Alī ap. *Bāk.* 10, 1. 8; Khaṣībī: ^{c}*abd Ṭaha wa al-Yāsīn* [*Diw.* 2b]; *Muzhir*, I, 180; *Al-Ṭāsīn*; and *nūr Ṭāsīnī* [Khaṣībī, *Diw.*, 18a]).

REMARK

On the process of interiorization (*taḍmīn*)[6] specific to semantic symbol making in Semitic languages, especially Arabic, cf. Khaḍir Ḥusayn, ap. *Majalla de l'Ac. de langue Arabe*, Cairo, 1 (1934), 180–99, and my studies:

a. in *Eranos* (Zurich): "Le Temps dans la pensée islamique," 1949 [*Opera Minora*, ed. Moubarac, Beirut 1963, 2:606–12; "Time in Islamic Thought," trans. Ralph Manheim, in *Testimonies and Reflections*, ed. Herbert Mason, Notre Dame, 1989, 85–92], for the words *waqt, ḥāl, wajd*; "L'Esprit dans la pensée islamique," 1946 [called, "L'Idée de l'Esprit dans l'Islam," *O.M.* 2:562–65; "The Idea of the Spirit in Islam," trans. Manheim, in

6. In the fragment Stf [Sulamī's *Tafsīr*] 84, Ḥallāj explains that true "closeness" (*qurb*) is achieved by a mental "approach." Which is not external annexation of the object by gradual analysis of its differentials but inner substitution of oneself for the object, by being transported into the midst of it in a mental decentering analogous to the Copernican decentering of Ptolemy's system of understanding the world. This method is the basis of all of Ḥallāj's parables, from those in the *Ṭawāsīn* to the parable of the crescent moon (Stf., no. 6). It is not an intellectualization detached from the experience of love's ecstasy; it is a conversion from a system of rectangular coordinates to one of polar coordinates (cf. the cartography of the seven Iranian *kishwār*, ap. G.Budé [II, 1943, 122–43]; cf. review *Arabica*, 1943, no. 1).

Mason, *ed. cit.*, 74–79]; "L'Onirocritique," 1945 [*O.M.* 2:554–61; "The Interpretation of Dreams"]; "L'Homme parfait," 1948 [*O.M.* 1:107–25; "The Perfect Man"], p. 300 ff. of the *Eranos Yearbook* for the chronograms of Maryam, "290," and of the Seven Sleepers, "309"; translated into Arabic by ᶜAR Badawi, Cairo, undated). [See also, on these subjects, "The Notion of 'Real Elite' in Sociology and in History," in *The History of Religions: Essays in Methodology*, ed. Eliade and Kitagawa, Chicago, 1959; reprinted in Mason, *ed. cit.*, 57–64).

b. in *Dieu Vivant* (Paris); "Le Pèlerinage" ["The pilgrimage"] and "Soyons des sémites spirituels," cahier XIV [*O.M.* 3:823–30; "Let Us Be Spiritual Semites"], on literal biblical exegesis.

c. in the *Roseau d'Or* (Paris): "L'Expérience mystique et les modes de stylisation littéraire," 1927 [*O.M.* 2:371–87; "Mystical Experience and The modes of Literary Stylization"].

d. in *Etudes carmélitaines* (Paris): "La Syntaxe intérieure des langues sémitiques et le mode de recueillement qu'elles inspirent," 1949 [*O.M.* 2:570–80; "The Inner Syntax of Semitic Languages and the Mode of Meditation They Inspire"]; "Le Coeur," (*qalb*) 1950 [*O.M.* 2:428–33].

e. in *Lettres d'humanité*, G. Budé (v. 2, 1943, 122–43), Paris: "Comment ramener à une base commune l'étude textuelle de deux cultures, l'arabe et la gréco-latine" [*O.M.* 1:172–86; "How to Find a Common Basis for the Textual Study of Two Cultures, the Arabic and the Greco-Latin"]; trans. into Turkish by Burhan Toprak; reprinted in *Revue du Caire*.

f. in the *Mardis de Dar el Salam*, Cairo: "Valeur de la parole humaine en tant que témoignage," cahier 1, 1951 [*O.M.* 2:581–84; "The Value of Human Speech as Witness"]; "Les Feuilles archéologiques d'Ephèse et leur importance religieuse pour la Chrétienté et l'Islam," cahier 2, 1952 [*O.M.* 3:104–18; "The Archeological Excavation of Ephesus and Its Importance for Christianity and Islam"].

2

ANALYSIS OF THE LEXICON

1. Inventory of the Technical Terms

A. Classification According to Origin

1) QUR^ᵓĀN

The lexicon's principal source, the one to be consulted first, is the Qurᵓān. These Muslims knew it by heart and would assiduously recite it in order to create a setting for their daily meditations.[1] In forcing themselves to recite the text uninterrupted from start to finish (*khatm*) they aimed to achieve the discipline of *istinbāṭ*,[2] the immediate elucidation of the meaning of each verse, considered in context, at its place among the other verses. As in the Ḥanbalite rule, "Do not (like the critical commentators) look for two separate passages from the Qurᵓān in order to juxtapose them; read the Qurᵓān from beginning to end."[3] Those who meditate a text to live by it tend to employ a simultaneous, synthetic consideration of the whole, instead of piecemeal, analytic consultation of isolated elements, the legal cross-referencing preferred by lawyers.[4]

In the lexicon, we have seen that some well-known mystical terms were borrowed from the Qurᵓān: *dhikr, sirr, qalb, tajallī, istimāᶜ, istiqāma, istiwā, iṣṭināᶜ, iṣṭifā, ṣidq, ikhlāṣ, riyā* (8:49), *riḍā, khulq, ᶜilm, nafs muṭmaᵓinna* (89:17), *sakīna, tawba, daᶜwä, yaqīn, Allāh = Nūr* (24:35) = *Ḥaqq* (22:6).[5]

Moreover, by direct derivation, the Qurᵓān supplied *khulla* (4:124), *tawakkul* (3:153), *futuwwa* (from *fitya*, 18:9), *ṭams, ṣūra, dunūw*, (53:8),

1. Muslim Khawwāṣ (d. c. 200) explains the method very well: "At first, since my reading of the Qurᵓān lacked sweetness, I began to read as if Muḥammad were dictating it to me; then, as if I could hear Gabriel announcing it to Muḥammad; finally, as if I could hear God Himself; 'and all the sweetness was given to me'" (Shaᶜrāwī, *Al-ṭabaqāt al-kubrä* [Cairo, 1305], I, 61 [*Recueil*, 1929, p. 10]).

2. *Passion*, Fr 3:198/Eng 3:185; Sarrāj, *Lumaᶜ*, 85 ff.

3. Malaṭī, f. 375, Cf. Goldziher, *Vorlesungen*, Eng. trans., 69 n 2.

4. Put back into this overall picture, each element is still appreciated according to its proper nuance, discerned beforehand by analysis. Therefore, when a proposition of Islamic dogma passes from Arabic into Turkish, its syntactical order can be changed without damage to the conceptual hierarchy of the corresponding ideas—provided that the translator has elucidated the subject in advance.

5. Note that the terms *waraᶜ, khāṭir, firāsa, ḥaqīqa, ᶜaql, fikr, maᶜnä, maᶜrifa* are absent from the Qurᵓān.

ladunnī (from *ladunnā*, 18:64), *ḥāl* (from *yaḥūl*, 8:24), *ṭabīᶜa* (from *ṭabaᶜa*, 4:154), and *ṣayhūr* (from *yuṣhar*, 22:21); the *fuqahā* and *mutakallimūn* used the same process of etymological derivation for their respective vocabularies. The Qurᵓān is also the source of the following pairs of opposites: *ẓāhir-bāṭin* (57:3), *ṭūl-ᶜarḍ* (57:21; 40:3), *qabḍ-basṭ* (2:246), *maḥw-ithbāt* (13:39), *ṣabr-shukr* (3:136–38), *fanā-baqā* (60:26–27).

There is no need here to point out the antique, foreign elements (Aramaic[6] and Persian[7]) within the Qurᵓānic vocabulary because these words were almost certainly Arabized well before the seventh century A.D.

Two objections might be raised to the preceding list. First, each of the terms appears only in the Qurᵓān: identifying them as the seeds of large and complex mystical theories would seem excessive. Response: In the Qurᵓān they are *mutashābihāt*, "ambiguous terms" that stop the reader and do not yield to the first analysis. The process of *istinbāṭ*, the frequent, complete rereading of the text with a view to "swallowing" after much "chewing,"[8] brings the intelligence, in the course of each new recitation, into violent contact with these words. The troublesome terms must be absorbed at any cost; therefore the verbal resources already assimilated by reading the rest of the Qurᵓān are made to crystallize around them. This phenomenon of crystallization occurs constantly in the mind of any careful reader, whether of a poem, code, or catechism: the difficult words are the important ones; when brought to light they are the key to the passage. The intelligence attacks them like knots in order to explain and understand the whole, eventually to participate in the guiding intention of the author.

Secondly, there is the objection that quotations of Qurᵓānic terms can be mere pretexts, smokescreens used by innovators to hide the extraneous sources of their condemnably borrowed theories. Response: With certain pseudo-mystics, the possibility of a more or less undeniable deception of this type is not to be excluded.[9] But such a phenomenon of mental

6. Talmudic or Christian; cf. below, sec. 1. c. See studies by Fraenkel; Dvorak.

7. ᶜA. M. Kindī has already pointed out *istabraq*, *sundus*, *abāriq*, *namāriq*, and the Abyssinian (*sic*) term *mishkāt* (*Risāla*, 95; cf. Maᶜarrī, *Malāᵓika*, 24). It is much less certain that the *sidra* (*muntahā*) is the "white *Homā*," or that the *sirāṭ* is the Chinvat Bridge; and one ought at least to decide between Darmesteter (*Hautes Etudes* XXIII), who makes *Haurvatat* into *Hārūt*, and Blochet, who turns the same word into *al-Khiḍr*...

8. Cf. Kraemer (*RMM* XLIV, 51).

9. Theosophical tendency, perceptible in the Mānī and Ibn ᶜArabī, who fail to understand that access to a mystical goal depends above all on the judicious choice of one way, which strengthens the will in its unwavering aim. They imagine, to the contrary, that they will find surer access to union with the divinity by using all ritual means at once. This syncretist eclecticism prevents them from perceiving the gradual, irreparable, transforming differentiation along the road, between those who prostrate themselves on the "Way of the Cross" and those who are stretched out under the Juggernaut's chariot.

decay[10] cannot provide the basis for a valid explanation of the growth of any religion's dogma. Every religion, like Islam, has at its foundation a specific body of "prophetic" preaching. From this source it offers each adept an identical structure intended for the realization *ab intra* of a way of life. The sructure is characterized by "individualizing points" on the basic design of the catechism, and by "vital points" of contact with social reaction. These points are marked precisely by the *mutashābihāt,* terms that are said to be ambiguous because each believer may elucidate their meaning through a devoted effort of his whole being: by engraving them onto his memory, testing them with his intellect, putting them to work in his conduct.[11] Having asserted this, one may concede that certain lukewarm and disillusioned believers have made Qurʾānic *mutashābihāt* the locus for parasitic grafts, as they artificially joined foreign concepts to their decaying religious systems.

II) EARLY *NAḤW*

The second source is all of the purely Arabic disciplines of the first development of Islamic civilization: early grammer (before Sībawayh), the reading of the Qurʾān, pre-Ḥanafite jurisprudence, and the critique of the *ḥadīth* (before Yaḥyā Qaṭṭān).[12] It was grammar that furnished the mystics with the specialized meanings of the following terms (some are Qurʾānic): *ḍamīr, huwa huwa, ṣifa* (opp. *waṣf*), *ḥaqīqa* (opp. *majāz, maqāl*), *shāhid,* (opp. *mithāl*), *jamᶜ* (opp. *farq*), *maᶜrifa (opp. nakira*), *ḥulūl, ḥāl, rasm, ᶜilla, khafī* (opp. *jalī,* concerning *shirk*), *tajallī, iqtirān, mulḥaq, ishāra.*[13]

III) EARLY *KALĀM*

The third source is the purely Arab theological schools before ᶜAllāf and Naẓẓām: Khārijī and Murjiʾī, Qadarī and Jabarī. The words they clarified for the mystics are *ᶜaql, ᶜadl, tawḥīd, ᶜaraḍ* (opp. *dhāt*), *ṣifa* (opp. *naᶜt*), *ṣūra,* (opp. *maᶜnä*) *qadīm* (opp. *muḥdath,* Qur. 21:2), *tanzih, ᶜaẓama, thubūt, wujūd* (opp. *ᶜadam*). Other terms refer to very old legendary themes, crystallized by certain *ḥadīth* in the second century A.H.; we cannot be sure whether they came from pre-Islamic Arab or foreign sources. E.g.: *subuḥāt al-wajh,*

10. Which enters religious consciences that are gnawed by doubt, during periods of decadence, not at a beginning.

11. Cf. the verse of the *shemaᶜ Israel.*

12. *ᶜAlīl,* etc.

13. *Passion,* Fr 3:13/Eng 3:6, and index.

durra bayḍā, kibrīt aḥmar, shabb qaṭāt, ism aᶜẓam,[14] *dīk abyaḍ, ᶜanqā mughrib;*[15] and invocations like *yā munawwir al-qulūb, dalīl al-mutaḥayyirīn, ghāyat al-suᵓāl wa'l-maᵓmūl.*[16]

IV) HELLENISTIC LEARNING

The fourth source is the scientific teaching of the time, presented in a sort of κοινή [*koine*], or technical Aramaic lingua franca, that eastern philosophical syncretism constructed little by little over the first six centuries A.D.[17] by copying terms from either Greek or Persian. This syncretism is not exclusively Hellenistic, but contains Iranian (and perhaps Sogdian) elements; nor is it purely Neoplatonic or Hermetic, as some of its components are gnostic, "Bardaiṣanian,"[18] or Manichaean. It is more secular than religious, althouth it borrows certain Christian, pagan, and Mazdean ritual terms.[19] It is one, with its disparate elements combined into a single encyclopedic classification. Examples are, in medicine, the Syro-Persian terms of the school of Jundisābūr;[20] in the zodiac, *kadkhodā* (Persian), borrowed as the antithesis of *haylāj* (Greek: ὑλικός [*hulikos*]);[21] the books of Agathodemon (Hermeticism), which were combined with the books of Jāmāsp (Mazdeism).

Founded on the Aristotelian scientific canon and Hellenistic medicine and alchemy, these technical teachings were rapidly translated from the Aramaic into Arabic.[22] They influenced Islam along two lines. Gnosticism (astrology, alchemy, talismans) affected extremist Shiite sects; metaphysics, Sunni theologians.[23] Examples:

14. *Passion*, see index.

15. Ibn al-Kalbī (ap. Ibn Mukarram, *Lisān*, see under *ᶜanq*) gives a pre-Islamic etymology; ᶜA. M. Kindī (*Risāla*, 12) gives a Buddhist origin.

16. *Jawshan kabīr* of Hādī Sabziwarī, lith. 1267, p. 75, 78, 393.

17. As early as the sixth century A.D. Aramaic was overcoming Greek in the Eastern dissident churches. In the eleventh century, Arabic would take its place.

18. *Dayṣāniyya of the Fihrist* [cf. ch. 2 n 143].

19. Fundamental point: there was no direct, autonomous action of Greco-Syriac paganism or Persian Mazdeism on Islam; the propagating force of those two religions was already completely spent by that time. It was through the intermediary of Eastern philosophical syncretism that certain pagan and Mazdean terms were brought into Islam; they first had to encapsulated and cleansed by various initiatory teachings: Ḥarranian gnosticism, eastern Manichaeism (which, at the same time, in the Byzantine lands, was producing the movement of the Paulicians-Bogomils) and neo-Mazdakian communism (the Khurramiyya, converted c. 245 by Dindān to Ismaili Qarmathianism). On the other hand, we shall see that for a brief period there may have been some direct action of Hinduism on Islam (see below, sec. 3.E).

20. E. G. Browne, *Arabian Medicine*, 34–35 (cf. 28, 33).

21. *Passion*, see index.

22. Ibid., Fr 3:14–15/Eng 3:7–8.

23. Muᶜtazilites; and even the Syrian monophysite Christian, like Yaḥyā ibn ᶜAdī, who is a sort of pre-Averroist.

a) *Literal borrowings*. Arabic terms artificially diverted from their usual meanings (*ᶜilla, ṣūra, istiḥāla, iḍmiḥlāl, kawn* [opp. *fasād*], *ṭabīᶜa* [the four temperaments], *rawāʾiḥ* [chemical effluvia]); Arabic equivalents forged from corresponding Arabic root-material (*huwiyya, anniyya, talāshī, taʾal-luh, waḥdāniyya*);[24] words simply transcribed and Arabized (*jawhar, isṭaqsāt, kunnāsh*).

Borrowings classified by subject: astrology (*aflāk, adwār, akwār, nawrūz, zīj*,[25] *mihrijān, jawzahar, kardāj*, etc.); medicine[26] (*kunnāsh* [in Syriac = *jāmī* in Arabic], *tawallud, naẓar* [opp. *khabar*], *istidlāl, tarbiya* [= cosmetics], *aqrābādhīn, bazzahrd, tiryāq*); logic (the ten categories, or *dawāʾir*, of the pseudo-Empedocles); political morality (books of *akhlāq*, the Hellenized Fürstenspiegel of Anushirvan and Buzurjmihr; cf. Miskawayh; *dīwān, wazīr*);[27] asceticism (*jihād al-nafs* of Ibn al-Muqaffaᶜ; macrocosm and microcosm; *anwār* [celestial, incorruptible, spiritual substances, separate intelligences,[28] as opposed to the *ajsām* in the works of ᶜAli ibn Rabban and Jibrāʾīl Bukhtyishūᶜ [Bukhtīshūᶜ];* *Taḍmīr al-maydān* of Ibn Ḥayyān]).

b) *Structural parallels*. The doctrine of the opposites (light and darkness, books of *maḥāsin wa aḍḍād*); the discipline of the secret (starting with the Elchasaites and among the Manichaeans: *katmān, ifshā al-sirr*); the doctrine of countable causes (without *tasalsul*, but with the negation of the [virtual or actual] infinite, beginning with ᶜAlī ibn Rabban),[29] from which comes the role of causality in Ḥanafite law,[30] as well as medical etiology and therapeutics, perhaps imitated by the mystics for the "maladies of the heart"; the doctrine of the transmigration of souls that contaminates certain theologians, both Muᶜtazilite (Ibn Ḥāyiṭ, Ibn Yānūsh) and Qarmathian (Abū Yaᶜqūb Sijzī allows it, if within a given species);[31] spiritual, astrological determinism of movements and destinies: God himself cannot suspend the laws (*falak*) (therefore, the irresponsibility of souls [*ibāḥa*]).[32]

* See Browne's *Chahār Maqāla*, p. 145, on this name.

24. See below, n 156 and related text.

25. *Zīj shahryār*, trans. Tamīmī.

26. *Fihr*, 295.

27. The analogies pointed out between *fiqh* and Romano-Byzantine law, between *consensus prudentum* and *ijmāᶜ*, between *utilitas publica* and *maṣlaḥa*, are only approximations.

28. This specialization contradicts the usage of the *mutakallimūn*, as well as Hinduism.

29. *Firdaws*, ch. 7.

30. Santillana.

31. Bīrūnī, *Hind*, 31.

32. The same slightly Mazdean, fatalist nuance is found among the Qarmathians: irresponsibility in man corresponds, in God, to indeterminacy. The first Muslim mystics, on the other hand, believe in the free responsibility of man, predestined in God. And the Hindus exaggerate man's freedom so much that it becomes a power of liberating self-creation.

2. The Method of Interpretation

A. The Guiding Principles: Chances of Error, Pseudo-Borrowings

The preceding inventory is no more that an attempt to classify the data of the problem to be solved. Only a complete study of the early Islamic mystics' authentic works (enumerated here in chapter 4) will permit us, as we construct the lexicon of their Arabic, to answer the endlessly argued question of foreign influences[33] on Sufism's development.

The philological method is the only one that will permit the presentation of serious evidence, i.e., evidence that will be able to bring the specialists into agreement if certain rules are strictly observed:[34]

i) After indicating literal coincidences between two texts and justifying them chronologically and geographically, one must still demonstrate that there was a real genealogical kinship between the thoughts carried in those texts. Without that demonstration, the question remains unanswered.

ii) Gathering a list of items, accumulating examples of parallelism between the schematic formulas in two works, does not prove that a didactic relationship existed, that the two authors were teacher and pupil.

iii) An observation after the fact (given results and ramifications in society) that the guiding intentions of two prominent mystics have converged does not show that an agreement was made, or a word given; in short, that there was collusion. Two sincerities can be alike, without allegiance, and both be right.

These rules must be observed by literary critics who wish to avoid confusing original work with plagiarism. Not all writers are pirates dealing in themes from legend. Novelists do not necessarily sink into unconscious ventriloquism in imagining they can invent (as it must be admitted they can); nor poets, in believing they hear an inspired voice from within.

The cautionary measures are even more important for a historian of scientific methods; without them he risks confusing the inventor's imagination with the skill of the man who puts the invention to valuable use, the industrialist with the engineer, the capitalist with the technician.

They are absolutely indispensable to anyone wishing to savor and compare the works of mystical writers. The scholar will not succeed as long as

33. As foreign, that is, to the Arab world as to Islam. Imitation, *ad extra*; influence, *ab intra*.

34. They do not seem to be strictly observed by Kremer, *Culturgeschichtliche Streifzüge auf dem Gebiete des Islams* [*C.S.*], 1873.

he only classifies technical terms and compares the structure of the authors' statements of dogma; he must personally redo the moral experiment,[35] reliving the experience by putting himself, at least hypothetically, in the place of his subjects, in order to gain a direct, axial understanding of the consequences of their rules for living.

In comparative literature, especially in the field of popular myth, it is admitted, a little too easily,[36] that imitation of *X* by *Y*, or borrowing, has taken place, on the sole evidence that identical separate elements, such as the princess with golden hair or Tom Thumb, are found at the same spot in the fabric of two different fairy tales. If this purely formal comparative method is to be adapted to the study of philosophical and mystical lexicons, it must be changed profoundly. Two sailors from different counties, on a brief shore leave, can swap stories in sign language in the time it takes to buy each other a drink. Two philosophers will communicate more slowly, have more trouble making contact, perhaps need time for reflection. Two mystics will understand each other with even more difficulty: they must form judgments of each other and test the sincerity with which they put their rules for living into practice. Each must see the results of the other's rule.

When a storyteller composes a fable — groups themes, characters, and anecdotes in certain circumstances of time and place — it is said that the fable has sprung entirely[37] from his creative fancy. No set of axioms justifying the arrangement of images needs to be assimilated in order for listeners to understand. Therefore the fable, though transposed into other idioms and civilizations, can still be recognized by its basic structure.

When a philosopher or learned man organizes his research and constructs a theory, the ideas collected are concepts that have been elaborated over time and removed from the material from which they were once abstracted. Their arrangement no longer depends upon a narrative sequence of specific occurrences, accepted in order and without argument, as in the case of fairy tales.[38] The ideas are arranged in general logical categories; another mind, in order to penetrate such a theory, must climb the scaffolding of its rational logic, discovering the base, joints, and niches along the way. For example, in order for a historian of scientific methods to affirm that the Arabs borrowed a certain algebraic solution from the Indians,

35. Ghazālī explained this well in his *Munqidh*.

36. Because the subject of these tales is not pure anarchic subjectivism. There are commonplaces for all of humanity, principles of probability for the imagination, a common sense assumed even in the wildest fantasies.

37. Although in most countries an unprepared native audience cannot understand its own theater.

38. And many listeners cease to enjoy even these, after experiencing real events that contradict the arbitrary narrative line.

he must show not only that the givens of the problem, as presented among both groups, more or less coincide,[39] but that the structural process used to find the solution was the same.[40]

A fortiori in mysticism. In my view, in order for Nicholson to assert that a tenuous introspective definition or a new technical differential, such as the *fanā bī'l-Madhkūr* of Sufism, was borrowed from India (Patañjali's *dhyāna*), he must show not only that the same isolated elements exist in two authors, as he would have to do in the case of pure, imaginative fancy; and that the constructive process used to introduce this new differential was analogous, as if the mystical definition were a hypothetical scientific postulate; but also that the authors demonstrated the convergence of their guiding intentions by an equal conviction in their rules for living, and, if they were contemporaries, that they personally showed a burning mutual desire to convince each other:[41] he must prove in effect that the two were interpermeable.

Moreover, mystics do not, like literary authors, only consider intellectual themes for their own sake,[42] or, like scientists, only seek a solution that will generalize their ideas.[43] They consider the reality that practicing a constructive method can enable them to discover. One last, purely religious problem therefore arises: the reality that the mystic seeks is only known to have been achieved when we can observe the consequences, personal and social, of his life.

B. Some Fortuitous Coincidences

ISOLATED TECHNICAL HOMONYMS

i) *By a fortuitous coincidence of two independent thoughts with a limited register of corresponding images*[44]

The primordial point: *kha* (Sanskrit); *neqodā rishōnā* (talmudic); *nuqṭa aṣliyya* (Ḥallāj): coincidental terms, without any real kinship among their respective processes of formation.

39. Because the problem will arise *a priori* in every thoughtful mind independently undertaking an examination of the science in question.

40. Since there may be several independent processes leading to the same result (the demonstrations of a proposition, in mathematics; the various routes of an ascent, in mountain climbing).

41. This is the true mystical goal of sincere apologetics (cf. Leibniz and Bossuet, and, more deeply, the cases cited in *RMM* XXXVI, 57). The poetic outrageousness of the Arabs overshoots this goal in the odd legend of the two friends mentioned by Stendhal (*De l'amour*, book 2, ch. 53, "fragments"), excerpting from the *Kitāb al-Aghānī* [Fr. *Le Livre des chansons*].

42. Art for art's sake.

43. The passion for discovery; for the hunt (more than the catch), for the game (more than the stakes), for the search (more than the truth).

44. Images of universal human experience.

The archtypical man: *insān qadīm* (Manichaean); *adam qadmōn* (Kabbala); *insān kāmil* (Jīlī): same remark.[45]

ii) By borrowing for a particular purpose, without subsequent parallels of usage

The Highest name of God: *shem hamforash,* or the ineffable tetragram (Kabbala); *ism a^{c}ẓam* (Sufism).

The column of light: "central column" (Talmud); "column of praise" (var. *^{c}āmūd al-ṣubḥ*: Manichaean; *^{c}āmūd al-nūr*: Tustarī);[46] the role of the dawn[47] in the *Nuṣayrī* theogony.

The sparkling of wine (*tasha^{c}shu^{c}*) poured into a cup: symbol of theophany, through *talbīs* and *takhmīr* (as much for the Nuṣayrīs as for the Sufis) = the opalization or irisation of the (human) water into which the divine wine is poured (*Passion,* Fr 3:49, 53 I 24, 308 n 3, 353 n 1/Eng 3:41, 45 I 23, 290 n 74, 335 n 10).

Decorative motifs such as these, set into two systems of dogma, do not necessarily play the same role in both contexts. During a plea, if a lawyer takes up the opposing party's position word for word, he is not implying that it is as valid as his own. The habit does not make the monk, nor the note the song: we could not infer, simply because two authors have used the same words,[48] that there was even an understanding between them; *experimental* verification is required.

PARALLELS IN THE MANNER OF PRESENTATION

i) By natural, functional coincidence, when reason is properly exercised by both mystics on the same body of typical patterns with common themes (life, death, distributive justice)

These parallels are mentioned by Ghazālī in his *Munqidh,*[49] on the sub-

45. Cf. the invocation "God of gods, Lord of lords," which is found simultaneously among the Sabians (Ibn al-Ṣabbāḥ, ap. Shahrastānī, II, 47) and the Sufis (Ibn Adham, ap. *Passion,* Fr 3:15/Eng 3:8). Cf. the *ẓuhūr kullī,* the "clothing of spiritual light," which is found, having appeared by different processes, in Christianity, in Manichaeism, among the Sufis (Junayd, "Dawā": *libās al-nūr; kiswa* of Ḥallāj and Wāsiṭī), and among the Yogis (Patañjali, II, sec. 52). *A fortiori* we must absolutely refuse to see borrowings in paired words like "divine light," "illumination of the heart," "silence and solitude," and "God and the Beloved," which are common to mystics all over the world. Merx, Andrae, and Wensinck (*Dove,* P. lxxxiv, 11), seduced by Reitzenstein's hypothesis that the initiation rites of all forms of early Asian religious mysticism had a common source, applied it inappropriately and supposed it confirmed the opinion that such word-pairs were borrowings, as had already been suggested by certain esoterically minded historians of freemasonry in the beginning of the nineteenth century.

46. *Passion,* Fr 3:301/Eng 3:283; Kremer, *C.S.,* 39.

47. Dussaud, *Noseïris,* 88.

48. The problem of homonyms and synonyms (*Passion,* Fr 3:93 ff./Eng 3:82 ff.).

49. Cairo edition, p. 19; here B. de Meynard's translation (p. 38) is insufficient [*Recueil,* p. 94].

ject of some maxims he was said to have stolen from ancient philosophers: "The truth is that *some of them*[50] are the fruit of my own meditations, and, as the proverb says, 'The hoof sometimes[51] falls in the hoofprint.'" In other words, the range of the intellectual process and the rhythm of discursive thought are more or less commensurable and synchronous in those devoted to serious reflection, since the operation of reason is the sole means of understanding among men. Science — true, experimental science — is not the precarious and artificial result of a blind entangling of atoms. It is a collective conceptual construction that is always growing; since its beginnings we have been working on it together, and that work is at the very heart of our being as thinking creatures. We assimilate and elaborate our individual experiences according to analogous processes, in order to put them into accord. For example:

Perinde ac cadaver ["like the corpse"]:[52] "Mithl al-mayit fī yaday al-ghāsil," said Tustarī, well before St. Francis of Assisi and St. Ignatius of Loyola. Asin struggled to discover a common source (St. Nilus and St. John Climacus), but for solitary men living in groups and dying without gravediggers, the case was of sufficient immediacy to suggest the image.

Breath control: Patañjali's *prānāyāma*, rhythmic *dhikr* on the breathing pattern "hū! hā! hī!" in modern Islamic orders, and recitation of the Lord's prayer in the exercises of St. Ignatius Loyola. Patañjali practiced this discipline to make the will master the reflex of breathing, because he considered[53] the link between breath (*prāna*) and the actualization of thought (*vṛtti*) to be indissoluble. The Muslims practice it to concentrate their ecstatic hearing (*samā*ᶜ) because, during recitation, the alternation of breathing[54] best scans the heart's three vocalizations of the divine *H*. St. Ignatius practiced breath control[55] to tighten the frame around his mental contemplation by fixing the manner of recitation and the average length of prayers said aloud. The three motives and goals are different; the only common trace is regularization of breathing. All mystics are ascetics: they know that they have bodies to tame and that as long as the human body lives, it breathes.

ii) By borrowing, to rival each other in zeal and discover who is right

50. *"Some others,"* he adds, "are found on our books of sacred law (*al-kutub al-shar*ᶜ*iyya*); and *most, as to their meaning,* figure in the writing of the Sufis."

51. Often, not always, not for everyone. This is not the relativism of Protagoras.

52. Asin, *Bosquejo . . .*, Zaragoza, 1903, 38–39; Goldziher, *Vorlesungen*, Eng. trans. 132 n 51; Hartmann, *Darstellung des Sūfitums*, 31, 103; Kīlānī (ap. Shaṭṭanawfī, *Bahja*, 79); Rinn, *Marabouts*, 90.

53. It is an asceticism of the breath, not of the heart (*anāhata*, seat of the *sattva*: *Yoga* III, sec. 34), as in Islam. Cf. Kremer (*C.S.*, 49).

54. Cf. the regular swaying of the torso of a child reciting a lesson in Qurᵓānic school.

55. *Spiritual Exercises*, fourth week, third method of prayer.

For example:

Vegetarianism (*tanaḥḥus*):[56] common to Christian, Manichaean, and Muslim ascetics. Among the Manichaeans, as St. Augustine indicates,[57] its exact purpose was to free the points of divine light imprisoned like captives in the dark matter of the vegetables. The disciples of St. Anthony gave it an entirely different meaning, that of bodily mortification for the ascetic himself. The Muslims agreed with the Christians, with certain nuances:[58] a sort of "perpetual vow" of vegetarianism (*qūt*) was the means by which the members of a Shiite mystical sect, the ᶜAbdakiyya Sufis[59] of Kūfa, bore witness to the ardor of their wait for the imminent coming of the Mahdī.

CONVERGENCES OF GUIDING INTENTION

i) By concordance in the development of morals and dogma

For example:

The wager (on the hypothesis of eternal life): Pascal and Ghazālī, moved by the same apologetic compassion for unbelievers, formulated this idea in the same terms and patterns, although Pascal knew nothing of Ghazālī.[60]

ii) By legitimate borrowing

The borrower feels the richness of an argument barely outlined in the book in which he finds it; having meditated, he in turn takes it up, strengthens it, gives it full weight. Some of Ghazālī's arguments that remained sterile in Islam were made fertile in this way by the Jew, Bahya ben Paquda,[61] and the eastern Christian Bar Hebraeus.[62] The same arguments gave better results to the coreligionists of the two borrowers than to those of the inventor. Another example:

The replacement of the *ḥajj* (the pilgrimage of sacred law) by devotional activity, a thesis of Ḥallāj's school of mysticism: An outstanding ex-

56. Ibn Sīda, *Mukhaṣṣaṣ*, XIII, 101.

57. *Confessiones*, III, 10; VIII, 6; cf. VII, 9, his remarks on the Christian *logos* and its Neoplatonic homonym.

58. Ascetic rivalry (to convince the adversary of the superiority of one's doctrine, by struggling to show greater abnegation) implies no doctrinal concession. Roberto de Nobili's method [cf. below, n 240], understood in this way, has no relation to the "Chinese rites" and "Malabar rites," both dangerous experiments.

59. Malaṭī, f. 162.

60. Asin tried to find, in either the *Pugio fidei* or Herbelot, the intermediary who might have introduced Ghazālī to Pascal . . . with no success.

61. See his *Hidāya*.

62. Wensinck, *The Book of the Dove*.

ample of guiding intention outlined by predecessors (in order to combat the *ᶜumūm al-maghfira's* lax inclinations)[63] and given full weight by Ḥallāj himself. It first appears with Ḥasan Baṣrī, who remarks[64] that the only "blessed pilgrimage" (*ḥajj mabrūr*) is the one from which the pilgrim returns as an ascetic in this world and desiring the next life. Ibn al-Munkadir[65] calls this pilgrimage "the one that wins passage to Paradise." Soon we find moral counselors giving practical advice of greater and greater boldness: Abū Ḥāzim Madanī advises a young man to abandon the pilgrimage and devote the money intended for travel expenses to supporting his mother.[66] Bishr Ḥāfī suggests[67] that a large sum hoarded for the pilgrimage[68] be distributed as alms. In a very lovely parable, Dhū'l-Nūn Miṣrī speaks[69] of a man from Damascus who gave up the pilgrimage in order to relieve the distress of a famished neighbor *hic et nunc.* The mystic says that God, solely for the sake of this man, who had "made the pilgrimage in spirit" (*ḥajja bihimmatihi*), granted a pardon to the pilgrims gathered at ᶜArafāt that year. Finally Ibn ᶜAṭā, commenting on a gloss by Jaᶜfar on Qur. 3:96, notes, "Whoever has deprived himself of everything for God sees the road of the *ḥajj* open wide before him, for *there* is the foundation (*qiwām*) of the call (to all Muslims) to the *ḥajj*."[70] Ḥallāj's thesis, which I have analyzed elsewhere at length,[71] is the correct dogmatic conclusion to be drawn from these premises.[72]

3. The Role of Foreign Influences

A. The *a priori* Thesis of Iranian Influence

The proper share of certain external influences on Islamic mysticism remains to be assigned.

63. Repudiated by Ramlī (*Passion*, Fr 3:223 n 11/Eng 3:211 n 266).
64. Makkī, *Qūt*, II, 119.
65. Ibid., II, 115, 118.
66. Hujwīrī, *Kashf*, 91.
67. Makkī, *Qūt*, I, 92. One of the Sālimiyya, probably at the time of the Qarmathian occupation of Mecca, advised giving up the pilgrimage "rather than aiding the enemies of Islam" Ibid., II, 117, I. 23). The advice was recently (after 1916) followed by opponents of the Malik of the Ḥijāz.
68. "Supplementary" or "surplus," says Makkī's text, which seems, to attenuate the advice incautiously.
69. Ibn al-Jawzī *Muthīr al-gharām*, ap. Ibn ᶜArabī, *Muḥāḍarāt*, I, 218. Cf. ᶜAlī ibn al-Muwaffaq (Makkī, *Qūt*, II, 120–21).
70. Baqlī, I, 107.
71. *Passion*, index, s.v. *ḥajj*.
72. When that conclusion was condemned, Makkī defined the purity of real intention (*ḥaqīqat al-ikhlāṣ*) required for the pilgrimage (*Qūt*, II, 115) as follows: "spending legitimate wealth for the love of God, keeping one's hand empty of all barter that might preoccupy the heart and distract the attention (*hamm*)."

Ghazālī[73] defines mysticism as the thorough, inner examination of religious experiments and of their results in the practicing believer. If we adopt his definition, we must recognize that in any religious milieu where there are sincere and thoughtful souls, cases of mysticism will be observed. Therefore, it is impossible for mysticism to be the exclusive privilege of one race, language, or nation. It is a human phenomenon, on the level of the spirit, that those physical boundaries could not contain. We cannot accept the exact sense of the overly popular theory of pro-Aryans like Gobineau and anti-Semites like Friedrich Delitzsch,[74] that the Semitic peoples are completely unfit for the arts and sciences in general,[75] and that mysticism in the Semitic religions is of Aryan origin. Naturally, the theorists deny the authenticity of Islamic mysticism, which is portrayed as a form of the racial, linguistic, and national reaction by the Aryan peoples, particularly the Iranians, against the Arab Islamic conquest. Renan, P. de Lagarde, and more recently Reitzenstein, Blochet, and E.G. Browne, have helped to spread this theory.[76]

It is an *a priori* theory that wrongly generalizes from a few special cases.[77] It assumes the indemonstrable idea that Iran in the seventh century A.D. was peopled solely by Aryans with an entirely Aryan culture.[78] In reality Shiism, which is presented to us as a specifically Persian Islamic heresy, was propagated in Persia by pure Arab colonists, who had come from Kūfa to Qum.[79] The Kurds and Afghans, pure Iranians by race, have always been anti-Shiite. The lists of great Muslim thinkers said to be of "Persian origin," because their *nisba* refers to a city in Persia, are misleading.[80] Most of these men thought and wrote only in Arabic, and were no more separate from the Islamic world, whether they were the sons of clients (*mawālī*)[81] or Arab colonists, than was Lucan of Cordova or Augustine of Tagaste from the Roman. Incensed heresiographers[82] have imagined numerous "Mazdean survivals" that "conspirators" are supposed to have smuggled into Islam; Firdawsī's *Shāhnāmeh*, celebrated as the hand-

73. *Munqidh.*

74. *Die Grosse Taüschung.*

75. The distinct Semitic reserve in these matters is not lack of imagination but respectful deference to the initiative of divine omnipotence.

76. The only person who has tried to support the theory with precise arguments is Inostranzev, *Iranian Influence on Moslem Literature,* trans. G.K. Nariman, Bombay, Taraporevala, 1918.

77. Diffusion of technical procedures in architecture, carpet making, metallurgical arts, floral decoration (narcissus preferred to the rose), the musical scale, the setting for stories (*Hezārafsāneh*).

78. Neither physical nor cultural anthropologists accept this.

79. Goldziher, *Vorlesungen*, Eng. trans., 212 n 125.

80. The Panturanians have recently raised the stakes, claiming Fārābī, Ibn Sīnā, Bukhārī, and Zamakhsharī as Tartar national treasures . . . Even the Shuᶜūbiyya used to speak of equality.

81. On the Arabization of *mawālī*, see Goldziher, *M. Stud.* I, 101 ff., 147 ff.

82. Baghdādī.

book of this Iranian nationalism,[83] demonstrates above all an archeological enthusiasm, almost as impartial as the Trojan patriotism of Virgil writing the *Aeneid.*

Finally, this theory, supposedly erected to the glory of the Iranian race, would lead us to perceive unconscious disloyalty in its most illustrious representatives. The theory insinuates that the great Muslim thinkers of Iran, contrary to their explicit statements, gave allegiance only for appearances' sake to orthodox Islam, and that they made considerable efforts to twist and mold it to their narrow, national bias. The explanation is psychological, and it will not convince anyone who has lived in intimacy with the works of these great men. No one's loyalty is greater than Sībawayh's in Arabic grammar, Isfahānī's in Arab folklore, Ṭabarī's and Fakhr Rāzī's in Qurʾānic exegesis. These Persians did nothing to alter the purity of early Islam; in fact they went to greater lengths than anyone else in self-denial and the sacrifice of personal inclinations, in order to safeguard the universalism of their beliefs. It would be rather presumptuous to argue that they did not succeed.[84]

The limited truth, unduly generalized by the theory of Aryan superiority, is that the general grammatical characteristics (vocabulary, morphology, syntax) of our Indo-European languages determine that when an idea is expressed in them, its outer form will differ entirely from its clothing in a Semitic language. The idea's Aryan presentation, the only one familiar to Western orientalists, is periphrastic, made of words with unstable, shaded contours and changeable endings, words fit for apposition and combination. Very early on, verbal tenses in these languages became relative to the agent, egocentric, polytheistic; the words also have a didactic order, and are arranged in long hierarchical periods by means of graduated conjunctions. The Semitic presentation of the idea is gnomic, employing rigid words with immutable and always noticeable roots. The few changes allowed are internal and abstract: consonants are interpolated for the general meaning, vowels altered for the precise shade.[85] The conjunctive role of particles is inseparable from the vocalic changes in endings; verbal tenses,

83. The works of supposed nationalists like Ibn al-Muqaffaʿ, Rūdagī, Miskawayh, Ḥasan Ṣabbāḥ are filled with a universalist spirit, either Hellenistic or Qarmathian. Even an arch-nationalist like the poet Mihyār Daylamī was writing characteristically when he finished a line, *"sūdad al-Furs wa dīn al-ʿArab,"* [Glory is ours from both sides] "Persian noble titles (in this world), and the Arabs' religion (for the next life)!"

84. We find what are basically the same stages of a growing "mobilization" of the literary theme, among Aryans and Semites: *epic* (= *qaṣīda*), *drama* (= *qiṣṣa* alternating between prose and verse), *romance* (= *maqāma*); in the first stage, only the memory of the listener is involved; in the second, the actor or reciter goes to work on the intelligence of the spectator; in the third, the reader's will itself is seized. But among the Aryans the form is capricious and the foundation precise; while among Semites the form is rigid, the foundation capricious, unreal.

85. *Passion,* Fr 3:90 ff./Eng 3:79 ff.

even today, are absolute (they concern only the action) and theocentric (they affirm the transcendence and imminence of the One Agent); and finally, word order is lyrical, with phrases parceled into staccato formulas, condensed and autonomous. Whence the misunderstanding of those who, unable to perceive the powerful, explosive concision of Semitic languages, pronounce them unfit for mysticism. They are, after all, the languages of revelation of the transcendent God, of the Prophets,[86] and of the Psalms. And the Psalms, historically, are the mystical text most widely known among men.[87] In Islam, the *Fātiḥa* is a psalm,[88] the two suras of *Ubayy* are psalms, as are the *muᶜawwidhatayn*. The *munājāt* of the first Sufis are psalms as well.

Unable to hold the racial and national ground, the partisans of Iranian influence retreat to linguistic territory; they can show only that certain languages (Semitic) are less appropriate than others (Aryan) for the didactic exposition of ideas; a rather secondary observation in religious matters, particularly in mysticism. Like Christianity, Islam has been preached in all languages, including those least like Arabic,[89] most stripped of grammar, such as Chinese. Mysticism, more than any proselytizing mission, can do without long grammatical periods; in the extreme case, onomatopoeia is enough: the cry that is understood if it is from the heart.[90]

In neither the grammar nor the literature of the conquered provinces was there a serious reaction against the Arab conquerors' Islamic doctrine. For one or two generations, almost imperceptibly, writers of Greek (Syria) and Persian[91] (or *huzvaresh* in Mesopotamia) continued to be employed at keeping the financial records concerning deeds to land, just long enough for new civil servants capable of writing Arabic to be trained. The Raqqāshī family, famous preachers in Persian, would quickly learn to excel in Arabic sermons on the Qurʾān, in Baṣra.[92]

B. Requirements for Demonstrating Foreign Influence

In summary: In order to prove that a linguistic influence from a foreign

86. Wensinck (*Dove*, p. xlvi) goes very far in his search for a Hermetic origin of an image in Bar Hebraeus, who is alluding to Ezekiel's "Ancient of Days."

87. Wensinck (*Dove*, p. xxii) omits reference to this.

88. A bitter enemy like ᶜA. M. Kindī (*Risāla*, 141) admits this without realizing it.

89. The Panturanians succeeded in writing perfectly orthodox Muslim catechisms in pure Turkish.

90. Popular preachers do not take lessons in diction or rhetoric.

91. Muqaddasī, 133.

92. Jāḥiẓ, *Bayān*, I, 168: though Ḥasan Baṣrī sometimes spoke in Persian (Ibn Saᶜd, VII, 123), Ḥallāj no longer had fluent use of the language (*Passion*, Fr 1:212–13/Eng 1:168). List of the great *mawālī* ap. ᶜ*Iqd*, II, 64.

source entered, permeated, and operated within a system of dogma in a given milieu, it must be shown:[93]

i) historically, that there was daily social contact and ferment between the two milieux. If this contact was not intellectual, it must at least have been practical; at a certain time, translators must have effected a *transposition*, borrowing stories and verbal elements from the foreign idiom.

ii) philosophically, that religious disputants and apologists adapted various concepts and partial, incompletely formulated theories from the foreign idiom. It is therefore important that this idiom should have contained, directed, and transported analogous dogmatic constructions. Only such an intellectual and moral affinity[94] makes possible a hybridization of the conquered milieu and the religion of the conquerors.

The first condition is met for the Aramaic (and the Arabic) of the Jewish and Christian circles (desert tribes, manufacturing colonies in cities), as well as the Mazdean (*huzvaresh*) and especially Manichaean circles (manufacturing colonies in cities), which were allied to the schools of eastern syncretism (dispersed physicians and philosophers). The condition is not met for the Pracrits of India (only one Indian merchant colony: Baṣra).[95]

By the criteria of that condition, the Hebrew-Christian milieu was the most important in relation to early Islam, because, at the time, it possessed analogous sketches of theology[96] and theoretical mysticism, and above all an admirable and widely read manual of prayer, the Psalms. In the second rank were the syncretist Helleno-Manichaeans, who were trying to annex theology and mysticism to their synthetic philosophy.

C. The Hebrew-Christian Milieu: Asceticism and Theology

We must first examine the possible influence on the Muslim believers' ritual intentions of the Hebrew-Christian group, the Arabic or Aramaic-speaking *ahl al-kitāb*, with whom the Qurʾān specifically authorizes[97] the pursuit of exegetical discussion. In practice, even conscientious commen-

93. *RMM*, XXXVI, 40 ff.; *Passion*, Fr 3:7, 257/Eng 3:xii, 243.

94. This would be a tolerable definition of a word much abused since Goethe.

95. Nor for Syria's peasants, who are supposed to have remained pagan (?), according to Dussaud's rash hypothesis: his equation Nāzirenī-Nuṣayrī falls apart because, as I discovered in the field, the *jurʿat al-Nāzirān*, northwest of lake Ḥums, still exists, without any geographical or etymological connection to the country of the Nuṣayrīs (*RMM*, XXXVIII, 272).

96. There is no precise textual basis for Kremer and Becker's hypothesis on Christian theology's influence on Maʿbad and Ghaylān (Qadarī school). Galtier, in his study of the *Thousand and One Nights* (*Mémoires*, Cairo, 178–79), has shown the inanity of the "Talmudism" that Chauvin supposes to be in the legend of Mālik ibn Dīnār.

97. Qur. 10:94; 5:18. See a work by Biqāʿī allowing references to Christian and Jewish scripture, in order to avoid the wave of *ḥadīth qudsī* (cf. Steinschneider, *Pol.*, 390). Biqāʿī, *Naẓm al-durar*.

tators like Mujāhid[98] and Muqātil[99] were reproached for these discussions, which were called dangerous. But a series of historical and legendary examples establishes the reciprocal curiosity, the awareness of an intellectual and moral affinity, that I believe to be indispensable for the beginning of doctrinal hybridization between two milieux.

Geiger,[100] Kaufmann,[101] Merx,[102] Wensinck, and Hirschfeld[103] have insisted on this affinity, for the Hebraic milieu; Merx, Asin, and Becker,[104] for the Christian.

HEBREW-CHRISTIAN ELEMENTS[105] (IN ARABIZED ARAMAIC FORM)[106]

i) *Literal borrowings* (*theological and ascetic words*). — Arabized words (nouns ending in *-ān*, or of the form *fāᶜūl*; adjectives ending in *-ānī*): *Qurᵓān, Raḥmān, ṭūfān, furqān, burhān, sulṭān*; *lāhūt, nāsūt, nāmūs*; *fārūq, jabrūt, malakūt*; *hākūl* (*haykal*); *kawn* (= *kyānā*, meaning both nature and person); *ṭūbā, rabbānī, rūḥānī, nafsānī, juthmānī, shaᶜshaᶜānī*; *waḥdāniyya, fardāniyya, rahbāniyya*; *ᶜubūdiyya, rubūbiyya, ulūhiyya, kayfūfiyya*. And

— Arabic words borrowed from Aramaic patterns or types, and then specialized: *sāᵓiḥ, rāhib, ghulām,* (deacon), *ṣawmaᶜa, ᶜukāz, tarbiya, sarīra* (truth), *ṭabᶜ* (from which comes *ṭabīᶜa*); *Bārī, bariya*.

ii) *Structural analogies*. Eschatological meditations on Hell and Paradise (Qurᵓān; literature of the *kutub al-zuhd, al-ahwāl, al-tawahhum*);[107] methods for the examination of conscience (*muḥāsabat al-nafs*);[108] scapular (*khirqa*, beginning with Ibn Ḥarb);[109] rosary (*subḥa*, beginning with Junayd); the talmudic rule of the blue and black threads for breaking the fast; Farqad's

98. Dhahabī, *Iᶜtidāl*.
99. Muqātil, *mutashābih*, explanation of the *sakīna*.
100. *Was hat Mohammed aus dem Judenthum aufgenommen*, 1833.
101. *Gesch. der Attributenlehre in der Jud. Relig.*, 1877.
102. *Grundlinien der Sufik*, 1892.
103. *Jüdische Elem.*, 1878; *New Researches*, 1902.
104. *Der Islam*, III, 374–99; *Christentum und Islam*.
105. We give the terms that figure in the Qurᵓān first.
106. Note the general "warping" of the radicals' meaning, as they pass from Aramaic into Arabic: *RḤM* (love; compassion); *ṢBR* (hope; endurance); *FRQ* (to save; to separate); *ḤMD* (to thank; to glorify); *SDD* (equity; exactitude).
107. In which Muslim ascetics are not trying to imitate Christian monks but to be their rivals in *rahbāniyya*, in accordance with a Muslim method inspired by the Qurᵓān.
108. Asin transforms the analogy into a borrowing and presumes that St. Ignatius of Loyola copied his way of noting personal examination, on a double-entry table, from Suhrawardī (*Bosquejo*, 40). As if the idea of a double-entry table were not a commonplace of any rational method.
109. V.i.

ṣūf (Christian tendency);[110] the *muraqqaᶜa*. The Arabic Gospel translations *used in Islam*[111] at the beginning (Ibn Qutayba,[112] Warrāq, Sulamī,[113] Ibn Jahḍam,[114] Ibn Ḥazm, Ghazālī) have not yet been studied seriously. Wensinck is now trying to prove that Stephen bar Sudaili, Isaac of Ninevah, and St. John Climacus were read by Muslims.[115] I have pointed out Aramaisms in Junayd's syntax.[116]

iii) Fertile hybridizations. During the first two centuries, Arab Muslims and their Christian compatriots lived among one another in Taghlib, Ḥīra, Kūfa,[117] Najrān,[118] Ṣanᶜā.[119] It seems established that hermitage architecture was copied; the first *khānqāh* were at Ramla (Abū Hāshim) and Jerusalem (Ibn Karrām). Until about 250/864[120] Muslim mystics went to consult Christian hermits on theology: ᶜAbd al-Wāḥid ibn Zayd, ᶜAttābī, and Dārānī recorded curious encounters.[121] While the anecdote about Bisṭāmī in Rūm[122] may be apocryphal,[123] the one about Ḥallāj in Jerusalem appears to be authentic.[124] The caliphal decrees[125] requiring distinctive clothes for Christians put an end to this life in common. Muḥammad ibn Faraj ᶜĀbid (d. 282 A.H.), answering Muḥammad ibn Isḥāq Kūfī,[126] asked, "From what source does such wisdom (*ḥikma*) come to damned monks?" "Legacy of the fast, which you find so painful." And Ibrāhīm ibn al-Junayd (died c. 270), editor of the *Kitāb al-ruhbān* of Burjulānī (d. 283), said[127] he found as an epigraph to one of Burjulānī's books (that same book, no doubt) these meaningful lines: *Mawāᶜiẓu ruhbān* ...

110. V.i.
111. For Christian recensions, see, Graf, *Christlich. Arab. Lit.*, 1905.
112. *Taʾwīl*, pp. 262, 270, 181.
113. *Jawāmiᶜ*, ms. Laleli 1516, f. 165b (= Matt. 8:22).
114. *Bahja*, ms. Damascus.
115. Cf. Nöldeke, *Aram. lit.*, *in Kult. Gegenw.*, 113. Since Wensinck (on Isaac of Ninevah), no one has pursued the study of possible Syriac models (hagiography, discourses on morals, philosophy). Tor Andrae undertook research on the subject, echoes of which are found in his posthumously published book on Sufism, *I Myrten-trädgården*, Stockholm. The great *Geschichte der christlichen arabischen Literatur* by Georg Graf (Rome, 1952) is a valuable source for the Arab period, to be combined with the recent discoveries in the Sinai (cf. Mourad Kamil, *Les Mardis de Dar el-Salam*, II [1952], Cairo, 205–18).
116. *Passion*, ch. 14, Fr 3:357/Eng 3:339.
117. Lammens, *Moᶜawia*, 156, 256, 300, ff. Cf. studies of L. Cheïkho.
118. Mission of Euphēmion (Ibn ᶜArabī, *Muḥāḍarāt*, I, 131, 94; *RHR*, XXVIII, 13).
119. Ibn ᶜArabī, *Muḥāḍarāt*, I, 182.
120. Afterwards, the "visit to the convent" is no more than a Bacchic theme for poetry.
121. Ibn ᶜArabī, *Muḥāḍarāt*, II, 353–54, 39.
122. Ms. Paris 1913.
123. Like the stories of Ḥasan Baṣrī's conversion and Maᶜrūf's burial in ᶜAṭṭār.
124. *Passion*, Fr 1:162–63, 3:233/Eng 1:121–22, 3:220.
125. De Goeje, *Conquête de la Syrie*, 148.
126. Cf. *Iᶜtidāl*, s.v.
127. *Ḥilya*, under the name Muḥammad ibn Faraj ᶜĀbid.

Monks' sermons, accounts of their acts,
true tidings from condemned souls.
Sermons that cure us as we gather them,
though the prescription comes from someone damned.
Sermons from which the soul inherits a warning (*ᶜibra*)
that leaves it anxious, wandering among the tombs.
Sermons, though the soul hates to be reminded of them.
that incite the heart they have discovered to suffering.
Take this for yourself, you who understand me: If you know how to defend yourself from evil,
hurry! Death is the first visitor to be expected.

[*Recueil*, 1929, 14–15]

A certain number of ascetic Islam's early works seem to be free transpositions of Christian writings: the *Ṣaḥāʾif Idrīs wa Mūsā*, Wahb's false Psalter (*Zabūr*),[128] and his *Mubtadā* and *Isrāʾīliyāt*; the *Akhbār al-māḍiyīn* of the Murjiʾite ᶜUbayd Jurhumī,[129] and especially the parables attributed to Jesus, which Asin published under the title *Logia D. Jesu . . . agrapha*, of which almost identical versions can be found in Dustuwāʾī (d. 153), Muḥāsibī, (d. 243), and Jāḥiẓ (d. 255).[130]

D. Near-Eastern Syncretism: Sciences, Philosophy, Hermeticism

Muslim believers had an affinity for a second group, the technical teachers (medicine, alchemy, abstract mathematics, astrology) of the Near-Eastern syncretist milieu defined above. Renan, working with Chwolsohn's confused data, was the first to perceive the milieu's existence;[131] Horovitz[132] and Wensinck[133] have recently defined its characteristics. It held the precious deposits of the corpus or organon of the science of nature, which, as a descendent of Hellenistic experimentation, was cast in the Aristotelian mold. The Neoplatonists had already, in the third century, annexed certain elements of Hermeticism;[134] the Manichaeans, in the fourth century, astrological and gnostic elements (Renan says "Elcha-

128. Ibn ᶜArabī, *Muḥāḍarāt*, I, 237; cf. Ghazālī, *Iḥyā*. Cf. mss. Oxford Nicoll 79; London Supp. 261; Paris 1397 (Cheïkho).

129. *Fihrist*, 89.

130. Asin, *Logia*, nos. 6, 53; Muḥāsibī, *Naṣāʾiḥ*, 6b; *Bayān*, III, 72.

131. *JAP*, 1853, 5th series, II, 430.

132. *Über den Einfluss der griechish. Philos. auf die Entwickl. des Kalam*, 1909.

133. *Book of the Dove*.

134. I have grouped some pieces of information in appendix 3 of Festugière's *Hermétisme*, Paris, 1943, 384–400, to be complemented by P. Kraus, *Jābir*, Cairo (IFAO).

saite").* In the sixth century, the corpus itself, literally translated from the Greek into Aramaic during the Syriac national awakening, was being taught in the same way at various centers in Syria, Mesopotamia, and the area of Susa; these were medical, alchemical, and semi-initiatory centers where Jewish and Christian (especially Nestorian) teachers came into contact with semi-pagans (Ḥarrānians), Bardaiṣanians (*dayṣāniyya*), and Manichaeans.[135]

Upon making this contact with Jews and Christians, the Muslims hesitated somewhat to imitate them. Throughout the second century of the Hijra, some isolated individuals, some *zanādiqa*, Ibn abī'l-ᶜAwjā, Ibn al-Muqaffaᶜ, Jābir, and, to a lesser extent, the extremist Shiites, took the risk. Ibn Muᶜāwiya adopted the astronomical calculation of the new moon.[136] Jābir used isolated letters of the alphabet to represent, in fixed systems of notation (alchemical, algebraic, syllogistic,[137] and medical),[138] the permanent natural functions of things.[139] Finally, Ibn al-Ḥakam rediscovered the Aristotelian theory of the process of sensation (*mizāj al-ajsām*) and perceived the immateriality of the concept (*sunḥ*).

It was only in the third century that a work of fiction adapted from the Qurᵓān, the romance of the Sabians, allowed the generalization of contacts between Islam and the scientific syncretist milieux. The school of Ḥarrān, persecuted in 148 and 159,[140] was summarily ordered to convert to Islam; in 208 its members succeeded in convincing the Caliph Maᵓmūn that they were descended from the monotheistic Sabians mentioned in the Qurᵓān[141] and that they should have the same status as Christians and Jews, with whom debate was legal.

The ruse worked. In the same period, an Ibāḍite from Fārs, Yazīd ibn abī Unaysa, announced[142] the imminent arrival of true "Sabianism," "not

*On this point, it seems (since the deciphering of the Codex Manichaicus Coloniensis in 1970) that Renan may well have been right as to the origin of these elements, since the Mughtasila of al-Ḥasīḥ (see *Fihrist*, p. 340), among whom Mānī was raised, are now known to be identical to the Elchasaites of Christian heresiography; on the question of the identity or nonidentity of the sects Elchasaites, Mughtasila, Mandaeans, Sabians (*Ṣābat al-Baṭāᵓiḥ*), see, e.g., S. N. C. Lieu, *Manichaeism*, 30–32. None of which answers the question that Massignon raises (see ch 2 n 143) of amalgamations within Muslim tradition of Bardaiṣan and Ibn Maymūn, both of whom were referred to as Ibn Dayṣān.

135. Cf. the odd, semi-Manichaean gospel fragment, in *Ikhwān al-ṣafā*, IV, 115–17.

136. This work, p. 141.

137. Which makes the old grammarians indignant (Yāqūt, *Udabā*, III, 105–24, after Tawḥīdī).

138. Tables of medicines.

139. Which presupposes the concept of nature (*tabīᶜa*), of the natural properties of things (a concept absent from early Muslim *kalām*). It is the idea of *jafr* rationalized (cf. *Passion*, Fr 3:105/Eng 3:95, and the idea of *Ars magna* in Ramon Lull); see the collation given at the end of this chapter.

140. Destruction of its great shrine.

141. Qur. 2:59; 5:73; 22:17; seeming to mean, according to Bīrūnī (*Āthār*), the Mandaeans or Mughtasila of Wāsiṭ [known since 1970 to be a false identification].

142. Shahrastānī, I, 183.

that of Wāsiṭ or Ḥarrān," which was supposed to absorb Islam and reconcile all sects and castes. By about 210 ᶜAbdallāh ibn Maymūn al Qaddāḥ, a man from Mecca, was dying in prison in Kūfa after founding the astonishing secret society[143] that was supposed to realize this ideal program: the Qarmathians or Ismailis.[144]

For two centuries, under severe Ismaili discipline, Hellenistic "Sabianism," in the threefold form into which it was organized by Qarmathian propaganda, diffused the following throughout Islam: an expanded spirit of scientific research;[145] syncretism that reconciled all religious confessions by using a methodically graduated theosophical catechism;[146] and initiatory communism that propagated a ritual of companionship and an understanding among trade organizations, and led to the institution of the political Ismaili imāmate, or Faṭimism. Ismailism's egalitarian religious tolerance is well defined by the encyclopedia of the *Ikhwān al-ṣafā*,[147] by the apostolate of *Nāṣir-i-Khusraw* (d. 481),[148] by the politics of Ḥasan ibn al-Ṣabbāḥ (d. 518), founder of the sect of the Assassins, whose "new propaganda" could still argue for "Sabian" universality of *khalīliyya*.[149] The wars of the Crusaders clipped the wings of Faṭimism;[150] the same stroke saved Sunni orthodoxy, which was being threatened. On the other hand, the great scientific teaching favored by the Faṭimids passed to Europe and infused initiatory eastern elements[151] into the corporative movement in our early universities.

How much did eastern syncretism, at least in the transitional forms[152] of Hellenistic Sabianism and Qarmathian Ismailism, affect the Muslim mystics?

143 There is research to be done as to whether the society was somehow connected to the alleged "Bardaiṣanians" mentioned by Ibn al-Nadīm (*Fihrist*, 339), because Ibn Maymūm was sometimes called "Ibn Dayṣān."

144. See my *Bibliographie qarmate* [*Opera Minora*, 1:627–39].

145. Highly developed zoology; medicine (opposed to *ṭibb al-Nabī* and to *ṭibb rūḥānī*); logic (opposed to grammar); astronomical calendars (opposed to *taᶜbīr*) and Indian *jafr* (as opposed to Arab *anwāʾ*).

146. Graduated pedagogy (as opposed to Qurʾānic school); politics and Hellenized constitutional law (as opposed to *fiqh*).

147. Casanova dates the modified version c. 450; we know that the basic material is older because Tawḥīdī (d. 414) already knew and appreciated it (Bahbahānī, ms. London add, 24,411, f. 182b).

148. *Zād al-musāfirīn*.

149. Extract of his *Fuṣūl arbaᶜa*, ap. Shahrastānī.

150. It was not the Sunni caliph of Baghdād but rather the Faṭimid anticaliph (who had destroyed the Holy Sepulchre in 1009), who was stricken by the taking of Jerusalem.

151. Contemporaries knew of this: Joachim of Flora, in Messina in 1195, learned from a man returning from Alexandria "that the Patarenes (Cathars) had sent agents among the Saracens to come to an understanding with them" (*Expositio in Apocalypsin*, cap. IX, ed. Venice, 1527, p. 134).

152. The translations themselves had very little immediate effect: three centuries would pass before a Plotinian text like the *Theology of Aristotle* (translated into Arabic in the third century A.H.) affected any Muslim mystics. Then it had influence thanks to two linked series of intermediaries: hybrid philosophers like Fārābī, Miskawayh, and Ibn Sīnā; and syncretist encyclopedists

In the third century A.H., at the time of their first encounter, early Islamic mysticism and Hellenistic philosophical sycretism possessed independent lexicons and opposed doctrines.

Lexicons. Mystics use the terms of classical *kalām* in their ordinary senses, not in the specialized manner proposed by the philosophers: e.g., *kawn*, instantaneous existentialization (not genesis, natural growth, opp. *fasād*); and *ṭabīᶜa*, habit imposed upon a creature, as a visible seal or distinguishing mark (not one of the body's four internal humors). The mystics also follow the rules of Arabic grammar in choosing their terms, unlike the translators of philosophy, who divert usage artificially. *Taʾalluh*, for example, meaning "mystical union" to the Muᶜtazilite Masᶜūdī[153] and the Ḥallajian Wāsiṭī,[154] is taken by the hellenistically inclined ᶜAlī ibn Rabban to mean "devout fervor";[155] *waḥdāniyya* (which means, in dogma as in mysticism, "the pure divine essence"),[156] is chosen as the translation of the Greek ἕνωσις (*henosis*, "unification"),[157] which the mystics had rendered as *ittiḥād*.[158] Sunni *mutakallimūn* and *rūḥāniyya* employ meanings opposite to those given by the physicians under Hellenistic influence for the following paired terms: *rūḥ—nafs, ṭūl—ᶜarḍ, ṣūra—maᶜnä* (Hellen.: *hayūlā—ṣūra*), *walī—nabī, ḥaqq—ḥaqīqa,*[159] *athar—khabar.*[160]

Doctrine. The mystical proposition of *nuqla* (cf. *sūq al-ṣuwar* is in contrast to Hellenistic metempsychosis (*tanāsukh*).[161] The mystical thesis of divine, liberating friendship (*khulla*) cannot be identified with the idea of the soul's anarchic emancipation (*khalīliyya=ibāḥa*). In the fourth century A.H., some Qarmathian infiltrations were made: ultra-intellectualist psychology depersonalized the soul, reducing *rūḥ* to *ᶜaql*[162] in Tirmidhī and Tawḥīdī; overly rationalist theology exhausted and attenuated divine transcendence,[163] limited the science of knowing God (Ghazālī's *laysa fī'l-imkān*), and compartmentalized God's power (Neoplatonic *ithbāt al-maqādīr* in Suhrawardī of

---

like the Ikhwān al-ṣafā: Both schools flowed together in Ibn ᶜArabī. Ḥātimī's minor work on Aristotelian sayings quoted by Mutanabbī is a mere witty game.

153. *Tanbīh*, 387.

154. Baqlī, I, 515: *sarāʾir mutaʾalliha*; and the pseudo-Muḥāsibī, ap. *Riᶜāya fī taḥṣīl*, ms. Cairo II, 87, at the beginning: *"mutaʾallih"*.

155. *Firdaws*, preface; cf. Tawḥīdī, this work, ch. 4, sec. 3.A.

156. *Passion*, s.v.; also this work, v.i. (Miṣrī, Tustarī, Junayd).

157. *Liber de Causis*, 67, 75.

158. Ḥallāj, ap. Baqlī on Qur. 37:7.

159. *Passion*, Fr. 3:307 n 1/Eng 3:289 n 65.

160. Or *khabar-naẓar* (ibid., Fr 3:310, 341–42/Eng 3:292, 323–24).

161. Ibid., Fr 3:27/Eng 3:19 (Ibn Junayd, *Shadd al-izār*, 10–12).

162. *Passion*, Fr 3:24/Eng 3:15.

163. Ibid., Fr 3:83 n 5/Eng 3:73 n 137.

Aleppo). Finally, the Covenant[164] and the Nocturnal Ascent,[165] two essential points mentioned but unexplained in the Qurʾān, became the means by which Qarmathian exegesis penetrated the Islamic mystical milieux. As early as the third century, Tustarī perilously[166] likened the Covenant (*mīthāq*) to the Qarmathian doctrine of the preexistence of souls, which were said to emanate and then be reabsorbed as divine, luminous particles. Though Ḥallāj did not adopt this idea,[167] Wāsiṭī used it in his teaching.[168] When the Ḥallājian thesis of divine transforming union was condemned by law, the mystics returned to Qarmathian exegesis: from the Qurʾānic Ascension's *qāb qawsayn*[169] they extracted the idea that mystical union was complete even without the transfiguration of the soul's substance, that union went no further than the moment of perfect intellectual vision[170] when the cluster of discourse that defines the divinity for us is dissolved in the void, at the precise moment the senses' ecstasy begins.

After three centuries of sustained struggle by Kharrāz,[171] Ḥallāj,[172] Tawḥīdī,[173] Ghazālī,[174] and Suhrawardī of Aleppo[175] — and at the very moment the Faṭimids' and Ismailis' political power was crumbling — Ibn ʿArabī made decisive,[176] irremediable concessions, which surrendered Islamic mystical theology to the Qarmathians' syncretist monism. He depicts all of creation, no longer souls alone, as emanating from God through a five-stage cosmogonic evolution, the correlative of a rational, symmetrical clarification of the science of God. As for mystical union, we are supposed to become God again by an inverse movement, an ideal five-stage involution that sums up all of creation in our thought.[177] After Ibn ʿArabī, and thanks to him, the Hellenistic syncretist vocabulary would dominate.[178] The concern

164. Ibid., Fr 3:116/Eng 3:105.
165. Ibid., ch. 14.
166. Ibid., Fr 3:301/Eng 3:283–84.
167. Ibid., Fr 3:113/Eng 3:101–2.
168. Ibid., Fr 3:157–58, 375–76/Eng 3:145, 357.
169. Ibid., ch. 14.
170. *Taḥṣīl*, a word rejected by Ḥallāj (Kalābādhī, no. 17 [in *Essai*, 1st and 2nd eds., appendix]) and allowed by Qurashī.
171. Against Tirmidhī.
172. Against Sālimiyyan concessions.
173. True precursor of Ghazālī.
174. *Passion*, ch. 14.
175. Who is the last nonmonist (*tarjīḥ, munājāt*), in spite of the encyclopedic tendencies that his adversaries exploited before Saladin, the conqueror of the Faṭimids, to have him executed as a Qarmathian. After Suhrawardī, the vocabulary, for example, of Ibn al-Fāriḍ, the poet, or of Ibn Ḥammūya, the chief of an order, is unconsciously infected with monism.
176. Prepared by Semi-Qarmathian works, themselves suspect, of the Spanish school: Ibn Barrajān; Ibn Qasyī, (author of the *Khalʿ al-naʿlayn*, which is preserved, with a commentary by Ibn ʿArabī, in Ms. Shāhid ʿAlī, 1174); Ibn al-ʿIrrīf; and Musaffar Sibtī.
177. *Passion*, Fr 2:414 n 3/Eng 2:395 n 101.
178. "The misdeeds of Hellenic culture," denounced by Suhrawardī of Baghdād in a contemporary work.

to be in theoretical agreement with it would win out over introspection during ritual practice and analysis based on experiment. Although hindered by the fervor of believers like ᶜIzz Maqdisī, Yāfiᶜī, Ibn Sīmaᵓūna, Zarrūq, Niyāzī and Nābulusī, the theory forcibly made experimentation conform.

Ibn Taymiyya, Ibn al-Qayyim, and Dhahabī, in the eighth/fourteenth century, justly stigmatized the Qarmathianism of Ibn ᶜArabī and his disciples; the only error of these commentators was their simultaneous reproof of early mystics as resolutely anti-Qarmathian as Ḥallāj and Ghazālī. (Note that the latter was indeed haunted by an esoteric tendency.)

The responsibility for the divorce between ascetic discipline (ritual and moral) and mystical theology lies with Ibn ᶜArabī's school, which elaborated a subtle theoretical vocabulary aimed at unverifiable cosmogonies and "ideogenies," and gnostic hierarchies that are beyond experiment (Farghānī, Jīlī, Kawranī).[179]

The school consummated the schism between the Muslim mystics' callings and their effect on society. The Qarmathian discipline of the secret was substituted for the duty of brotherly correction; mysticism became an esoteric science not to be divulged,[180] the preserve of closed circles of initiates and intellectual fossil groups,[181] Gobineau-Verein or Stendhal Clubs of ecstasy, opium dens of the supernatural.

E. Hinduism and Islamic Mysticism

This last problem is not the least delicate. Unlike the experimental scientific and philosophical information collected from Greece and Iran, India's contributions had not been incorporated into Near-Eastern syncretism by the eighth century A.D., the time of Islam's sudden expansion. The case of Hinduism[182] is therefore exceptional: it had the opportunity to exercise an independent influence upon Islam, through a direct channel to its mysticism.

William Jones[183] suggested this possibility, but he did not seriously dem-

179. *Arḍ samsam*; arithmomancy.

180. Lines of Sīdī Majdhūb, v.s. herein p. 11.

181. Nevertheless, among the Sanūsīs, there are social, or rather political, ramifications.

182. And not of a Buddhism, which I believe must be excluded. In the eighth century, Buddhism in India (Hsuan-Tsang) was in an advanced state of decay. The arguments set forth are easily dismissed: of the translation of the *Kitāb al-bud* of Lāḥiqī we have only the title; the hypothesis of the *nauvihāra* of Balkh has now been abandoned; the resemblance of the Sufi's *kashkūl* to the Buddhist beggar's bowl may be fortuitous; the legend of Ibn Adham, the "beggar prince" of Balkh, is an adaptation of the Manichaean version of the story of the Buddha (*Barlaam and Joasaph*), not a direct imitation; finally, a passage from Jāḥiẓ cited below (ch. 4, sec. 6) and used by Rosen, Nicholson, and Goldziher [*Vorlesungen*, Eng. trans. 142] to advance the theory of Buddhist influence, is in fact directed at Manichaean ascetics.

183. *Asiatic Researches*, 1803, III, 353 ff., 376.

onstrate an influence with his comparison of later monist Sufism and the Vedānta school, or of Jalāl Rūmī's and Ḥāfiẓ's poetry and the *Gīta Govinda*; Tholuck, then Kremer,[184] Rosen, and recently Goldziher, have shown that they accept the hypothesis to various degress.[185]

What ideas can we be certain were exchanged between Hinduism and Islam? What were the social hybridizations of these ideas in practice? Of what does pure Hindu mysticism, especially Patañjali's, consist? Finally, what must we think of Bīrūnī, who connects several specific texts, mostly of Patañjali, to sayings of the Muslim mystics Bisṭāmī, Ḥallāj, and Shiblī?

Scientific information was directly exchanged between India and Islam during a very short period (100–180 A.H.). Knowledge was transferred through Baṣra while Sind belonged to the caliphs and before the Hellenistic syncretist corpus was translated into Arabic.

Exchanges observed in mathematics: "Indian" numbers (*devanāgarī*);[186] some astronomical tables translated by Fazārī in 154/771;[187] astrological information (Indian *jafr*, instead of the *anwā*ʾ; *namūdhār*); calculation of sines (instead of chords) in trigonometry. Borrowing of information in medicine (observations of Charaka[188] and Mashqār)[189] and erotology,[190] perhaps after encapsulation in Pahlavī translations in the manner in which borrowing is proved to have taken place in romances (*Pañchatantra, Jātakas*) and in moral and philosophical writings.[191]

And that is all. Bīrūnī, commenting on the sketchy information available to his predecessors Zurqān Mismaʿī[192] and Iranshahrī,[193] emphasizes that the Muslims' knowledge of India, even after three centuries of contact, is superficial. A reading of the *Fihrist* leads one to agree. Indian astonishes: Muslims, though interested by its bizarre customs[194] and natural wonders,[195] do not seek to understand it. The philosophical school of skep-

184. Following Dozy and anticipating Salmon, he adopts the false date attributed by Langlès to Abū Saʿīd ibn abī'l-Khayr's apostolate in Khurāsān: 200/815 instead of 400/1009.

185. The thesis of the Hindu origin of Islamic mysticism was pushed to extremes by Max Horten, in *Indische Strömungen*, (*Wallesers Mater. zur Buddhismus*, Heidelberg, XII, 1927). For the period after the conquest, Tarachand, Yusuf Husain, Khaliq Ahmad Nizami, and Masud Husain have made studies of reciprocal influences. Cf. above, in ch. 2, sec. 5. E. A Ḥallājian resurgence in eastern Bengal was remarked upon in my *Gandhian Outlook and Techniques*, New Delhi, 1953, 78.

186. Bīrūnī, *Hind*, trans. I, 174.

187. Ibid., p xxxi; II, 15. Before Ptolemy was translated.

188. *Fihrist*, 303. ʿAlī ibn Rabbān had made a translation (Bīrūnī, *loc. cit.* p. xxxi-xxxii).

189. Quoted by Jibrāʾīl Bukhtyishūʿ.

190. XXIX *figurae veneris*, in Yamanī, *Rushd*, ch. 7. Cf. the *āsannas*.

191. Cf. *Fihrist*, 245. And Abū Sharm, ap. Jāḥiẓ, *Bayān*, I, 51.

192. Samʿānī, s.v.

193. Add Kindī to the list.

194. Bīrūnī, *Hind*, trans., I, 179–82.

195. *ʿAjāʾib al-Hind* by Ibn Shahriyār. Indian vocabulary introduced into Arabic by sailors: *shaṭra*, parasol; *kūt*; *fūṭa*; etc.

tics drawn to Hinduism, the Sumaniyya (introduced into Baṣra by Jarīr b. Ḥāzim Azdī,[196] 120–140 A.H.), was an aberration that disappeared quickly after offending the conscience of theologians such as Jahm.[197]

Horten's conjectures[198] on the Indian origin of the skepticism of some of the *mutakallimūn* are useless.[199] Kremer's and Margoliouth's, on the poet Maᶜarrī's supposed conversion to Hinduism,[200] remain unverified.

Direct contact stopped in the third century. Hinduism, with its complex idolatry and causal chains intertwined *ad infinitum* (*karma, saṃsāra*), found itself losing metaphysical ground to Islamic occasionalism's forceful witness to a living, threatening, transcendent, and personal God. In science, by 180–200 A.H., Arab translators of Hellenistic syncretism[201] possessed a doctrine that was clearer, fuller, and more homogeneous than the one maintained in the Indian schools. The syncretist doctrine was also closer to Islam: it taught the search for causes (but not actual infinity) and the one divinity (not explicitly transcendent), supreme giver of order and prime mover; it had an astronomic calendar (which was homogeneous, unlike the multiple astronomic days of the Hindus); it used less time-consuming methods of calculation and more condensed lists of predicaments and causes of error; its egalitarian political theory unified social morals and behavior (without the compartmentalization of the caste system) and finally justified requiring the whole community to observe the fast and pilgrimage, where Hinduism would have considered those acts to be supererogatory (*nafal*), strictly optional and individual.

The first serious cases of fertile hybridization between Hinduism and Islam appeared in India as a result of Muslim missionary activity. There were two types of these cases, mystical and Qarmathian:

Sunni Mystics: in Cranganore and Maldives, conversion of the Moplahs (Mapillas) by the disciples of Mālik ibn Dīnar (d. 127); in Gujarat, conversion of the Dudwalas and Pinjaras by Ḥallāj (d. 309); in Trichinopoly, of the Labbais by Nathar Shāh (d. 431/1039); in Porto Novo, of the Marecars; in Cutch, of the Momans, by Yūsuf al-Dīn Sindī (seventh/thirteenth century). Then came the missionary work of the orders (on which see below).

196. *Aghānī*, III, 24; Kremer, *C.S.*, 34.

197. In Ibn Ḥanbal, *Radd ᶜalā'l-zanādiqa*, the beginning. Cf. Naẓẓām and Muᶜammar (Murtaḍā, *Munya*, 31–32).

198. *Philosoph. Systeme*, 1912, 177, 274, 608.

199. The skepticism of early Islamic *kalām* comes from an occasionalism of Qurᵓānic origin (*Passion*, Fr 3:75, 96/Eng 3:65, 85; cf. "Méthodes de réalisation artistique ... de l'Islam," in *Syria*, 1921). Hindu skepticism on the other hand has a mystical foundation: it denies substances at first, then accidents, then sensations, only in order to liberate the consciousness from the labor of conceptual elaboration.

200. He refused to kill a flea (*Luzūmiyyāt*, I, 212; cf. Margoliouth, *Letters*, 1898).

201. The few Hindu elements to be found encapsulated there had passed through the Pahlavi language and had been cleansed by Manichaean teachings (*Kalīla and Dimna, Sindbad*).

Qarmathians: in the time of Harūn al-Rashīd, Ismailis began to take refuge in the Sind:[202] conversion of the area around Moltan (c. 200), where there are still some *Dāūdpōtras* of Khairpur (cf. Bahāwalpūr and Baluchistan); conversion of the Bōhoras of Gujarat by ᶜAbdallāh Harrāzī (460/1067); of the Wakhan and Afrīdī tribes by Nāṣir-i-Khusraw (473/1080); of the Khojas of Gujarat by two neo-Ismaili apostles, Nūr Satagar (d. 535/1140) and Ṣadruddīn (d. 834/1430).

Propagandists of these two types gave rise to several phenomena of social hybridization.[203] Some low castes[204] that had been converted to Islam combined the strict canon with Hindu customs; some vain practices slipped into Sunni mysticism (Mehdevis,[205] Rawshaniyya, Nūrbakhshiyya).

The Qarmathian syncretist catechism had already been adapted by its Muslim founders to the other forms of monotheism, to Ḥarrānian paganism, and even to Mazdeism. It was effortlessly annexed to the Hindu theogony. Among the Khoja caste, ᶜAlī became the tenth avatar of Vishnu, in anticipation of the strange syncretist encyclopedias later concocted in Persian (e.g., the *Dabistān* of Mobed Shāh[206] and the Mazdean *Desātīr*).[207]

In the sixteenth and seventeenth centuries, the Sanskrit classics appeared in various translations in the language of the Muslim conquerors, Persian,[208] with encouragement from Fayzī, the brother of Akbar's minister, Abu'l-Faḍl (*Baghavad Gīta, Rāmāyana*), then from Prince Dārā.[209] On the other hand, versions of various *qiṣaṣ*, Muslim hagiographical tales, were made immediately in the popular Indian dialects. The tale of Ibn Adham was translated into Kashmiri, that of Ḥallāj into Urdu.[210]

Hindu responses to certain kinds of Muslim men of letters are insignifi-

202. *Dastūr al-munajjimīn.*

203. Arnold has forcefully proved that it was not the conquerors' brute force that assured Islam's progress in India; Kāfūr's persecutions in the Mahrat country (1305–6 A.D.), Aurangzeb's in Rajpoutana, and Tippo Saheb's in Mysoor accomplished nothing. If Sikandar's (d. 1417) in Kashmir and Jattmali's (1414) in Gaur had more success, it is because they coincided with the conversions of princes.

204. Momans, Bōhoras, Khojas, Moplahs.

205. *Passion*, 1st ed., 86 n 1 [and for revisions of earlier thinking on the Manṣūrīs, cf. 2nd ed. Fr 2:288/Eng 2:275].

206. In the seventeenth century; 1st ed., Calcutta, 1224/1809 [bib., s.n., Fānī].

207. Published in Bombay in 1818 [bib., s.n., Firuz Bin Kaus].

208. Before that, there were only two translators of Indian mystic authors into Arabic: Bīrūnī, of whom more will be said below, and Rukn Āmidī (d. 615/1218) whose *Mirʾāt al-maᶜānī*, translated from the *Amṛtakunda* of a Yogi, was later imitated by Ibn ᶜArabī (Brockelmann, *G.A.L.* I, 440, 443).

209. The Muslim-Hindu "conversations" of prince Dara Shukuh with the Kabirpanthi Baba Laᶜl Das (whose tomb I saw in old Qandahar in 1945) have been published and translated (by myself, with Huart) in *JAP*, 1926. Cf. my *Recueil*, 1929, pp. 160–64 for his Persian translation of the Upanishads. We know that in reaction to Hindu pantheism, Islamic mysticism in India repudiated the *waḥdat al-wujūd* (existential monism) in favor of *waḥdat al-shuhūd* (testimonial monism: Simnani, ᶜAlī Hamadhani, Serhindi, Iqbal).

210. Cf. cat. Luzac, XIII, no. 310.

cant compared to the popular conversions achieved by the Islamic mystics. It was they who increasingly led the Hindu masses to Islam. Colonies of Muslim holy men, after fleeing Persia during the Mongol invasions, grew and multiplied in Northern India; from the seventh/thirteenth century onward, the hermits' example of austerity and ministering gentleness converted Hindus, who founded villages around their masters' sacred tombs:[211]

Muᶜīn Chishtī (d. 634) in Ajmer; Quṭb Kākī in Delhi; Jalāl Tabrīzī (d. 642) in Bengal; Farīd Shakarganj (d. 664), the ancestor of the Kīlānī *"sayyids,"* in Pākpattan; Jalāl Surkhpōsh (d. 690), ancestor of the Bukhārī *"sayyids,"* in Ucch (Bahāwalpūr); Muḥammad Gīsūdarāz in Belgaum; Abū ᶜAlī Qalandarī in Panīpat (d. 725); Shāh Jalāl Yamanī at Sylhet in Assam (d. 786); ᶜAlī Hamadhānī in Kashmir (d. 791); and ᶜAbdallāh Shaṭṭārī (d. 818).

In India, Islam was spread not by war but by mysticism and the great orders of mystics: Chishtiyya, Kubrāwiyya, Shaṭṭāriyya, and Naqshabandiyya. To follow the "Centuriators" of Magdeburg and describe local devotion to India's Muslim holy men as "survivals of idolatry"[212] and "pagan infiltrations,"[213] is to forget that victors can only obtain a social reconciliation with the vanquished by giving while asking for nothing in return, and by lending without hope of gain. It is also to forget the two liberating ideas that the converts were bound by their consciences to hold:[214] a sovereign and transcendent God, and an individual immortal soul. With two others, perhaps: the notions of supernatural grace (*prasāda*) and of devotion to a personal God (*bhakti*).[215]

Islamic mystical influence beneficially pushed toward the reconciliation of castes, in humble vocations like Baba Kapur's (d. 979/1571) in Gwalior, and brilliant apostolates like Kabīr's (d. 924/1518). Though a student of the Hindu Ramananda, Kabīr taught hymns to his disciples, the Kabīrpanthīs, in which they could celebrate the one God — the personal God Who answers prayers, has characteristics, and is accessible through transcendent revelation, rather than the supreme, indifferent, quasi-virtual divinity perceived by the schools of polytheistic syncretism. The hymns of the Sufi Farīd Shakarganj were incorporated into the *Adi Granth* of the Sikh sect (Nānak, d. 946/1539), which tried to reintegrate the Kabīrpanthī apostolate into Hinduism. No doubt the modern polemic of the Arya Samāj,[216] fighting for

211. In the fifteenth century, there were Hindu pilgrims to the tomb of the martyr prince Salar Masᶜūd, called "Ghāzī Miyān," defeated and killed 14 Rajab 424/1033 in the battle of Bahraich (Oude) by idolaters.

212. Pirzadas, Ḥusayn Brahmanis, Satya Dharma.

213. Tomb of Ḥasan Abdāl in Attok.

214. More so than in the very limited apostolate of the Syro-Chaldean Christians of Meliapor.

215. See the polemic of Grierson and Kennedy on this subject, in *JRASB*, 1907–8. Tara Chand has recently begun to study the problem.

216. Arnold, *Preaching of Islam*, 2nd ed., 439.

souls against Islam in the center of India, especially at Bundelkhund, demonstrates that the old Indian paganism is not dead. But the social reform of the *satyagraha*[217] ("civil vindication of the truth through self-sacrifice"), now preached by a pure Hindu ascetic, Mohanlal Karamchand Gandhi, shows how close some kinds of Hinduism have come to a Muslim religious and mystical ideal:[218] social action is directed not towards freeing ourselves as individuals but towards our communal salvation; actions are founded on the dogma of the personal soul's immortality, and the soul is devoted to a sort of spiritual "holy war" through the fast and the practice of the sacrificial virtues accessible to illiterates.[219]

It might be asked whether Indian mysticism as presented by Patañjali's commentators did not help Kabīr move toward the disciplined, transcendent monotheism of Islam. I hope an Indianist will compile documents on the subject; in conclusion I will simply present a brief account of the characteristics of postvedic Hindu mysticism:

Already in the Upanishads, the problem mysticism raises is not of positive unification of the soul through purifying the heart, but simply of preliminary meditation, the negative eradication of all mental images or intellectual movements *ad extra.* This mysticism is original[220] insofar as it repudiates all foreign elements, metaphysical or ritual. Consideration of the substance or the attribute, the objectivity of sense-data or the permanence of personality, God's grace or transcendence, is deliberately refused. The mystical experience, strictly confined to the psychological consciousness, makes a direct attack on the "bond," the human mind's conditioning to the flesh, by which freedom of thought is paralyzed. The mystic wants to eliminate[221] the imposed relation that couples thought to a given object of perception; he attempts to do without the external, partial realities that the mind constantly needs in order to maintain an ordinary, intermittent awareness of itself.

In this mystical system, the question of mind–matter dualism, though not stated in metaphysical terms, is understood. The mind is implicitly affirmed to be superior *a priori* to matter, as is (angelic) intuition to (human) understanding. The mystic seeks to free his consciousness from the servitude of the five senses and the yoke of discursive effort.

217. See *RMM,* XLIV, pp. 55–63.

218. As Dr. Abdul Majid has shown, in the *Modern Review,* Calcutta, Nov. 1920.

219. Cf. Ḥasan Baṣrī, Muḥāsibī, and Ḥallāj for an analogous doctrine (*Passion,* Fr 3:228 ff., 222 ff., 228 n 4/Eng 3:216 ff., 210 ff., 216 n 300).

220. Its first lucid presentation to Muslims is by Abūl-Faḍl, in his *Āyin-i-akbarī,* trans., III, 127 ff.

221. In Christian terms, the conceptualization of the *logos* in the mind must be freed from the preliminary process of *informing* an image. The mystic aims to unsheathe the conscious subject from the perceived object, which is supposed to disappear.

Does psychological consciousness have length, or continuity, or permanence? The question was soon set aside. The soul's permanent individuality (*ātman*), as well as the substantiality of the soul and heart (*manas*),[222] became blurred in the Nyāya school and were rejected by the Mīmāṃsā and Vedānta schools.[223] Finally, the Sāṃkhya school, for greater simplicity, after denying the *ātman* and analytically enumerating twenty-four graduated forms of material nature (the *prakṛti*), thought it sufficient to add one last form, the *purusha*: simple, instantaneous, and impersonal consciousness of the truth, divisible into pieces through multilocation.

The Nyāya school provided a sketch of Indian mysticism's goal. A decisive critique of the discursive intellect's imperfect functioning led to the search for *apavarga*, the "final emancipation" from the sadness caused by intellectual error. The goal became precise with the Sāṃkhya school. It is *sattvāpatti*, "actualization of psychological consciousness," the purely intuitive "truth without content" described by Bīrūnī.[224] The *purusha* must attain this state by control over the conceptual process.

Patañjali, adept in the principles of the Sāṃkhya school,[225] gave Hindu mysticism its classical form in his *Yoga-Sūtra*,[226] in which he sets *samādhi asaṃprajñāta* (see below) as the goal of the mystical search.

Patañjali presents four sets of preliminary training exercises, which must be combined. The senses are mastered through abstinence (*yama*); intentions are bound by ritual vows (*niyama*) dedicated to one of the gods (*īśvara*); the limbs are made supple by being placed in various rigid postures in turn (84 *āsana*); the breathing reflex is regulated by the will. This ascetic training eliminates phenomena extraneous to the perceived goal and facilitates the pursuit of it. Learning to regulate the breath teaches the adept, after he has used abstraction (*pratyāhāra*) to make his thought a sheath for the five senses, to concentrate his mind at will.

The mystical experimentation properly called "synergy"[227] begins here, with constraint of the consciousness, or *samyama* ("synderesis"): (1) The first stage is contemplation (*dhāraṇā*), in which thought consists of only three things — a conscious subject (*purusha*), a state of consciousness (*sattva*), and an object (of some sort) of which the subject is conscious (*bud-*

222. Considered two of the nine substances (*dravya*).

223. According to Buddhism, the soul is merely an artificial aggregate of five attributes (*skandhas*) without a substance to support them. Symmetrical concept of envelopes of personality in Tustarī (*Passion*, Fr 3:24–25/Eng 3:17–18; but here God occasionalistically creates their unity).

224. It is not enough.

225. Borrowing from the Vedāntists, he adds the notion of the "three *guṇas*" of *prakṛti* (*sattva, tamas, rajas*) and the idea of *īśvaras* (perfect ideal beings, divine models to be venerated, virtual figures, children of Brahmā and Māyā).

226. I quote the English translation of M. N. Dvivedi, Tattva Vivechaka Press, Bombay, 1899, iii + 99 + vii pages, where Ramananda Saraswati's commentary is used.

227. *Conscientia* in the etymological sense.

dhi).[228] (2) The next state is absorption (*dhyāna*), in which thought becomes only two things — a conscious subject and an object of which one is conscious.[229] (3) The final stage is psychological ecstasy (*samādhi*), in which thought becomes the object of which one is conscious, by a gradual transformation.[230]

The final transformation takes place (for *vṛtti*) in three stages, corresponding (for *purusha*) to three new aspects of the conscious subject:

a) *nirodhapariṇāma* (for *vṛtti*): When thought has become identified with the object of thought, consciousness is placed in a state of suspension with regard to that object. It is torn away and realizes that the object (which thought has just become) is in itself not absolute, permanent, or necessary. This perilous leap from the mental trampoline, this rapture into the void, corresponds in the *purusha* to *dharmapariṇāma*, "the subject's transformation in the property (= haecceity)* of the object."

b) *samādhi saṃprajñāta* (for *vṛtti*): "conscious psychological ecstasy." The consciousness becomes rooted in indifference towards the object with which its thought has become identified. At an increasing frequency, the consciousness makes thought alternate between moments of suspension outside the object and moments of identification with it. Through this process, the consciousness learns to be insensitive to suspension and resumption of attention to an object; the change corresponds in the *purusha* to *lakshanapariṇāma*, "the subject's transformation in character** (= ipseity)."

c) *samādhi asaṃprajñāta* (for *vṛtti*): "unconscious psychological ecstasy." The consciousness achieves supreme simplicity, in which states of suspension and resumption of thought pass over it without a trace. This simplicity corresponds in the *purusha* to *avasthāpariṇāma*, "the subject's transformation in condition (= the Real)" = *kaivalya*. In this state of "solitude," the three qualities (*guṇas*) of nature (*prakṛti*) are reduced to one, the *sattva*, a state of consciousness that is as pure as the conscious subject (*purusha*) is purified.[231]

With a view to comparison, I shall now try to transpose Patañjali's vocabulary into the technical language of Islamic mysticism:

*"Haecceity" serves principally to make clear that Massignon means propriété, "property," in a sense that happens to be obsolete in common usage, in both French and English.

**Or characteristic. For "haecceity" and "ipseity," see *Passion*, Fr 3:85/Eng 3:75 and index of technical terms (*annīya*, *huwīya*); Lalande's *Vocabulaire technique de la philosophie* (*entries for eccéité, ipséité*); Massignon's *Muḥāḍarāt*. "Haecceity" and "ipseity" have sometimes been synonyms, but in Massignon's usage, haecceity is simply what distinguishes the individual from all others, the outer contour of its ipseity, or inner selfhood.

228. *Yoga*, III, sec. 1.

229. Ibid., III, sec. 2.

230. Ibid., III, sec. 3–13. The term *vṛtti* is explained herein, in ch. 2, sec. 2. B., and ch. 2, sec. 2. E.

231. *Yoga*, III, sec. 55.

ātman = *nafs*; both "soul" and "self."
manas = *qalb*; both "heart" and Intellect."
purusha = *rūḥ*; in the double sense of "mind" and "spirit" in Islam.
vṛtti = *istinbāṭ*, *ᶜirfān*; elucidation, discursive assimilation of the object of thought.
sattva = *naẓar*, *ruᵓya*; "state of consciousness."
buddhi[232] = *manẓūr*; "the object of which one becomes conscious."

The admirable internal malleability of Semitic radicals will permit a schematization of the long preceding description of *samyama's* three stages. In Arabic, one need only perform grammatical operations on the roots, which do not change in themselves:

a) In the state of "contemplation" (*dhāraṇā*) there remains only *nāẓir*, *naẓar*, and *manẓūr* (= *dhākir*, *dhikr*, *madhkūr*; or *ᶜārif*, *ᶜirfān*, and *maᶜrūf*; or *mushīr*, *ishāra*, and *mushār ilayhī*; or *muwaḥḥid*, *tawḥīd*, and *muwaḥḥad*).[233]

b) In the state of "absorption" (*dhyāna*) there remains only *nāẓir* and *manẓūr*. This is the *fanā ᶜan al-dhikr*.

c. In psychological ecstasy (*samādhi*): (1) the state of suspension is the *bayn* or *tajrīd* of Ḥallāj;[234] (2) the alternation of suspension and resumption of thought is Sayyārī's *jamᶜ wa tafriqa*;[235] (3) unconscious ecstasy is Ḥallājian *tafrīd* (not *tawḥīd*)[236] and Sayyārī's *jamᶜ al-jamᶜ* (absolutely not to be confused with the transforming *ᶜayn al-jamᶜ*).

Nicholson's use of *fanā* and *ghayba* as equivalents of Hindu words is to be rejected. As Ḥallāj observed,[237] the Arabic terms are complex and extremely ambiguous. Moreover, in Islam, *fanā* means either "annihilation of thought in its Object" (*fanā bi'l-Madhkūr*, *ᶜan al-dhikr*: Tustarī, Junayd, Ḥallāj), or "annihilation of the Object in thought" (*fanā bi'l-dhikr*, *ᶜan al-Madhkūr*: Bisṭāmī, Sarrāj). Here, in Hinduism, it would mean strictly "thought's self-annihilation, through a cycle of suspension and resumption" (*fanā bi* [and *ᶜan*] *al-jamᶜ wa'l-tafriqa*).[238]

The difference is this: in Islam God is the transcendent Real. Islamic mysticism cannot make that revelation abstract. At the threshold of liberation from the flesh, the Muslim mystic's conscience can no longer ignore

232. Ibid., II, sec. 17 [IV, sec. 21].
233. *Passion*, Fr 3:102 ff., 87, 143/Eng 3:91 ff., 76, 131; *Ṭaw.*, VIII, 6.
234. *Ṭaw.*, VI, 7.
235. Hujwīrī, *Kashf*, 252.
236. *Ṭaw.*, VI, 7–8.
237. Ap. Sulamī on Qur 52:47.
238. One might argue that, the *shahāda* being precisely a choice for the mind, and therefore an alternation (suspension and resumption, *nafy* and *ithbāt*), the *fanā bi'l-tawḥīd* that Abū ᶜAlī Sindī taught to Bisṭāmī is quite close to the Hindu idea.

the absolutely real Object, the superabundant Truth reflected in his thought. The conscience must burn in that Truth, to be transfigured or destroyed. For Patañjali, the mystical method was stripped of metaphysics and ritual; it was limited to establishing a remarkably balanced and precise introspective formula for the liberation of a man's spiritual nature from the bonds of flesh, the mind's complete renunciation of all created things. The method concedes that, in exchange, certain practitioners of the preternatural (not to be examined here) may suddenly find that their thoughts have extraordinary powers over all of nature (second sight, miracles, which are of secondary importance). Patañjali insists that the purpose of mysticism is not to obtain miraculous powers but to maintain the consciousness in a state of absolute simplicity.

With unusual honesty, in the beginning of his preparatory exercises,[239] Patañjali permits something that his masters of the Sāṃkhya school reject: semiritual reliance on an *īśvara*, a legendary or historical god or hero, as an admired example. This recourse to the *īśvara* is allowed for stimulation and discipline of vows and devotional acts, but Patañjali states that it would be of no use in *samādhi*: the *īśvara* is an effigy of the imagination, and it would become a vain idol, in which the consciousness would admire itself alone.

The true position of Patañjali's mysticism is as follows: it has no conclusion; in the end it offers a glimpse of a negative state obtained by high-frequency cycles of thought that remove all images from the consciousness. This mysticism is the intuitive destruction of idols and idolatry, the complete ascetic experiment pushed to the threshold of ecstasy: mortification of the flesh, extinction of images, perfect denial of the will. Just as Greek rationalism, among the teachers of Socrates, led to an experiment *ad extra* with the possibility of monotheism, Hindu mysticism among Patañjali's disciples led to a demonstration *ab intra* that polytheism is inane.

The mysticism of the *Yoga-Sūtra* is devoid of *shaṭḥ*, the supreme feature of monotheistic mysticism in Islam. *Shaṭḥ* is a positive state of mental intermittency, accompanied by dialogue, in which the isolated soul receives the supernatural visitation of a transcendent Interlocutor. In spite of the declarations of the theosophists who translated Patañjali, thinking they could understand him as a syncretist ally, his school prepared many souls in these Indian regions, enslaved as they were to all idolatrous divinizations, including the cruelest and vilest, to desire[240] the dogmatic revelation of the personal God.

Patañjali's mysticism is an admirably practiced asceticism of the con-

239. *Yoga*, I, sec. 24, 37; II, sec. 45.

240. Cf. Roberto de Nobili (d. 1656), who submitted to the ascetic rule of the Sannyasis in order to demonstrate, by an *ad hominem* argument comparable to Pascal's "wager," Christ's superiority as an *īśvara*, a simple, ideal model [cf. above, n 58].

sciousness. Neoplatonic mysticism seems more comprehensive but is more limited. To accomplish the transformation of substance through ecstasy by which it is claimed that unification with the One may be achieved, the Neoplatonists use only philosophical concepts.[241] These, being naturally inoperative, are overestimated and become idols, in order to make the transcendent operation succeed. Only[242] mystics belonging to the three groups of Semitic monotheism, which are founded on the revelation to Abraham, admit that God alone transfigures consciousness during ecstasy by substituting His fiat for the soul's. This doctrine of mystical union, taught categorically in Christianity and fiercely contested among Jews,[243] was distinctly set forth in Islam.[244]

The table of Arabic-Sanskrit transposition given above will make it possible to examine the only serious demonstration yet attempted, that mystical union in Islam is of Hindu origin. It is in the admirable work on India by Bīrūnī (d. 440/1048). Some of the furtive analogies[245] he sketches in passing can be quickly set aside: between Sufi *fanā* and some verses of the *Baghavad Gīta*;[246] between the Sāṃkhya school's critique of Paradise and the Sufi statement (Bisṭāmī's) that "the recompense of Paradise is not a good thing, because, with it, something other than God becomes a distraction, and concentration is fixed on something besides the absolute Good";[247] between the Sufis' doctrine of miracles[248] and Patañjali's. This is the principal passage:[249]

> The Sufis use Patañjali's method[250] in the matter of (unifying) concentration on God. They say, "As long as you are working out your expressions, you have not affirmed the one God; and you will not have affirmed Him until He has taken over your expressions by making you renounce them, so that neither the (created) enunciator nor its (human) expression survives." Some of their statements favor the doctrine of unification. For example, one mystic, when asked a

241. Besides certain adventitious forms of theurgy of dubious character.

242. The Chinese mysticism of Chuang-Tzu has just begun to be studied. Negro animist mysticism is rudimentary (*RMM* XLIV, 10, n 2).

243. Ascetic inspiration.

244. *Passion*, Fr 3:51/Eng 3:44.

245. To the Christian doctrine of expiation (trans., II, 161); a quote from Basidiyo (text, p. 26).

246. Trans., I, 76, 82, 87–88.

247. Trans., I, 62. He himself remarks that "the premises were different." In the same way we might compare the *sphoṭa* (*Yoga*, III, sec. 17) with the Muslim *jafr*, and the *nirodha* (*Yoga*, III, sec. 9, eighth article of the Way [*mārga*], suppressing pain at its cause, the end of *karma's saṃsāra*, rest) with the *bayn* and *bīkār* of the Druze.

248. Trans., I, 68.

249. Text, 43.

250. Except Abū'l-Faḍl, who analysed the *Yoga-Sutra* briefly, the only Muslim after Bīrūnī who seems to have studied it is Ḥusayn ibn Muḥammad, the Persian author of the *Baḥr al-ḥayāt*, written in the eighteenth century (Luzac catalogue, XXIII, no. 867).

question about the Truth, answered, "How could I not notice Him who is my 'I' in haecceity and who is not my 'I' in localization? If I insist on this, my insistence separates me from him! If I do not insist, my negligence stuns me, and I become improperly familiar with unification (in God)." Abū Bakr Shiblī responded, "Cast everything away, and you will join Us completely! Not being, you will be! Because news of you will come from Us, and your act will be Our act." And Abū Yazīd Bisṭāmī, when asked, "How did you acquire these favors?" answered, "I removed my soul ('carnal soul,' *nafs*), as the serpent sheds its skin; then I considered my essence. And now you see, my 'I' is He!"

Certainly Bīrūnī had some right to discuss Patañjali. He had translated the entire *Yoga-Sūtra* from Sanskrit into Arabic under the title *Kitāb Pātanjal al-Hindī fi'l-khalāṣ min al-amthāl.*[251] (Long passages are reproduced in his studies of India, which still exist in manuscript at Constantinople.)[252] His title for the book, which means *Liberation from the Images,* is quite a good translation of the Sanskrit *Vṛttinirodhā.*[253] But what is the real worth of the four textual comparisons quoted above? The first text is by Ḥallāj; I have analyzed its theory of the *shahāda,*[254] which surpasses Patañjali's *samādhi* in that it describes not only renunciation of the soul but also actual transformation in God. The second text, anonymous and probably late, is perhaps a commentary on Ḥallāj's *Anā'l-Ḥaqq.*[255] The third, by Shiblī, is, like the second, an elliptical condensation of Ḥallāj's thesis. The last, by Bisṭāmī, in spite of its outrageous conciseness, is monist only in appearance.[256] Nevertheless, Hindu analogies[257] could be found in his method.

Appendix: Table of the "Philosophical" Alphabet (*JAFR*)[258]

Sources: Naṣībī, *Jafrjāmiᶜ*, London ms. Or. 2333; Baqlī, *Shaṭhiyāt,* 22 ff., Ibn Sina *Nayrūziya* (cf. *Mémorial Avicenne,* IV, Cairo, 1952).*

*When clarifications or additions from this article are particularly helpful, I have inserted them, in brackets.

251. The critical edition of the Arabic translation by Bīrūnī of Patañjali's *Yoga-Sūtra* (with Sanskrit facing page) was remarked upon by J. W. Hauer (and H. H. Schaeder) in *OLZ,* 1930, 273–82.

252. Köpr ms. 1589; recopied in the margin of sec. 52 (*Sīrat al-shaykh al-kabīr* = Ibn Khafīf) but not mentioned in the printed catalogue of the library, p. 116.

253. Patañjali, *Yoga-Sūtra,* II, sec. 27.

254. *Passion,* Fr 3:143, 246/Eng 3:131, 232.

255. *Passion,* Fr 3:55–56, 71/Eng 47, 62.

256. Below, ch. 5. Critique of his *"anā huwa,"* in *Passion,* Ḥallājian Text II, Fr 3:71/Eng 3:62.

257. Sindī, who taught him *fanā bi'l-tawḥīd* (Qush I, 107–8), had arguably been in contact with Hindus. But his *nisba* refers to Sind near Abīward. (Yq. III, 167).

258. The letters are in the order of the *abjad,* the old Semitic and numerical order. (a) the two senses (*ṭūl, ᶜarḍ*), and typical words in Ḥallāj, Tirmidhī, etc....; Naṣībī is indicated by N., Baqlī by

alif = 1. The basic element that is a part of every composition (*ma'lūf*). The one; theoretical unity, *a parte ante* (*azal, fardāniyya*). grammar (gr.): prefix of the first person. Hebrew (Hebr.): bull [i.e., the animal], teaching. Christian (Chr.): convenience, foundation.[259] Cf. *fatha* (*manṣūb*). *Bārī* (Ibn Sīnā).

bā = 2. Introduction. Putting into relation (*aṣl li'l-ta'līl*, N.). gr: *li'l-ilṣāq*. Hebr: house, visitation. Chr: house.[260] *ᶜAql* (Ibn Sīnā).

jīm = 3. That which complements. Beauty (*jamāl*, N). Hebr: camel. Chr: fullness of elevated things (*gamma*). *Nafs* (Ibn Sīnā).

dāl = 4. The equilibration of created things (N). Their permanence (*dawām*). Hebr.: gate, tablets. Chr; genesis of created things (*delta*).[261] *Ṭabīᶜa* (Ibn Sina; *hayūlā* for the Ismailis).

dhāl = 700. What is fundamental in the thing or idea (*dharra, dhāt*, N).

hā = 5. "ah"; the guide that straightens (*hudā*). The enunciation of the subject ("I") (*huwiyya* BS, *ᶜaql, ᶜadad tāmm*, N). gr: silence, third person suffix. Hebr: window. Chr: he who is in the creation[262] (*epsilon*). *Al-Nāṭiq* (Ismaili ms). *Bārī bi'l-iḍāfa* (Ibn Sīnā).

wāw = 6. Oath. Unconditioned connection (*wujūd muṭlaq, isrā*, N). gr: *li'l-ᶜaṭf* [conjunction]. *li'l-jamᶜ fī'l-ḥukm dūn tartīb fī'l-zamān*.[263] Hebr: ankle, sign. Chr: the Sign (*digamma*). Cf. *ḍamma* (*marfūᶜ*). *ᶜAql bi'l-iḍāfa* (Ibn Sīnā).

zā = 7. Realization. Growth, increase (*zuhd, ziyāda*, N). Hebr: javelin, life. Chr: life[264] (*zeta*). *Nafs bi'l-iḍāfa* (Ibn Sīnā).

ḥā = 8. Actual or enlivening inspiration (*ḥāl, waḥy, ghayth shāmil*, N). Hebr: the living. Chr: the living (*ēta* = 8).[265]

**khā* = 600. Good; immortality. (*khayr dā'im*, N), (*khi* = 600).

ṭā = 9. Primordial purity of God; sanctity, felicity of the contented; bounty

---

BS. (b) grammatical meaning. (c) Hebraic meaning. (d) Christian meaning and Greek equivalent. (c) and (d) according to Apa Saba (= St. Sabas?), *Les mystères des lettres grecques* (Coptic Arabic manuscript at Oxford, Huntington, 393), trans. Hebbelynck, Louvain, 1902, 127, 132. Cf. St. Pachomius, in *Patrol. lat.*, XXIII, 87, 95, 98; and St. Jerome, Ep. 30 ad Paulam. (e) Ibn Sīnā is marked *in fine*, in italics.

This fundamental presentation was redone in fascicule 4 of the Institut français du Caire's *Mémorial Avicenne*: "La Philosophie orientale d'Ibn Sina et son alphabet philosophique," 1–18. Ibn Sīnā shows the origins, both Arab (symbolism of the twenty-eight mansions of the zodiac) and Islamic (the fourteen isolated first letters of certain Qur'ānic suras), of this attempt to form a "symbolic logic" tabulating the process by which the events of the sublunar world come to occur, and he demonstrates the relation between that process and the Arabic grammarians' *ishtiqāq akbar*.

259. Ḥallāj (Qur. 7:1, *Ṭaw.*, VI, 25).

260. Ibn ᶜAṭā, ap. Sarrāj, *Lumaᶜ*, 88.

261. Jaᶜfar (ap. Baqlī, on Qur. 112:1); Ḥallāj (*Ṭaw.*, I, 15).

262. Tirmidhī (ap. Sulamī on Qur. 20:1). Cf. *Ṭaw.*, IX, 2.

263. Qarāfī (ap. Qāsimī, *Uṣūl*, 44).

264. Ḥallāj (*Ṭaw.*, VI, 25).

265. Ḥallāj (*Ṭaw.*, I, 15); Qushayrī (ap. Baqlī on Qur. 45; cf. 44).

(*ṭahāra, ṭūbä*).[266] The letter was exchanged in Arabic with the Hebrew *ṭeṭ* (*ṭā*) = beauty. Good (Chr.) (*thēta* = 9). *Hayūlä* (Ibn Sīnā).

**ẓā* = 900. The *via remotionis*. Appearance of God (*ẓuhūr, tanzīh* N).

yā = 10. Intellectual allegiance offered [conforming adherence]. God's help (*yad al-qudra*); divine speech (BS). gr: *li'l-iḍāfa*; possessive suffix, third person prefix. Hebr. the hand, the principle (*yod*). Chr. the Lord, Yahwe.[267] Cf. *kasra* (*majrūr*). *al-Qāyim*. *Ibdā*ᶜ (Ibn Sīnā).

kāf = 20. The appropriate statement or expression of an idea (*kāfī*). The idea of the fiat (*Kun*! N). gr: comparison. Hebr: meanwhile. Chr: Ecclesiastes.[268] *Takwīn* (Ibn Sīnā) [the structure imprinted on all that is created].

lām = 30. An idea's becoming explicit, in its comprehension (*taḍammun*). The gift of grace (*mujādala, ālā, abad*), divine transfiguration (N), divine disguise (BS). gr: *ḥarf al-tajallī*. Hebr: instruction (*lamed*). Chr: the immortal.[269] *Amr* (Ibn Sīnā) [the divine commandment].

mīm = 40. The determination of an idea, in its extension (*muṭābaqa*); its divine status, its name (*ism, maqām, mulk, maḥall*); emergence of the action of the spirit (BS). gr: sign of the past participle. Hebr: water, soul. Chr: about Him and by Him.[270] *Khalq* (Ibn Sīnā) [the created universe].

nūn = 50. Access to union. Accomplishment of the fiat. Consummation by fire (*tamattu*ᶜ *bi ittiṣāl*, N). gr: sign of the passive; of the indefinite (*tanwīn*); corroborative suffix, Hebr: the fish in the sea. Chr: the eternal.[271] *M* + *Y* (Ibn Sīnā).

sīn = 60. Everlasting glory of God (*sanā*), the manifestation of His names (N); preaching. gr: sign of future tense. The Hebrew and Syriac letter *samekh*, meaning promise, assistance (Chr: strength and succor), disappeared in Arabic and was replaced by *sīn* (obedience to the Commandments), which was doubled (see *shīn*).[272] (*Xi* = 60).

ᶜ*ayn* = 70. Fixed essence; the original meaning (*ma*ᶜ*nä*); the source of the intellect (BS). Hebr: eye, perennial spring. Chr: same as in Hebrew.[273]

266. Wāsiṭī, Qushayrī, ap. Baqlī (on Qur. 26); Tirmidhī, ap. Sulamī (on Qur. 20:1).

267. Baqlī on Qur., sūras 19, and 36; cf. Ḥallāj (*Ṭaw.*, VI, 15; *ya*ʾ*wa, Akhb.*, 39).

268. Baqlī on Qur. 19.

269. Meaning established by the Nuṣayrīs (catechism of Wolf). Cf. Ḥallāj on Qur. 7:1, and *Ṭaw.*, VI, 25.

270. Meaning established by the Nuṣayrīs (Muḥammad) and adopted by Ḥallāj on Qur. 7:1; and *Ṭaw.*, p. 38, 86; *tajallī bāṭin al-malkūt li'l-mulk*. Cf. Naṣībī; cf. *Ṭaw.*, I, 15; VI, 27; *Akhb.*, 46 [51]).

271. Cf. "Piscis assus, Christus passus."

272. Meaning established by the Nuṣayrīs (Salmān). Qushayrī, according to Baqlī (on Qur. 27). Taqdīs: Salsal. Ibn Sina makes it the *kun*.

273. Meaning established by the Nuṣayrīs (ᶜAlī). Baqlī on Qur. 19; cf. *Ṭaw.*, VI, 25.

(*omicron* = 70 + *omega* = 800). *Tartīb bi'l-Amr* (Ibn Sīnā) [the concatenation imprinted on the universe by the *Amr*].

★*ghayn* = 1000. The mystery of the divine plan, the assigned limit (*ghayb, ghayra, ghāya*, N).

fā = 80. The link joined or made, the disposition of language [causal linkage]. gr: *li'l-taᶜqīb, tartīb, tasabbub*. Hebr: mouth (*peh*). Chr. word, image (*pi* = 80 + *phi* = 500).[274]

ṣād = 90. Sincerity (saying the truth); exact discrimination (*ṣidq, ittiṣāl wa infiṣāl*); the spirit (BS). Hebr: justice (*tsāde*). Chr: truth and sanctity (*psi* = 700 + *sampi* = 900).[275] *L* + *M* + *K* (Ibn Sīnā).

★*ḍād* = 800. Separation. Being deprived of God's presence (*ḍāllūn*).

qāf = 100. What is decided, imposed, assured; said, certified (*qāla, qāhir*, N) (*Ṭaw*. X, 19). Hebr: call (*qof*). Chr: sure vocation (*qoppa* = 90). *Pre-assembly of all* (= *S* + *Y*) (Ibn Sīnā).

rā = 200. What is divided, given out by lot [the announced lot]. The message (*rabb; iddā al-ḥuqūq, rasūl ṣadūq*, N); the differentiation of the attributes (BS). Hebr: head (*resch*). Chr: the beginning. *Return to the One* (= Q + Q) (Ibn Sīnā).

★*shīn* = 300. Personal destiny, voluntary fate (*mashīᵓa, mashhūd*, N) (*Ṭaw*. X:19). gr: pause (disapproval, remembrance). The double in Arabic, when the Hebrew *sīn* was made into two letters; obedience to the Commandments (Chr: same as in Hebrew: *sigma*).

tā = 400. Signal of ecstasy, discovery, return to God (*tawba*, N). gr: prefix marking the second person; sign of the feminine; sign of the oath. Equivalent in Arabic of the Hebrew *taw* (*ṭā*) = the end, the conclusion, the signature (Chr: the consummation: *tau*).[276]

★*tha* = 500. Consolidation, bearing fruit (*thubūt, thamara*, N).

The *lāmalif* [*lā*], the "last consonant" (Tirmidhī, quest. 141), of which the grammatical function (*ḥarf al-salab*) is pure indefiniteness, *nakira*,[277] the inverse of the *alif-lām* [*al*], the article, whose grammatical function is pure determination (*adāt al-taᶜrīf*).[278] For Ibn ᶜArabī (*Fut*, I, 83), *alif* + *lām* = *wujūd* (*muṭlaq* + *muqayyad*).

The alphabet was used cryptographically in this way in order to denote and combine various bits of metaphysics, as if by algebra. The practice

274. Cf. Qarāfī (ap. Qāsimī, *Uṣūl*, 44).

275. Ḥallāj (on Qur. 7:1); Jaᶜfar, ap. Baqlī on Qur. 112; cf. on Qur. 19, Ḥallāj (*Akhb.*, 46 [51]; *Ṭaw.*, VI; IX, 1).

276. Ḥallāj, ap. *Akhb.*, 39.

277. Tahānuwī, s.n. Which is why Ḥallāj says, "the knowledge of (isolated) consonants is in the *lām-alif*. . . " Cf. *Ṭaw.*, XI, 1.

278. *Al-tajallī li'l-āḥād.*

turned into kabbalistic magic[279] under the influence of Shiite gnostic dreamers confusing the use of acronyms with the possession of objects. On this sort of magic, see principally Ismaili and Ḥurūfī texts.[280]

279. Like circles and range formulas.

280. *Ikhwān al-ṣafā*, III, 138–40 (ᶜ*ilal*); Faḍl Allah, *Jāwīdān* (cf. Huart, *Textes ḥoroūfis*, 189). Cf. the mystical Balaybalan alphabet of Muḥammad Bakrī (Sacy, *Notices et extraits* . . . , IX, part 1, 365–96. Cf. Sacy, *Druzes*, II, 86. Goldziher, *ZDMG*, 28, 782. On the two Qurʾānic pentads, *KHY*ᶜ*Ṣ* [sura 19] and *ḤM*ᶜ*SQ* [sura 42], see *Mémorial Avicenne*, IV, 6–8. [Cf. *Passion*, Fr 2:191/Eng 2:181.] On the seven doubled Arabic letters, see *Hégire d'Ismael*, 1939, 37–39.

3

GENERAL CONCLUSIONS

1. The Innate Originality of Islamic Mysticism

A. Liturgy

The long inventory above allows us to affirm that the Qurʾān, through constant recitation, meditation, and practice, is the source of Islamic mysticism, at its beginning and throughout its growth. Complete recitals (*qirāʾa*)[1] and frequent "rereadings" of the text, which is considered sacred, were the foundation of Sufism, and from these activities developed its distinctive characteristics: reading in groups in a loud voice (*dhikr, rafᶜ al-ṣawt*) and the regular sessions established for "recollection," *majālis al-dhikr,* in which practitioners recited sections of the Qurʾān, as well as prose and verse on related themes for meditation.

These sessions quickly evolved into the traditional spiritual concert or oratorio (*samāᶜ*). The affective or emotional part of collective meditation grew, to the detriment of the introduction (preparing the place of meditation) and the conclusion (formulating practical resolutions). The practitioners had a legitimate desire to form a liturgical relation to God; to relive, through solemn collective psalmody, the angel's indirect dialogue with Him Whom the Prophet's consenting soul had heard and obeyed with mute fervor. But the spiritual concert had its dangers. Teachers of Sufism such as Miṣrī, Junayd, and Ḥallāj said again and again that only on condition of self-mastery could a humble soul attract, if God wills, the unpredictable grace of *shaṭḥ,* the divine speech that attacks the soul directly through the unwitting reciter's voice, in the form of the consecrated words. Whether or not *shaṭḥ* leads the soul to ecstasy (*wajd*) is a detail of little importance, as Junayd and Ḥallāj remarked.[2]

Unfortunately, the *samāᶜ* was not always conceived in this way; in the fourth/tenth century the Khurāsānian Malāmatiyya[3] were denouncing the

1. Reading of the whole text, without pauses or intercalations; practice of the theory of *istinbāṭ* (*Passion,* 1st ed., 43 n 8; 2nd ed. Fr 3:197/Eng 3:185).

2. *Passion,* Fr 3:253/Eng 3:239.

3. Kharkūshī, *Tahdhīb,* f. 12b.

Sufis of Baghdād for throwing themselves into *samāʿ* and *dhikr* with the kind of secret pleasure or spiritual lust that Ḥallāj had already judged and condemned, particularly in these lines:[4]

> It is You, not my *dhikr*, You, who take me to ecstasy!
> Oh! That my heart may never become attached to my *dhikr*!
> *Dhikr* is the median pearl (of a finely wrought gorget) that hides You from my sight,
> When thoughts of it allow my mind to be encircled.

For these Sufis of Baghdād, sessions of *dhikr*, like certain Welsh revivals, were supposed to bring listeners to ecstasy by force, almost mechanically. The absolutely essential thing, *shaṭḥ*, which is the source of *maʿrifa*, was confused with ephemeral accessories: the physical tremor of ecstasy (*wajd*) and the loss of sensory perception. Starting in the fifth/eleventh century, the types of *dhikr* formulas that were used to obtain the loss of the senses spread and diversified with the development of the orders. *Dhikr* were litanies of the names of God, and they have been the subject of numerous studies in the West. I have noted elsewhere the formula used by the neo-Ḥallajian *ṭarīqa*.[5] It is important to remember that the main procedure for attaining ecstasy remained the chanting of the words from the Qurʾān.

In the seventh/thirteenth century,[6] groups under the influence of charlatans from India began to use stimulants and depressants, such as the hashish, coffee, and opium (*banj, asrār, maslakh*) condoned by some of the Qalandariyya. These narcotics served only as supplementary aids, intellectual stimulants, or tools for hypersensitization of the hearing.

What were the results of this disorientation of mysticism in the fourth/tenth century, this deviation towards the stubborn pursuit of ecstatic trances? In addition to the preternatural phenomena (telepathy, prediction, conjuring of objects, etc.) common to all kinds of mysticism (and discussed elsewhere),[7] there were certain salient original traits specific to Islam.

The oldest is the *raqṣ*, the ecstatic "dance" of jubilation.[8] In the beginning there may have been some sincere, spontaneous cases of this kind of ecstasy. But since then, several religious orders have been artificially attempting to reproduce the original circumstances by forced, concerted theatrics. The circular dance of the Mevlevis, to the sound of the *nay* (small flute), is well known. It has recently been considered an imitation of planetary rotations and orbits (*sic*).

4. *Ṭaw.*, 170.
5. *Passion*, Fr 2:34–35/Eng 2:28–29.
6. Jawbarī, *Kashf*, ms. Paris 4640, f. 23a.
7. *Passion*, Fr 1:199 ff., 338 ff./Eng 1:155 ff., 291 ff.
8. *Passion*, Fr 1:632–33/Eng 1:583–84.

The second trait, more suspect, is the *tamzīq*, the ecstatic "tearing of clothes" during a trance. The practice is dangerously close to hysterical exhibitionism. Shiblī tried in vain to prove that it was canonically permissible (in the presence of Ibn Mujāhid, who told the story to Ibn ᶜIsä).[9] He saw it as a manifestation of divine arbitrariness comparable to David's slashing the horses in Qur. 38:32. We might see it in the same light as the screaming ecstasies, much like sorcery, that discredit the *dhikr* sessions of the Rifāᶜiyya (Baṣra), Bayūmiyya (Cairo), and ᶜIsāwiyya (dialect "Aissawas," Meknes)[10] in the eyes of the reasonable Muslim public.

The third trait is the extremely suspect *naẓar ilä'l-murd* ("Platonic stare"), a mute, serene gaze at the beautiful faces of the novices sitting in the first row of the circle of initiates (*ḥalqa*). The stare is performed either before (to provide images for stimulation), during, or after ecstasy. In spite of condemnations by the wisest observers, it was accepted under various pretexts. In answer to the critics, Abū Ḥamza (d. 269) taught[11] that looking at what might not be desired was permitted, in order to mortify the desire itself (*sic*, this is morose voluptuousness). To enter into ecstasy, Aḥmad Ghazālī (d. 517) like to place a rose between himself and the novice's face, as a sign of separation.[12] Ibn Ṭāhir Maqdisī in the twelfth century, and then Nābulusī in the seventeenth, strained to make these esthetes' acrobatics appear legal; they were responding to various scandals caused by such practices, and a lowering of the public's opinion of certain Islamic orders.[13]

B. Allegories

The Qurᵓān[14] is also the source of Islamic mysticism's typical allegories: the fire and light of God (Qur. 28:29; 24:35); the veils of light and darkness placed over the heart (41:4; 39:8); the bird, symbol of the soul's resurrection, or rather its immortality (2:262; 3:43; 67:19); water from the sky (50:9 etc.); the tree representing man's vocation and destiny (28:30; 14:29; 36:80); the cup (*kaᵓs*), the wine (*sharāb*), and the salutation (*salām*; *qawl* 36:51), symbols of the special ceremony in which the privileged saints (*muqarrabūn*) are enthroned in Paradise (56:18, 25; 76:21). Certain

9. *Ḥilya*; Ibn al-Jawzī (preface to the *Ṣafwa*) reproaches Abū Nuᶜaym for putting this anecdote, as well as texts by Muḥāsibī (*Maḥabba*) and Anṭakī (translated here, below), into his collection.

10. Tremearne's recent studies lead one to think that these practices are in fact infiltrations from animist sorcery.

11. See his anecdotes collected in the *Kitāb al-muntammīn* of Aḥmad Dīnawarī (d. 341; Tagr., II, 334; Ibn Qutayba, *Taᵓwīl*, 458) and reproduced by Sarrāj (*Maṣāriᶜ*, 14, 21, 63, 76, 88, 100, 108, 120–25, 142–43, 166, 227).

12. Ibn al-Jawzī, *Nāmūs*, XI.

13. *Passion*, Fr 3:254/Eng 3:240

14. And not Pahlavi literature at all.

images peculiar to Ḥallāj are also linked to the Qurʾān, such as the mountain path (*ghirbīb*, Qur. 35:25), and the new moon (*hilāl*)[15] as a symbol, generally, of the revelation, and, more specifically, of the appearance of God discovering himself to the soul.

One of these allegories had an exceptional flowering. The enthronement ceremony of the privileged saints in Paradise became the correlative of the mystic's itinerary (*safar*) in this world. The source of the allegory is the *ḥadīth al-ghibṭa*.[16] Certain saints in Paradise will enjoy the greatest glory, which will be conferred on them at the *yawm al-mazīd*.[17] The theme, borrowed from Raqqāshī by Ibn Adham,[18] condensed by Ibn Ḥanbal, and taken up again by Miṣrī,[19] bursts into magnificent fullness in Muḥāsibī's *Kitāb al-tawahhum*.[20] After a solemn procession out of the communal Paradise and a banquet served by the Angels, the chosen friends of the divine Essence are greeted by Its own voice.[21] It celebrates their worthiness and brings them into familiarity with It.[22] Kharrāz, Tirmidhī,[23] and Ḥallāj still permitted this allegory, which subsequently shrank and withered because of polemics about divine union and the preeminence of the saints.[24]

In the fifth/eleventh century we begin to find the allegory hidden by the very curious poetic symbolism of the monastery (*dayr*),[25] intended to forestall canonical censure. After a long journey, the saints leave their walking sticks at the door of a monastery, enter, and drink wine poured into goblets by cup-bearers (the sāqī = the Angels). Then, by candlelight (*shamᶜ*), a mysterious being suddenly appears and greets them. He has the solemn, beautiful features of a young man (*shabb qatāt, tarsābacheh* in Persia, *shammās* in the Maghreb).[26] The saints prostrate themselves[27] before this Idol, which contains the divine Essence.[28]

This form of the allegory is remarkable. Its features were exaggerated (but, contrary to current orientalist opinion, not invented) by the extreme sensuality of the Persian poets.[29] It combines the Qurʾānic setting of the

15. *Passion*, Fr 3:102–3/Eng 3:91–92; cf. the Jewish Feast of the New Moon.

16. *Passion*, Fr 3:218/Eng 3:206.

17. Syn.: *ziyāda, ziyāra, iḥsān*; it is the "day of *tajallī* in Paradise," says the gloss in the *Sīra Ḥalabiyya* (I, 453).

18. Dāwūd Ṭāʾī also speaks of the "wine of joy" (ᶜAṭṭār, I, 222).

19. "The cup of love" (Makkī, *Qūt*, I, 225; ᶜAṭṭār, I, 126).

20. F. 152–71 of the ms. Oxford Huntington 611.

21. And no longer by the voice of a *munādī*.

22. He gives them not only the vision (*ruʾya*) but also life together (*munādama*).

23. *Khātam* (*Khatm*), quest. 74, 119, 128, 129; and ap. *Ḥilya*, s.n.

24. *Passion*, Fr 3:220–21/Eng 3:208.

25. Ibid., Fr 3:255–56/Eng 3:241–42. Cf. Shushtarī, *Dīwān*.

26. Shābistarī, *Golshan-i-rāz*, ch. 15 (syn.: *butt, wathan, dumiya*).

27. Cf. Abū Ḥulmān (*Passion*, 1st ed., 362; cf. P Fr 2:62–3, 140–41/Eng 2:55–6, 130–31.

28. Cf. the adoration of the *Rawḍa*, a sacred virgin, among Ismailis.

29. *Jashm, lab, zulaf, rukh, khaṭṭ, khāl* (Shābistarī, *op. cit.* ch. 13).

yawm al-mazīd with the poetic scenery of the Christian convent, to which the pre-Islamic Arab poets and their Bedouin caravan leaders used to come for wine.[30]

2. Concordance of Mysticism's Basic Problems with Those of Dogmatic Theology (*Kalām*)

Because mysticism is simply inner experimentation upon the proper practice of a religion, it is always possible[31] to make a tabular one-to-one concordance of mystical *termini technici* (*iṣṭilāḥāt*) and the corresponding theoretical *loci* (*masāʾil*) of dogma.[32] I have pursued this work in detail for the first three centuries of Islam.[33] The results confirm the existence of a strict parallel in development between Islamic dogma and mysticism.

The principal results can be summarized as follows:

a) Experimental concepts of mysticism that correspond to the problems of dogma

Divine justice (*ʿadl*); conciliation of precept and decree — *riḍā* (Hasan), leading to discussion of the reality of the *aḥwāl* (Miṣrī, Muḥāsibī; against Junayd); *tawakkul* (Shaqīq), leading to discussion about the permissibility of the *aksāb* (Thawrī, Muḥāsibī, Tustarī; Tirmidhī; against Shaqīq, Ibn Karrām, Nūrī); for or against "poverty".[34]

How can we reconcile divine "movement" of our actions with the transcendence of the divine act? Hasan's *tafwīḍ*. How does God move us? In preeternity (Ibn Sālim's *tafʿīl*, Wāsiṭī's *qidam al-muḥdathāt*, Abū ʿAmr Dimishqī's *azaliyyat al-anwār*), or by an innovation of grace (actual: *takhlīq* of Ibn Karrām; actualized: *taqaddum al-shawāhid* of Fāris), or by the Ḥallajian fiat. How does the divine "motion," inserted between the two *khāṭir*, operate in man? As an opportune memory (*fāʾida*), an intellectual light (*anwār*), or a persuasive presence (*shawāhid*).[35]

b) The dogma of divine unity

How can the incomparability of (*balkafiyya*) of revealed attributes be affirmed? the mystical experience of *tanzīh*: the anitithetical attributes (Abū

30. Abū Nuwās perversely amalgamated this literary tradition and the glorification of antiphysical love. Cf. ch. 4 n 514.

31. As I have indicated in the *Actes du IVe Congrès International d'histoire des religions* (1912), Leiden, 1913, 121–22.

32. The same sort of concordance should be made for mystical terms and their *loci* in the *ḥadīth* (*isnād, mursal, samāʿ* and in the *uṣūl al-fiqh* (*dalīl, niyya, istinbāṭ*).

33. *Passion*, ch. 11 and 12.

34. *Passion*, Fr 3:239 n 6/Eng 3:225 n 31.

35. *Passion*, Fr 3:120 ff., 34/Eng 3:108 ff., 26–27.

Ḥamza's *qurb wa bu^c^d*, Kharrāz's *ghayba wa ḥuḍūr* and *fanā wa baqā*; *takhalluq* [*bi asmā Allah* or *bi akhlāq Allah*]). Passing from *tajrīd* to *tawḥīd* (Ḥallāj). Is the attribute "love" essential (Qur. 36:25)? Inseparability of the attributes and the essence (Ḥallāj).[36]

Modes of the transforming union (Kharrāz's *^c^ayn al-jam^c^*; *ḥulūl al-fawā^ɔ^id* (Muḥāsibī, Ibn Karrām), then *ẓuhūr al-anwār* (Tustarī, Tirmidhī, Wāsiṭī), finally *tajallī al-shawāhid* (Ḥallāj, Fāris). What becomes of the human personality (*nafs, ruḥ; anā, anniyya*).[37]

Is the Qur^ɔ^rān created or uncreated? Experimental differentiation among *ma^c^nä, lafẓ*, and *nuṭq* (Ibn Ḥanbal, Muḥāsibī; Ḥallāj).[38]

c) ESCHATOLOGICAL PROBLEMS

Is faith enough for salvation? Experimental information about the necessary minimum of hope (Yaḥyä Rāzī's *rajā*) and attrition* (Tustarī's *tawba*). Distinction between *^c^aql* and *qalb*, between *mu^ɔ^min* and *^c^ārif* (Ibn Karrām, Muḥāsibī, against the majority, whose opinion was followed by Tustarī and Tirmidhī). Will it be possible to see the divine essence? Notion of the transfiguring *tajallī* (Rabāḥ, ^c^Abd al-Wāḥid ibn Zayd) as opposed to merely intellectual awareness (*ru^ɔ^ya*). What will be the recompenses of Paradise? Notions if *iḥsān, iṣṭifā^ɔ^iyya, ghibṭa*.[39]

d) LEGAL STATUS OF ACTS

Is the use of naming, which applies the name to the named thing, always legitimate? Is Qur^ɔ^ānic *ḥikāya* permissible? Concept of the *da^c^wä*, legitimate preaching of the *huwa huwa* (Tustarī, Ḥallāj), differentiation of *^c^ilm* and *ma^c^rifa*. Notions of *istimā^c^* and *istinbāṭ*. The problem of observation (*taḥaqquq*), as distinguished from reality (*ḥaqīqa*) and the Real (*Ḥaqq*). Attributability of acts, responsibility of agents.[40]

e) POLITICS

Differentiation of prophet and saint: the characteristic of infallibility and the grace of impeccability. Equality of rank among the prophets.[41]

Certain experiences of the mystics have even contributed to the found-

* "Attrition" in the sense of incomplete penitence for one's sins, based on fear of retribution.

36. *Passion*, Fr 3:141 ff., 117 ff./Eng 3:128 ff. 105 ff.

37. *Passion*, Fr 3:181, 32 ff., 23 n 2, 52 ff., 375–76/Eng 3:169, 25 ff., 16 n 29, 44 ff., 356–58.

38. *Passion*, Fr 3:154 ff./Eng 3:141 ff.

39. *Passion*, Fr 3:159–61, 24 n 2, 162, 176, 218/Eng 3:146–48, 17 n 36, 149–50, 163–64, 206.

40. *Passion*, Fr 3:93–94, 192, 70, 197, 85–88/Eng 3:83, 180, 60, 185, 74–77.

41. *Passion*, Fr 3:211–12, 220–21/Eng 3:199, 208–9.

ing of schools of dogmatic theology; Faḍliyya, Bakriyya, Karrāmiyya, Sālimiyya. I have shown that in this sense Ḥallāj was recognized as the true leader of a school (Ḥallājiyya).

3. List of Dogmatic Criticisms Incurred

The precise moral and dogmatic range of the theses experimentally established by the Muslim mystics can be measured by the censures they incurred from various jurists and canonical authorities.

The Imāmīs were the first to react. They condemned Ḥasan Baṣrī for three theses: *wa^cẓ*, or the precept of fraternal correction (without dissimulation or violence); *riḍā*, the state of reciprocal contentment between God and the soul; Ḥasan's "compromise" between predestination and free will.[42]

Next, they condemned Abū Hāshim ᶜUthmān ibn Sharīk of Kūfa. He had offended them by his monastic rule (*khānqāh*), his habit (*ṣūf*), and his doctrine of physical premovement (*jabr*).[43]

Nevertheless, there were still mystics among the Imāmī traditionists at Kūfa until about 220/835. Most notable were Kulayb, ᶜAbdak, ᶜAbdallah ibn Yazīd ibn Qinṭāsh Hudhalī, and the illustrious poet Abū'l-ᶜAtāhiya of the Butriyya Zaydī sect.[44] Nevertheless, as early as the third/ninth century, Imāmīs and Zaydīs had agreed that the mystics were to be outlawed.[45]

The Khārijites accepted some ascetic penitential practices, but they condemned Ḥasan Baṣrī for his refusal to revolt, his submission to authority, and his theory that the intention is more important than the external work.[46] The Khārijites never ceased condemning mysticism.

The Sunnis were much more divided. The first censures had their source in the strict traditionist (Ḥashwiyya) circles where the mystics were classified as *zanādiqa* (Manichaeans), a subclass of the Rūḥāniyya ("spirituals"). Abū Dāwūd Sijistānī (d. 275), author of the *Sunan*, condemns[47] a "group of four [*sic*] *zanādiqa*": "Rabāḥ,[48] Abū [Muḥammad][49] Ḥabīb, Ḥayyān,[50] Ḥarīrī, and Rābiᶜa." Among the group are two saints who have be-

42. Ṭabarsī, *Iḥtijāj*, 167–68, 170, 172, 161.

43. Bahbahānī, *Khayrātiyya*, f. 241b. See however *Passion*, Fr 3:119 n 4/Eng 3:107 n 66. Jaᶜfar's bull [edict] (*Ṭarāʾiq*, I, 112).

44. Muḥāsibī, *Makāsib*, f. 87; and *Passion*, Fr 1:361/Eng 1:314.

45. *Passion*, Fr 2:22, 44/Eng 2:16, 38.

46. Below, ch. 4, sec. 3.

47. In Dhahābī, *Iᶜtidāl*, s.n. Riyāḥ (*sic*).

48. Marked with two dots instead of one, making it Riyāḥ; the passage shows that he meant Rabāḥ Qaysī.

49. Thinking of Ḥabīb ᶜAjamī, I suggest this intercalation.

50. Marked Ḥibbān. He probably meant Ḥayyān Qaysī (*Passion*, Fr 3:126/Eng 3:114), a shortening of the name Abū'l-ᶜAlā Ḥayyān ibn ᶜUmayr Qaysī, the *rāwī* of Ibn ᶜAbbās and Ibn Samura (Ibn Saᶜd, VII, 137, 165).

come universally revered. The heresiographer Khashīsh Nasaʾī (d. 253) explains this condemnation of the mystics. Some, he says[51] [he is speaking of Dārānī], pretend that by virtue of meditation (*fikriyya*) they may enjoy (in this world) the spiritual life of God, the angels, and the prophets, and dine with the houris. Other mystics, he says, including Kulayb and Rabāḥ, teach that when love of God has supplanted all other attachments in the heart (*khulla*), legal bans are no longer valid (*rukhaṣ*). And some, such as Ibn Ḥayyān, teach a method of ascetic training (especially of the diet) that so mortifies yearnings for the flesh (and repugnances) that when the training is finished the "ascetic" gains licence to everything (*ibāḥa*). Another group [including Rabāḥ and Kulayb] maintains that the heart is distracted when mortification becomes too vigorous; it is better to yield immediately to one's inclinations;[52] the heart, having experienced vanity, can then detach itself from vain things without regret.[53] One last group, according to Nasaʾī, affirms that asceticism (*zuhd*) is applicable only to things forbidden by religious law, that enjoying permitted wealth is good[54] and that riches are superior to poverty.[55]

These more or less tendentious charges are aimed at the quietist deformation of mysticism: *khulla, ibāḥa, tafḍil al-ghanī.*

At first, the accusations of Sunni Muʿtazilite heresiographers were directed only at individuals. Kahmas (d. 149) was indicted for holding that God could be perceived "by the sense of touch" (*mulāmasa*); ʿAbd al-Wāḥid ibn Zayd (d. 177) was faulted for his claim that it was possible to see God "in this world, in proportion to one's good works," which leads to *ḥulūl*; Abū Shuʿayb Qallāl (d. c. 170), for maintaining that "God rejoices in or is saddened by" the acts of His saints.[56]

In the following century, Muʿtazilite theologians became more generally and violently critical. They stigmatized the "mystical states and stations" professed by Dhū'l-Nūn Miṣrī, the superiority of saints to prophets affirmed by Ibn abī'l-Ḥawwārī,[57] and the doctrine of transforming union (*muṭāʿ*) preached by Ḥallāj. Bisṭāmī (*subḥānī, janna, miʿrāj*), Kharrāz (*taqdīs, ʿayn al-jamʿ*, and Tustarī were sentenced to banishment; finally, Ḥallāj and Ibn ʿAṭā were put to death.

Moderate Sufi writers subsequently began to reserve a chapter of their

51. In *Istiqāma*, extract ap. Malaṭī, f. 160–67.

52. Cf. the Rasputinism so frequent among Slavs (even Soloviev is inclined to it: *Trois entretiens*, Fr. trans. Tavernier, 56–60).

53. Ibn Adham interrupts a fast to receive a friend (Thawrī, ap. Makkī, *Qūt*, II, 177, 180). Cf. Dārānī (in Makkī, *Qūt*, II, 174–75).

54. "Eating delicious dishes in an incitation to find satisfaction in God" (*sic*: Dārānī, ap. Makkī, *Qūt*, II, 177–79).

55. Proposition of Yaḥyä Rāzī. Cf. *Passion*, same references as in n 34.

56. Ashʿarī, *Maqālāt*, f. 97a.

57. Ibn al-Jawzī, *Nāmūs*, XI.

manuals for the special heretical dangers to which one is exposed by mysticism. Sarrāj, in his *Lumaᶜ*,[58] makes a list: *tafḍīl al-ghanī, fanā* ([*ᶜan*] *al-ᶜubūdiyya, al-bashariyya, al-awṣāf*), *ḥulūl* (*bi'l-anwār, bi'l-shawāhid, bi'l-mustaḥsanāt*), *tafḍīl al-walī, ibāḥa, faqd al-iḥsās,* the question of the *Rūḥ*.

In the *Ghalaṭāt*,[59] Sulamī makes the same list more systematic. He adds *ruᵓya fī'l-qulūb* and *shaṭḥ*. On the other hand, he defends[60] the legality of the following "dispensations" (*rukhaṣ*): *raqṣ, samāᶜ, ᶜurs, naẓar ilā'l-murd*; Hujwīrī only mentions them [with *tamzīq* (*kharq*)] in his *Kashf*[61] in order to register his disapproval. In the *Iḥyā*, Ghazālī takes the same position as Sulamī, more or less.

Ibn Ṭāhir Maqdisī, in the *Ṣafwa*, also justifies the dispensations (*mizāḥ, tamzīq, raqṣ, samāᶜ*; a small piece on the *naẓar*). He was the first to give the characteristic formula of spiritual discipline, "obedience is more important than observance" (*"al-khidma afḍal min al-ᶜibāda"*); therefore, in spite of the resulting scandal over pharisaism, a spiritual guide can tell a disciple not to say a certain prayer, not to go to the mosque on a given Friday, not to make the pilgrimage, if God (and his own soul) command it.

On the subject of later Sufism, it is useful to consult Turkumānī (*Lumaᶜ*),[62] Shāṭibī (*Iᶜtiṣām*), and ᶜAbdarī (*Mudkhal*),[63] who made long lists of the *bidaᶜ*, innovations, for which they reproached the mystics. On Sufism in Turkey there is Hammer's analysis, published long ago, of the arguments between the schools of the religious jurist Abū'l-Suᶜūd and the mystic Berkevi, and the twenty-one points for which the canonical authority Qāḍizādeh reproached the mystic Sīwāsī in 1066/1656.[64] In the last hundred years, analogous polemics have appeared periodically, in a slew of pamphlets in Egypt, Mecca, and Java-Sumatra.

4. Specialized Appropriation of Technical Terms

The doctors of sacred law and dogma make numerous complaints against the mystics. The one most important here concerns the special meaning, the incomparable experimental flavor, that the mystics suppose adheres to and inheres in each technical term or set of root letters chosen from the vast resources of ordinary Arabic language. In mystical thought, these terms are not simply images stripped of their sense objects, or schematized frames for rational concepts. Above all, they are allusions pointing to

58. Ed. Nicholson, 409 ff.
59. Ms. Cairo VII, 228. Cf. *Passion*, Fr 3:249/Eng 3:235, and all of ch. 13.
60. *Sunan*, ap. Ibn al-Jawzī, *Nāmūs*.
61. Nicholson trans., 416 ff.
62. *Lumaᶜ fī'l-ḥawādith wa'l-bidaᶜ*, ms. Cairo, *taṣaww.*, no. 701.
63. These two books were printed in Cairo.
64. Hammer, *Gesch. Osm. Reich.*, VI, 679, and V, 576.

the spiritual realities, the sanctifying virtues, that only the persistent practice of a concerted rule for living can allow the mystic to discover and savor, as he gradually acquires them. He must put the words into practice before he can understand them. This doctrine of the *aḥwāl* and the *maqāmāt*, which Miṣrī and Muḥāsibī made explicit, is characteristic of all mysticism. It is congenital to Sufism.

The ability, which poets possess, to engrave the characteristic mark of personal experience of the universe onto common words, is even greater in mystics. This phenomenon can be seen as early as Ḥasan Baṣrī, who used ordinary words,[65] such as *fiqh, niyya, nifāq, riḍā,*[66] for internal experiment and moral introspection, by which he deepened their range remarkably. Ibn al-Mubārak[67] did the same for *qirāʾa*[68] and *futuwwa,* Shaqīq for *tawakkul.* The new usage was explained in definitions that were later modified and refined by the nuances of successors' personal experiments.

These terms have no absolute worth out of context. They are valuable only in relation to their common goal, like distance markers on a road. On the "soul's road towards God" they represent successive stages. Each one of them can be understood by gradual assimilation; Harawī's *Manāzil al-sāʾirīn* systematically explains how the meaning of a single word is deepened as the mystical experiment progresses.

The technical terms undergo a gradual warping. Their deliberate, growing appropriation for a meaning more and more personal and enlivening to the reader is only one stage on the way to the happy conclusion of the inner journey. The reader is given a direct warning (*ᶜibra*) intended to awaken his conscience; his thought is dissociated from the appearances and forms of human actions and works. His attention is focused on the inner part of his actions, on the divine grace giving a distinct mode to what is actualized in him. Ḥallaj notes, "When works are considered, He for Whom the works are accomplished is lost from sight. When He in Whose sight we act is considered, the consideration of acts becomes invisible." That is the goal.

Finally, in all phrases or actions, even those that appear the least important, the attentive mystic grasps the anagogic sense (*muṭṭalaᶜ*), which is a divine call. Then a dialogue begins between the humble, meditating soul and the transcendent, divine Wisdom. For the soul, words take on the fullness specific to their momentary reality, in which God is heard to speak; the soul reforms its vocabulary in the image of the divine speech. At the threshold of mystical union, the phenomenon of *shaṭḥ* intervenes.

65. Not artificial words, as in Ibn ᶜArabī's later school.

66. Makkī, *Qūt,* I, 153; Sh. *Ṭab.,* I, 29; *Passion,* Fr 3:44/Eng 3:36.

67. Makkī, *Qūt,* I, 251.

68. *Taqarraʾa* in the sense of *tanassaka* (Goldziher).

An exchange, a switching of roles through love, is offered; the consenting soul, without suspecting it, is invited to desire, and to express in the first person, the point of view of the Beloved Himself. *Shaṭḥ* is the supreme test of the soul's humility and the seal of its election.

The first sketches of *shaṭḥ* appear in Ibn Adham and Rābiᶜa; Bisṭāmī describes his intoxication at a glimpse of it; Ḥallaj gives undeniable instances of *shaṭḥ*, of which he also provides penetrating psychological analyses. Shiblī alludes to *shaṭḥ* frequently.[69]

After Shiblī, cases of it in Islamic mysticism become rarer, and their value declines. The *shaṭḥiyāt* attributed to Kīlānī, Rifāᶜī, and Ibn ᶜArabī are almost unreadable in comparison to those of their great ancestors. The giddy pride that already intrudes in Bisṭāmī and Tustarī pushes those later mystics to make embarrassingly puerile statements:[70] "My foot is on the neck of all the saints," "Here am I, the Throne of God," etc. They submit to the theologians and make every effort to maintain the distance between inaccessible divine transcendence and acts of worship; then, in revenge, they take pride in being at least beyond the range of other men.

5. The Question of False Attributions

A. *Ḥadith Mursal* and *Ḥadīth Qudsī*

Shaṭḥ is ecstatic language: the mystic claims to be a simple mouthpiece, the inert bearer of another voice, a channel for the word of God. The phenomenon of *shaṭḥ* is the key to two of early Islam's particular features, studied in *ḥadīth* under the names *ḥadīth mursal* (loosened)[71] and *ḥadīth qudsī* (sacred).

In the third century A.H., the founders of the critical science of the *ḥadīth* indignantly denounced various "falsifiers" (*waḍḍāᶜun*) for inventing and spreading statements supposedly of the Prophet, which, of course, they would have been unable to trace by genealogy (*isnād*) from witness

69. The most complete collection of the theopathic speech (*shaṭḥiyāt*) of the first Muslim mystics is the one compiled by Rūzbihān Baqlī (d. 606 A.H.) during his great labors on Ḥallāj. It appeared in Arabic under the title *Manṭiq al-asrār bibayān al-anwār*; then in Persian (with alterations) as *Sharḥ al-shaṭḥiyāt*. H. Ritter has reproached me for not publishing these texts, after using them for so many years. No "Lexicon of Mystical Terms in Islam" could be published before an edition of Baqlī's work. H. Corbin and A. R. Badawi are considering one. [*Sharh-e shathiyāt*, H. Corbin, ed., Tehran and Paris: Institut Franco-Iranien, *Bibliothèque iranienne*, XII, 1966. The Arabic text of the *Manṭiq* has not yet been edited.] I was at least able to give an analysis of Baqlī's two collections, in "La vie et les oeuvres de Rūzbehān Baqlī" in *Florilege Pedersen*, Copenhagen, 1953, 282–86 [*Opera Minora*, II].

70. How infinitely preferable is the humble response of Naṣrābādhī, when he was told, "There is nothing in you of what makes true lovers": "It's true, I have nothing of theirs except their sobs; and those sobs set me afire" (Qush. 172).

71. Goldziher, *Muh. Stud.*, II, 141.

to witness back to the putative source. Certainly there were counterfeiters, motivated, for example, by economic interest, political ambition, sectarian bias, and even the perverse desire to deceive.[72] The *muḥaddithūn* identified an additional category of fraud, to be distinguished from the others: *ṣāliḥūn*, pious men, inventing *ḥadīth* "in order to touch the hearts of the people," and fabricating imaginary *isnād* in order to spread their sayings. These are either simple calls to prayer, penitence, or love of God, or promises of comprehensive indulgences (*rukhaṣ*) in exchange for the performance of supererogatory acts.[73] The mentality of these falsifiers is more complex than that of the others, and it merits more careful study.

In the third century, some of the pious men, being caught in the act, had, at least according to their admissions, fabricated *isnād*, as the cases of Abū ᶜIṣma ᶜAbdī,[74] Jawbiyārī, and Ghulām Khalīl apparently show. They illustrate the eventual absorption and perversion of a psychological process having its origin, and its early permissible forms, in the preceding centuries. With the caution of men of the world, the pious falsifiers were trying to use legitimate chains of transmission as a protective cover. They wanted to continue to tap and channel information about dogma and custom from their preternatural source: the divination or mysticism and states of dreaming or ecstasy in which they consulted Muḥammad and other deceased prophets, and even questioned God supernaturally.

There were several methods to evoke the prophets, most notably Zuhrī's,[75] used by Ibn ᶜUkkāsha in the famous dream in which he consulted Muḥammad. (Ibn Ḥanbal attested to this event's authenticity before Mutawakkil.)[76] The earliest mystics published communications directly obtained from a dead prophet as *ḥadīth mursal*, i.e., authoritative prophetic texts permitting no dispute.[77] The commentator allowed himself to "loosen" or shorten the *isnād*, because the *ḥadīth's* content was so convincing.

The second case is *ḥadīth qudsī*: in the statements collected in mystical experiments, God speaks directly, in the first person (and not indirectly, quoted as an interlocutor, as in the Qurᵓān). Here, a grave problem is posed by direct mystical union (superior to indirect prophetic revelation). Most of the first Muslim mystics did not dare to make an open claim to it. Ḥasan Baṣrī and the pseudo-Jaᶜfar gave their *aḥādīth qudsiyya* as *marāsil* (of Muḥammad). After trying to be more straightforward, Ibn Adham

72. Goldziher, *Vorlesungen*, Eng. trans., 43–45.

73. Mālik ibn Dīnār was already reproaching Abān ibn abī ᶜAyyāsh for this (Dhahabī, *Iᶜtidāl*, s.v.). Cf. *Passion*, Fr 3:218–19./Eng 3: 206–7.

74. Goldziher, *Muh. Stud.*, II, 155–56.

75. And Ibn Sīrīn's: the *istikhāra*, which, if performed in private, remained legal.

76. Malaṭī, *Tanbīh*, f. 28–30.

77. Resulting in this sense of the word *mursal* (cf. *asmā mursala*, as opposed to *muḍāfa*, in ᶜA. M. Kindī, 34; and the *maṣlaḥa mursala* of the Malikites).

retreated[78] and gave a *ḥadīth qudsī* as a *mursal* of John the Baptist. Others gave them as sayings of David, Idrīs, etc.[79] Dārānī, taking more extreme measures, refused to divulge any of his ecstatic experimental results (*tankīt al-ḥaqīqa*), except those explicitly confirmed by Qurʾānic and traditional authority. Bisṭāmī confessed them in the same way, emitting Qurʾānic words almost completely removed from their contexts as choppy, ecstatic cries in the first person. Tirmidhī, without giving further details, said that his results were a confirmation of the traditional discipline he was imposing upon his inner life. Like the others, Ḥallāj had found *aḥādīth qudsiyya* through mystical experimentation; he alone was honest enough to publish them as such. They are his *Riwāyāt,* of which the *isnād* is *ilhāmī* (ecstatic);[80] he set forth not a historical succession of dead witnesses but a contemporaneous ensemble of phenomena in which divine grace is affirmed.[81]

The traditionists' critical polemic against the "apocryphal" *aḥādīth* of the mystics is of a great importance. As the arguments become more and more acrimonious, they underscore an irremediable divergence of points of view. Ḥammād ibn Salama stigmatizes the "ignorance" of the *quṣṣāṣ.*[82] Yaḥyā ibn Saᶜīd Qaṭṭān, speaking of Mālik ibn Dīnār, Muḥammad ibn Wāsiᶜ, and Ḥassān ibn abī Sinān, declares that "the most condemnable thing about the conduct of the pious with respect to *ḥadīth* is that they accept them from any source."[83] Posed like this, the problem raises two questions, one of method and one of morality.

If the *muḥaddithūn* had succeeded in imposing their method and eliminating all *ḥadīth* with apocryphal *isnād* from the "authentic" collections, believers would now have only dried meat[84] to feed meditation: a few prescriptions concerned only with hygiene and civility, sandal cleaning,

78. Makkī, *Qūt,* II, 67.

79. Cf. Jalāl Rūmī attributing his lines to Shams Tabrīzī, Musaffar Sibtī attributing his *Maḍnūn ṣaghīr* to Ghazālī.

80. *Passion,* Fr 3:344–52/Eng 3:327–34.

81. In the beginning, the *ḥadīth qudsī* was an indirect means of putting "theopathic speech" into circulation by tracing it to Holy Scripture, in which God spoke in the first person. This aberrant branch of the *ḥadith* played a fundamental role in the history of Sufism, and, more generally, in the history of prayer formulas and forms of devotion in Islam. It has not yet been studied systematically. An elementary study by Zwemer (in *MW* 1922, 263–75) refers to the following monographs on the *ḥadīth qudsī*: Ibn ᶜArabī (G.A.L. I, 441; there is the collection of *Arbaᶜīn* by his disciple Qunyawī); Munāwī (Gotha ms.); Madanī (*Athāfī sīniyya,* printed in Ḥaydarābād, 1323); Nabhānī (*Jāmiᶜ*). There are some *aḥādīth qudsiyya* among the Imāmīs (*Khuṭbat al-bayān*). There are references below for the study of the most important *ḥadīth qudsī* (list, ch. 3, sec. 5. B.): the *ḥadīth* of the *kūnī* (ch. 4 sec. 3. D.), the *ḥadīth al-ghurba* (ch. 5, sec. 1. B.), the *ḥadīth al-ᶜishq,* the *ḥadīth al-ikhlāṣ* (ch. 4, sec. 5. A.) and the *ḥadīth al-abdāl* (above, ch. 1, s.v. *BDL*). Cf. also Abū Dharr (in *Ḥilya,* VI, 163, life of Shihr); Rāghib Pasha, *Safīna,* 162. [See William A. Graham's *Divine Word,* and relevant findings in Juynboll's *Muslim Tradition.*]

82. Except for Bunānī, (Ibn al-Jawzī, *Quṣṣāṣ,* s.v.).

83. Dhahabī, *Iᶜtidāl,* s.v.

84. *Qadīd.* The word is used to Abū Madyan of Tlemcen.

and the right wood for making toothpicks. Purely formal criticism of *isnād* is ideally no more than a servant who sweeps the house. If it becomes the basis for constituting the corpus of Islamic tradition, and if a given religious precept's social rank and importance are simply made to correspond to the degree of soundness of its textual transmission, the result is the undue elimination of the most important precepts. In theory and in private judgment, the acceptability of a witness should be examined before the content of his testimony,[85] but in practice and in society the content must take precedence. In order to obtain exceptionally valuable testimony in a court of law, there is no hesitation to change the manner of questioning witnesses, or even to force their confessions. A method of historical criticism that only accepts the accounts of witnesses who are professionally honorable,[86] summoned and recorded by proper procedure, will miss[87] most of the unusual events and, in recording the others, will fall into all possible traps of prejudice and personal interest, which the forgers of documents will have set for gullible, positivistic investigators.

Next, the question of morality. The *ahl al-ḥadīth* school, from Yaḥyā Qaṭṭān to Ibn al-Jawzī and Dhahabī, condemned the "perversity" of authors who, like Raqqāshī, Namīrī, Murrī, Muḥāsibī, and, later, Makkī and Ghazālī, had cited apocryphal *aḥādīth* in their works. They would have been reprehensible only if they had acted knowingly (as Ibn Ṭāhir Maqdisī seems to have done),[88] which is not the case of Muḥāsibī or Ghazālī. For these two teachers, the important thing was not to know whether a quotation was reproduced word for word, complete and unabridged, or whether *X* or *Y* had first put it into circulation, but to appreciate and taste its worth as a rule for living, by ceasing to quibble over the form in order to experience the sense.[89] Of course Ghazālī stuffed his *Iḥyā* with *ḥadīth* whose *isnād* is indefensible. The point is secondary; the *Iḥyā* is not a manual of textual criticism but a guide for moral edification. Ghāzalī took little care over the genealogy of the quotations he was collecting, and very great care over their moral significance for the reader. He was writing not for curious amateur archeologists but for consciences avid for moral meditation.

We are led to one last question: how to assess the guilt of those moralists who knowingly became *waḍḍāᶜūn*, or inventors of *ḥadīth*. It is no doubt

85. *Passion*, Fr 1:341/Eng 1:294.

86. *ᶜUdūl* of Islamic jurisprudence.

87. As if, in order to understand a diplomatic negotiation, the historian could permit himself to read only ministerial telegrams printed in the "blue" or "yellow" books; cf. a battle according to the operational memoranda of the military command; a parliamentary debate according to official newspapers; any biography according to the documents intended for administrative archives (city hall, notaries, police).

88. *Ṣafwa*. Cf. Maysara, a sufi of ᶜAbbādān (Goldziher, *M. St.*, II, 394).

89. Cf. also Ibn Sīnā and the philosophers.

a mistake, an act of cowardice, to disguise the invention of an *isnād*; but the preliminary, venial fault should not compromise the *ḥadīth* itself, which will have currency among believers by virtue of its content, not by reason of its date of origin.[90] *Aḥādīth* are essentially rules of conduct, condoned *hic et nunc.* Is it permitted to invent an imaginary sentence, if it is related to a case of conscience? The question is such that it engages the whole problem of artistic invention and personal originality of style. Solutions vary enormously between civilizations derived, on the one side, from Indo-European linguistic tradition, and, on the other, from Semitic tradition.

The Semitic tradition since Abrahamic and Mosaic monotheism was introduced[91] has restricted all creative initiative and innovation to God alone. Except for revelations planned and solemnly brought to pass by Him, all private inspirations, especially the profane fancies of the poets, are treated with extreme mistrust. The Aryan tradition, from the beginning polytheistic, idolatrous, and favorable to individual liberty, has been satisfied with fables, artistic and literary fictions, painting or sculpture, drama or romance. All of these things are denounced by the Semites either as man's blasphemous usurpation of the role of God, the only giver of life, or as a sacrilegious conception of the truth of God, when He is suspected of telling fables[92] to His servants.

Through deeper meditation, the Muslim mystics conquered their repugnances and came to admit that the fact of divine omnipotence did not exclude the exercise and celebration of His gifts to men. The artist is but a perishable image of what the saint may become: the free and living instrument of the one Poet, the creative Power. Parables, even about God, may be told, as long as the teller forgets himself, and the parables cause the hearers to think of Him.

This attitude is explained very well at the end of Plato's *Gorgias* (sec. 79): "... Listen, then, as they say, to this very lovely story. Perhaps you will believe it is a fable, but for me it is a *true story,* and I wish you would regard all I am going to tell you as the truth."[93] The mystics conceive the parables of their catechism as true prophecies that will be verified in time, but which can only be said to be "true" insofar as they have been realized. The truth of their parables is observed *a posteriori* in what they produce in society, in the swarm of imitations, the teeming variety of images, synonyms, and viable applications they provoke in those who have listened to them attentively. This truth is difficult to grasp, alas; the experience of it is

90. Like a museum piece in an antique shop.
91. Artistic imagination was intense among the Chaldeans and Phoenicians.
92. The question of the "historical" books of the Old Testament.
93. Cf. the tale of Er the Armenian; and that of Thespesios (in Plutarch, *Delays*).

limited to those who are found worthy, or who have been humble enough to admit their unworthiness in advance.

B. Authors Responsible for
Certain Famous *Aḥādīth Qudsiyya*

Abū Dharr: *"man taqarrab ... shibran ... dhirāᶜan ..."* (Muḥāsibī, *Riᶜāya*, 12a, attributes it to Ibn Musayyab);* Ḥanbal V, 153; Nabhānī, *Jāmiᶜ*, no. 30).

Kaᶜb: *"anā jalīs man dhakaranī"* and the *ḥadīth al-jumjuma* (according to *Ḥilya*, s.v.).

Ḥudhayfa: *"yad Allah maᶜ* (var: *ᶜalä) al-jamāᶜa"* (Ḥanbal, I, 406; taken up by Ibn ᶜIyāḍ, according to Malaṭī, 143; Ibn Baṭṭa ᶜUkbarī, *Sharḥ wa ibāna*); and the *ḥadīth al-ibtilā* (Cf. *Passion*, Fr 3:127 n 2/Eng 3:115 n 123; Muttaqī, *Kanz*, V, 164; attributed by Ibn al-Jawzī, *Mawḍūᶜāt*, to Yamān ibn ᶜAdī).

Ibn Masᶜūd: *"ṭūbä liman lam yushghil qalbahu bimā tarä ᶜaynāhu ..."* (Muḥāsibī, *Riᶜāya*, 15a; later attributed to Jesus; cf. Asin, *Logia*, no 20).

Ḥasan Baṣrī: *"man ᶜashiqanī ᶜashiqtuhu ..."* (according to ᶜAbd al-Wāḥid ibn Zayd; ap. *Ḥilya*, s.v.; included[94] by Ibn Sīnā in his *ᶜIshq*); *"tarjīḥ midād al-ᶜulamā ᶜalä dam al-shuhadā"* (Manjanīqī, ap. Suyūṭī, *Laᵓālī*,[95] s.v.; then admitted as a *ḥadīth* via Ibn ᶜUmar, according to Kürküt, Ḥarīmī; cf. Ḥasan's pronouncement to the contrary, in Ibn Qutayba, *ᶜUyūn*, II, 295); *"yā muqallib al-qulūb, thabbit ..."* (according to Ibn Saᶜd, IV, 128; Ibn ᶜIyāḍ made it a *ḥadīth*, according to the *Ḥilya*); *"Khayr al-umūr awsaṭuhā"* (*ᶜIqd*, I, 250, according to Goldziher, *RHR*, XVIII, 193).

Yazīd Raqqāshī: *ḥadīth ghibṭat al-mutaḥābbīn* (Makkī, *Qūt*, I, 222; compare Nabhānī, *Jāmiᶜ*, no. 31).

Ibrahim ibn Adham: *"Kuntu samᶜahu wa baṣarahu"* (according to Muḥāsibī, *Maḥabba* [see herein, ch 5 n 72], cf. Makkī, *Qūt*, II, 67; accepted by Bukhārī); *"al-ᶜārif fārighan ..."* (Id.; cf. *Passion*, Fr 3:15/Eng 3:8).

Fuḍayl ibn ᶜIyāḍ (cf. *supra*): *"udhkurūnī adhkurukum"* (according to the London Or ms. 8049, f. 30b).

Aḥmad Jawbiyārī: *"uṭlubū al-ᶜilm, walaw bi'l-Ṣīn"* (accepted by Ibn Karrām; Dhahabī, *Iᶜtidāl*, s.v.).

Yaḥyä ibn Muᶜādh Rāzī: *"man ᶜarafa nafsahu, faqad ᶜarafa Rabbahu"* (according to Suyūṭī, *Laᵓālī*, s.v.; Ibn ᶜArabī, *Muḥāḍarāt*, II, 369).

Sahl Tustarī: *"mā min āya ... illā walahā arbaᶜ maᶜānī"* (according to Tustarī, *Tafsīr*, 3, 6; accepted by Ghazālī, *Ladunniyya*, 16).

Muḥammad ibn Yūnus Kadīmī (d. 286, at 100 years of age): *"uṭlubū'l-ḥawāᵓij*

---

* *"rawiya Abū Hurayra ...,"* Smith's ed., p. 20.

94. *Talbīs*, 181. Sarī extracts a portion "of one of the revealed books" (Qush., III, 165).

95. Suyūṭī, *Durar*, 199; Ghazālī, *Iḥyā*, I, 6.

ʿind ḥisān al-wujūh" (accepted by Sulamī, Ibn Sīnā [*ʿIshq*]; cf. Dhahabī, *Iʿtidāl*, s.v.).

C. Initiatory *Isnād*, al-Khiḍr, the *Abdāl*

The deception of false attributions was perhaps excusable in mystics who had no civic heroism from which to benefit, but who nevertheless wished, under borrowed names, to initiate their contemporaries into the experiences of their spiritual lives. Unfortunately, the practice spread to areas in which authenticity was fundamental. One such problem, hotly debated, especially from the fifth/eleventh century onward, was initiatory *isnād*, the "chain of mystical supports" attaching orders, link by link, to the most venerated saints, the Companions, and the Prophet.

Muḥāsibī's works (*Naṣāʾiḥ*) prove that, in the third/ninth century, the question of initiatory *isnād* was not yet being raised, and, as a correlative,[96] that the taking of a special habit (*khirqa, shuhra bi libās*) was no more than a voluntary act of certain individuals. The institution of collective hermitages, as at ʿAbbādān, and the writing of manuals for the communal life, came long before the solemn affiliation of orders and the ritual wearing of habits.

In the fourth/tenth century, Jaʿfar Khuldī gave[97] the first known initiatory *isnād*, a sort of written *samaʿ*. He declared that the *tābiʿūn* (among others Anas ibn Mālik, d. 91), through Ḥasan Baṣrī (d. 110), Farqad Sinjī (d. 131), Maʿrūf (d. 200), and Sarī (d. 253), had transmitted the mystical doctrine to Junayd (d. 298), Khuldī's teacher.

Shortly thereafter, Daqqāq gave Qushayrī[98] the following genealogy for what he more explicitly called his "*akhdh al-ṭarīq*" (initiation): (1) the *tābiʿūn*, (2) Dāwūd Ṭāʾī, (3) Maʿruf, (4) Sarī, (5) Junayd, (6) Shiblī, (7) Naṣrābādhī.

In the following century, at the time of the foundation of the great orders, this chain was prettified, as ludicrous details were added to the rare, confirmed facts about the orders' origins. Here is the chain in its traditional form:[99] (1) ʿAlī, (2) Ḥasan Baṣrī, (3) Ḥabīb ʿAjamī, (4) Dāwād Ṭāʾī, (5) Maʿrūf, (6) Sarī, (7) Junayd, (8) Abū ʿAlī Rūdhbārī (d. 322), (9) either Abū ʿAlī Kātib (d. 340) or Zajjājī, (d. 348), (10) Abū ʿUthmān Maghribī (d. 373), (11) Abū'l-Qāsim Gurgānī (d. 469).[100]

This *isnād* of the *khirqa* was soon criticized. Step 1–2 is false: Ḥasan and ʿAlī never met[101] (Ibn Diḥya, Ibn al-Ṣalāḥ, Dhahabī). Step 3–4 is false: Ḥa-

96. Muḥāsibī, *Masāʾil*, 237–44.
97. *Fihrist*, 183.
98. Qush., *Risāla*, 158; the same, ed. Anṣārī, III, 245; IV, 36.
99. ʿAlī Burhānī, *Zahra, in fine*; Ibn abī Uṣaybiʿa, *ʿUyūn*, II, 250.
100. Cf. rem. of Jāmī, 347.
101. This work, ch. 4, sec. 3.

bīb died in Baṣra, Dāwūd lived in Kūfa (Dhahabī).[102] Step 4–5 is false: Maᶜrūf never went to Kūfa (Dhahabī).[103] Step 5–6 is dubious: Sarī was only the indirect disciple of Maᶜrūf.[104]

A second *isnād*, otherwise identical to the first, replaces steps 1–4 by the line of ᶜAlid Imāms up to ᶜAlī Riḍā (b. 183, d. 203 at Ṭūs), who is supposed to have taken Maᶜrūf (d. 200) as his doorman (after Maᶜrūf's conversion) and to have clothed him in his own *khirqa*. Ibn al-Jawzī (in his *Faḍāʾil Maᶜrūf*) and Dhahabī point out the chronological impossibilities of this ridiculous legend, which Qushayrī accepts.[105]

Two sorts of falsification that the later mystics frequently committed may be included here. One is to put certain sayings and poems under the *isnād* of a respected name, in order to avoid censure by the theologians.[106] The list of examples includes the *tafsīr* attributed to Imām Jaᶜfar (from the fourth/tenth century—see below); the *khuṭab* that Ṭabarsī attributes to ᶜAlī, which perhaps are by the Imāmī Mufaḍḍal; the false *Dīwān* of ᶜAlī, which contains pieces by Suhrawardī of Aleppo;[107] "letters," lightly accepted as authentic by Mehren, from Ibn Abī'l Khayr[108] to Ibn Sīnā, and from Ibn Sabᶜīn to Frederick II. The authenticity of Ibn ᶜArabī's letters to Fakhr Rāzī is also problematic.[109]

The other falsehood is to treat the most compromising works of daring mystics as apocrypha. Shaᶜrāwī, for example, declared without any supporting evidence that the *Fuṣūṣ* were not by Ibn ᶜArabī.[110] Nabhānī has recently tried to reject Nābulusī's authorship of the *Ghāyat al-maṭlūb*.[111]

The importance of these critical corrections must not be exaggerated. They remove an awkward overlay of arbitrary details, but they hardly change the curve of the historical development of mystical ideas, as the tradition represents them. The Muslim mystics themselves were not embarrassed to confess their uncertainty as to the intermediaries from whom they

102. This work, ch. 4, sec. 2.

103. In reality Maᶜrūf was the disciple of Bakr ibn Khunays, disciple of Bunānī.

104. This work, ch. 4, sec. 6.

105. Qush., I, 82–83. Cf. the supposed interviews of Junayd with Ibn Kullāb and with Abū'l-Qāsim Kaᶜbī (Ibn al-Najjār; Subkī; Yāfiᶜī, *Nashr*, II, 377); the legend of Aḥmad Sibtī, brother of Hārūn (*Futūḥāt*, I, 668); the legend of the *ahl al-ṣuffa*.

106. Jīlī's *ᶜayniyya*, attributed to Kīlānī.

107. E.g., the *Dawāka fika* (Turkumānī, *Lumaᶜ*; Nābulusī, *Kashf al-sirr al-ghāmiḍ*); imitated in Turkish by Niyāzī: *"Dermān arārdam"* (first *shīniyya*).

108. *Traités mystiques*, 1891, III, sec. 3; cf. Goldziher, *Vorlesungen*, Eng. trans., ch. 4, 153 n 120; and his apocryphal quatrain against the *madrasas* (though he had had the Niẓāmiyya created), in which the Qalandars are named, though their order was founded in the thirteenth century. Langlès, followed by Dozy and Salmon, put Ibn abī'l-Khayr two hundred years before his real dates.

109. Goldziher, *Vorlesungen*, Eng. trans., IV, 153–54 n 124. Margoliouth accepted (*Early Development*, 186–98) the authenticity of Nafzī's *Mawāqif*, reproduced and presented by Ibn ᶜArabī and ᶜAfīf Tilimsānī as if they were of the fourth century; I cannot agree with him.

110. In Shaᶜrāwī, *Laṭāʾif*, II, 29.

111. Preface to the *Madāʾiḥ*.

might have received the *khirqa.* The idea of an uninterrupted chain is quite foreign to Qurʾānic occasionalism, and the mystics accepted it only in order to answer traditionist objections. Perhaps it was infiltrated into their midst, as it was into the other guilds, by the ᶜAlid propaganda of the Qarmathians. In the table, which seems to be of Faṭimid origin, of the XVII patrons of the major organizations, there are several mystics: Dhū'l-Nūn Miṣrī (V), Ḥasan Baṣrī (VII), Abū Dharr (XIII), Abū'l-Dardā (XIV).[112]

Many mystics, finding it repugnant to use justifications as artificial as these *isnād,* say boldly that they have received their *khirqa* from al-Khiḍr (or Khaḍir).[113] The real meaning of this pretense is transparent. "Al-Khiḍr" is the traditional name of the anonymous figure shown, in the Qurʾān, to be the recipient and keeper of the *ᶜilm ladunnī,* a saint of God, and, as the guide given the responsibility to direct Moses[114] (Qurʾān 18:64–81), superior to the prophets. The mystic initiated by al-Khiḍr is sanctified, emancipated from the tutelage of prophetic law. It is an axiom of Sufism that al-Khiḍr is immortal,[115] because he is the supreme spiritual counselor who dictates the formulas of prayer to the heart.[116] According to Simnānī,[117] his complete name is Abū'l-ᶜAbbās Balyān ibn Qalyān ibn Fāligh al-Khiḍr.[118]

The *khirqa khiḍriyya* proves that the certified transmission of mystical initiation by *isnād* was only an ancillary argument, for external use. However, the Muslim mystics do not deny that at any given instant there is a precise

112. See Goldziher's introduction to Sijistānī's *Kitāb al-muᶜammarīn*; see also *Kutub al-futuwwa,* for example, the one by ᶜUbaydallāh Rifāᶜī (1082 A.H.: Damascus manuscript Ẓah. taṣ. 81).

113. Book by Shaᶜrāwī (*Khiḍriyya,* p. 13) devoted to those in contact with Khiḍr: Ibn Adham, Miṣrī, Bisṭāmī, Jurayrī, Tirmidhī, Kīlānī, Ibn ᶜArabī, Shādhilī. Cf. Khark., 213a, ᶜAṭṭār II, 92–94; Ḥazm IV, 180. *Khaḍir* = "Elianic Spirit" (n.b., *Khiḍr* is a vocalization to be rejected). The Islamic solution to the problem of "spiritual guidance" is provided from the eschatological point of view represented by Elias (Khaḍir is St. Elias of the Carmel) in all of Christian tradition. Much research has convinced me of the basic eschatological importance of the Qurʾān's sura 18, devoted to the Seven Sleepers of Ephesus, for understanding not only the psychology of the Prophet but also the social evolution of the generations of Muslims, during the thirteen centuries in which that sura has been read, every Friday, in every mosque. The sura's second part is a treatment of this problem of spiritual guidance (*irshād*) and of the priority of the spiritual guide (here Khaḍir, i.e., Elias: the spirit of Elias, as with St. John the Baptist) over the prophet legislator (here Moses). Cf. in *Analecta Bollandiana,* 1950, II, 245–60: "Les Sept Dormants, apocalypse de l'Islam"; and, in *Les mardis de Dar el Salām,* Cairo, 1952, II, "Les fouilles archéologiques d'Ephèse et leur importance religieuse pour la Chrétienté et l'Islam," 1–24. On Khaḍir, cf. the *Iṣāba*; Nuᶜmān-b-Muṣṭ. Köprülüzadeh, *Al-ᶜadl fī ḥāl al-Khaḍir,* (ms. Köpr. [3] 145); Kamālpashazadeh, *Kashf al-ḥāḍir fī amr al-Khaḍir,* Hakimoghli ms., 937. Cf. Ḥallāj on the *sīns* in Yā Sīn and in Mūsā (*Akhbār,* 28). The problem of the *Abdāl* is tied to that of Khaḍir. On the *ḥadīth al-abdāl,* consult the sources indicated above, s.v. *BDL* (and Khaṭīb II, 182).

114. Remark of Rabāḥ Qaysī (Sh. *ṭab.* I, 46).

115. *Passion,* Fr 2:347/Eng 2:330. Allusion to Ibn al-Jawzī's book against this belief (*ᶜAjālat al-munṭaẓir fī ḥāl al-Khaḍir,* cited in Ibn ᶜAṭā Allah, *Laṭāʾif,* I, 87).

116. A. Ibrāhīm Taymī (Makkī, *Qūt,* I, 7). Ibrāhīm Khawwāṣ (Qush. III, 53; cf. I, 71, IV, 173).

117. Apud *ᶜUrwa,* extract in Abulfazl, *Ayin-i-akbarī,* trans. Jarrett, III, 376.

118. He "renews his youth" every 120 years in 240, 120, 1 A.H., 120, 240, 360 . . .). He incessantly travels the world and was therefore nicknamed, among Christians in the Middle Ages, the "Tervagant" (hypothesis of J. Ribera). He likes the *raqṣ* and practices alchemy. See Vollers's work.

hierarchy of the sanctifying graces, which the divine omnipotence dispenses in various places on the earth, while insuring that the number of recipients of grace remains constantly fixed.[119] This is the famous theme of the *abdāl*, the apotropaic saints, who succeed one another by permutation (*badal*) and constitute the spiritual pillars without which the world would collapse.* In Islam, the doctrine is older than it is generally believed; in spite of what Ibn Khaldūn[120] says, it is not necessarily of Imāmī origin. By the fourth/tenth century it was already traditional,[121] was accepted by the Sālimiyya and the Ḥanbalites, and had assumed a great variety of forms differentiated by their complex, previous elaboration. It was mentioned explicitly[122] as early as the third/ninth century, in connection with the *ḥadīth al-ghibṭa* (taught by Ḥasan Baṣrī, Yazīd Raqqāshī, Ibn Adham, and Wakīᶜ),[123] the Abrahamic *khulla*, and the "three fundamental virtues."[124]

In the doctrine's oldest form, there were "forty" *abdāl*, "forty" being the traditional Semitic number that designates penitence and expiation.[125] Three hundred *nuqabā* and seventy *nujabā* were subsequently put under the authority of these *abdāl*, and seven *umanā* (var.: *abrār, awtād, akhyār*), four or three *ᶜamud* (var.: *athāfi*), and one *quṭb*, (*ghawth*) over them; the geographical distribution and administrative roles of the figures vary with each author.[126] These concepts represent a work of the mind parallel to those performed by the Nuṣayrīs (on the four *arkān*) and Qarmathians. Maghribī's remark that the head of the hierarchy knows his subordinates, "but they do not know him," refers to a Masonic principle that is applied, it must be admitted, in Ismaili secret societies; it remains unproved that thematic borrowing occurred.

* See Massignon, "The Notion of 'Real Elite' in Sociology and in History." For reference, see "Remark," ch. 1.

119. Among the Druze, this idea became the idea of the invariable number of souls (immediate compensation for the deaths by births, with immediate reincarnation of souls).

120. Muqaddima, de Slane trans., s.v.

121. Passion, Fr 3:221–22/Eng 3:209–10; Muḥāsibī, *Masāᵓil*, f. 233; *Maḥabba*, f. 6; Tirmidhī, *Rasāᵓil*, f. 180, 319; Junayd, ap. Kal. 54; Suyūṭī, *Khabar dāll*, in *Machriq*, XII, 194 ff. (article in bib., s.n. Anastase.)

122. Ibn abī'l-Dunyā specifies the "Abrahamic" moral virtues of the forty *abdāl*; they surpass others, not by their number of prayers, fasts, mortifications, or model behavior, but by the sincerity of their continence, good will, heart's peace, and fraternal advice to all Muslims *"ibtighāᵓa marḍāt Allah"* (Suyūṭī, *Khabar dāll*, in *Machriq*, XII, 204. Ibn abī'l-Dunyā, in his *Kitāb al-sakhā* [Anastase p. 201], gives a shorter recension of the text, as a *ḥadīth* of Ḥasan, through Ṣāliḥ Murrī). Maᶜrūf, Dārānī, Nibājī, and Bishr Ḥāfī tried to define the *abdāl* (Anastase, 200–204).

123. *Passion*, Fr 3:218/Eng 3:206.

124. Suyūṭī, op. cit., XII, 204 (Sulamī); cf. *Passion*, Fr 3:31, 44/Eng 3:24, 36.

125. See the Old and New Testaments, s.n.; Qurᵓān, s.n. arbaᶜīn; the "forty martyrs" in eastern toponymy.

126. See various theories: Kattānī's (d. 322) in Sh. *Ṭab.*, I, 110; Abū ᶜUthmān Maghribī's (d. 373), in Tahānuwī, *Kashshāf*, 846; Makkī's, in the *Qūt*, I, 109, II, 78; Tirmidhī's in Baqlī, I, 501. Cf. Jāmī, 21. The assembly of universal intercessor saints (*ḥaḍra*) is now thought to be composed of Kīlānī, Badawī, and Dasūqī, with Rifāᶜī as president.

We know that the saints particularly venerated by Ibn Adham were Mālik ibn Dīnār, Bunānī, and Sikhtiyānī; by Bishr Ḥāfī: Wuhayb ibn al-Ward, Ibn Adham, Ibn Asbāṭ, and Muslim Khawwāṣ.[127] According to the Makkī,[128] the Sālimiyya venerated Ibn Adham and Shaqīq, Miṣrī, Bisṭāmī, and Tustarī.

127. Tagr. I, 413.
128. *Qūt,* II, 76 (s.v. *khulla*).

4

THE FIRST MYSTICAL VOCATIONS IN ISLAM

Introduction

It is clear from the preceding chapters that a study of the lives of the first Muslims called to mysticism is of primary importance to anyone wishing to analyze the formation of Sufism's technical language. The historian of the arts need not exhaust himself over artists' biographies in order to study and appreciate the fabric of a popular song of even the technique of a classical work. Nor is he obliged to enquire whether Layla was as beautiful as Majnūn says she was, whether the painter of the *Embarkation for Cythera* had visited Cerigo, or whether Abū Nuwās really liked to take part in the licentious scenes described in his poetry. The basic question will not have been decided; the work's intrinsic value will not suddenly have come to light. The same is true in the study of science and philosophy, even legal, moral, and political philosophy; the historian can give an appraisal of the range and economy of a system without detailing the intentions that directed its maker's behavior. The arts and sciences touch man accidentally; they graze our surface.

Mysticism is not the same. It is an experimental science, a method of introspection; it aims by definition at reality itself, at the very heart of man, the intention under the intonation, the smile under the mask. Behind a person's conduct it seeks a grace that comes only from God. Therefore, an appraisal of each subject's degree of sincerity, an examination that makes every conscience transparent, is basic to the study of mysticism. To proceed we must be able to rely on a detailed inquiry into the lives and extant works of those who claim to teach it. Chapters four and five outline an investigation of the distinctive figures of Islamic mysticism at its beginnings.

1. Qurʾānic Foundations

A. The Qurʾānic Parables and the Problem of Muḥammad's Inner Life

If Christianity is fundamentally[1] the acceptance and imitation of Christ

1. Except among the historical Ebionites and the Sabbatarians of today.

before the acceptance of the Bible, Islam on the contrary is the acceptance of the Qurʾān before the imitation of Muḥammad, as the Prophet himself explicitly declared. He insistently taught the verses[2] emphasizing the strict dependence (and inferiority) of his person in relation to his mandate.[3]

We must therefore examine whether the Qurʾān itself suggests themes for mystical meditation before arguing whether Muḥammad had an inner life leaning towards mysticism.

Europeans unfamiliar with Semitic concision, with the brief lightning flashes of the Psalms[4] for example, communally suppose that the Qurʾān has no mystical tendencies; in other words, that there are no passages meant to be taken in an anagogic (*muṭṭalaᶜ*) sense.[5] But many allegorical passages,[6] contained in various suras both Meccan and Medinese, will be perceived, if we reflect even a little attentively (*a fortiori* if a believer meditates), to be more than simple anecdotes offered to the imagination, verifiable definitions presented to the intelligence, or legal and moral injunctions against our desires. Such verses (*āyāt*) are condensed but expressive parables containing an *ᶜibra*, an "admonition." One must consent to accept them before they will be understood; as a result, their vehemence proves repellent to the haughty and pharisaic minds of the *fuqahā*. Purely legal commentators, in general, also neglect them. E.g.:

Parables of Vocations: "*There* is a true reminder for him who has a heart for it, and who knows how to pay attention!" (50:37).[7] Build in the heart an edifice "founded on duty to God, not on a piece of earth, which will collapse" (9:109). Life in this world is like running water, like the harvest set out to dry (6:99: 10:25; 13:43; 57:19). At the ritual sacrifice in the pilgrimage,[8] "it is not the blood or flesh of the victims, but piety, that rises to God" (22:38). "A pardoning affectionate word is worth more than alms that cause a wound" (2:265).

Separating the good from the wicked: The different fates reserved for sincere hearts and deceitful ones (2:263, 266, 267, 268; 68:17), for those who rely on God for support and those who count on themselves (39:30; 18:31–40): the first are like sprouting seeds (48:29), like kernels that bear fruit (2:263), like growing trees (14:29); the second are like the deaf and

2. Qur. 28:86; 7:188; 3:138; 6:107; 41:5; 47:21; 72:21, 24.

3. Whence the legitimate inductions of the Wahhābīs in their reform of the *ṣalāt ᶜalā'l-Nabī*, and of the mystics, who expect saintliness alone to bring about a perfect accomplishment of the law announced by the prophets (*tafḍīl al-walī*).

4. *Qanādīlu ruhbān . . . fī manāzili'l-quffāl.*

5. *Passion*, Fr 3:187–88/Eng 3:175.

6. With Ibn ᶜAbbās, Qur. 13:28 is allegorized as follows: "Water is knowledge, and the streams are men's hearts" (*ᶜAwārif*, I, 61); cf. Ḥasan on sura 102, and a literalist like Ibn Ḥanbal on the anagogic sense of names such as *Kawthar, Ṭūbā, Kāfūr.*

7. See his role in Muḥāsibī (*Riᶜāya*, f. 4b).

8. Goldziher, *Vorlesungen*, Eng. trans., 18–19; and the whole verse Qur. 2:172.

dumb, like captives, like lost men groping to find their way by flashes of lightning (2:117–119) or following a mirage; like swimmers awash in a dark sea (24:39–40) or travelers bitten by an icy wind (3:113); their house is as fragile as a cobweb (29:40). At the last day, these souls, empty of good actions, will call after the first group in vain, like the mad virgins crying after the good virgins, "Wait for us, that we may borrow from your light!" (57:13).[9] Sura 36 mentions not only the sadness of the martyred apostle who thinks of the hardening of his executioners (verse 24) but also the painful censure God reserves for some (*yā ḥasratan,* 36:29; 3:150, 8:36; 19:40; 69:50; 39:57)[10] and the greeting[11] He addresses (*qawlan*) to others (36:58).

And the parables of the resurrection: God, who gives life to sterile earth with water (16:67; 41:39) and produces fire from green wood[12] (36:80), will be able to bring souls back to their bodies like tamed birds[13] (2:262). These parables, with guiding intentions independent from, but parallel to, those of certain psalms and verses of the gospel, are meant for everyone; for the most part, they are ascetic rather than mystical advice.

But there is more in the Qurʾān. There are mentions of clearly illuminative and even ecstatic phenomena: (a) God exposes Muḥammad's secret thoughts as He sounds the Prophet's heart.[14] (This examination of conscience is admittedly involuntary, but it is accompanied by an undeniable mental doubling, in which the spiritual personality of the subject admits that there is another, sovereign Presence [93:6–10; 33:37; 80:3].) (b) The hidden circumstances[15] and unknown supernatural significance of certain events are suddenly revealed to the soul.[16] (c) Mention is explicitly made of the inner miracles effected by the grace that comes to certain prophets: speech within (*iqrā*); *sharḥ al-ṣadr* or expansion of the chest; external prun-

9. Subject of one of the sermons of Manṣūr ibn ʿAmmār (d. 225; *Fihrist,* 184).

10. Question raised by Ṭabarsī, 122.

11. Question raised by Muḥāsibī (*Passion,* Fr 3:178/Eng 3:166; herein ch. 3, sec. I. B.).

12. Allusion to the Burning Bush.

13. Cf. Ḥallāj (*Ṭawāsīn,* p. 27).

14. Qur. 33:37 (cf. *Passion,* Fr 3:199 n 8/Eng 3:187 n 15).

15. Cf. the strange meditations of the first mystics on the "mortal trouble" of Mary before the birth of Jesus (Qur. 19:23): *"yā laytanī mittu qabla hadhā!"* [*Recueil,* p. 55] "O, would that I had died before that!": before they sinned by wrongfully suspecting me (Ibn ʿAṭā); before I had to think of someone (= my child) other than God (Kharrāz); before I had to ask for something (= dates), instead of remaining (as before) abandoned to God (Ibn Ṭāhir); before they worshipped my son, separate from God (Jurayrī; cf. Baqlī, II, 8; Sh. *Ṭab.,* I, 93). And Wāsiṭī's commentary on the barren date palm that gave Mary fresh dates (Qur. 19:25): he says it is an image of the pure conception of Jesus within her, a pure gift of God (*rizq*), not an advantage (that she was seeking, *ḥaraka*) or something acquired (*kasb,* with respect to which she would have been avaricious) (Baqlī, II, 8).

16. Description of Satan's fall; description of the rivalry of the Angels desiring to serve Mary in the Temple; words of the Annunciation; contestations of Abraham and Noah with God; discussion between Moses and his guide.

ing of the heart,[17] which is circumcised by faith. Finally, (d) there are cases of rapture, such as the central event in Muḥammad's vocation, the night journey (*isrā*) to Jerusalem, and to the *qāb qawsayn*.

I have shown elsewhere[18] how the greatest Muslim mystics concentrated their Qurʾānic meditation on these themes, as they tried to find in their own hearts the states of the soul that had been the favors of grace to some of the prophets.

Nothing more can be affirmed. The Qurʾān raises the question of purifying (*ikhlāṣ*) the profession of monotheistic faith, and that of habitually conforming to the will of God (*ṭumaʾnīna, riḍā*, state of grace); we can therefore say that the Qurʾān mentions certain mystical phenomena but does not explain their occurrence in history.[19] In particular it supplies no decisive documentary evidence on the evolution of Muḥammad's inner life (as proved by Hubert Grimme's failed attempt).[20] The secret of his soul, which was devoted to such an extraordinary destiny, has remained sealed to us.[21] Sura 53 contains no cries of mystical love, and we cannot easily adopt Ghazālī's hypothesis that Muḥammad was at first a "passionate lover of his God," wandering in solitude on Mt. Ḥirā and drunk with desire for union.[22] But we must not, like the many orientalists led astray by the *fuqahā's* partisan reasoning, deny the sincere and lasting vehemence of Muḥammad's devotion, indicated by his severe discipline and frequent supererogatory prayers after midnight (*tahajjud*). Like all true leaders, he was hard on himself, and sometimes even on his harem. Goldziher and Lammens have recently brought to light some traditional tales of the luxury of his "court," of his and his Companions' softness; the stories are picturesque, but they first appeared as highly suspect polemical arguments, used and probably invented by the shameful second-century A.H. school of *muḥaddithūn* most notably represented by Wāqidī (d. 207) and his "secretary" Ibn Saᶜd (d. 230). These men were exclusively occupied in seeking apostolic precedents for licentious sumptuousness, especially the silks, jewels, henna, antimony, and perfume of the profligate governors and vizirs on whose subventions the school survived.[23] Ḥātim al-Aṣamm gave an early warning about them to the *qāḍī* Ibn Muqātil of Rayy.[24] Muḥāsibī's vibrant

17. *Passion*, Fr 3:19–20/Eng 3:12–13; Ghazālī, *Munqidh*, 7; cf. Qur. 5:10–11.

18. *Passion*, Fr. 3:213 ff., 312/Eng 3:200 ff., 294–95.

19. *Passion*, Fr 3:39/Eng 3:31.

20. Goldziher (*Vorlesungen*, Eng. trans., 80–81) thinks his attempt might help to reconstitute the chronological order of the suras. — Only if we begin with the axiom that predestination and freedom are contradictory, against which all the religious experience of believers protests.

21. *Passion*, Fr 3:199 n 7, 315, 320/Eng 3:187 n 14, 297–98, 302–3.

22. Ghazālī, *Munqidh*, 33.

23. Wāqidī was a commensal of the Barmakids. See Goldziher's discussion of Ibn Saᶜd, in *Vorlesungen*, Eng. trans., 125–26 n 30.

24. Yāfiᶜī, *Nashr*.

pages stigmatize[25] the unspeakable motives in their hearts, which were devoted to the flesh. A profane desertion of all that is sacred lurked beneath their specious historical criticism of the supposed poverty of Islam's first champions. That poverty was real, in fact was inevitable[26] among fighters as hardened as them, condemned to forty years of ceaseless skirmishing and extended military expeditions.

The diversity alone of the Muslim mystics' reflections on Muḥammad's inner life shows how mysterious the problem has remained. What the Prophet's public life attests should be noted: proven will, self-control,[27] moderation and prudence, perspicacity and readiness to forgive, patience and forethoughtfulness, in short all the capacity to maneuver of a chief in war and a chief of state.[28] His abilities were disciplined by the deepest faith, but we must not claim without proof, like certain neo-Muslims of India, that his faith was combined with personal practice, on a heroic scale, of the Sermon on the Mount.[29] On the other hand, the Qurʾān mentions that ideal of saintly Christian mildness and does not find fault with it.

B. Is the Monastic Vocation to Be Rejected? The *Ḥadīth* of *Lā Rahbāniyya*

The Qurʾān, while condemning some erroneous Christian opinions, clearly states that among those monks "who are humble" (5:85) are to be found the Muslim believers' closest friends.[30] On the other hand, those monks "who consume another's goods, and those who hoard wealth" will be condemned to hell (9:34). It is not monasticism that is condemned *a priori* but only bad monks. Nothing in the Qurʾān limits the legality of the monastic life to Jews and Christians; certainly nothing allows bad Muslims to escape the damnation pronounced for thieves and misers. An opinion to this effect was declared in public by Abū Dharr, during ʿUthmān's caliphate,[31] and no matter how flagrant the doctrinal hypocrisy under certain Umayyads may have been, all ancient commentators on the Qurʾān adopted

25. Herein ch. 5, sec. 1.

26. Cf. the "luxury" of Napoleon's marshals on campaign.

27. Hypotheses of epilepsy, self-hypnosis, or a hyperexcited imagination have been worked out by sedentary psychiatrists who know nothing of life in desert camps and the positive ingenuity that must be marshaled in a band of bedouin, simply to remain its leader.

28. But it has been said gratuitously that he demonstrated the adroitness of a legislator in the "dosage" of his Qurʾānic prescriptions; the accusers miss the fundamental point that Muḥammad *did not make* the Qurʾān.

29. On this subject, for modern alterations to the school of Ameer Alī, who was too impressed by Protestant missionary attacks (Pfander), see the rough, but more honest, portrait of Muḥammad by Kamāl-al-Dīn (*Islamic Review* of Woking, 1917, p. 9–17).

30. Moreover, the opinion is common in pre-Islamic Arab literature.

31. Herein p. 109.

it. Muqātil (d. 150), giving rules for Qurʾānic exegisis, says that, "Every time you read the word *ruhbān* in the Qurʾān, you must understand it to mean *al-mujtahidīn fī dīnihim*, the believers who make an effort to practice their religion with zeal."[32] Many pious figures are called *rāhib* without any pejorative intent.[33]

Western orientalism also makes much of a *ḥadīth, "la rahbāniyyata fī'l-Islām"* ("No monasticism in Islam"), in order to prove that *rahbāniyya* was censured by the Qurʾān and forbidden by Muḥammad, and therefore that Sufism was a foreign import. I shall briefly examine the origin of this *ḥadīth*; no competent Islamologist has offered a strict defense of its authenticity, and it seems to have come into use later than the second century, since the Imānī attacks do not mention it.[34]

The statement, "No manasticism . . . ," to which Sprenger,[35] following Ḥarīrī,[36] has given so much notoriety, first appears in Ibn Saʿd's writings[37] about the ascetic ʿUthmān ibn Maẓʿūn Jumaḥī.[38] Abū Dāwūd (d. 275) changes it to "No celibacy . . ." (*"lā ṣarūra . . ."*)[39] in order to corroborate his posthumous attacks against Rabāḥ and Rābiʿa and his new exegesis of Qur. 57:27 (*"rahbāniyya,* which was not prescribed for them").

The attenuated variant of the *ḥadīth*, "Monastic life for my Community is holy war (*jihād*),"[40] seems to have appeared even later.[41] How, exactly, is *rahbāniyya* defined for writers of Arabic?[42] It is life in a hermitage (*ṣawmʿa*)[43] and a vow (*nadhr*) to abstain from sexual relations. It may include even "abstention from eating meat, and forty-day retreats,"[44] as well as wearing a hair shirt (*musūḥ*). Lexicographers hostile to asceticism define *rahbāniyya*[45]

32. Malaṭī, 122. In fact, *tarahhub* = *taʿabbud* in all dictionaries.

33. Abū Bakr Makhzūmī, *"rāhib Quraysh"* (d. 94; Goldziher); ʿAmmār ibn al-Rāhib (Ibn ʿArabī, *Muḥāḍarāt* [*Muḥaḍ.*], II, 62); Dārimī (d. 243), *"rāhib al-Kūfa"*; cf. Murdār, *"rāhib al-muʿtazila."* *Qiss*, on the other hand, was pejorative (see below, sec. 3. C, n 296 and related text).

34. Khūnsārī, *Rawḍāt*, II, 233.

35. *Mohammad*, I, 389.

36. *Maqām*, XLIII; Sacy, in a note, reproduces only the *ḥadīth* of ʿAkkāf Hilālī, where the word in question does not figure (ed. 1822, 497); cf. Ibn al-Athīr, *Usd*, IV, 3.

37. *Ṭabaqāt*, ms. Sprenger, f. 258 = vol. III, part 1, p. 287. The classical form is given by Zamakhsharī (*Fāʾiq*, Ḥaydarābād, 1324, I, 269) and Ibn al-Athīr (*Nihāya*, Cairo, 1311, II, 113).[— Snouck.]

38. Died in the year 2. The Prophet is supposed to have said it to him before the Hijra, in Abyssinia (*sic*! Muir, *Life*, 1858, II, 107 n).

39. *Sunan*, I, 173; II, 195. Cf. Goldziher, *M. St.*, II, 395; and *RHR*, XVIII, 180; XXXVII, 314 ff.

40. Tholuck, *Ssuf.*, 46.

41. Wensinck sees fit to bring to my attention three parallel *ḥadīth*, in Muslim (ch. *imāra*, no. 122), Tirmidhī (ch. *faḍāʾil al-jihād*, no. 17), and Dārimī (ch. *jihād*, no. 6), which conclude with a condemnation of the believer who abstains from going to war and makes a voluntary retreat (*iʿtizāl*). This word seems to me to refer to the political abstentionists of the years 657–61, not to ascetics.

42. See also Ibn Sabʿīn's work cited by Maqqārī (*Anal.*, I, 594).

43. Zamakhsharī.

44. Baqlī.

45. Fīrūzābādhī, *Qāmūs*; cf. *Lisān al-ʿArab*.

as "making oneself a eunuch (*ikhtiṣā*)"[46] and "voluntarily binding oneself with chains (*iᶜtināq bi'l-salāsil*)."[47] In reality, the Arab monastic life is based on vows of chastity[48] and seclusion: it is the eremetic life. Islam is so little opposed to it that a temporary vow of chastity[49] is imposed on pilgrims during their stay on sacred ground in Mecca.[50] All the orthodox schools of jurisprudence allow the *iᶜtikāf*, "pious retreat." Their manuals treat the aforementioned types of vow under the heading *nudhūr* ("vows"). The word *rahbāniyya* was at first sufficiently free of suspicion to have been used as the name of one of the three styles of Qurʾānic chant (*alḥān al-qirāʾa*): *ghinā, ḥidā, rahbāniyya*.[51]

The decisive reason for the word's acceptance was that it figures, with all its letters, in a celebrated Qurʾānic verse (57:27), unanimously interpreted by the exegetes of the first three centuries A.H. as giving permission and praise. A tendentious interpretation, too easily accepted by contemporary orientalists, made the verse into a confirmation of the pejorative, restrictive *ḥadīth* quoted above. The verse must be examined closely. Here is a literal translation of it:

Then . . . Jesus, son of Mary; and We gave him the gospel, and in the hearts of

46. Cf. two Christian heretics of the East: Sabas the Massalian and the Arab Valesius. I think in this case there was not mutilation but only perforation: the *tathqīb al-iḥlīl* of the Qalandariyya, with infibulation by a chain (*silsila*). The name of this latter group, "calendars," appears in ᶜAṭṭār, Suhrawardī Baghdādī (*ᶜAwārif*), and Najm ibn Isrāʾīl ("*mulḥaqīn*"). The order was founded by Jamāl Muḥammad ibn Yūnus Sāwijī (of Sāva) at Damascus (Qanawāt) in 616 A.H. After Sāwijī's death at Damietta (630), Jamāl Derguzīnī succeeded him, then Muḥammad Balkhī. They were persecuted (cf. Sauvaire, *JAP*, 1895, I, 378, 409). Ibn Khaldūn cites the prophecies of one of them, Bājirqī. Another Qalandar, Bahā Zak. Multānī, had disciples including the poet Fakhr ᶜIrāqī (who went to India, d. Damascus 699 A.H.) and Fakhr al-Saᶜādāt Ḥusayn Ghawrī, author of the *Qalandarnāma*, and Ḥasan Jawāliqī, founder of the *Khānqāh Siriyāqūs* (NE of Cairo) c. 722 A.H. (a line of *shaykh al-shuyūkh*). Other *khānqāhs*, called *Qalandarkhānas* were founded in Istanbul, in Baghdād (in 762 A.H. according to ᶜAzzāwī; this one became a *tekke* of the Mevlevis in 1017 A.H.), and in Jerusalem (at Birkat Mamilla in 793 A.H.; cf. *Revue des Etudes Islamiques*, 1952, 89). The *salsabīl* of Sanūsī contains the *dhikr* of the Qalandariyya of today (which is a sort of "sign of the cross" evoking the "Five of the Mantle"). They are Mukhammisa, extremist Nuṣayrī Shiites, who took refuge in northeast Baluchistan near the Khyber Pass (according to Ghalib Amīn Ṭawil of Latakia, and confirmed by Ansari at Agra, June 1945; also Abdulbaki, *Qaygusuz*, 163–65).

47. One of the oldest features of Arab asceticism: Goldziher, M. St., II, 395; Ibn Wāsiᶜ and ᶜUtba; Ḥallāj (*Passion*, Fr 1:524/Eng 1:477).

48. I have studied the problem of the vow of chastity in Islam in *Etudes carmélitaines* ("Mystique et continence"), Paris, 1952. The only Muslim order to make a permanent public vow of chastity was the Qalandariyya, who are very late (our thirteenth century); the master infibulated the novice with a small iron chain (*ṭawq*) as the *qufl* of his chastity. On the ideal of virginity, cf. Ḥallāj (*asrārunā Bikrun*: Stf 159, 191).

49. Cf. the *ᶜuzzāb* of the first century; and among the Ibāḍites.

50. Considering the antiquity of the *ḥajj* as a mystical symbol, I am willing to see in the Muslim vow of chastity an extension of the pilgrims' temporary vow, and in the special costume an extension of the *iḥrām*, which implies chastity.

51. Ibn Qutayba, *Maᶜārif*, 265.

> those who followed him We placed (*jaᶜalnā*) (the seeds of) readiness to forgive (*raʾfa*), compassion (*raḥma*), and the monastic life (*rahbāniyya*). It was they who instituted it (*ibtadaᶜūhā*); We only prescribed (*katabnā*) it for them in order to make them desire[52] to conform to what pleases God, but they have not followed the obligatory method of this rule for living (*riᶜāya*); to those among them who have remained faithful We have given their recompense, but many among them have been sinners.

The phrase is long, full of nuance, and grammatically impeccable. Its meaning explicitly confirms the Qurʾān's double judgment of monks. Here is a remarkable text, placed by Muḥāsibī at the beginning of his *Riᶜāya,* a book intended precisely to rediscover for believers the "method" (*riᶜāya*) that God had willed and the monks had lost:

> And each duty God demands of his servants, and each order given especially to some of them — God commands that these be preserved and put into effect. This is the "method that is God's due," which is, intrinsically as in practice, a canonical obligation for us. God finds fault with those among the Israelites[53] who instituted a monastic life that He had not made obligatory for them, and then did not observe it exactly; and He said, "We did not prescribe the monastic life that they have instituted."
>
> There is disagreement about this verse. Mujāhid interprets it to mean, "We had only prescribed it for them in order to make them desire to conform to what pleases God, and it was they who (then) instituted it. God placed in them, *for their own good,* (the seeds of) the monastic life, and He reprimanded them later for having abandoned it." But Abū Imāma (Bāhilī) and others make this commentary: "We did not prescribe it for them, i.e., *it is not We* who prescribed it; they have instituted it only in order to please God, and *nevertheless,* God has reprimanded them for abandoning it." And this second opinion is the more likely; it is the one upon which the majority of the Community's doctors agree.
>
> Therefore God said, "They have not followed the method required for this rule of life." If God reprimanded them because they did not follow a rule that He had not even made an obligation or a part of the sacred law, what then will He do to those who abandon obligatory duties, which, if neglected, bring His wrath and the punishment of separation from Him? And he has made piety (*taqwā*) the key both to the performance of these duties and to all felicity, in this world and the next . . .[54]

52. Insofar as they should desire it; in case they should desire it; this is not a commandment or precept but a piece of advice. *Ibtighāʾa* is a semantic correlative of *ibtadaᶜūhā.*

53. Disciples of Jesus.

54. *Riᶜāya,* f. 3b.

The text is fundamental. It provides the two early opinions of Mujāhid and Abū Imāma, and it shows that in both cases the Qur'ān praises the *rahbāniyya* of the Israelites as a pious work, canonical in the first case, supererogatory (*taṭawwu*ᶜ) in the second.

Muḥāsibī gives precedence to Abū Imāma's exegesis of *ibtdaᶜūhā*, but Abū Isḥāq Zajjāj (d. 310)[55] puts it in a secondary position:[56] "The standard commentary[57] on this subject says that certain believers who could not bear the (impious) conduct of their rulers took refuge in hidden dens or cells and instituted this kind of life. Then, since they had promised themselves to a supererogatory work (*taṭawwu*ᶜ) and had undertaken it, they were obliged to accomplish it (as in the case of the vow of an extra fast, which must be kept)." But Zajjāj, on his own initiative, suggests another interpretation as the primary one:

> *Rahbāniyyatan ibtadaᶜūhā* is an ellipsis for "they instituted the monastic life, it is they who instituted it," as one says, "I saw Zayd; and ᶜAmr, I greeted him"; *mā katabnāha ᶜalayhim* means, "*We* absolutely did not prescribe it for them," and *hā*[58] stands for *illā ibtighā'a riḍwān Allāh*, giving the sense, "We had prescribed for them only that they should desire to conform to what is pleasing to God." *Ibtighā'a riḍwān Allāh* here means, "God's Commandment (in His revealed law)."

Zajjāj's second interpretation, which tends to place the monastic life outside of divine providence and strip it of all praise,[59] would triumph over the others with assistance from the polemic among theologians about *jaᶜalnā* and *katabnā*. Muqātil had defined the verbs as synonyms,[60] and most Murji'ites, like him, taught that both words communicated God's physical premovement of all acts of the heart and body. The Muᶜtazilites also took them as synonyms, but, unlike the Murji'ites, they weakened their meaning. Jubba'ī adopted Mujāhid's thesis and had no objection to admitting that *ra'fa*, *raḥma*, and *rahbāniyya* were all governed by *jaᶜalnā*; according to this school, *jaᶜalnā* = "We have given man the power to create (on his own . . .)";[61] the verb governs the first two objects slightly differently from the third (*rahbāniyya*). The great grammarian Abū ᶜAlī Fasawī (d. 377), be-

55. Zajjāj, of dubious finances (*Talbīs*, 135).

56. *Lisān*, I, 421–22.

57. I have translated *tafsīr* as "standard commentary."

58. From *katabnāhā*.

59. Cf. an antimonastic pronouncement attributed to Ibn al-Ḥanafiyya, though he was the head of the Murji'ites (Ibn Saᶜd, *Ṭabaqāt*, V, 70).

60. On Qur. 58:22 (in Ibn al-Farrā, *Muᶜtamad*). *Katab* = *taᶜabbad* according to Tustarī (152; to constitute as a ritual) = *faraḍ* according to Muḥāsibī and Zamakhsharī, *Fā'iq* (cf. above, n 37).

61. In Zamakhsharī, loc. cit.

cause of his prejudice against mysticism, preferred to rally to Zajjāj; "*Rahbāniyyatan,*" he says, "is the object of an understood verb. It is an ellipsis for '*they instituted* the monastic life: it is they who instituted it.' *Rahbāniyyatan* cannot be in apposition to the preceding objects because 'what God has placed in the heart could never be instituted [= introduced, modified] by man.'"[62]

Finally, Zamakhsharī,[63] developing Fasawī's premises by renouncing the postulates of Muᶜtazilism,[64] proposes that *jaᶜalnā* = *waffaqnā* and separates *rahbāniyyatan* from the group of direct objects.[65] He cuts the passage in two and changes the second half, making four fragments arranged in the order 1, 2, 4, 3: "*rahbāniyyatan–ibtadaᶜūhā–illā ibtighāʾa riḍwān Allāh–mā katabnāhā ᶜalayhim.*" By the syntactical figure he calls *istithnā munqaṭiᶜ*[66] (an "exception"* severed by an interjection), he obtains the following sense: "As for the monastic life, it is they who instituted it out of desire to please God; We did not make it a canonical duty for them." The monastic life is then a reprehensible innovation that Muslims must prevent themselves from imitating.

Most modern *tafsīr,* even mystical *tafsīr,* follow Zamakhsharī; in order to separate *rahbāniyyatan* from *jaᶜalnā,* Ṣāwī[67] declares, "Mildness and compassion, unlike the monastic life, are not gains that man can acquire (and augment; they are divine attributes)." But the Indian Muhāʾimī (d. 710/1310) was still maintaining the old tradition when he gave the reading, "As for *rahbāniyyatan,* it is We who placed it in their hearts, but they instituted it (too early). *Ibtadaᶜūhā,* before it was ordered by a clear revealed text; 'We had prescribed it for them only because it contains within itself the desire to please God,' for it reinforces the practice of canonical duty."[68]

Our lengthy inquiry can be closed by some indirect proofs: in the Qurʾān, the expression *ibitghāʾa riḍwān Allāh,* "from desire to please God," is used constantly as praise,[69] and the mystics before the fourth century A.H. understood it in that sense. Bishr Ḥāfī (d. 227) used to say, "Do you plan to do this from desire to please God, or for your personal satisfaction?"[70] When Ibn abī'l-Dunyā (d. 281) was speaking of the indirect apos-

* As in Wright's grammar, index, under "exceptive sentences."

62. In Ibn Sīda, *Mukhaṣṣaṣ,* XIII, 100; *Lisān,* I, 421. This goes directly against the grain of ᶜAllāf's Muᶜtazilism (*Passion,* Fr 3:121/Eng 3:109).

63. *Tafsīr,* III, 165.

64. Though he himself was a semi-Muᶜtazilite.

65. Goldziher finds the pejorative *bidᶜa* (already) in *ibtadaᶜūhā* of this verse (*M. St.,* II, 23 n 6).

66. *Passion,* Fr 3:99/Eng 3:88.

67. IV, 138; cf. Baqlī, II, 311.

68. *Tafsīr raḥmānī,* II, 324.

69. Qur. 3:156, 168; 5:2, 18; 48:29.

70. Makkī, *Qūt,* I, 92.

tolate the saints had undertaken among other Muslims, he described inner virtues they exercised *"ibtighāʾa marḍāt Allāh."*[71]

Finally, there is the use of *rahbāniyya*, always as a word of praise, among the mystics of the third century A.H. Burjulānī wrote a *Kitāb al-ruhbān*, and the cautious Junayd could still say, at the end of his *Dawā*, "The friends of God ... have their eyes perpetually fixed on their prescribed duty as servants, in the monastic life (*rahbāniyya*). God blamed those who had embraced that life and failed to execute its obligations, thereby neglecting the prescribed method." Anṭākī, in the first chapter of his *Dawā*, had said even more energetically, "That is the true *rahbāniyya*, which is not speech but silent action."[72]

C. Some *Termini a quo*: *Ṣūf, Ṣūfī, Ṣūfiyya*

1) THE WEARING OF THE *Ṣūf* AS A SIGN OF PENITENCE

Until the third century A.H., the *ṣūf*, an undyed rough wool garment, was not so much a regular monastic uniform as the mark of a personal vow of penitence. Muḥāsibī still maintained that singling oneself out in such a manner might conceal pride.[73] It seems that pilgrims to Mecca wore the garment.[74] Ibn Sīrīn (d. 110) is supposed to have criticized some contemporary ascetics who wore it "in order to imitate Jesus": "I prefer to follow the example of the Prophet, who wore cotton (*quṭn*)."[75] He was speaking of ᶜUtba[76] and Farqad Sinjī (d. 131), Ḥasan Baṣrī's intimate disciple, to whom Ḥammād ibn Salama (d. 165) said, "Then rid yourself of that christianism!"[77] Ibn Dīnār on the other hand did not consider himself pure enough[78] to wear the *ṣūf*.[79] Thawrī wore it, but Shiite tradition (in a saying attributed to Jaᶜfar) reproaches him for putting it deceitfully over a garment of silk.[80]

Beginning in the third century A.H. the *ṣūf* of white wool became a known and respected piece of religious clothing, said to have been worn

71. Herein, ch. 3, n 122. Cf. *ibtighāʾa wajh Allāh* of Ḥudhayfa (Ḥanbal, V, 391).

72. And when Ibn Qutayba speaks of a false *rahbāniyya*, *"al-rahbāniyya al-mubtadaᶜa,"* it probably means that he envisages a different, true one.

73. *Masāʾil*, f. 237–44.

74. *Aghānī*, 1st ed., XI, 61 (cited by Nöldeke, *ZDMG*, XLVIII, 46).

75. *Ḥilya*: extract ap. *Manār*, XII, 747.

76. Sh. *Ṭab.*, I, 46.

77. Ibn ᶜAbdrabbihi, *ᶜIqd*, I, 177; III, 247.

78. Pun (*ṣāfā*).

79. Sh. *Ṭab.*, I, 36.

80. Khūnsārī, I, 233, 316.

by Moses, they by Muḥammad. Mystics avid for penitence preferred the *muraqqaᶜa*, a motley assortment of rags stitched together.[81]

II) THE PERSONAL TITLE *al-Ṣūfī* IN THE FIRST THREE CENTURIES

Abū Hāshim ᶜUthmān ibn Sharīk Kūfī Ṣūfī, d. at Ramla c. 160/776 (Jāmī, 35).
Jābir ibn Ḥayyān Kūfī Ṣ. and his disciple Saʾiḥ ᶜAlawī Ṣ.,[82] alchemists (*Fihrist*, 354, 359).
Ibrāhīm ibn Bashshār Khurāsānī Ṣ., disciple of Ibn Adham (Ibn ᶜArabī, *Muḥāḍ.*, II, 346).
Abū Jaᶜfar Qāṣṣ Ṣ., disciple of ᶜAbd al-Ṣamad Raqqāshī (Jāḥiẓ, *Bayān*, I, 168).
ᶜIsä ibn Haytham Ṣ., Muᶜtazilite (Murtaḍä, *Munya*, 45).
Abū Ḥamza M ibn Ibrahīm Ṣ., disciple of Muḥāsibī, d. 269 (Tagrib, II, 47).
Abū ᶜAA Aḥmad ᶜAbd al-Jabbār Ṣ. (al-Kabīr), student of Muḥāsibī and Ibn Maᶜīn, teacher of Dāwūd; died at the age of 100 in Baghdād in 306 (Samᶜānī, 357a).
Abū'l-Ḥasan Aḥmad ibn Hurmuz Ṣ. (al-Ṣaghīr), d. Baghdād 303 (id.).
Muḥammad ibn Hārūn Ṣ., teacher of the Shiite Sinānī, who trained Ibn Bābūya (*ᶜIlal*).
Abū ᶜAA Shīᶜī Ṣ., the Qarmathian Dāᶜī in Ifriqiya, d. 297.

III) THE COLLECTIVE NAME *Ṣūfiyya* BEFORE THE FOURTH CENTURY

Muḥāsibī (d. 243) cites two of the Kūfan Ṣūfiyya, Ibn Qinṭāsh and ᶜAbdak, in order to criticize the excessive severity of their doctrine of the *makāsib*.[83] Jāḥiẓ (d. 255) gives a list of noteworthy ascetics (*nussāk, zuhhād*), then a seperate list[84] of "Ṣūfiyya": Kilāb, Kulayb, Hāshim Awqāṣ, Abū Hāshim Kūfī, and Ṣāliḥ ibn ᶜAbd al-Jalīl. At first, therefore, the collective name designated a certain group among the ascetics of Kūfa. A century later it meant the organized body of mystics in Baghdād (Junayd, Makkī, and Ibn ᶜAṭā were part of it; Kharrāz, Tustarī, and Ruwaym claimed not to be).[85] In the fourth century, the word spread over all of ᶜIrāq.[86]

IV) ETYMOLOGY

Each of these terms, *ṣūf, al-Ṣūfī, Ṣūfiyya*, seems to have evolved indepen-

81. *Passion*, Fr 1:143–44/Eng 1:103.
82. See *Fihrist*, 143, on his other disciple Muḥammad ibn Yaḥyä Munajjim of Sāmarrā, editor of his *Kitāb al-raḥma*.
83. *Makāsib*.
84. *Bayān*, I, 94.
85. Jāmī, s.n.
86. Kharkūshī, *Tahdhīb*, f. 12b.

dent of the others until the fourth century. For the word *al-Ṣūfi* alone, there is perhaps more than one etymology. Used as the name of a pure ascetic like Abū Hāshim, it is no doubt derived from the "wool" of his cloak. As the name of a chemist like Ibn Ḥayyān, it suggests the "purification" (*ṣāfä, ṣūfiyya*) of red sulphur. These two etymologies were linked quite early if it is indeed true that Ibn Dīnār had already made the pun on "Sufism" and "purity" that would be employed by Tustarī[87] and Sarrāj,[88] and then in the famous *qaṣīda* on mysticism of the Karrāmī poet Abū'l-Fatḥ Bustī.[89] Other, less defensible,[90] etymological sources have been suggested: *ṣaff awwal*, the first row before God; *ahl al-ṣuffa*, the "people of the bench" in the mosque in Medina: Banū Ṣūfa, a bedouin tribe; the Greek word *σοφος* (*sophos* — Merx); *ṣūfa* and *ṣūfān*, employees of the church. ᶜAbd al-Qāhir Baghdādī in the eleventh century[91] was able to collect a thousand different definitions of the word "Sufism"; Nicholson, in the twentieth, seventy-eight.[92] These curiosities of literature and dogma are irrelevant to the semantic history of the vocable.

V) THE FIRST TRACES OF COLLECTIVE ORGANIZATION[93]

mawāᶜiẓ, moral sermons: Ḥasan Baṣrī and Bilāl Sakūnī.

ḥalqa, a room for pious meetings: Jaᶜfar b. Ḥasan Baṣrī.[94] The first *ḥalqa* for the *samāᶜ* (spiritual concert) was established in Baghdād by Abū ᶜAlī Tanūkhī, a friend of Sarī (d. 253).[95]

majlis al-dhikr, hermitage for brief retreats: Ḥasan;[96] ᶜIsä ibn Zādhān at Ubulla, c. 120.[97]

ṣāwāmiᶜ, conical cells (syn. *kūkh* and *duwayrāt*), imitated from the Melkites.[98] In about 150, ᶜAbd al-Wāḥid ibn Zayd's disciples made the first cluster of these, in a *ribāṭ*, a monastery with defensive walls, at ᶜAbbādān (an Arabo-Persian word meaning "the pious men"). The monastery

87. Ap. Yāfiᶜī, *Nashr*, II, 341.
88. Bustānī, *Dāʾira*, s.v.
89. Bīrūnī, *Āthār*, s.v.
90. Kalābādhī, *Taᶜarruf*, ms. Paris Supp. pers., f. 65a–69b.
91. Subkī, III, 239.
92. *JRAS*, 1906, 303–48.
93. The first form of Muslim asceticism was militant; generally, the mystics sequestered themselves only after participating in holy war on the frontier. They took to hermitages that were fortified because near dangerous borders. From Ibn Adham to Shaqīq to Ḥallāj, mystics were militants.
94. Jāḥiẓ, *Bayān*, I, 195.
95. Tagrib, II, 25.
96. *Qūt*, I, 149.
97. Ibn ᶜArabī, *Muḥāḍ.*, II, 59.
98. Qallāl, in Jāḥiẓ, *Ḥayawān*, IV, 146.

quickly became famous: Ḥafṣ ibn Ghiyāth (d. 194) mentions it;[99] prayers performed there (*al-ṣalāt bi ʿAbbādān*) were especially valued;[100] Wakīʿ (d. 197) went there to make a retreat of forty nights;[101] Sahl Tustarī made a visit.[102] It seems to have been destroyed by the Zinj (260 A.H.).[103]

maṭāmir, silos, caves (syn. *shikāft* in Persian), imitated from the Nestorians.[104] Kalābādhī speaks of the Shikāftiyya ascetics of Khurāsān.[105]

khānqāh, monastery: at Ramla in Palestine about 140: Abū Hāshim, who had come from Kūfa; then perhaps Abū ʿAbbād, the teacher of Ibn Adham, and Abū Jaʿfar Qaṣṣāb.[106] In Jerusalem, Ibn Karrām built a monastery about 230.

minbar (*kursī*): the first chair of Sufi doctrine in the mosques; Yaḥyā Rāzī in Cairo (d. 258), and Abū Ḥamza in Baghdād (d. 269).[107]

2. General Picture of Islamic Asceticism in the First Two Centuries

A. Among the Ṣaḥāba: Abū Dharr, Ḥudhayfa, ʿImrān Khuzāʿī

We must first dismiss the stories, invented after their time, about the as-

99. Dhahabī, *Iʿtidāl*, s.n. "Jaʿfar ibn Muḥammad."
100. *Qūt*, II, 121.
101. ʿAbbās Dūrī, *taʾrīkh*, ap. Shiblī, *Ākām*, 150.
102. *Tafsīr*, 26.
103. It is amazing indeed that the collective name *ṣūfiyya* should first appear in Alexandria in 199 A.H. (Kindi, 162, 440; Mez, 269) to designate puritans in revolt. Around ʿAbbādān the word designated the *muṭawwiʿa*, "civic volunteers" from Baṣra, who formed groups in the shadow of the hermits' prayers. Not until a century later was there an attack, by the famous Ibn Waḥshiyya (pseudonym of the extremist Shiite Ibn al-Zayyāt) in his *Filāḥa Nabṭiyya* (ms. P., 2803, 22b–23b), against the "Ṣūfiyya" for their proud, false, and parasitic laziness (Nöldeke sees a bookish borrowing from a Greek text of Eunapios against Christian monks). The hermitage of ʿAbbādān (now an oil refinery) was named after a man called ʿAbbād. The greatest masters went there on retreat: Muqātil ibn Sulaymān (d. 158: *Tārīkh Balkh*, ms. P. afp. 115, 52a), Ḥammād ibn Salama (d. 167: *Iʿtidāl*, I, 278), Bishr Ḥāfī (Ghazālī, *Kīmyā*, trans. Ritter, 171). Ibn al-Mubārak imitated it at Marv (Naw Ribāṭ: cf. Samʿ). ʿAbbādān was the model imitated by Abū Hāshim ʿUthmān ibn Sharīk Kūfī at Ramla in Syria (one of the sites suggested for the Qurʾānic "Rabwa" of Jesus) c. 150 A.H. Ramla (destroyed c. 560 A.H.) was the center for ascetics in Syria (*ahl al-shām*) and was visited by Sarī Saqaṭī, Ibn Khafīf (when Rūdhbārī lived there), and Ibn al-Jallā; Wajīhī heard Ibn Fātik there. After Ramla, the Karrāmiyya founded *ribāṭs* at Jerusalem, in Khurāsān, and at Dīnawar. Then the Kāzarūniyya constructed their great network of pious hostels. In ʿAbbādān, the recitation of the *tasbīḥ* entailed repeating not the "*subḥān Allah*" but the "*ḥasbī Allah*" (counting with pebbles and dates), which made Naẓẓām indignant (Ibn al-Jawzī, *Ḥumaqā*, 106). Sahl Tustarī justified this *dhikr* as *tawakkul* (Qur. 9:129; 39:38), declaring that it was the *taqallub* of the Seven Sleepers (Qush. 90). According to Muqaddasī, the earth at ʿAbbādān was composed of silt from Jerusalem. Ḥammād ibn Salama, nephew of Ḥamīd Ṭawīl, was considered one of the *abdāl*; via Thābit (of Ṣuhayb) he taught the *ziyāda* (of Paradise) and the vision of God (*shābb amrad*) (*Iʿtidāl*, s.v.).
104. Qallāl, loc. cit. (above, n 98).
105. *Taʿarruf*, loc. cit. (above, n 90).
106. Blochet, *Esotérisme*, 245.
107. *Qūt*, I, 166; Tagrib., II, 25.

ceticism of Bilāl, Abū Hurayra, and the first four caliphs; but some clear cases can still be observed among the Ṣaḥāba.[108] For example, Abū'l-Dardā ᶜUwaymir ibn Zayd recommended *tafakkur* (meditation) and preferred piety (*taqwā*) to forty years of ritual observance (*ᶜibāda*). He said, "What clearly shows that God despises the world is that only in the world do we offend him, and without renouncing the world we obtain nothing from Him."[109] Someone consulted his wife, Umm al-Dardā, saying, "There is an incurable pain in my heart, hardness of heart; and hope is too far away"; she replied, "Go among the tombs to see the dead."[110]

Abū Dharr Jundub Ghifārī is an even more marked case, celebrated by Saᶜīd ibn Musayyab[111] and Thawrī. "It is through asceticism that God makes wisdom and goodness enter men's hearts," he said. "Three men are beloved of God: he who returns secretly to give alms to a beggar he has first refused, when the beggar had asked in the name of God alone, not in the name of some kinship; he who prays after a long night march; he who perseveres in combat until he is victorious. God hates three men: a lascivious old man, an insolent poor man, an iniquitous rich man."[112] Abū Dharr claimed to have learned five[113] precepts from the Prophet: "Pity the poor, spend time with them, think of the lesser men before the greater, tell the truth, say the *ḥawqala*."[114] He condoned and practiced the fast, to prevent hardening of the heart; he recommended the *iᶜtikāf* (spiritual retreat in a mosque). Muḥammad is supposed to have said to him, "If they knew what I know, they would laugh little and weep much, they would not commit foolish acts in bed with women, and they would keep to the company of God"; at which Abū Dharr concluded, "By God! I would like to be a pruned tree!" But the Prophet criticized him for his desire for celibacy:

— "A recompense is reserved for you, for living with your wife."
— "How could I expect a recompense for my sinful desires?"

108. Cf. Bukhārī, IV, 76 (*riqāq*). Ibn Masᶜūd left sayings with mystical tendencies, such as his *qirāʾa* of Qur. 24:35; there are quotations in Muḥāsibī (*Riᶜāya*, f. 13a), Makkī (*Qūt*, I, 148: on allegorical meaning): cf. Ibn al-Jawzī, *Quṣṣāṣ*.

109. Sh. *Ṭab.*, I, 23 (the saying would be taken up by Anṭākī); Jāḥiẓ, *Bayān*, I, 145 (taken up in the *risāla* attributed to Ḥasan).

110. Jāḥiẓ, *Bayān*, III, 81 (it becomes a *ḥadīth*, according to Muḥammad ibn Yūnus Kadīmī, ap. Dhahabī, *Iᶜtidāl*, s.n.; Ḥarīrī, *Maq.*, XI). Umm al-Dardā Juhayma bint Ḥayy Awṣābiya, d. c. 80 (Dhahabī, *Ḥuffāẓ*).

111. *Qūt*, I, 255. The statement *"taqarrab shibran ... dhirāᶜan ..."* is attributed to Ibn Musayyab by Muḥāsibī (*Riᶜāya*, f. 12a); Ibn Ḥanbal (V, 153) gives it as one of Abū Dharr's.

112. Ḥanbal, V, 153.

113. Seven, in Ibn Saᶜd's account (quoted in Goldziher, *Vorlesungen*, Eng. trans., 41).

114. Ḥanbal, V, 170; cf. V, 145. He even gives a *ḥadīth qudsī*: "O my servants, you are all sinners — ask forgiveness of me; you have gone astray — ask me the way. You can do nothing, and everything is in my power!" (V, 154).

— "If God wills, he will give you a good and beautiful child, a recompense of which you would in no way be the cause."[115]

From his asceticism, Abū Dharr drew the logical conclusions concerning society. Against the profane hypocrisy of the politicians in the entourage of Muᶜāwiya, who was then *walī* of Damascus, he boldly affirmed that the Qurʾānic threats (9:34) against theft and avarice concerned not only evil, rich infidels, but also rich Muslims who live wickedly.[116] For his criticisms and his claim that ᶜAlī's right to the caliphate gave him precedence over everyone else, Abū Dharr was exiled from Damascus, where he had lived since 13/634.

The younger Ḥudhayfa ibn Ḥusayl al-Yamān (d. 36/657) is a highly balanced and defined model of the Muslim mystic.[117] There would be later developments of his theses on science ("the science that we practice"),[118] on the intermittency of faith (which must be revived by daily *istighfār*),[119] and on the different sorts of hearts subjected to temptation (*fitan*):[120] "the uncovered heart (of the *muʾmin*, 'believer'), which remains pure like a flame; the uncircumcised heart (of the impious *kāfir*), caught in its sheath; the warped heart (of the *munāfiq*, the 'hypocrite'); and the smooth heart[121] (of the *fāsiq*, the 'occasional sinner')."[122] In politics, Ḥudhayfa rectified Abū Dharr's opinion: he forbade calls to revolt against unjust leaders, but, anticipating Ḥasan, he also recommended expressing disagreement with their injustices and disapproval of their lies.[123] He put his principle into practice in the case of ᶜUthmān, whose stewardship he criticized, saying, "He acted against the advice of the Companions, governed badly without consulting them, rewarded those with no right to reward." When ᶜUthmān became irritated and summoned him to appear, Ḥudhayfa recanted and appeased him. His excuse for retreating was that he wanted to preserve the peace and unity of the Community. He said, "I buy my religious virtue (*ishtarī dīnī*) piece by piece, for fear of losing it all." This crafty bedouin ruse made

115. Ḥanbal, V, 154, 172, 173, 169. Ibn Ḥāyiṭ declared it *"azhad min al-Nabī"* (Ḥazm, IV, 197).

116. Ibn Saᶜd, IV, 166; Ḥalābī, *Sīra*, I, 306.

117. On Ḥudhayfa, cf. my *Salmān Pāk*, Paris, 1933, 24 n 2, where I suppose that Ḥudhayfa was a Shiite. One might ask whether there was not a rift between Salmān and Ḥudhayfa at Madāʾin (where they are now buried in the same tomb); a rift analogous to the one between Kaysāniyya and Sabaᶜiyya, in the circles of initiate-artisans; cf. on this my "Futuwwa," in *La Nouvelle Clio*, Brussels, 1952, 182–83.

118. Ḥanbal, V, 406.

119. Following the Prophet's example (ibid. V, 393, 394). Cf. Bukhārī, IV, 80 (*riqāq*).

120. Muttaqī, *Kanz*, I, 120.

121. *Muṣfaḥ*, which is flat, on which everything slips, and where "faith grows like a purpura in clear water, and hypocrisy like an ulcer in pus and blood."

122. The first statement of the legal problem of the *fāsiq* (cf. *Passion*, Fr 3:188/Eng 3:176).

123. Ḥanbal, V, 384.

Naẓẓām indignant,[124] but it is easily excused. Ḥudhayfa meant, "I abandon one piece of my virtue in order to keep another, which I consider more important," i.e., "I cease to maintain my criticisms, although they are well founded, in order not to threaten the union of our community."[125]

He was obviously a partisan of concessions[126] and an opportunist, permitting the pursuit of well-being simultaneously in this world and the next; Ḥudhayfa was nevertheless the true forerunner of Ḥasan Baṣrī. He stigmatized twelve hypocrites from among the Ṣaḥāba, as well as the unjust emirs.[127] Claiming to quote Muḥammad, he repeated a bitter prediction of the imminent end of time.[128] He was the first to write down the *ḥadīth al-ibtilā*: "When God loves one of his servants, he tests him with suffering . . ."[129]

ᶜImrān ibn Ḥaṣīn Khuzāᶜī (d. 52/672)[130] is a model of the man who gives his life entirely to God. Sent to Baṣra under ᶜUmar as part of the judiciary, then name *qāḍī* by Ibn ᶜĀmir, he soon resigned after involuntarily committing an injustice. (He also paid an indemnity to the victim.) ᶜImrān was ill and bed-ridden for the last thirty years of his life, and admirers of his growing resignation would visit him. One of them, Muṭarrif, naively expressed his disgust at the sight of ᶜImrān: "Nothing prevents me from visiting you (frequently) but the sight of your illness." ᶜImrān responded, "Because God makes me find the illness good (*aḥabba dhālika ilayya*), I find it good (lit., 'I love it'), coming from Him." Ḥasan Baṣrī was his disciple; Ibn Sīrīn considered him the most virtuous Ṣaḥābi living in Baṣra and called him *mujāb al-daᶜwa* ("he whose prayers are answered"). For a long time, ᶜImrān refused to have his pain relieved by *kayy*, cauterizations (perhaps he had abscesses), because the Prophet was hostile to them. In the year 50, as a white-haired old man, he yielded to his friends' insistence and allowed himself to be cauterized; not only was his pain not relieved, he told Muṭarrif, but also he was deprived of a spiritual consolation that had sustained him, the *taslīm* of the angels appearing around his head to greet him at the end of every prayer. Then God pardoned him, and he was given the *taslīm* again shortly before his death. This description of his simple, exquisite life is taken from Ibn Saᶜd, an author generally hostile to

124. Ibn Qutayba, *Taʾwīl*, 25, 47.

125. He is the first to celebrate the *Umma* (Ḥanbal, V, 383).

126. He denies the *isrā* via Jerusalem, against the opinion of Abū Dharr and Zarr ibn Ḥubaysh (ibid. V, 387, 156).

127. Ibid., V, 390, 384.

128. In the same *ḥadīth*, Qatāda saw only a foretelling of the *ridda* of 633 A.D.

129. Muttaqī, *Kanz*, V, 164. And his curious parable of the penitent fisherman, who, from fear of God, has himself burnt, and his ashes cast into the sea; God pardons him because of his fear (Ḥanbal, V, 383). Cf. Titus, according to the Talmud (Drach, I, 232).

130. Ibn Saᶜd, *Ṭabaqāt*, VII, 5 [there is another version in Ḥanbal, IV, 427]; Ibn al-Athīr, *Usd*, IV, 137.

mystics. ᶜImrān represents the first flowering of the inner life to be found in authentic stories about the Ṣaḥāba.

Later hagiographers preferred to summarize the period of the Companions in two legends of highly dubious authenticity: first, that of the *ahl al-ṣuffa,* "people of the bench," or "of the veranda," a name designating some *muhājirūn* who had voluntarily impoverished themselves.[131] They were supposed to have remained poor and to have met frequently in a corner of the mosque at Medina for their devotional exercises. Sulamī had collected their names, in a separate work devoted to them;[132] Muḥāsibī, Ibn Karrām, and Tustarī accepted the legend's authenticity, and Abū Nuᶜaym, Ibn Ṭāhir Maqdisī, and Subkī[133] later defended it.

The second legend is that of Uways Qaranī,[134] the ascetic from the Yemen whose odor of sanctity[135] was carried all the way to Muḥammad. Only after the Prophet's death did Uways come to the Ḥijāz; he died fighting for ᶜAlī at Ṣiffīn (31/657). The first author to write about him was Hishām Dustuwāᵓī (d. 153). Mālik called Uways's very existence into doubt, and his *aḥādīth,* though accepted by Ibn ᶜIyāḍ, were refused as "weak" by Bukhārī.[136] Many later works collected Uways's *manāqib.*[137] Gurgānī venerated him and invoked his name to induce ecstasy.

B. Among the *Tābiᶜūn*: Ascetics of Kūfa, Baṣra, and Medina

From the year 40/660 to the year 110/728, cases of asceticism multiplied. Faḍl ibn Shādhān could count eight notable ascetics at Ṣiffīn,[138] including four partisans of ᶜAlī: Rabīᶜ ibn Khaytham, Harim ibn Ḥayyān, Uways Qaranī, ᶜĀmir ibn Qays; two partisans of Muᶜāwiya: Abū Muslim Khawlānī and Masrūq ibn al-Ajdaᶜ (who later made a retraction); and two neutrals: Abū ᶜAmr Aswad ibn Yazīd Nakhaᶜī and Ḥasan Baṣrī.

131. Qur. 54:8.

132. Hujwīrī, *Kashf,* 81–82; cf. *Ḥilya,* part II, ms. Paris 2028. The case of Ṣuhayb may be historical; Aḥmad Ghazālī (d. 517), in a sermon, in order to insinuate the superiority of saints to prophets, shows Isrāfīl bringing Muḥammad the "keys to the treasures," and Muḥammad begging in vain for something with which to open "the souls of Ṣuhayb and Uways" (Ibn-Jawzī, *Quṣṣāṣ,* f. 118 [*Recueil,* p. 97]).

133. Ms. Berlin 3478.

134. Uways, cf. *Al-maᶜdan al-ᶜadanī* (ms. no. 4978; Asᶜad 1690); *Manāqib Uways* of Lāmiᶜī (cat. Rieu).

135. Ḥadīth of the *"nafas al-Raḥmān."* He is supposed to have ripped out the same tooth Muḥammad had broken at Uḥud (cf. Ibn ᶜUkkāsha's vision). Ibn Saᶜd, VI, 11–114. Dhahabī, *Iᶜtidāl,* s.v.; ᶜAṭṭār, I, 15–24. Accepted by Faḍl ibn Shādhān (Jazāᵓirī, *Ḥāwī al-maqāl,* ms. London 8688, 22b).

136. Ms. Köpr. majm. 1590.

137. ᶜAṭṭār, I, 23.

138. Khūnsārī, *Rawḍāt,* I, 233; same list in Dhahabī, *Iᶜtidāl,* I, 130.

It is possible to correct and complete this list of the first *zuhhād* (syn. *nussāk*, *ʿubbād*) and *quṣṣāṣ*, thanks in particular to Jāḥiẓ[139] and ibn al-Jawzī:[140]

i) Ascetics of Kūfa: [ʿAmr ibn] ʿUtba b. Farqad; Hamām ibn Ḥarth; Uways Qaranī; ʿAlqama b. Qays Nakhaʿī; Ḥuṭayṭ b. Zayyāt, tortured by Ḥajjāj in 84;[141] Saʿīd b. Jubayr. The best known is Abū ʿAA Rabīʿ b. Rāshid Khaytham (d. 67); he gave up his belief in legitimacy before God's will at Karbala, and he converted a sinful woman who had come to tempt him.[142]

ii) Of Damascus: Kaʿb Aḥbār, who wrote down the *ḥadīth al-jumjuma*, among other scriptural parables;[143] his student Khalīl ibn Miʿdān; Bilāl ibn Saʿd Sakūnī, teacher of Awzaʿī and preacher; and Maṣqala, Ruqba's father. Then the movement slowed, quickening again only with the disciples of Ibn Adham and Dārānī.

iii) Of Baṣra: ʿĀmir ibn [ʿAbd] Qays[144] and Bajāla ibn ʿUbda ʿAnbarī; ʿUthmān ibn Adham; Aswad ibn Kulthūm; Ṣila ibn Ushaym ʿIdawī and his wife Muʿādha Qaysiyya;[145] Ḥayyān ibn ʿUmayr Qaysī.[146] The *qāṣṣ* Abū Bakr ʿAbdallah ibn abī Sulaymān Shikhkhīr Ḥarrashī Hudhalī; his sons, Bakr, ʿAlā, and especially Muṭarrif, (d. 87 or 95). Madhʿūr b. Ṭufayl, a friend of Muṭarrif; ʿAṭā b. Yasār, Muwarriq ʿIjlī; Jaʿfar and Ḥarb b. Jarfās Minqārī; Jaʿfar ibn Zayd ʿAbdī, Bakr ibn ʿAA Muzanī, Harim b. Ḥayyān,[147] Ḥasan Baṣrī, ʿIsä b. Zādhān, Maskīna Ṭafāwiya.[148]

iv) Of Mecca: ʿUbayd ibn ʿUmayr and Mujāhid ibn Jubayr Makhzūmī ([d. 104] whom Ḥasan and Muhāsibī admired), a student of Ibn ʿAbbās and the editor of his *tafsīr*. Mujāhid used to say, with his palm opened wide, "The heart is in this form. If a man commits a sin, it becomes like this," and he curled up one finger; "then another sin, like this," and he curled up another finger; then three, then four. Finally, at the fifth sin, he closed the fist with the thumb and said, "Then God seals the heart."

v) Of Medina: Tamīm Dārī, the first *qāṣṣ*;[149] Abū Yūsuf ʿAA b. Salām

139. *Bayān*, I, 190–94, 197; III, 98.

140. *Quṣṣāṣ*. cf. Dhahabī, *Ḥuffāẓ*.

141. Tagrib.

142. Sarrāj, *Maṣāriʿ*, 146. His mosque in Qazwīn (Goldziher, *M. St.*, II, 352; I, 227, 287); cf. ʿAwnī and Ḥurayfish, *Rawḍ*, 203 (cf. 84).

143. Asin, *Logia D. Jesu, in fine.*

144. Ṭabarī, I, 2924: a vegetarian and chaste; does not go to the mosque on Friday.

145. Sarrāj, *Maṣāriʿ*, 136–37.

146. Ibn Saʿd, VII, 137, 165.

147. He is confused with Jābir ibn Ḥayyān, ap. Khashīsh.

148. Ibn ʿArabī, *Muḥāḍ.*, II, 59. Add Ṣafwān ibn Maḥraz Māzinī, Aswad ibn Sarīʿ, and ʿUbaydallāh ibn ʿUmayr Laythī, whose native country is not specified.

149. The details of Tamīm Dārī's biography ought to be collected. He was the first writer of sermons in Islam, also the author of a brief apocalypse (*ḥadīth al-jassāsa*) and the teacher of Shihr ibn Ḥawshab (who was also Salmān's *rāwī*; Ibn Ḥawshab [d. 111 A.H.] had an interest in *jafr*). Tamīm is buried in Bayt Jibrīn. It is known that the Prophet had promised him the territory of Hebron (tomb of Abraham), whence the famous *waqf Tamīmī*, on which see *Revue des études islamiques*, 1951, 78–82.

(d. 43), a former Jew; Muslim b. Jundub Hudhalī, *qāṣṣ* of the mosque; ᶜAA ibn Shaddād ibn al-Hādī (d. 83).

vi) Of the Yemen: a. M. Wahb b. Munabbih Ḍimārī (d. 110), who was a Qadarite for a time.

There is no extant historical detail for most of these names; the exceptions are Rabīᶜ ibn Khaytham, Muwarriq,[150] ᶜAlqama, Muṭarrif,[151] Mujāhid, Wahb,[152] and especially Ḥasan Baṣrī (to be studied separately). During this period asceticism was simple, and the interiorization of ritual was still rudimentary: Qurʾānic meditation provoked the flowering of some *ḥadīth*, and there were cases of retreats, abstinence, and supererogatory prayer.[153]

C. The Ascetics of the Second Century A.H.
Classification

From 80/699 to 180/796, Muslim asceticism grew and gained strength. It was characterized by not being separate from the Community's daily life: all ascetics were led to perform the duty of brotherly correction (*naṣīḥa*); each *zāhid* was called to become a preacher, a *qāṣṣ*. The second century, especially at Baṣra, was the century of preachers. Without an official mandate and before the ᶜAbbasid regulation of the Friday sermon, they gave the *khuṭba* to arouse the fervor of believers. The spontaneous movement of the *quṣṣāṣ*,[154] so profoundly popular and later so maligned,[155] was the foundation of apologetic religious instruction in Islam (Qurʾānic school and Friday sermon),[156] just as the seminaries of the Karrāmiyya and the Qarmathians, in the following century, would become the foundation of the Islamic *madrasas* and universities. The *quṣṣāṣ* preached in the open air, converting the people by telling anecdotes in rhymed prose (*sajᶜ*).

The ascetics or "servants" (*ᶜubbād*) began to attract the attention of the public, which gave them different names suited to their various habits of mortification and zeal: readers of the Qurʾān (*qurrāʾ*) exciting themselves to public contrition (called *bakkāʾūn*, "weepers"), and preachers attacking

150. Jāḥiẓ admired this saying of his: "I have been asking God for an urgent favor for forty years. He has not given it to me, but I do not despair. — ? — I renounce what is not my affair."

151. His doctrine is well developed: *tafḍīl al-ghanī*; *uns*; the true *saʾiḥ*; dialogue of the living and the dead (Ibn ᶜArabī, *Muḥāḍ.*, II, 270).

152. There have been no critical editions of his works (*Mubtadā*; fragments of an *Isrāʾiliyāt*, ap. *Ḥilya* and *Iḥyā*). See his doctrine of *ᶜaql*, a better tool to serve God (cf. Ibn ᶜAṭā); on Moses in the Sinai (see Baqlī, I, 273); on the heart, the dwelling-place of God (Tirmidhī, *ᶜIlal*, f. 202a).

153. The invention of *wird* by Ibn Sīrīn.

154. Goldziher, *Muh. Stud.*, II, 161 ff.

155. By the critics of the *ḥadīth*, Ibn Ḥanbal (Makkī, *Qūt*, I, 151) and Ibn al-Jawzī (*Quṣṣās*), who at least perceives the importance of the movement. Ghazālī is the only one who fully realizes the moral value of their "apostolic missions."

156. ᶜAnbarī, an official preacher (*khaṭīb*), uses Ḥasan's *mawāᶜiẓ*.

the imagination by eschatological descriptions (*quṣṣāṣ*). Among those who came to listen in passing were doctors of the law (*fuqahā*) personally conscientious about morality, keepers of the tradition who were truly devout, and genealogists (*nassābūn*) with a taste for odd anecdotes.

1) ASCETICS OF BAṢRA

a) *Nussāk*: the mystic disciples of Ḥasan Baṣrī: Muḥammad ibn Wāsiᶜ (d. 120 fighting in Khurāsān), Mālik ibn Dīnār (d. 128), Farqad Sinjī (d. 131);[157] and the less intimate disciples, Thābit Bunānī (d. 127) and Ḥabīb ᶜAjamī (d. 156). Then, the group of Ibn Dīnār's disciples: ᶜUtba ibn Abān ibn Damᶜa,[158] Rabāḥ Qaysī and his saintly friend Rābiᶜa Qaysiyya, ᶜAbd al-Wāḥid ibn Zayd, and Saᶜīd Nibājī.

b) *Bakkāʾūn*: Abū Juhayr Darīr, who died chanting the Quʾrān;[159] Ṣubᶜam (d. 146); Kahmas b. Ḥasan Tamīmī ᶜĀbid (d. 149);[160] Hishām Qurdūsī (d. 148), a *rāwī* of Ḥasan; Haytham ibn Nammāz, a disciple of Yazīd Raqqāshī; Ghālib b. ᶜAA Jahḍamī; Ziyād b. ᶜAA Namīrī (d. 150);[161] and especially Abū Bishr Ṣāliḥ Murrī (d. 172), a disciple of Yazīd Raqqāshī, whose moving eloquence gained him lasting fame.[162]

c) *Quṣṣāṣ*: (Waᶜīdīs = semi-Qadarites). The Raqqāshī family, whose traditional eloquence in Persian was soon surpassed by their eloquence in Arabic:[163] Yazīd ibn Abān R. (d. 131), disciple of Ḥasan and teacher of Ḍirār b. ᶜAmr, Ḥajjāj ibn al-Furāfiṣa, Murrī, and Wakīᶜ; Faḍl ibn ᶜIsä b. Abān R., head of the Faḍliyya school,[164] and his son ᶜAbd al-Ṣamad R.

d) Semi-Qadarite moral interpreters of the law, students of Qatāda: Mūsä b. Sayyār Uswārī, a commentator, in both Arabic and Persian, on the Quʾrān. His son, the *qāṣṣ* Abū ᶜAlī ᶜAmr b. Faʾid Uswārī, made Quʾrānic commentary in public for thirty-six years; he began with the second sura but was unable to finish. Filling his explanations with allegories (*taʾwīlāt*)

157. His *ḥadīth* on the 500 virgins wearing the *ṣūf* who came to Jerusalem (quoted by Lisān al-Dīn ibn al-Khaṭīb, *Rawḍa*, 31a; also Maqdisī, *Muthīr*, ms. Paris 1669, f. 35a), not unlike the companions of St. Ursula; extracts from his book, in Shiblī, *Ākām*, 107; Baqlī, *Tafsīr*, f. 278b. Samᶜānī reads Farqad Sabakhī, not Sinjī.

158. Called *Ghulām* (deacon): his attrition (*ḥuzn*) is reminiscent of Ḥasan's. He bound himself in chains and wore the *ṣūf*. He was killed on the *jihād* at Qaryat al-Ḥabāb (*Ḥilya*). His prayer (*Qūt*, I, 10).

159. Thaᶜlabī, *qatlä*.

160. Founder of an ephemeral school (Samᶜānī, 377b; Qalhātī, *loc. cit.* [= *Kashf*, cited in P Fr 3:254 n 2/Eng 3:240 n 43].

161. Who justified his being a *qāṣṣ* by quoting Anas ibn Mālik (*Qūt*, I, 151); cf. Dhahabī, *Iᶜtidāl*; Jāḥiẓ, *Bayān*, III, 81; Ibn al-Najjār, ms. Paris 2089, s.v. Note that Anas ibn Mālik is one of Yazīd Raqqāshī's sources (Kalābādhī, *Akhbār*, f. 8, 16). Ziyād Namīrī and the *taṣliyat ᶜalä Ibrāhīm* (Sanūsī, *salsabīl*).

162. Jāḥiẓ, *Bayān*, II, 38.

163. Ibid., I, 159, 167, 168.

164. The school is condemned as Qadarite by Ibn ᶜUyayna.

and anecdotes (*akhbār*), he sometimes remained for several weeks on a single verse.[165] There was also Abū Bakr Hishām b. ʿAA Dustuwāʾī (d. 153), who collected many important parables from the Gospels; and his disciple Jaʿfar b. Sulaymān Ḍabʿī (d. 133), a student of Farqad[166] and a friend of Rābiʿa.

e) Muʿtazilite theologians: ʿAmr ibn ʿUbayd (d. 143); his disciple ʿAbd al-Wārith b. Saʿīd Tannūrī, whose student Abū Maʿmar recorded tales about Rābiʿa.[167]

f) Strictly Sunni *muḥaddithūn*: Ayyūb Sikhtiyānī (d. 131),[168] whose first efforts Ḥasan had admired and whom Ibn ʿUyayna called "the greatest of the *tābiʿūn*"; Sikhtyānī's disciple Wuhayb b. Ward Makkī, venerated as a saint by Bishr Ḥāfī. Yūnus ibn ʿUbayd Qaysī (d. 139), another of Ḥasan's disciples, and ʿAbdallah ibn ʿAwn ibn Artabān[169] (d. 151, who, with Sikhtiyānī and Sulaymān Taymī,[170] constitute Aṣmaʿī's celebrated group of the "four" founders of the *ahl al-sunna waʿl-jamāʿa*. Ḥammād ibn Zayd (d. 179) and Ḥammād b. Salama[171] (d. 165), also noteworthy Sunnis, had feebler contact with ascetic ideas; but Ibn Salama trained Wakīʿ ibn Jarrāḥ (d. 197), a fine theologian and a Ḥanafite in law, whose *Kitāb al-zuhd*[172] and reasoned conversion to mysticism[173] almost anticipate Ghazālī.

g) Semi-Murjiʾite Sunni *quṣṣāṣ*: Ibn Sīrīn's students and Sulaymān b. Ṭuhmān Taymī (d. 143),[174] who wrote the *tasbīḥiyāt* and was Faḍl Raqqāshī's son-in-law.[175]

h) *Nassābūn* and philologists; Abū ʿAmr ibn al-ʿAlā (d. 154), who was converted through Quʾrānic meditation (*taqarraʾa*); and his disciple ʿAbdalmalik Aṣmaʿi (d. 216).

II) ASCETICS OF KŪFA

a) Shiite mystics (Zaydī): First, the famous Abū Isrāʾīl Mulaʾī ʿAbsī[176]

165. Jāḥiẓ, *Bayān*, I, 196.

166. Ṭabarī, I, 410.

167. Sarrāj, *Maṣāriʿ*, 181.

168. Ibn Qutayba, *Taʾwīl*, 93, 120; Sarrāj, *Masāriʿ*, 8.

169. Who condemns those who wept for Ḥusayn at Karbala (Ibn Baṭṭa ʿUkbarī, *Sharḥ*, bib., s.n. ʿUkbarī).

170. Who was excluded, as a Murjiʾite, by Ghulām Khalīl (*Sharḥ al-sunna*) and Ibn Qutayba.

171. Hostile to Thawrī (Makkī, *Qūt*, II, 152).

172. In which he writes that during the *miʿrāj*, Muḥammad saw some of the damned with their lips being cut by incandescent scissors: they were *quṣṣāṣ* who had not practiced what they had preached.

173. He proposes a preeminent role for the saints in the divine plan for creation (*Passion*, Fr 3:219/Eng 3:206–7).

174. Jāḥiẓ, *Bayān*, I, 167; Ibn Qutayba, *Maʿārif*, 240.

175. Samʿāni (s.v., *qāṣṣ*) gives the following series of *qāṣṣ* at Medina: Muḥammad ibn Kaʿb Qaraẓī (d. 108), Abū Ḥarza Yq. ibn Mujāhid Makhzūmī, Abū Ibrahīm ibn Sulaymān.

176. Abū Isrāʾīl Ismāʿīl ibn abī Isḥāq Khalīfa (Ibn Saʿd, VI, 202, 231, 265; Samʿānī, s.n.; Ḥanbal, IV, 168).

(b. 83,[177] d. c. 140), whose excessive doctrine of the *iᶜtikāf* was quickly rejected.[178] then the Shiite Ṣūfiyya: Kilāb; Kulayb [b. Muᶜāwiya Asadī Ṣaydāwī, the teacher of Ibn abī ᶜUmayr Azdī,[179] "the ascetic," and of Ṣafwān b. Yaḥyā Kūfī, "the keeper of the fast";[180] Kulayb was the author of a *Kitāb al-maḥabba wa'l-waẓāᵓif* and a *Kitāb bashārat al-muᵓmin*]; Ibn Qinṭāsh and ᶜAbdak, founder of the vegetarian ᶜAbdakiyya sect. Jābir ibn Ḥayyān and Faḍl ibn Ghānim can be inserted here; they transmitted mystical sayings attributed to Imām Jaᶜfar.

b) Semi-Murjiᵓite Sunni Sūfiyya: Hāshim b. al-Awqāṣ, whom Bukhārī rejected as a *rāwī*; Abū Hāshim ᶜUthmān b. Sharīk Kūfī (d. c. 160), who taught Manṣūr ibn ᶜAmmār and was venerated by Kharrāz;[181] Dāwūd Ṭāᵓī, an ex-Ḥanafite versed in various disciplines of canon law[182] who was converted and spent twenty years in solitude before his death (in 165); Ibrāhīm Taymī, author of the *Musabbiᶜāt*;[183] ᶜAwn ibn ᶜAbdallah; Ibn Shaddād's student Dharr Hamdānī Marhabī, and especially his son Abū Dharr ᶜUmar (d. 150),[184] preacher and theologian,[185] whose disciple Ruqba ibn Maṣqala said that those who listened to him believed they were hearing "the trumpet of the Last Judgment"; Ruqba himself "obeyed him as if he were God."[186]

c) Pious anti-Murjiᵓite *muḥaddithūn* who put limits on the use[187] of the Ḥanafite *raᵓy*: The great Sufyān b. Saᶜīd Thawrī, (d. 161) head of a school;[188] he studied with Wuhayb b. Ward, Ḥajjāj b. Furāfiṣa, and Yūnus b. ᶜUbayd, and he taught Ibn ᶜUyayna Hilālī (d. 198), Ibn ᶜIyāḍ, (d. 187) and Dārānī. Ibn ᶜUyayna's student Abū Thawr Kalbī (d. 240) gave some ephemeral prestige to Thawrī's legal school,[189] which was widespread among mystics; Ibn Khu-

177. The year after the *yawm al-jamājim*.

178. *Passion*, Fr 3:240/Eng 3:226–27; Bukhārī, IV, 98.

179. *Tusy's list*, 265. His disciple Abū'l-ᶜAbbās Faḍl ibn ᶜIsā Shādhān Azdī Rāzī (d. c. 275) wrote a *Kitāb al-qira'āt*, unfortunately lost (cf. *Fihrist*, I, 26, 27, 31, 231), which was the fundamental work on the early recensions of the Qurᵓān. He violently attacked the Sunni mystics Ḥasan Baṣrī and Ibn Karrām, along with the philosophers and the Qarmathians (*Tusy's list* 254–55; Dāmād, *Iqāẓāt*, 130; Khūnsārī, *Rawḍāt*, II, 210; on his son ᶜAbbās, see Dhahabī, *Qurrāᵓ*, 64a). Equally esteemed by the Ḥashwiyya and the Imāmīs, Ibn Shādhān was attacked by the Imāmī Jaᶜfar Ṭūsī for giving importance to the *ḥadīth al-ghār* (Qur. 9:40), which puts Abū Bakr in the most prominent position.

180. *Tusy's list*, s.v.

181. Bahbahānī, *Khayrātiyya*, 241a (according to Abū'l-Maᵓālī, Ibn Ḥamza in his *Hādī*, and Nasafī, ap. *Taṣfiyat al-qulūb*).

182. Ibn Qutayba, *Maᶜārif*, 257; teacher of Isḥāq Salūlī (d. 204).

183. *Qūt*, I, 7.

184. Student of ᶜAṭā and of Mujāhid, teacher of Wakīᶜ.

185. *Mutakallim*; condemned as such by Abū Usāma Kūfī (d. 201), disciple of Ibn Shaddād (Harawī, *Dhamm*, f. 116b).

186. Jāḥiẓ, *Bayān*, I, 144–45, 188; II, 158, 166.

187. Rectifying it, as Najjār corrected Jahm.

188. Adversary of Abū Ḥanīfa (Subkī, II, 39, l. 8) and Ibn abī Laylā (Qut. *Maᶜarif*, 273). Associated with two mystics, Ibn Adham and Abū Hāshim; his disciples attacked Shaqīq.

189. Ibn Ḥanbal's comment on this subject.

bayq Anṭākī, Ḥamdūn Qaṣṣār, and Junayd were Thawrites in law. There was also Abū ᶜAA ᶜAmr b. Qays Mulaᵓī (d. 146), a student of ᶜIkrima[190] (d. 105); and Bakr b. Khunays, Bunānī's disciple and Maᶜrūf Karkhī's teacher.

d) *Nassābūn*: Abū ᶜUmayr Mujāhid ibn Saᶜīd (d. 144), disciple of Shaᶜbī and teacher of Haytham b. ᶜAdī (d. 207) and of Dāwūd b. Muᶜādh ᶜAtakī, one of Ḥallāj's sources.[191]

III) ASCETICS OF THE ḤIJAZ

In Mecca, there are few ascetics besides Ḥajjār and Ibn Jurayj Makkī (d. 150), the author of the first *tafsīr*,[192] one of Muḥāsibī's sources.

In Medina: Muḥammad ibn Kaᶜb Qaraẓī; Aᶜazz; ᶜAA b. ᶜAbd al-ᶜAzīz ᶜUmarī; Abū ᶜĀmir Nubātī; and especially Abū Ḥāzim Maslama b. abī Dīnār Aᶜraj Madanī (d. 140), the first Sufi master after Ḥasan Baṣrī, according to Kalābābhī.[193] In Madanī's circle was Ibn al-Munkadir Taymī (d. 130),[194] a disciple of the *ṣaḥābī* Jābir b. ᶜAA Ansārī and the teacher of Faḍl Raqqāshī and Sulaymān b. Harim Qurashī.[195] ᶜIsä b. Dāb Laythī (d. 171), a *nassāb* whose works on the *ᶜāshiqūn* ("illustrious lovers")[196] are cited in the *Fihrist*, wrote an unusual piece[197] entitled *Al-fityat al-tawwābbūn, The Young Penitents.* It is about ten young Medinese libertines, Sulaymān b. ᶜAmr Qurashī and his friends, who suddenly renounce the world; but only their dramatic conversion scene is presented without any explanation of motives or results. Laythī's mysticism is rudimentary, expressed in a simple unified language quite close to that of the *Dīwān* of Abū'l-ᶜAtāhiya (d. 213).

IV) ASCETICS OF KHURĀSĀN

Among the *jund* from Baṣra and Kūfa who settled in the Arab military colonies in Northeastern Iran, mystical vocations appeared after 145/762,

190. From whom we have a very strange parable concerning the resurrection: God will revive a drowned man whose bones, having washed up onto the beach, will be eaten by camels whose turds have been burned (Ibn al-Jawzī, *Ṣafwa*, ms. Paris 2030).

191. *Passion*, 1st ed., 337 n 6 [a French version of Qushayrī's note, contained in *Essai*, Arabic supplement, Q 3 (*Risāla, bāb al-jawᶜ*, index, s.n., Muḥ. ibn Bishr). Massignon later said that this note was to be suppressed: *Passion*, Fr 3:266/Eng 3:250]; ms. Paris 2089, f. 107a.

192. Makkī, *Qūt*, I, 159.

193. *Taᶜarruf*; *Qūt* II, 56; Jāḥiẓ, *Bayān*, I, 94, III, 97; Tagrib., 378.

194. His definition of *ᶜaql* (Tirmidhī, *ᶜIlal*, 211a).

195. Author of the famous *ḥadīth* of the pomegranate (Dhahabī, *Iᶜtidāl*, s.v.): "And as for him who retires to pray on an island on which God brings forth a spring and a pomegranate tree — if he eats a pomegranate and succeeds in dying prostrate, it is this grace obtained (*and not his efforts*) that will procure salvation for him." The pomegranate is the fruit symbolizing Paradise (Tustarī, *Tafsīr*, 14–15).

196. *Fihrist*, 90–91, 306; Tagrib., I, 464

197. Discovered and published by L. Cheïkho, in *Machriq*, XI, 260–64.

twenty years after the first theological movements (Jahm, Muqātil). The first mystic was Ibrāhīm ibn Adham ᶜIjlī (d. 160/776), a pure Arab[198] of the Tamīm tribe who was born in Balkh. His favorite models were Ibn Dīnār, Bunānī and Sikhtiyānī, all from Baṣra. Ibn Adham came to ᶜIrāq to receive the teaching of Ḥajjāj ibn Furāfiṣa and Abū Shuᶜayb Qallāl, and to Mecca for Abū ᶜAbbād Ramlī.[199] He lived for a long time in Jerusalem,[200] then went into retirement, to live on the *ḥalāl* ground[201] of Mt. Lukkām, at Jebla near Laodicea. The influence of his powerful personality will be studied below.[202]

The second man called to mysticism was Ibn al-Mubārak[203] (b. 108, d. 180), Wuhayb ibn Ward's disciple and an anti-Malikite Ḥanafī, author of a *Kitāb al-zuhd* and teacher of Naᶜīm ibn Ḥammād.

The third was Fuḍayl ibn ᶜIyāḍ (d. 187), a disciple of Abān ibn abī ᶜAyyāsh[204] and Thawrī. Ibn ᶜIyāḍ came to live at Kūfa and finally died on retreat in Mecca after losing his son, ᶜAlī (who died chanting the Qurᵓan in high fervor).[205]

Throughout the second century A.H., the mystics still indistinguishable

198. His genealogy: ibn Adham ibn Manṣūr ibn Yazīd ibn Jābir. A characteristic of the legend of the Buddha was later attributed to him (legend of the beggar prince of Balkh; cf. the legend of his departure for the hunt, according to Ibn Manda, ap. Tagrib., I, 428.

199. Tales of Ibn Bashshār.

200. Maqdīsī, *Muthīr*, ms. Paris 1669, f. 35b, 126a.

201. Land duly given, after its conquest, to the Community (and not as a fief to an individual; cf. Anṭākī, *shubuhāt*). Note that before his arrival, the mystical movement barely existed in Syria, a powerful argument against the supposed imitation from the Orthodox Christian monasteries of Palestine.

202. Hallauer's monograph should be reviewed in light of two sources now published: the *Ḥilya* (VII, 367–94; and VIII, 1–57) and the *Tārīkh Dimashq* (abridged) of Ibn ᶜAsākir (II, 167–96). Ibn Adham fled from Balkh in 132 (during Abū Muslim's revolt) and joined his sister, a pure Arab of the Banī ᶜIjl, in Kūfa (*Aghani*, 2nd ed., XII, 106–7), where she had a son, the poet Muḥammad b. Kunāsa Asadī. The other stages of Ibn Adham's life are well known, except the journey he is supposed to have made, shortly before his death, to the Baḥr Lūṭ (= the Dead Sea, the *paneremos* of the Essenes and the first Christian Palestinians). That visit might have made another Khurāsānian, Ibn Karrām, decide to come to Segor. Ibn Adham was killed in *jihād* on the Syrian coast and buried at Jebla. His tomb, which I visited there, was enriched under the Mamlūks and Ottomans by the addition of a great mosque and *waqf* (later parceled out, c. 1930; photograph by Nieger [in *Essai*]). In the fourteenth century (Yāfiᶜī) an order was founded under a name derived from Ibn Adham's, the "Edhemiya," which developed *zāwiyas* in the major Ottoman cities, notably Jerusalem (where the *zāwiya* still existed in 1917: *Rev. Et. Is.*, 1951, 93).

203. He fought the Qadarites and Murjiᵓites, the Khārijites and the Shīᶜa (it was he who classified them as such, according to Ghulām Khalīl, *Sharḥ al-sunna*; cf. Sh. *Ṭab.*, I, 59); he was also against the Jahmites (Ālūsī, *Jalā*, 60). Ibn al-Mubārak is the source of a rigidly traditional ascetic current running from his teacher, Sulaymān Taymī, through Sufyān Thawrī and Sufyān Ibn ᶜUyayna, students of his, and Wakīᶜ, to Ibn Ḥanbal. Through the latter, the current would influence all of Ḥanbalism (cf. *Kitāb al-zuhd* of Ibn Ḥanbal, ed. Cairo, 1357, 400 pp.). Ibn al-Mubārak ought to be studied. His tomb is at Hīt, a curious and very archaic city on the Euphrates, where a Karaite ghetto survives, near some tar pits.

204. Makkī, *Qūt*, 29. He trained Muslim Khawwāṣ, the teacher of Bishr Ḥāfī.

205. Thaᶜlabī, *Qatlā*.

from the humble troupes of homeless poor[206] and ordinary worshipers camped in the mosques did not draw the criticism of the theologians and doctors of sacred law. Nevertheless, mystics from Ḥasan to Ṣāliḥ Murrī, with their sermons invoking contrition and their supererogatory penance, were called Waᶜīdiyya and, as such, confused with the Qadarites, when they were in fact semi-Qadarites. In addition, the punctilious traditionists were suspicious and saw indirect criticisms of their own literal-mindedness in sayings like ᶜAmr ibn Qays Mulaᵓī's,[207] "The *ḥadīth,* 'In keeping my heart for company, through my heart I reach my Lord,' is dearer to me than the solutions to fifty legal problems." Ibn ᶜIyāḍ openly attacked the *ahl al-ḥadīth.*[208] The ultimate doctrinal consequence of mysticism (i.e., divine union) was already appearing in Kahmas, Kulayb, Rabāḥ, and Rābiᶜa, whom the orthodox doctors of the third century condemned collectively, *post mortem,* as *zanādiqa.*

3. Ḥasan Baṣrī

A. Sources for His Biography, Chronology of His Life

I) SOURCES

There is no definitive account compiled by his disciples. Qatāda, Ibn ᶜAwn, Yūnus and Ayyūb provide a few notes. Scattered mentions — deferent but also reserved, distant, or hostile — are made by *muḥaddithūn* like Ibn Saᶜd (d. 230; *Ṭabaqāt,* VII, 114–29) and Ibn Shādhān (d. c. 275; lost work);[209] by commentators and historians like Abū'l-Yaqẓān (d. 190)[210] (whose work is used by Ibn Qutayba [d. 276; *Maᶜārif,* 225, 273, 286]) and Ṭabarī (d. 310; *Taᵓrīkh,* III, 2488–93 and passim); and by theologians like Jāḥiẓ (d. 255; *Bayān;* II, 34–39, 50–54, 88, 154, III, 66, 68–71, 75, 76, 79, 82, 83, 86). The remarks of later hagiographers such as Abū Nuᶜaym Isfahānī (d. 430; *Ḥilya,* v. III) must be used with great caution.[211]

II) CHRONOLOGY OF THE LIFE OF ABŪ SAᶜĪD ḤASAN B. ABĪ'L-ḤASAN YASĀR MAYSĀNĪ BAṢRĪ

Year 21/643. Birth, probably at Medina; his father is Yasār, a Mesenian

206. Their fraternal rules for communal life (bread, salt, ashes; women raise their veils, as before relatives); cf. *Passion,* Fr 3:241; 1:562–63; 2:122/Eng 3:227; 1:515–16; 2:110–11. Jāḥiẓ (*Bayān,* III, 3) sees these customs (*nār al-tahwīl*) as a *shuᶜūbī* infiltration.
207. Tagrib., s.a. 146.
208. Sh. *Ṭab.,* I, 67.
209. Extracts in Khūnsārī, *Rawḍāt,* II, 210; *Tusy's list,* 255.
210 *Fihrist,* 94.
211 Ibn al-Jawzī did not write a *Faḍāᵓil Ḥasan Baṣrī,* as Brockelmann erroneously inferred from his *Kitāb al-quṣṣāṣ.* [See GAL2 and bib., Ibn al-Jawzī, *al-Ḥasan al-Baṣrī.*]

slave of Zayd b. Thābit Anṣārī (or rather of Ḥumayl b. Qaṭana); his mother is Khayra, said to be Umm Salama's servant.[212] Yasār is freed after his son's birth.

Ḥasan is brought up in Baṣra (where he falls and breaks his nose). He supposedly meets Ḥudhayfa (d. 36 at Madāʾin) there as well.

Year 35. He passes through Medina at the time of the *yawm al-dār.*

Years 37–41. Returns to Baṣra. During the conflict among the Companions of the Prophet, he imitates the neutral attitude adopted by Aḥnaf ibn Qays Tamīmī (d. 67),[213] whom the *walī*[214] made his representative to the Baṣran *jund* (Banū Saᶜd, of the Tamīm) in Khurāsān (Aḥnaf ibn Qays comes back to live in Baṣra from 37 to 44). Ḥasan develops ties to him, to Abū Bakra, and, especially, through Hayyāj ibn ᶜImrān Burjumī,[215] to ᶜImrān Khuzāᶜī (d. 52), the former *qāḍī* of the town, whose admirable resignation to God's will so impressed the inhabitants.[216]

Years 50–53. He goes on *jihād* near Kābul, fights in Anduqān and Andaghan, and in Zābulistān with Samura ibn Jundub (who returns to Baṣra in 53 and dies there in 60).

Year 60. Having returned to Baṣra, he protests against the manner of Yazīd I's selection.

Years 65–85. His great period of oratory and doctrine. He associates himself with Muṭarrif Ḥarrashī (d. 87), ᶜAṭā ibn Yasār (d. 94), and even with Maᶜbad Juhanī, the head of the extremist Qadarīs.[217] Very soon, following the example of ᶜAbdallah ibn ᶜUmar (d. 74), he explicitly dissociates himself (*tabriya*) from those Qadarīs;[218] the semi-Qadarīs Ghaylān and ᶜAmr ibn ᶜUbayd imitate Ḥasan's attitude.

Years 81–82. He refuses to participate in Ibn al-Ashᶜath's insurrection against the cruelty of the *wālī* Ḥajjāj,[219] although his friends ᶜAṭā Mujāhid[220]

212. Ibn Khallikān, I, 139; ᶜAṭṭār, I, 24.
213. Ibn Saᶜd, VII, 66.
214. ᶜAbdallāh Ibn ᶜĀmir (29–44 A.H.), then Ziyād (Tagrib., I, 96, 142).
215. Ibn Saᶜd, VII, 109; Ḥanbal, IV, 428; Dhahabī, *Iᶜtidāl,* s.n.
216. See above, sec. 2. A.
217. Executed in 83 as a partisan of Ibn al-Ashᶜath.
218. Ibn Baṭṭa ᶜUkbarī; Harawī, *Dhamm,* 126b, 127a.
219. Ibn Saᶜd, VII, 119.
220 Imprisoned until Ḥallāj's death.

and Saᶜīd ibn Jubayr[221] do take part, along with Ṭalq ibn Ḥabīb ᶜAnazī[222] and ᶜAmr ibn Dīnār.[223]

Years 86–95. Ḥajjāj's police suspect him; he is pursued and must go into hiding.[224]

Year 99. He is named *qāḍī* of Baṣra momentarily, at the accession of ᶜUmar II, as a replacement for ᶜAdī ibn Arṭāh. He resigns and is succeeded[225] by Iyās ibn Muᶜāwiya (d. 122).

Death of his brother Saᶜīd.

Year 101. In a resonant sermon he expresses disapproval of Ibn al-Muhallab's anti-Syrian excesses.

Year 110. Death, Thursday the first of Rajab (= 10 October 728); his body, washed by Ayyūb Sikhtiyānī and Ḥamīd Ṭawīl Khuzaᶜī, is buried in old Baṣra (now Zubayr); Ibn Sīrīn refuses to come to the funeral. Ḥasan is survived by three sons:[226] Saᶜid, Jaᶜfar, and ᶜAbdallah, who supposedly burns his father's books, in accordance with Ḥasan's last requests.[227]

B. List of Sources for His Works

1) SPURIA

Others, up to the present, have listed under Ḥasan's name only *spuria*:

a) Fifty-four *farīḍa*: in manuscripts, Paris 780, Köpr. 1603, Aya Ṣufiya 1642, Laleli 1703; Qaṭalān catalogue Cairo, 1332 no. 350 (p. 28); printed, Constantinople, 1259, 1260. An interesting brief ascetic work that in no way diverges from the main lines of Ḥasan's doctrine; but the manuscript in Paris mentions authors of the fourth/tenth century, and if the work has an authentic, early core, it is difficult to discern from the rest.

b) *Risāla fī faḍl ḥaram Makka* (*ilā'l-Ramādī*), ms. Ẓah. Majm. 38. An insignificant pamphlet on the *ᶜumra*, probably apocryphal.

221. Taken and executed in 94.
222. Semi-Murjiᵓite.
223. He was pursued, but he escaped.
224. *Aghānī*, IV, 40.
225. Ibn Saᶜd, VII, 116: Ṭabarī, II, 1347.
226. Jāḥiẓ, *Bayān*, I, 195; Ḥasan's grandson Jaᶜfar ᶜIsä (d. 217) is mentioned (by Dhahabī, *Iᶜtidāl*, s.n.)
227. Ibn Saᶜd, VII, 127.

c) Numerous fragments from Ḥasan figure, without indication of *isnād* or of origin in a specific text, in the works of Muḥāsibī, Kharrāz, and Tirmidhī.

II) LIST OF HIS AUTHENTIC WORKS:

a) Mawāᶜiẓ, *sermons in public.* Text collected and established in his lifetime[228] by his disciples[229] and published after his death by Abū ᶜUbayda Ḥamīd Ṭawīl ibn Ṭarkhān Khuzaᶜī (d. 142).[230] After their publication, the sermons were frequently quoted (notably by Jāḥiẓ) without *isnād*, which proves there was a *textus receptus* with copies in circulation.

ᶜUbaydallah ᶜAnbarī (d. 168),[231] the official *qāḍī-khaṭīb* of Baṣra, soon amalgamated the *rasāᵓil* of Ghaylān[232] with these sermons, and they seem to have been the basis for the diluted text of semi-Qadarī *rasāᵓil* that was sent, under Ḥasan's name, to the caliphs ᶜAbd al-Mālik and ᶜUmar II.[233]

b) Tafsīr, *glosses on the Qurᵓān.* Ḥasan's glosses on the Qurᵓān were coordinated in the form of *tafsīr* by the Muᶜtazilite ᶜAmr ibn ᶜUbayd.[234] In the fourth century, two additional *risālas* were known under Ḥasan's name, one about the numbering and division of the verses (*fī'l-ᶜadad*), the other about their chronological order (*nuzūl*).[235] His *qirāᵓa* was original; numerous examples of the special characteristics of his reading are given in the *shawādhdh* of Ibn Khālawayh.[236]

c) Masāᵓil, *question/response.* Ḥasan's private teaching on dogma and the morals prescribed by canon law seems to have survived, in its original form of *quaestiones* or *masāᵓil,* because of Muᶜadh ibn Muᶜadh's teacher, Ashᶜath ibn ᶜAbdalmalik Ḥamrānī (d. 146); Yaḥyä Qattān expressed esteem for this edition.[237] The *masāᵓil* are the most likely source of the famous *sunan* or "rules for communal life"[238] later compiled in Ḥasan's name for the Bakriyya school. Ḥallāj cites a section (*kitāb al-ikhlāṣ*) on the pilgrimage,[239]

228. Ibn Saᶜd, VII, 126; Samᶜānī, 39.
229. Abū ᶜUbayda Bājī.
230. Muṭarrif's *rāwī*; teacher of Ḥammād ibn Salama.
231. Jāḥiẓ, *Bayān*, I, 161. ᶜAnbarī is a well-known theologian.
232. He had had an audience with ᶜUmar II (Khashīsh, ap. Malaṭī, f. 315–16).
233. Shahrastānī, I, 59; Murtaḍä, *Munya*, 12–14; *Aghānī*, VIII, 151. Cf. *risāla* of Muṭarrif to ᶜUmar II (Sarrāj, *Lumaᶜ*, 65) and a major *risāla* that the *Ḥilya* attributes to Ḥasan (cf. *Passion*, 3:242/Eng 3:228).
234. Ms. London 821.
235. *Fihrist*, 37, 38, 34.
236. Ms. Ḥamīdiyya 24.
237. Dhahabī, *Iᶜtidāl*, s.n.
238 Expression of G. Lioni Africano, *Descrittione*, III, ch. 43.
239. *Passion*, Fr 1:593/Eng 1:546.

and Kīlānī reproduces a fragment on "the forty-five errors to be avoided during canonical prayer."[240]

d) Riwāyāt, *Sayings*. In the manner of the *ahl al-ḥadīth*, most of Ḥasan's disciples transmitted his sayings only in the oral form of independent *riwāyāt*. *Logia* had to be compiled later, by the *bakkā* Hishām ibn Ḥassān Qurdūsī (d. 148), a student of Ḥawshab ibn al-Dawraqī. Wuhayb ibn Ward and Thawrī did not accept what Qurdūsī had collected, but Ibn ᶜUyayna did.[241] Another collection (*Maṣḥaf*), made by Abān ibn abī ᶜAyyāsh Fīrūz (d. 128 or 141)[242] and reedited by Abū ᶜAwāna Waḍḍāḥ (d. 170 or 176),[243] forced Ḥasan's *riwāyāt*, by fabricating *isnād* for them, into the classical form of the *ḥadīth* attributed to the Prophet; fifteen hundred of them were given with Anas ibn Mālik as an artificial link.[244] ᶜAbd al-Wāḥid ibn Zayd (d. 177) more honestly gave Ḥasan's *riwāyāt* as *marāsil*, without "completing" their *isnād*.

There are no other extant details on the other four compilers of the period: the Qadarī Mubārak ibn Faḍāla (d. 165), Abū Saᶜd, Abū Bakr Hudhalī, and Mukhtār ibn Filfil.[245]

Jābir ibn ᶜAbdallāh Yamāmī was exiled from Bukhārā for bringing out another edition of Ḥasan's *riwāyāt*, shortly after 200/185.[246] We know that Aḥmad Jawbiyārī forged a link of *isnād* through Abū Hurayra for various *marāsil* (perhaps complete fabrications), which he then passed to Ibn Karrām.[247]

As a general rule, *isnād* linking Ḥasan to the Prophet via Anas ibn Mālik, Abū Hurayra, or ᶜAlī are fabrications. Suyūṭī made great efforts to show[248] that Ḥasan had the opportunity to meet ᶜAlī and Ṭalḥa. Perhaps. But as Dhahabī showed, the only Companions whose *rāwī* he might have been are ᶜImrān Khuzāᶜī, ᶜAbd al-Raḥmān ibn Samura, and Abū Bakra; and, possibly, Nuᶜmān ibn Bashīr (2–67) and Mughīra ibn Shuᶜba.

240. *Ghunya*, II, 97.
241. Dhahabī, *Iᶜtidāl*.
242. Author discussed by his contemporary Ibn Dīnār and accepted by Ḥammād ibn Salama and Anṭākī.
243. Dhahabī, *Iᶜtidal*; Tagrib., I, 482; Ibn Qutayba, *Maᶜārif*, 252.
244. Makkī, *Qūt*, II, 141. Laying bare the formative process of the corpus of Sunni traditions, the future *Ṣaḥīḥ* of the third century. This collection of the *ḥadīth* of Anas ibn Malik and Ḥasan, celebrating chastity and condemning *liwāṭa*, was published three times: in the edition of Ḥasan's freedman Abū Makīs Dīnār ibn ᶜAbdallāh Ḥabashī (250 *ḥadīth*), published by Muḥammad ibn Aḥmad ibn Ḥabīb Qaffās (d. 286); and editions by Dāwūd ibn ᶜAffān Khurāsānī and Ghulām Khalīl.
245. Dhahabī, *Iᶜtidal*; Muḥāsibī, *Riᶜāya*, f. 10b.
246. Dhahabī, *Iᶜtidal*.
247. Herein, ch. 5, sec. 2.
248. *Itḥāf al-firqa*, Paris, 2800.

C. His Political, Exegetical, and Legal Doctrines

We are in the presence of one of the most powerful and complete figures of early Islam. The learned Sabian Thābit ibn Qurra (d. 288) made the wise judgment, "I envy the Arab nation for three men: ᶜUmar as head of state, Ḥasan as ascetic, and Jāḥiẓ as philosopher."[249]

Ḥasan was not only an ascetic. In addition to teaching the fine points of asceticism to Farqad, he taught *tafsīr* to Qatāda (d. 117), *kalām* to ᶜAmr ibn ᶜUbayd, and grammar to Ibn abī Isḥāq.[250] Abū Ḥayyān Tawḥīdī, who supplies these details,[251] comments,

> Ḥasan was a master not only of piety, asceticism, abstinence and forgiveness, union with god (*taʾalluh*)[252] and veneration of His inaccessibility (*tanazzuh*), but also of law, rhetoric, and advice for brotherly correction; his eloquence, still famous, was essentially practical; his sermons touched the heart and his style disturbed the intelligence.

Ḥasan's personality ripened during the great crisis of the early Islamic community. He was fourteen when ᶜUthmān was killed, and he was able to meet 70 survivors[253] from among the 313 combatants of Badr. He was the first to formulate the "Sunni" solution to the crisis of the years 36/656–41/661: his coherent political doctrine shows, psychologically, the source of his "conversion"[254] to mysticism and, socially, the marks of the first historical manifestation of Sunnism.[255]

249. Tawḥīdī, *Taqrīẓ al-Jāḥiẓ* (ap. Yāqūt, *Udabā*, VI, 69–70).

250. On his orthoepy, see *Fihrist*, 41; *Aghānī*, XVIII, 124; XXI, 60.

251. Tawḥīdī, ap. Yāqūt, *Udabā*.

252. Perhaps in this case the word has the attenuated philosophical nuance of "devotion" (herein, ch. 2 n 153–55 and related text).

253. The *Ḥilya* adds: "Most of them wore the *ṣūf*" (*sic*).

254. ᶜAṭṭār says that Ḥasan, who had been a jeweler, was converted while on a voyage to Rūm, at the funeral service for the emperor's son (ᶜAṭṭār, I, 25). But the description is borrowed from the *Syntipas* (sec. 137 — Chauvin, *Bibliographie* VI, 71 [*1001 Nuits*]; VIII, 139).

255. Cf. above all *Ḥilya*, II, 131–60. There are studies by H. H. Schaeder (in *DI*, XIV, 1–72) and by H. Ritter (*DI*, 1933). Ibn Taymiyya attributes to Ibn al-Jawzī some *Manāqib wa akhbār Ḥ. B.*, which seem to be lost (Salāmī, *Radd*, I, 348). It is very important to note that Ḥasan Baṣri, according to Balādhurī, was secretary to Rabīᶜ b. Zayd Ḥārithī, the governor of Khurāsān, and that he organized the colonization of Fars (Bayḍā; Khabr, where his brother Saᶜīd was buried) and Khurāsān by the Baṣrans. In Baṣra, he may very well have lived in the neighborhood called *al-Qasāmil*; his last descendent, Abū Yaᶜlā A-b-M ᶜAbdī ibn al-Ṣawwāf died there (in 490: Ibn al-Jawzī, *Muntaẓam*, IX, 103). Etymology: Qismīl (Wüst., *Reg.*, 375). Abū Nuᶜaym denies that Ḥasan was a Qadarite (*Kitāb dhabb al-qadar ᶜan Ḥ.-b-a. Ḥ.*, cited by ᶜAyn al-Quḍāt Hamadhānī, *Shakwā*, 35b). Abū ᶜAbdallāh Muḥammad ibn ᶜAbd al-Wāḥid Maqdisī wrote a *juzʾ fī man laqāhu min aṣḥāb ḤB* (Salāmī, *Radd*, I, 348). ḤB's *musnad* was published by the Mālikī Ismāʾīl ibn Ḥammād (d. 282): Ibn Farḥūn, 94); Ibn al-Qayyim cites a collection of his *fatwas* in seven books (*Iᶜlām*, I, 19). In 200 A.H., Jābir ibn ᶜAbdallāh Yamanī was chased out of Bukhara for declaring himself Ḥasan Baṣrī's disciple (*Iᶜtidāl*).

Ḥasan begins with the fundamental notion that the social body of Muslim believers (*umma*, "Community") is and must remain one; its distinctive feature is obedience to God, from Whom all power flows. Ḥasan states[256] (1) that all believers owe *equal* respect and obedience to the government's representatives, as long as their official decisions do not contravene the Islamic faith and even if their personal conduct is condemnable (contradicting the Khārijites and Imāmīs); (2) that every believer must , at all cost, remain united in his heart with his brothers; he must continue his brotherly participation in communal life, expressing, openly and without hesitation, the private judgments of his conscience concerning any sin committed by the leaders, in an effort to "advise" (*naṣḥ*) the Community about justice. Ḥasan does not call for tacit secession (*muᶜtazila*, of the year 657) or violence against the government (movement of Ibn Ashᶜath, of the year 700; cf. the Zaydīs). Believers must respect the political order and keep their place in it, even when they have been treated unjustly and find themselves obliged to deplore the personal conduct of those in control. Neither *khurūj* not *katmān*.

Therefore, Abū Bakr's imamate was doubly legitimate,[257] and ᶜUthmān is remembered as innocent.[258] ᶜAlī's election was valid, but he and Ṭalḥa share the guilt for the opening of hostilities in the Camel War. ᶜAlī was wrong to accept the arbitration (*ḥukūmat al-ḥakamayn*) at Ṣiffīn and right to exterminate the Shurāt at Nukhayla.[259] While Ḥasan solemnly exhorts the Baṣrans to remain subject to the Umayyads, he unequivocally observes that Muᶜāwiya has committed five grave offenses against the Community:[260] he

> abandoned the administration to his own creations, the *parvenus*; he monopolized authority without *mashwara*, without consulting either the Companions or the upright people; though he had been elected, he made the caliphate hereditary by leaving it to his son Yazīd, a drunkard with silken clothes who played the guitar; he make Ziyād (who was a bastard son of Muᶜāwiya's father) legitimate; he had Ḥujr [Ibn ᶜAdī] and his companions executed for cursing him twice.

Ḥasan always put his firmness into practice. Muṭarrif said expressively to Qatāda,[261] "Ḥasan is like the man who puts people on guard against the flashflood but stays with them in the riverbed (*wad*) (still dry, but which he knows will soon be submerged)"; Qatāda himself would say, "He for-

256. *Passion*, Fr 3:164–65, 202–3, 205 n 4/Eng 3:152–53, 190–91, 193 n 69.
257. Kīlānī, *Ghunya*, I, 68; Masᶜūdī, *Tanbīh*, 337.
258. Mubarrad, *Kāmil*, II, 144–45.
259. Ibid.; and II, 154.
260. Ṭabarī, II, 146; cf. Lammens, *Mo'āwia*, 104.
261. Ibn Saᶜd, VII, 103.

bade his fellow citizens to revolt, but when the revolt came, he stayed in the city."[262] Ḥasan courageously faced[263] the famous Ḥajjāj (*walī* after 75, d. 95), who was known for his autocratic cruelty. Summoned before Ibn Hubayra, Ḥasan was alone in daring to undercut Yazīd's memory.[264] But he refused, with equal firmness, to take part in the anti-Umayyad insurrection of Ibn al-Ashᶜath (81) or to condone Ibn al-Muhallabs's anti-Syrian excesses (101).[265] He clearly explained that penitence, rather than combat, would obtain divine redress of social injustices.[266] His position, which is mystical in the true sense, went unrecognized by factionalists and skeptics alike. Ibn Shādhān, for example, accused him of "wanting to flatter all parties," and Ibn abī'l-ᶜAwjā reproached him for "being unable to join any particular school."

Ḥasan also emphasized Muḥammad's role as head of state:

> "I call you to God," said Muḥammad to all the clans of the Quraysh. "I announce the imminence of His chastisement. I have been commanded to make war against men until they confess, 'No god but God!' (observe canonical prayer, and pay the legal tithe).[267] If they make the confession, their blood and their property become sacred to me, except as payment for debts incurred (by them). And the right to judge them belongs to God alone."
>
> Fear (*khawf*) guided the Prophet in his conduct with respect to God and prevented him from neglecting His command.[268]
>
> Those who could see Muḥammad saw him depart in the morning and return at dusk, never setting brick upon brick (*libna*) or reed upon reed (*qaṣāba*) (= building neither wall nor fence). A Sign (*ᶜalam*) rose up before him, and he hurried towards it. Save yourselves! Save yourselves! Make haste! Make haste! Where are you straying? Already the best among you are in advance, the Prophet has departed, and as for you, you are viler[269] every day (var.: every year)! Open your eyes! Open your eyes!
>
> Muḥammad had no trivet (on which to place his dishes), no pillow, and no doorman.[270]

Muḥammad is presented by Ḥasan as a warner and precursor; if he is idealized a little, he is also rightly depicted in the vehemence of his prose-

262. "While Muṭarrif gave his warning and then fled." Cf. Ibn Khallikān, I, 140.
263. Their meetings (Ibn Qutayba, *Taʾwīl*, 100; *Aghānī*, IV, 74; Samᶜānī, 397b; Ibn ᶜAbd Rabbihi, *ᶜIqd*, III, 16).
264. While Ibn Sīrīn and Shaᶜbī exercised *taqiyya* (Ibn Khallikān, *loc. cit.*).
265. Ṭabarī, II, 1391.
266. Ibn Saᶜd, VII, 119, 125.
267. *Ḥilya*. The part in parentheses seems to be something Ḥasan added to justify Abū Bakr.
268. Tirmidhī, *ᶜIlal*, 211a; Ibn ᶜAbd Rabbihi, *ᶜIqd*, I, 267.
269. *Tardhilūn*, which became a *ḥadīth* (Suyūṭī, *Durar*, 186).
270. Ṭabarī, III, 2426.

lytizing spirit.[271] Ḥasan professes no devotion to the legitimacy of the Prophet's person or descendents: the Qurʾānic verse 42:22 (*"al-mawadda fī'l-qurbā,"* a favorite argument of the Shiites) does not concern blood relations; the true meaning is, "You must love anyone who, by obeying God, comes close to Him."[272] In a commentary on Qur. 41:33, Ḥasan describes the Prophet as an example, which every believer is able to follow, of obedience to God: "The friend of God! God's intimate, this is he! He whose prayer God answers, he who preaches among men that by which God has answered his prayers, and who acts zealously according to it . . . he is God's lieutenant here below . . ."[273] On the other hand, Ḥasan repeats as a *ḥadīth mursal* of the Prophet the saying, "After me emirs will come who will announce their wisdom from high seats, while their hearts are filthier than carrion."[274] The tradition was directed at some *mulūk* of whom it was said, in Ḥasan's presence, that they excused themselves by claiming, "If our acts are accomplished in this way, it is that God so decreed it," which made Ḥasan cry out, "They have lied, those enemies of God!"[275]

His very rationalistic exegesis of the Qurʾān has marked positivist tendencies, perhaps accentuated by ʿAmr ibn ʿUbayd, the Muʿtazilite editor of the *tafsīr.* It is particularly useful to refer to Ḥasan's refutation of the fables about the first sons of Adam and to his remarks on Abraham, the *ibtilā* and the *mafdī* (Isaac, not Ishmael),[276] and Harūt and Marūt, who are not fallen angels but "non-Arab" princes (*ʿiljān*).[277] With his critical mind, Ḥasan saw the *taḥīyāt* ("salutations") ending the second *rakʿa* of the *ṣalāt* as an islamization of an earlier custom[278] intended for pagan idols.[279] His *qirāʾa* (partially preserved by Ibn Khālawayh) was rich in unusual punctuations and vocalizations. His exegesis, though critical, is firmly realist on several important points. On the vision of God (*ruʾya*), he was almost alone with Ibn ʿAbbās in affirming that it was really the divine essence (and not the angel) that Muḥammad beheld during his night journey.[280] Ḥasan dared to teach that in Paradise the elect would see the unveiled divine essence but without grasping it (*bilā iḥāṭa*).[281] "If the faithful thought that in the next life they would not see God, their hearts would melt with sor-

271. Ṭabarī invokes Ḥasan's testimony to decide several historical points related to the Prophet and his four successors (I, 1013, 1173, 1456, 1835, 1849, 2373, 2560, 2697, etc.).

272. Baqlī, s.v.

273. Baqlī, f. 325b, s.v. Cf. Muḥāsibī, *Naṣāʾiḥ*, 5b.

274. Jāḥiẓ, *Bayān*, I, 88.

275. Ibn Qutayba, *Taʾwīl*, 225; cf. Ibn Saʿd, VII, 125, 127.

276. Ṭabarī, I, 290, 316–17.

277. On Qur. 2:96; Ibn Qutayba, *Taʾwīl*, 223, 264.

278. Tirmidhī, *ʿIlal*, 170b.

279. Cf. Bīrūnī and Ibn Ḥazm on the repulsiveness of the external rites of the *ḥajj*.

280. ʿIyāḍ, *Shifā*, I, 159, 165.

281. Shaʿrāwī, *Ṭab.*, I, 29; which does not imply a contradiction (cf. Spitta, *Asharitentum*, 102).

row in this world!"[282] he does not appear to have broached the theological problem of the *ṣifāt* (divine attributes), and his Muᶜtazilite disciples, when presenting them, followed Jahm's detailed treatment.[283]

A few things should be kept in mind. Ḥasan's reading of the Quʾrān is a kind of dynamic meditation in which he assimilates the commandments that the sacred text has addressed to the prophets, and asks his disciples to apply these commandments to themselves.[284] Like Ubayy and Ibn Masᶜūd, he generalizes the "*mithl nūrihī*" (24:35) by means of the gloss "*fī qalb al-muʾmin.*"[285] On Qur. 102:1 he comments, "Your haste to haggle and ask higher prices (in the market) has made you postpone your visit to the tombs"; on Ṣāliḥ's camel (11:70) he says, "One man alone killed the camel, and yet God enveloped the entire people in punishment, as he had enveloped them in grace (by sending a messenger)."[286] "Indulgences" for reciting the Quʾrān, such as guaranteed forgiveness in exchange for reading Sura 36 at night, are attributed to him.[287]

Ḥasan Baṣrī counsels the strictest observance of ritual. But he demands that everyone precisely control all actions, not ritual alone. For him, the essential thing in an act is the intent (*niyya*),[288] which must be purified (*ikhlāṣ*) of vainglory (*riyā*).[289] Ḥasan puts the spirit before the letter, the *sunna* before the *farḍ*; his teaching, rooted in morals, blooms into an ascetic method of introspection. I have elsewhere examined his famous solution[290] of the mixed legal status of the *fāsiq* (the believer guilty of a grave offense), whose sin suspends him, making him susceptible to damnation like a hypocrite (*munāfiq*), until he has repented; Wāṣil and the Muᶜtazilites found a weaker solution, putting the *fāsiq* in a state of neutral equilibrium in which his heart has the freedom of complete indifference.[291]

Ḥasan does not possess the traditional list of five *farāʾiḍ* (established by Shāfiᶜī), but at least he recognizes, in addition to the *shahāda*, which is intended for God, eight canonical social obligations,[292] "about which there

282. According to ᶜAbd al-Wāḥid ibn Zayd (*Passion*, Fr 3:172–73, 178/Eng 3:159–60, 166).

283. According to what Ibn Ḥanbal says (*Radd*, f. 2b).

284. Cf. his prayer taken from Qur. 12:38 (Murtaḍā, *Munya*, 15).

285. Nöldeke, *Gesch. Qur.*, 273.

286. Jāḥiẓ, *Bayān*, III, 69 (cf. *risāla* said to be Ḥasan's), 67.

287. Since it contains the verse of the "fiat."

288. The *ḥadīth* at the beginning of Bukhārī's *Ṣaḥīḥ*: "Certainly works depend upon intent," even if "intent" is taken in the Ḥanafite sense of "premeditation of a ritual gesture," seems to be an echo of Ḥasan's statement, given herein (see below; n 299 and related text), "The intent is more effective than the work."

289. *Passion*, Fr 3:161, 164, 167–68/Eng 3:149, 152, 155.

290. Improved from that of Abū Bayhas (d. 94; Mubarrad, *Kāmil*, II, 179; Brünnow, *Charidschiten*, 30–31).

291. *Passion*, Fr 3:188–91/Eng 3:176–79; Ṭabarī, III, 2489; Jāḥiẓ, *Bayān*, III, 69; Kīlānī, *Ghunya*, I, 80; *Farq*, 97; Murtaḍā, *Munya*, 23; Shaᶜrāwī, *Ṭab.*, I, 29.

292. Ibn Baṭṭa ᶜUkbarī, *Sharḥ*.

is to be no discussion with innovators (*ṣāḥib bidᶜa*): the fast, prayer, the pilgrimage, the spiritual retreat at Mecca (*ᶜumra*), alms, holy war, barter (*ṣarf*), and arbitration (*ᶜadl*)." He places the *ᶜumra* on the same level as the *ḥajj*; he establishes the rituals of *shufᶜa* and *ghusl*.[293] He declares that legal sanctions cover sodomy and gives a supporting analogy (*ḥadd al-lūṭī = ḥadd al-zānī*), the oldest example of a syllogism (*qiyās*) in Islamic law.[294] He is very strict on the rules governing legal marriage (*nikāḥ*), and he tries to make Farazdaq divorce his wife.[295] For his disapproval of mixed gatherings, at which the poets of Baṣra used to meet in the company of married women, Ibn Burd (d. 167) calls him a *qiss* ("priest").[296]

His spoken rules for the correct ordering of daily human contact in the communal life (*muᶜashara*) were codified later by either the Bakriyya[297] or the Ṣūfiyya. The rules taught both groups that at all times the *dīn* (practice of religion) should include not only the canonical works but also certain ascetic restrictions (on eating) and works of mutual brotherly aid. For example, Ḥasan said to a man who wanted to leave a funeral procession because he saw that weeping women were approaching (the lament is a blameworthy innovation), "If you deprive yourself of a good action every time you perceive a sin, how can you make quick steps in religious practice. (*dīn*)?"[298] For Ḥasan, *adab* is more important than *farḍ*, "intent is more effective (for salvation) than works."[299] "It is because the believer thinks well of God that his works are good; it is because the hypocrite thinks ill (*sūᵓ al-ẓann*) of God that his works are evil."[300] Therefore he held the doctrine, which was answered sharply by the Ibāḍites, that it was very important for a dying man to say the *shahāda*.[301] Lax Muslims later drew from this recommendation (to put all confidence not in one's own works but in final thoughts of God)[302] the illusory and expedient Murjiᵓite "justification by faith." That thesis is very far from Ḥasan's thinking; for him faith is vacillating and intermittent; it must be revived constantly in the heart[303] by explicit acts of submission to God, such as the one with which he used

293. Ibn Qutayba, *Taᵓwīl*, 287, 251.

294. Haytham Dūrī, *Dhamm al-liwāṭ*; Qāsimī, *Majmūᶜ mutūn uṣūliyya*, 21 n 3, 120 n 4.

295. Ṭabarī, III, 2493; *Aghānī*, XVIII, 14, 47.

296. *Aghānī*, III, 34.

297. *Farq*, 201; Ibn Qutayba, *Taᵓwīl*, 179.

298. Jāḥiẓ, *Bayān*, II, 39.

299. *Qūt*, II, 152.

300. *Ḥilya*. The *ḥadīth* quoted by Nabhānī (*Jāmiᶜ*, no. 30) deforms the saying as follows: "I conform to what my servant thinks of Me: if he thinks well, the good is his; if he thinks ill, the evil is his."

301. His words to the dying Jābir Juᶜfī (in 96), in Shammākhī, trans. Masqueray, 182 n.

302. Who will come forth as a Judge of the separated soul (cf. *Passion*, Fr 3:246–47/Eng 3:232–33).

303. His resulting theses of necessary *istithnā* (*Iḥyā*, I, 91) and of *tafḍīl al-faqīr* (*Passion*, Fr 3:100–101 notes/Eng 3:89–90 notes).

to end meetings: as Ibn ᶜAwn reports, after telling a parable, Ḥasan would make it understood (*bi'l maᶜānī*)[304] by means of the concluding invocation, "O God, see in our hearts associationism, pride, hypocrisy, vainglory (of the eyes and ears), confusion, even doubt in Your religion! O Transformer of hearts, strengthen our hearts in Your religion,[305] make of our rites a true Islam!"[306]

Ḥasan took this position against two series of adversaries. First, against the routine and the blindly emotional pietism of certain Ḥashwiyya traditionists. He clearly disapproved of their *qiṣaṣ*, parables, when these became emotive sessions and chanted oratorios (*samāᶜ*); also their litanies (*awrād*) not based upon the Qurᵓān but composed according to personal taste, and their prolonged visits to cemeteries (*qubūr*). With sarcastic irony, he expressed mistrust of anything not rationally justifiable. Ibn Qutayba reports that, with Ḥasan present, one *muḥaddith*, Abū Salama ibn ᶜAbd al-Raḥmān, recounted the tradition, "according to Abū Hurayra, that the sun and the moon, on the Day of Judgement, would be turned upside down in Hell, like two bulls at the slaughterhouse!" Ḥasan said simply, "For what sin?" The traditionist insisted, "I have this on the Prophet's authority!" Ḥasan was silent, but the congregation was saying as one, "But Ḥasan is right. For what sin?"[307]

It was Ḥasan's principal polemic to attack the pharisaism of the doctors of the law, *fuqahā*, whose knowledge and works were devoid of all sincere intent; Farqad Sinjī recorded his invective against these frauds.[308] For Ḥasan, knowledge of the Qurᵓān was not an end in itself but a means to live better. "Faith is not an ornament to wear or a fashion to follow; it is what the heart venerates, it is the truth confirmed in our acts."[309]

> No man has true faith as long as he allows himself to reproach others for a fault he commits, or to decree for them a reform he has not adopted within himself. If he makes the decision, if he begins, there is no reformed fault that does not make him discover another offense to reform within himself. If he makes this resolution, he will concentrate on his own concerns, and not on the faults of others.[310]

The latter statement is not merely psychological analysis. It has moral

304. Ibn Saᶜd, VII, 115.

305. This saying became a *ḥadīth*.

306. Ibn Saᶜd, VII, 128.

307. Ibn Qutayba, *Taᵓwīl*, 121. The *muḥaddith*, Abū Salama ibn ᶜAbd al-Raḥmān, was the grandson of Ibn ᶜAwf (parallel story in Goldziher, *Richt.*, 68 with Kaᶜb in the role of Ibn ᶜAwf [*sic*: Massignon must mean "the role of Abū Salama"] and Ibn ᶜAbbās in that of Ḥasan).

308. *Qūt*, I, 153; attenuated ap. *Iḥyā*, III, 272, and *ᶜAwārif*, I, 63.

309. Famous statement [*Recueil*, p. 4], later attributed to Abū Bakr; the Wahhābīs used it.

310. Jāḥiẓ, *Bayān*, III, 70.

range; its intellectual midwifery is authentically Socratic and gently leads the hearer to the threshold of an examination of conscience. It is the link to Ḥasan's ascetic and mystical doctrine.

— "You — would you be satisfied with the state (*ḥāl*) in which you are now, if you were in it when death surprised you?"

— "No."

— "Do you struggle with yourself, do you strive to move from this state to another, in which you would be well disposed towards death, in case death were to come?"

— "Certainly I do, but not seriously."

— "After death, is there another place (besides this world) where you could ask for mercy?"

— "No."

— "Have you ever seen a sensible man satisfied with himself in the condition that satisfies you now?"[311]

D. His Ascetic and Mystical Doctrines

Ḥasan begins with disdain for this passing life and this perishing world, because the Prophets disdained it, and because God disdains what He has created separate from Himself.[312] "Be with this world as if you had never been in it, and with the next as if you were never to leave it." "O man, sell your present life for your life to come, and you will earn both lives; do not sell your life to come for your present life, for you would lose them both."[313] "God has put at his creatures' disposal three things,[314] which have become objects of their rejection (*taraᵓik*), but without which neither the prophets nor the solitary men (*ahl-al-inqiṭāᶜ*) would gain from their stay in this world. They are hope, death (*ajal*), and the night vigil (*sahar*)."[315] "What do you think of this world? Encountering its sorrows has prevented me from tasting its delights."[316]

His rule for living is characterized by scrupulous denial (*waraᶜ*)[317] and strict renunciation of all legally dubious actions (*shubuhāt*); more than that, it is asceticism (*zuhd*), a complete and universal abandonment of the world and all that perishes. In the self this is translated into continuous sorrow

311. Ibid., III, 72 [*Recueil*, p. 5].

312. Cf. the statement of Abū'l-Dardā quoted above [see n. 109 and related text], which is used again in the *risāla* said to be Ḥasan's (*Ḥilya*).

313. Jāḥiẓ, *Bayān*, II; 34; III, 68.

314. Ibid., III, 86.

315. Saying taken up by ᶜUtba: "Hope and the night vigil are two exceptional graces for the sons of Adam."

316. Versified by Abū'l-ᶜAtāhiya (*Dīwān*, 169).

317. Opp. *ṭamᶜ*.

(*ḥuzn*);* Thawrī learned from Yūnus that "Ḥasan was invaded by sorrow." "Continuous sorrow in this world is what makes a pious act fertile (*talqīḥ*)," he used to say. In addition to the scrupulous renunciation (*wara*ᶜ) that is the basis of religious ritual (*aṣl al-dīn*),[318] Ḥasan recommends fear (*khawf*) of God, because "nothing develops piety better," and attentive listening to the divine word (*istimā*ᶜ,[319] a "science that can be learned"). Then he lays the foundations of the "science of hearts" (ᶜ*ilm al-qulūb*) or mystical psychology.[320] The introduction of the notion of *ḥāl*, mental state, has been discussed above; Ḥasan also perceives the two motive forces of free choice (*khāṭirān*), the two types of suggestion (*waswās*),[321] and the two stable forms of a decision taken (*hamm*).[322] His definitions of the examination of conscience (*muḥāsaba*)[323] prepare the way for *Muḥāsibī's*: "The examination on the Day of Judgment will weigh lightly on those who have examined themselves in this world."

> When a believer suddenly comes upon something pleasing to him, he cries out, "Certainly you are pleasing to me, and I feel the need for you! Yet beware the ambush between you and me . . ." That is an examination *before* action. Then, when something has escaped him and he is taken aback, he says, "How could I have done that? Surely I shall never remove my guilt for it. No, I shall never come back to it, if it please God."

The constant operation of intellectual reflection (*fikr*)[324] in the believer's life is Ḥasan's base. "Reflection is the mirror that makes you see what is good and bad in yourself."[325] His sermons, which invite meditation almost entirely without the forming of sensuous images, are mostly calls to examine the conscience.[326] His most famous sayings are quoted here:

i.

Ah! If only I could find life in your hearts! Men have become like specters; I perceive a murmur, but I see nothing that loves. Tongues are brought to me

* "Attrition" in the religious sense. Massignon's translations for *ḥuzn* are *attrition* and *chargrin* or sorrow.

318. ᶜAṭṭār, I, 27.
319. Jāḥiẓ, *Bayān*, II, 154.
320. *Passion*, Fr 3:119–20, 168–69; 130, 118/Eng 3:107–9, 156–57; 118, 106.
321. In Tustarī, *Tafsīr*, 100.
322. Ghazālī, *Iḥyā*, II, 21.
323. Ibid., IV, 289.
324. Tirmidhī claims that Ḥasan even applied the Greek theory of the four temperaments to explain the influence of the fast on character (ᶜ*Ilal*, f. 209a).
325. As quoted by Ibn ᶜ*Iyāḍ* (in *Ḥilya*, s.n.).
326. His theory of *tadhakkur* (according to Ṣafadī, in Khūnsārī, II, 211).

in abundance, but I am looking for hearts. Your intellects go astray, seeking the butterflies of hell and the flies of covetousness.[327]

ii.

O son of Adam! Your religious life! Your religious life! That is your flesh and blood! O son of Adam! Glutton, glutton! You hoard and hoard wealth in the cellar of your house, you nourish your avarice, ride softened mounts and wear fine clothes ... May God have mercy on the man who is not shaken when he sees the actions of the multitude! O son of Adam! You will die alone! You will enter the tomb alone! You will be revived alone and judged alone! O son of Adam, it is you that are watched here,[328] it is you that I accuse (now)!

iii.

Converse with your hearts and maintain them, for they are quick to rust. Humble your carnal souls, for they tend to raise themselves up.[329]

This semi-public teaching had immense resonance. Islam has never known more sober and beautiful sermons (*khuṭab*), and Jāḥiẓ, as penetrating a judge as there has ever been, describes them as peerless in his *Bayān*.[330] An official *khaṭīb*, ᶜAnbarī, would soon found the art of Sunni homiletics on them. In comparison, the rasping, rebellious preaching of the Khārijites[331] displays superficial violence and hasty, shallow psychology. The sermons of the other mystics, Ṣāliḥ Murrī, ᶜAbd al-Wāḥid ibn Zayd, Manṣūr ibn ᶜAmmār, and Kīlānī, employ various points of eschatology, visions either terrifying or seductive, in order to disturb the imagination and reach the will. Ḥallāj, in his speeches of 296/908, is a lover of God wishing to rejoice in Him "beyond joy," in a vulgar world that does not recognize such love. But Ḥasan's sermons are addressed to the listeners' intelligence alone,[332] so that their will may be attracted; he succinctly and powerfully summons them to retire into themselves.[333] His

327. Jāḥiẓ, *Bayān*, III, 69; Ibn ᶜabd Rabbihi, *ᶜIqd*, I, 287.

328. Cf. the similar pronouncement of Muṭarrif (in Ibn ᶜArabī, *Muḥāḍ*, II, 281).

329. Jāḥiẓ, *Bayān*, I, 162; var.: "Hold a tight leash on your carnal souls, which are escaping; resist them, for if you yield to them, they will drag you to ruin. Sharpen them (the word "hearts" is missing here) with recollection (*dhikr*), for they are swift to lose their edge."

330. Ibid., I, 162; III, 68–72. Cf. Ṭabarī, III, 1400.

331. Ibn ᶜabd Rabbihi, *ᶜIqd*, II, 138–39.

332. "The wise man does not concern himself with opinion; if his wisdom is approved, he praises God; if it is disapproved, he praises God" (quotation ap. Ghulām Khalīl, *Sharḥ al-sunna* [and *Recueil*, p. 3]).

333. Cf. his anecdotes: his four amazements (ap. ᶜAṭṭār) [he was amazed by a child, a drunk, a *mukhannith*, and a woman]; the two tombs confused (Jāḥiẓ, *Bayān*, III, 76); his smile as he died (ap. ᶜAṭṭār).

phrases are condensed judgments, robust and sinewy; he resorts to assonance (*saj*ᶜ) only as often as the thought allows; he sacrifices nothing to style. Ḥasan is known to have had contempt for literary "inspiration,"[334] the "satanic" instinct that pushed Farazdaq to sharpen his satires and Ibn Rabīᶜa (d. 100) to sing of the physical charms of Qurayshī beauties.[335]

His sermons had consequences not only on morals and literature but also on the formation of dogma. For him the human personality is defined, essentially, not as a body composed of members but as a living, sapient heart (*qalb*). Here Ḥasan represents the beginning of Islamic spiritualism, soon to be clearly developed by ᶜAmr ibn Fāᵓid Uswārī.[336] The problem of the creation of human acts is also addressed in the sermons. God invests men with their actions, but this investiture (*tafwīḍ*)[337] becomes real and fertile only when men submit to the conditions of the covenant (*mīthāq*).[338] "God does not punish[339] in order (arbitrarily) to see His sanctions operate; he punishes infractions against His precepts." Therefore, the problems of *arzāq* and *ajāl*, and of *qadar*, are raised; I have shown[340] that Ḥasan, after some vacillation, clearly repudiated the Qadarī doctrine that his Muᶜtazilī disciples would later dilute and adopt. His pronouncements on the subject prepared the way for, but were not as distinct as, those of his mystic disciples, Miṣrī, Kharrāz, and Ḥallāj.

Between predestination and responsibility, between decree and precept, there is an apparent conflict. For Ḥasan it can be resolved by creating within oneself a special mystical state, *riḍā*, reciprocal acceptance and contentment between God and the soul. *Riḍā* is the name given in the Quᵓrān to the "state of grace" sought by the old Christian monks in their *rahbāniyya* (monastic life). This search for the perfect life before death made Imāmīs indignant. Abū Ḥamza Thumālī describes Imām Zayn al-ᶜAbidīn's irritation at seeing Ḥasan lay a claim to the sanctity that the Imāms considered their privilege.[341] An extremely important *ḥadīth qudsī* of Ḥasan, transmitted by ᶜAbd al-Wāḥid ibn Zayd,[342] says,

334. *Aghānī*, XVIII, 33; Yāqūt, *Udabā*, II, 389; Tagrib., 275, 299.

335. The only two lines of poetry later attributed to him are in fact by Muᶜrūf and Abū'l-ᶜAtāhiya (*Dīwān*, 96; cf. *Aghānī*, XVIII, 14; XIX, 15).

336. *Passion*, Fr 3:23/Eng 3:16.

337. Bāqir, ap. Ṭabarsī, *Iḥtijāj*, 167–68, 210, 231, 243; Ibn Qutayba, *Taᵓwīl*, 5; Baqlī, II, 213; Junayd, *Dawā* [*Recueil*, p. 4].

338. The expression *mīthāq al-ᶜulamā* (copied from the Covenant of the Prophets) is used by Ḥudhayfa and Ḥasan (Ibn Saᶜd, VII, 115; Ṭabarī, III, 2490).

339. *Passion*, Fr 3:130/Eng 3:118.

340. Ibid., Fr 3:120–21/Eng 3:108–9; Yāfiᶜī, *Marham*, I, 69–72; Malaṭī, 332.

341. Ṭabarsī, *Iḥtijāj*, 161.

342. *Ḥilya*, in which he is mentioned as a *gharīb*. Perhaps Mālik ibn Dīnār was already alluding to this *ḥadīth* when he claimed to have read in the Torah (*sic*): "We have incited you to desire Us, and you have not desired Us . . ."

As soon as My dear servant's[343] first care becomes the remembrance of Me, I make him find happiness and joy in remembering Me. And when I have made him find happiness and joy in remembering Me, he desires Me and I desire him, (*ᶜashiqanī wa ᶜashiqtuhu*). And when he desires Me and I desire him, I raise the veils between him and Me, and I become a cluster of knowable things (*maᶜālimā*) before his eyes.

Such men do not forget Me, when others forget Me. Their word is the word of the prophets, and they are the true heroes.[344] When I wish to inflict a calamity upon the inhabitants of the earth, they are the ones I remember in time to spare the earth that calamity.

This *ḥadīth* deserves reflection. It established a gradation in the mystical graces and an experimental method of sanctification that would be filled out in detail by Ibn Adham, and especially by Ḥallāj.[345] The word *ᶜishq*, "passionate desire," is noteworthy. It was the only word allowed by ᶜAbd al-Wāḥid ibn Zayd for speaking of God. He rejected the word *maḥabba*, "favorite love," as an unworthy Judeo-Christian survival[346] showing too much confidence in divine "favor" ([*niᶜmat Allah*] Qur. 5:20). Mālik ibn Dīnār, Muḍar Qārī, and Miṣrī suggested the term *shawq*, covetous love; *ḥabb* (*taḥabbub, maḥabba*) was nevertheless recommended by Abān ibn abī ᶜAyyāsh, Yazīd Raqqāshī, the pseudo-Jaᶜfar, and Rābiᶜa, and its triumph was sealed with Maᶜrūf and Muḥāsibī.

Here is another of Ḥasan's *ḥadīth*:[347]

Some servants of God can already see the elect who are in Paradise forever, and the damned tortured in Hell; these servants' hearts are contrite, their pains do not trouble them, their needs are light, their souls continent. They endure with patience, like a long rest, what few days they know are left to them. They pass the night in silent attentiveness . . . awake (for prayer); tears run down their cheeks, and they implore their Lord, "*Rabbunā*! *Rabbunā*!" During the day they are restrained, knowledgeable, pious, experienced. When examined, they are taken for sick men, but it is not they who are sick. Or, if they are indeed stricken by a disease, it is the disease of meditation on the next world, which has struck deep.

E. His Posthumous Influence

The attacks against Ḥasan Baṣrī began during his lifetime. Among Sunni moderates, even Ayyūb Sikhtiyānī, a disciple and friend, once capriciously

343. Diminutive: Ḥasan liked to use such names (Furayqid, Muwaylik).
344. Text: *abṭāl*. Should this not be corrected to read *abdāl*? Cf. ch. 1, sec. 2, under *BDL*.
345. *Passion*, Fr 3:48, 218/Eng 3:40, 206.
346. Ibn Taymiyya, in ms. Damascus Ẓah. taṣ 129, sec. VII.
347. Preserved by Zayādī. Quoted from the *Ḥilya*.

said that Ḥasan had split from the Qadarīs "on my advice, from fear of the police." Ḥamīd Khuzaʿī notes that the caprice was "regrettable for Ayyūb."[348] Indeed, it was simplistic and fatuous. Ayyūb also criticized some of Ḥasan's *isnād*.[349] Like Muṭarrif, he rejected Ḥasan's thesis of "the superiority of poverty."[350] Yielding to Abū Qulāba Jarmī's (d. 104)[351] exhortations on the subject, Ayyūb decided that it was necessary to find a trade, because "ease alone procures tranquility of spirit."[352]

Muḥammad Ibn Sīrīn (d. 110), another notable Sunni,[353] a castrator of sheep by trade,[354] disagreed with Ḥasan on many points. Ibn Sīrīn would not admit that a grave sin could put a believer in danger of damnation (*ashadd rajaʾan*, as opposed to *waʿīd*, *khawf*, according to Ḥasan);[355] he tolerated *taqiyya* in case of danger (as opposed to Ḥasan's *naṣḥ*, *iḥtisāb*);[356] he condoned certain purely emotive devotional practices, anecdotes (*qiṣaṣ*),[357] visions (*ruʾyā*), prayers in cemeteries, litanies (*awrād*, sing. *wird*),[358] oratorios (*samāʿ*); he rejected only artificial ecstasy accompanied by loud exclamations. Ḥasan condemned all of these things together as *bidaʿ* (heretical innovations).[359] We have already discussed Ḥasan's polemic against Ibn Sīrīn on the respective merits of *ṣūf*[360] and *quṭn*. In meetings (*majālis*) where Ḥasan spoke, the only subject was the life to come. Ibn Sīrīn led discussions[361] of historical traditions (such as the anecdote about ʿUdhrī love told by Ayyūb),[362] and his pietism bears no trace of the mystical desire for the divine perfections that explodes within Ḥasan.

Mālik pronounced in favor of Ibn Sīrīn, whom he greatly admired, and against Ḥasan, "whom the Qadarites led astray."[363] Ibn Ḥanbal, less preju-

348. Ibn Saʿd, VII, 122.

349. Ibn Qutayba, *Taʾwīl*, 93, 120.

350. Ibid., 211.

352. Who left him four recommendations: "No individual *raʾy* in *tafsīr*; excommunicate the Qadarites; be silent about the Companions (see *Passion*, Fr 3:223 n 6/Eng 3:211 n 261); allow no heretics among your listeners, for they would denature the meaning of your words" (Ibn Baṭṭa ʿUkbarī). This is the same Abū Qulāba whose authority is invoked by Ibn Saʿd (via Ḥammād ibn Zayd) for the phrase, which the Prophet is supposed to have said to ʿUthmān ibn Maẓʿūn, opposing *ḥanīfiyya samḥa* to *rahbāniyya* (see above, n 37–38 and related text).

352. Ibn Qutayba, *Maʿārif*, 228.

353. Ibn Saʿd, VII, 140–50.

354. Maʾlūf, ap. *Muqtabas*, VI, 316.

355. Ibn Saʿd, VII, 144.

356. Ibid., 118; Ibn Khallikān, I, 140.

357. Ḥājj Khalīfa (s.v., *zuhd*) remarks that Ḥasan was not a *qāṣṣ*.

358. *Qūt*, I, 81.

359. *Qūt*, I, 149; Ibn Saʿd, VII, 128 (against raising the voice or stretching out the hands during prayer).

360. See above, n 75–77 and related text. Ibn Saʿd, in contrast, has Ḥasan condemn the *ṣūf* (VII, 123); obviously a polemicist's invention (Muḥāsibī, *Riʿāya*, 111a).

361. Ibn Saʿd, VII, 121.

362. Sarrāj, *Maṣāriʿ*, 8; Ibn Qutayba, *Taʾwīl*, 411.

363. Ṭabarī, III, 2492.

diced, recognized that "Ḥasan never doubted the divine predetermination of all calamities (*muṣība*)";[364] Ḥasan would then be the father of the semi-Qadarism professed by Ja^cfar and Ibn Sālim. I think we can go further and state[365] that his supposed Qadarism is a legend, which his Mu^ctazilī disciples and Ḥashwiyya adversaries collaborated to invent.

He was reproached by the Khārijites, "who hated him,"[366] because of his disdain for their pragmatism (*tafḍīl al-niyya; shahāda*), his solution to the problem of the *fāsiq*, and his condemnation of all their rebellions.

The Imāmīs reproached him[367] for his criticisms of ^cAlī's policies; his "neutrality" between ^cAlī and Mu^cāwiya; his thesis that the dead of both parties (^cAlī, Ṭalḥa) in the "Camel War" were damned;[368] his requirement to practice "fraternal correction" (*wa^cẓ*), as opposed to their "permitted dissimulation" (*katmān*); his mystical doctrines of *riḍā* and *tafwīḍ*; his "concessions" to the Qadarīs and Jabarīs (which he did not make).

Not Ḥasan, but his disciples, were persecuted by Ḥashwiyya and Mālikite Sunni literalists for guiding ideas concerning the importance of meditation (*fikr*) in the religious life, and the reciprocal love (*khulla*) to be desired between God and the soul. Not daring to accuse Ḥasan directly, they maintained an acrimonious reserve for this great man, the patriarch of Islamic mysticism, whom Abū Ṭālib Makkī compares to Abraham.[369]

The people did not forget him. The Islamic orders of the following centuries called him their founder and the *ghawth*[370] of his time. The trade brotherhoods made him their seventh shaykh[371] and even, at times, their *pīr*.[372]

His disciples may be classified under three headings:

i) The mystics, those I believe to be the most faithful interpreters of his thought: Ibn Wāsi^c, Farqad, Abān, Yazīd Raqqāshī; Ibn Dīnār; Bunānī and Ḥabīb ^cAjamī. Then, at one remove, Ibn Dīnār's students: ^cUtba (d. 167), Rabāḥ, Rābi^ca, and especially ^cAbd al-Wāḥid ibn Zayd.[373] In the third

364. Yāfi^cī, *Marham*, I, 72; on the antithesis *iṣāba-khaṭā*, see *Passion*, Fr 3:126 n 3/Eng 3:114 n 115.

365. Ḥasan considers that Adam's sin was foreseen (Yāfi^cī, *Marham*; I, 70).

366. Ibn Sa^cd, VII, 127; see above, n 256 and related text. Aḥnaf ibn Qays had also been against them.

367. See above, text and notes at n 259 and n 341.

368. Ibn Shādhān.

369. *Qūt*, I, 149. See the very penetrating judgement on Ḥasan and Muḥāsibī (cf. *Passion*, Fr 2:370 n 1/Eng 2:352 n 109) by J. Leo Africanus.

370. ^cAṭṭār, Pavet trans., 29.

371. ^cUbaydallāh Rifā^cī, *Kitāb al-futuwwa* (written in 1082 A.H.).

372. "*Pīr al-mashā^ɔikh*" according to the chant of initiation into the trade (*zajal fi'l-shadd*, in Bouriant, *Recueil de chansons*, popular Arab songs, 1893, 5–7). The Yazīdī sect makes him their *Shaykh Sīn*, perhaps identifying him with the ancient Semitic god of the Moon.

373. See below, sec. 5. A.

generation, Ibn Zayd's students: the Bakriyya theological school, founded by his nephew and two eminent thinkers, the theologian Wakīᶜ and the mystic Dārānī.

ii) The Muᶜtazilīs, with their precursor, Abū'l-Khaṭṭāb Qatāda ibn Diᶜāma Sudūsī (d. 117), and their two founders, Abū ᶜUthmān ᶜAmr ibn ᶜUbayd ibn Bāb (d. 143) and Abū Ḥudhayfa Wāṣil ibn ᶜAṭā Ghazzāl (81–131). The overly famous legend according to which Ḥasan, in the manner of a village pedant, solemnly pronounced the excommunication of one or another of these three "dissidents" (*muᶜtazila*),[374] seems to be derived from a false etymology.[375] If such an event had occurred, neither Qatāda[376] nor ᶜAmr could have continued to consider Ḥasan[377] his master.[378] Finally there is Wāṣil, whose young age (twenty years) at the time of Ḥasan's last sermon suffices to refute the anecdote about him.[379] On three fundamental points, the Muᶜtazila strayed from Ḥasan's teaching: *fāsiq munāfiq, amr* distinct from *ḥukm, tafḍīl al-niyya.*

iii) Some Sunni *muḥaddithūn*: Ayyūb Sikhtiyānī (d. 131), and Ḥammād ibn Salama (d. 165), who was the teacher of ᶜAbd al-Karīm ibn abī'l-ᶜAwjā (d. 167), an unusual, original mind. Ibn abī'l-ᶜAwjā abandoned Ḥasan's doctrine, then briefly became a disciple of Jaᶜfar;[380] it is said he died a skeptic. To justify abandoning Ḥasan's doctrine, he would say, "My teacher was an eclectic, sometimes a Qadarī, sometimes a Jabarī; I do not think he ever adopted a firm doctrine."[381]

Ḥasan Baṣrī is the author responsible for several statements that now have the force of law in Islam. Taken for *ḥadīth* of the Prophet, they were incorporated into the *Ṣiḥāḥ*: *"Yā muqallib al-qulūb"*; *"Kull ᶜāmm tardhilūna"*; *"Tarjīḥ midād al-ᶜulamā"*; *"Man ᶜashiqanī."*[382]

4. The *Tafsīr* Attributed to Imām Jaᶜfar[383]

A. The Current State of the Textual Problem

In third-century "Sufi" mystic circles in Kūfa and Baghdād, some moral

374. The opposite story is also told: Ḥasan puts his Ḥashwiyya listeners "in penitence" (Ālūsī, *Jalā*, 236).

375. They "split from us" on the question of the *fāsiq*. The true etymology is *iᶜtizāl bayn al-manzilatayn* (*Passion*, Fr 3:189 n 6/Eng 3:177 n 37).

376. Who had first said, *"fāsiq = munāfiq"* (Murtaḍā, *Munya*, 23).

377. Makkī, *Qūt*, I, 106.

378. Ayyūb put ᶜAmr ibn ᶜUbayd on the index, as, in imitation of him, did Abū Ḥanīfa, Ibn al-Mubārak and Mālik (Harawī, *Dhamm*, 127a).

379. Steiner, *Mutaziliten*, 25.

380. See below, p. 141.

381. Ṭabarsī, *Iḥtijāj*, 172 [*Recueil*, p. 4].

382. Cf. ch. 3, sec. 5. B.

383. Abū ᶜAbdallāh Jaᶜfar Ṣādiq ibn abī Jaᶜfar Muḥammad Bāqir, b. 83/702, d. Medina, Shaw-

ḥadīth attributed to the sixth Imām, Jaᶜfar[384] (d. 148), giving mystical explanations of various obscure points in the Quᵓrān, began to circulate. In the following century they would come to constitute a *musnad min ṭarīq ahl al-bayt*[385] (a body of sayings of the Prophet collected and conserved by his family), a grandiose title for *ḥadīth* that must in fact be *marāsil*, because, as the *Ibāḍites* remark, the fourth Imām had no opportunity to hear anything from his father. Yaḥyā Qaṭṭān and Bukhārī reject Jaᶜfar's *ḥadīth en masse*; strangely, they are accepted by some rigid Mālikīs, such as ᶜIyāḍ[386] (see below for an explanation). Ibn Ḥanbal also accepts some of them.[387]

After Fuḍayl ibn ᶜIyāḍ,[388] the first of the Sunnis to mention them is Dhū'l-Nūn Miṣrī, who claims to have received them, through Faḍl ibn Ghānim Khuzaᶜī, from Mālik,[389] who is supposed to have received them from Jaᶜfar himself.[390] This chain seems very strange, and the composition of the collection of *ḥadīth* is still mysterious. Its authority, thanks to Miṣrī's edition, was considerable. Sulamī, in the preface to his *Ḥaqāᵓiq al-tafsīr*, speaks of Jaᶜfar's commentary as "detached verses, arranged in no order," but he quotes numerous passages from the text established by Ibn ᶜAṭā.[391]

---

wāl, 148/765. Jaᶜfar, a descendant of both ᶜAlī and Abū Bakr, is one of the only Shiite Imāms to be venerated in traditional Sunni devotional practice. The name *jaᶜfarī* was suggested for the Shiite religion in case Nādir Shāh's reconciliation had succeeded in permitting the placement of a fifth *muṣallā* for Shiism, next to the four Sunni ones at the Kaᶜba. The Sunnis accept the *kutub al-jafr, al-katf*, under his name. The Zaydīs have occasionally obtained this fifth *muṣallā* (Snouck, *Mekka*, I, 68).

384. Among the *ḥadīth qudsī* attributed to Jaᶜfar, specifically among those he received from Jābir (who is buried at Madāᵓin in the same grave as Salmān and Ḥudhayfa) and transmitted to ᶜAbdallāh ibn Maymūn Qaddāḥ (*Ḥilya*, III, 202; *Iᶜtidāl*, s.v.), there is one of considerable importance in dogma. In it, God says to the *qabḍa maᶜlūma* (= the handful of matter from which He made all of the elect), *"kūnī Muḥammadan, fa kānat,"* "'Be Muḥammad,' and it became him." This word *kūnī* (Muṣṭ. Yf. Salām, *jawāhir al-iṭṭilāᶜ* . . . *ᶜalā matn Abī Shujāᶜ*, Cairo, Tadāmun, 1350, p. 123) is the feminine of the Qurᵓānic word *kun* (be = fiat); it is directed at the first of human creatures, the "white pearl" (*durra bayḍā*) of another *ḥadīth*, the *ewigweibliches*, the sign of Mary (cf. "Textes prémonitoires et commentaires mystiques relatifs à la prise de Constantinople par les Turcs en 1453," in *Oriens*, VI, Leiden, 1953, 10–17. It is quite remarkable that early Qarmathian doctrine sees the *kūnī* as the first divine emanation (Van Arendonk, *De Opkomst . . . in Yemen*, 1919, 304–6), while a Sufi like Manṣūr ibn ᶜAmmār can make it a personification of the perfect houri of Paradise, "to whom the Creator of the human race said, *'kūnī, fakānat'*" (ap. Sarrāj, *Maṣāriᶜ*, 1301, 127, l. 14; note that Manṣūr ibn ᶜAmmār, the *rāwī* of Abū Hāshim Kūfī, was the teacher of ᶜAlī ibn Muwaffaq [d. 265; *Ḥilya*, IX, 325]). The Qarmathians, on the other hand, see in it the Perfect Man.

385. *Passion*, Fr 3:207 n 4/Eng 3:195 n 90; Dhahabī, *Iᶜtidāl*, s.v. Cf. *ᶜan baᶜḍ ahl al-bayt*, in Kharkūshī f. 155b.

386. This question is also linked to the strange (and ancient) mystical tradition according to which Mālik permitted the *samāᶜ*.

387. Ḥanbal; I, 77.

388. Dhahabī, *Ḥuffāẓ*.

389. The founder of the Mālikī rite.

390. One of these, which Dhū'l-Nūn repeated to his disciple Rabīᶜa ibn Muḥammad Ṭāᵓī, claims that ᶜAlī was the only legitimate caliph of the *rāshidūn* (Dhahabī, *Iᶜtidāl*, s.v.). It is difficult to imagine Mālik transmitting such a Shiite *ḥadīth*.

391. Parallel passages, ap. Baqlī, I, 48, 97, 107; II, 304.

Ḥallāj uses and develops important suggestions from the collection: from the lexical point of view, he adopts the use of the words *mashīʾa* (and not *irāda*), *maḥabba* (and not *ʿishq*), *azaliyya* and *ḥulūl*, and *Ḥaqq* (as a name for God).[392] From the structural point of view, he uses the Qurʾānic exegesis of the divine name *Nūr* (= *munawwir*) and *Ṣamad* (= *maṣmūd ilayhi*), and the word *ihdinā* (= *urshudnā ilä maḥabbatika*).[393] He takes up the parable of the twelve zodiacal houses of the soul,[394] and the dialogue-form of explanation of the *via remotionis* (*tanzīh*). Two passages of the *Ṭawāsīn* are inspired by these *ḥadīth*: first, Ḥallāj compares a saint reciting the Qurʾān to the Burning Bush. Second, when he writes "blink an eye out of the *where*" (2:7) for the nocturnal ascension in which Muḥammad "did not turn to look right or left" (6:2), he is developing Jaʿfar's statement, "He blinked his eyes to shield them from the (created) signs, trying to occupy them with God alone and not to turn (and look at) any detail of those signs."[395] There are texts of Jaʿfar on the *nūr muḥammadiyya* (*al-Qurʾān nusikha*), on *tajallī al-Qurʾān* (*tilāwa*, forty-one *anwār*),[396] and on *tawba qabl ʿibāda*,[397] that prefigure Ḥallajian theses; according to Ibn Ayyāsh, Ḥallāj referred to a *riwāya "min ahl al-bayt"* justifying his rule replacing the *ḥajj* with devotional acts.[398]

It is not easy to determine which of these *riwāyāt*, in Sunni mystic circles, are in fact of the sixth Imām of the Shīʿa. I have briefly summarized Jaʿfar's biography in the notes.[399] We can only say that he must not be

392. *Passion*, Fr 3:15, 130/Eng 3:8, 118; Baqlī, f. 156a, 265b. and on Qur. 2:160.
393. *Passion*, Fr 3:15, 145 n 1, 142–43/Eng 3:8, 132 n 65, 130.
394. Ibid., Fr 3:34 n 1/Eng 3:26 n 45.
395. Baqlī, on Qur. 17:1.
396. *Passion*, ch. 14, sec. IIIa, Fr 3:152, 15/Eng 3:139, 8; Baqlī, f. 265b.
397. Baqlī, on Qur. 1:4; 9:113.
398. *Passion*, Fr 1:585–86, 594/Eng 1:539–40, 547.
399. In 122/739, the Shiite legitimists of Kūfa, refusing to lend armed support to Zayd, ostentatiously seceded (*rāfiḍa*, secession) and declared Jaʿfar the one legitimate Imām. Jaʿfar himself broke with Abū'l-Jārūd, the confidant and editor of the *tafsīr* of his father Bāqir (d. 117), for being a partisan of Zayd. Jaʿfar then went to live in Medina on retreat. Surrounded by a more or less compromising circle of adepts, he was obliged on several occasions to disavow friendly interpreters of his thought. According to the orthodox Imāmīs, he designated four doctors of healthy doctrine, four pillars (*arkān*): Burayd ibn Muʿāwiya (d. 150); Zurāra ibn Aʿyān (d. 150), who later proclaimed Mūsā the seventh Imām; Muḥammad ibn Muslim ibn Rabāḥ; and Abū Baṣīr. On the same authority, Jaʿfar is supposed to have given his blessing to the theologian Ibn al-Ḥakam and to have favored, to varying degrees, Muʾmin al-Ṭāq, Abū Mālik Ḥaḍramī, ʿAlī ibn Manṣūr, and ʿAlī ibn Yaqṭīn (b. Kūfa 124, d. Baghdād 182, who edited his *Malāḥim*; *Tūsy's List*, 234). The orthodox accept Jaʿfar's *riwāyāt* from Abān ibn Taghlib, Abū Ḥamza Thumālī, and especially Mufaḍḍal ibn ʿUmar Juʿfī. They claim he excommunicated several *rāwīs* (Friedländer, II, 90). In contrast, the *ghulāt* Imāmīs publish their *riwāyāt* of Jaʿfar on the authority of Abū Shākir Maymūn (father of the founder of the Qarmathians) and Muḥammad ibn Sinān Ẓāhirī, a disciple of Mufaḍḍal. They affirm that Jaʿfar made Abū Shākir the tutor of his favorite son, Ismaʿīl. There are reasons to wonder whether the orthodox were not wrong about the whole line: the divergent opinions of the above-mentioned doctors (Ibn al-Dāʿī, *Tabṣira*, 422–423); Abū Shākir's intimacy with Jaʿfar, which they [the orthodox] admit; the close relationship between the Qarmathian *ibṭāl*

ruled out, absolutely and *a priori*, as the source of these sayings of mystical exegesis, because they show extraordinary doctrinal coincidences with his fragments invoked independently by both orthodox Shiites and the Ghulāt (Nuṣayrīs and Druze).* For example: in *ᶜadl*, the distinction between *amr* and *mashīʾa*;[400] on *tawḥīd*, the use of *tanzīh*;[401] in *al-furūᶜ*, the nonobligatory character of the *ḥajj*[402] and the calculated[403] determination (not empirical, with witnesses)[404] of the new moon; and finally, the condemnation of *qiyās* and *raʾy*.[405]

By whom was the corpus of these *riwāyāt* compiled? Perhaps by Jābir ibn Ḥayyān or Ibn abī'l-ᶜAwjā (d. 167) The case for Jābir is that he dedicated his books to Jaᶜfar; that one of his disciples in alchemy was Dhū'l-Nūn Miṣrī, the first editor of this collection; and especially that Jābir was called "al-Ṣūfī"[406] and wrote books on asceticism.[407] He (and not Harim ibn Ḥayyān) was probably the Ibn Ḥayyān denounced by the heresiographer Khashīsh Nasaʾī (d. 253)[408] for vaunting an ascetic training of the senses comparable to "the gradual conditioning of a racehorse" (*taḍmīr al-maydān*), at the end of which the ascetic is "as insensitive to the bitterness of vinegar as to the sweetness of date custard" and can do anything with no fear of punishment, no constraint to observe the Law.

But the case for Ibn abī'l-ᶜAwjā is strong, especially on textual evidence. He was a disciple of Ḥasan through Ḥammād ibn Salama; we know that Ibn abī'l-ᶜAwjā modified Ḥasan's doctrine (his *riwāyāt* do not contain the words *ᶜishq* and *tafwīḍ*, which Ḥasan uses). It is stated with certainty that he made and published a collection of *ḥadīth*[409] (the name under which it was published is not known; perhaps "Jaᶜfar"),[410] and that

*Nwyia comments, in the introduction to his edition (1968) of the *Tafsīr*, that Massignon here underestimates the "doctrinal coincidences": the two traditions, Shiite and Sunni, have preserved for all practical purposes the same work. Nwyia's lexicon of the *Tafsīr* accomplishes what LM carries out for Ḥallaj in ch. 1.

and the *nafy al-ruʾya* professed by the orthodox, disregarding Abū Baṣīr and Ibn al-Ḥakam, from the beginning of the third century; the Qarmathian *Nūr ᶜUlwī* and Jaᶜfar's *Allāh Nūr*, which are identical.

400. *Passion*, Fr 3:130/Eng 3:118; Nuṣayrī ms. Paris 1450, f. 12a.

401. *Passion*, Fr 3:138 n 5, 147/Eng 3:126 n 7, 134.

402. Ibid., Fr 3:209 n 6/Eng 3:197 n 114; and Makkī, *Qūt*, II, 117.

403. *Iltimās al-hilāl* following the tables brought out by Ibn abī'l-ᶜAwjā , under the name Jaᶜfar (*Farq*, 25; Kindī, *Qāḍīs*, ed. Guest, 538 l. 37, 533 l. 23, 534 l. 20; Ibn Jubayr, 162 l. 11, 167; Ibn Saᶜd, V, 21 l. 16). On Jaᶜfar's opinion, cf. Maqrīzī, *Ittiᶜāẓ*, 76 l. 14; Kindī, *Qāḍīs*, ed. Guest, 584 l.17; Ibn Taymiyya, *Majm, al-rasāʾil al-kubrā*, II, 157 (Goldziher); Ṭabaṭabaʾī, *ᶜUrwa wuthqā*, 419–21.

404. Sunni method.

405. Ṭabarsī, *Iḥtijāj*, 185–86, 183, 179.

406. *Fihrist*, 335: title of his *Kitāb al-raḥma*, Cambridge ms. 896.

407. Sāᶜid (d. 462), in his *Ṭabaqāt*, compares him to Muḥāsibī and Tustarī; cf. Ibn al-Qifṭī, 111, 127.

408. *Istiqāma*, ap. Malaṭī, 166.

409. *Farq*, 25.

410. With whom he was very close.

this collection had mystical tendencies and was often accused, in an apparent contradiction, of both *tashbīh* and *ta^cṭīl*. Ḥallāj would have to respond to the same charge.[411]

B. The First Editor: Dhū'l-Nūn Miṣrī[412]

SOURCES FOR HIS BIOGRAPHY

Kindī mentions him in his *Ta'rīkh al-mawālī al-miṣriyīn*. There are no extant biographies from Miṣrī's time, and the accounts by Ibn Khamīs and ᶜAṭṭār are stuffed with invention. The *Ṣarf al-tawahhum ᶜan Dhī'l-Nūn Miṣrī*[413] by Abū Hurrā ibn Suwayd Ikhmīmī is lost. Later monographs include *Kawkab durrī fī tarjamat Dh. N. M.* (ms. Ṭōpqāpū, 1378) and Suyūṭī's *Sirr maknūn fī manāqib Dh. N.* (ms. ᶜAshir Eff. 2051).

CHRONOLOGY OF HIS LIFE

Abū'l-Fayḍ (var. Fayyāḍ) Thawbān (var. Fayḍ) ibn Ibrahīm Miṣrī, called Dhū'l-Nūn,[414] was born at Ikhmīm in Upper Egypt, c. 180. Little is known of his life. Authentic details are missing about the circumstances of his and his brothers' vocations. His teacher of mysticism seems to have been Saᶜdūn, of Cairo.[415]

He learned certain *ḥadīth* with an *isnād* including Layth ibn Saᶜd, ᶜAbdallah ibn Lahīᶜa (d. 174), Ibn ᶜUyayna (d. 198), and Ibn ᶜIyāḍ. (d. 187), but we do not know who taught them directly to Dhū'l-Nūn. Perhaps it was the enigmatic Faḍl ibn Ghānim Khuzaᶜī.[416] Dhū'l-Nūn's works attest to his knowledge of the mystical literature of the time, including some of

411. See *Der Islam*, III, 251.

412. See *Ḥilya*, IX, 331–35; Ibn ᶜAsākir, V, 271–88. On his trial in Baghdād: Kindī, *Quḍāt Miṣr*, 453. And Kattani, *Fihris*, I, 234, for the monograph of Ibn ᶜArabī. His *mawāᶜiẓ* were compiled by a Mālikī, Muḥammad ibn Qāsim ibn Yāsur (descendent of the *ṣaḥābī* ᶜAmmār: Ibn Farḥūn, 248). On his tomb [photograph in *Essai*], which is preserved in the Qarāfa, cf. Ibn al-Zayyāt (*Kawākib sayyāra*, ed. Aḥmad Taymur, Cairo, 1907, 233–38, and 109–10). Following Yf. Aḥmad (1922), I studied the adjoining *turba* of Fakhr Fārisī, the Ḥallājian *muḥaddith* (d. 622 A.H.) who was Malik Kāmil's adviser during his interview with the *rāhib* (St. Francis) at Damietta. For centuries, Dhū'l-Nūn's tomb was one of the stages in the curious pilgrimages, in the form of a closed circle, which were undertaken in the great Muslim cemeteries, such as the Qarāfat Miṣr. The aim was to speed the arrival of Divine Justice, hoped for by the Martyrs of Desire. It should be noted that in the fourteenth century, popular legend had it that Dhū'l-Nūn was a contemporary and friend of Ḥallāj (Qūṣī ap. Shaᶜrāwī, *Lawāq*, I, 159); especially in Turkish poetry (*Rev. Et. Isl.*, 1946, 72, 74, 76).

413. *Fihrist*, 359.

414. The man with the fish, like Jonah.

415. Sarrāj, *Maṣāriᶜ*, 130.

416. Dhahabī, *Iᶜtidāl*, s.v.; herein, p. 139; Mālinī, 31.

Rābi^ca's poems, which he uses without naming the author. He traveled widely: to Mecca, Damascus, and the cells of the ascetics on Mt. Lukkām, south of Antioch.[417] Summoned by the state's Mu^ctazilite inquisition, he courageously affirmed the "uncreated" character of the Qur^ɔan.[418] The Egyptian Mālikite *faqīh* ^cAbdallah ibn ^cAbd al-Ḥakam (d. 214) condemned him for his public teaching of mysticism. Towards the end of his life he was disturbed again: arrested, transferred to Baghdād, and interned at the Maṭbaq prison, where the Baghdād Sufis, notably Isḥāq ibn Ibrāhīm Sarakhsī, were able to visit him.[419] Released by order of the caliph after a brief interrogation, Miṣrī came back to Cairo to die (in 245/856).[420]

HIS WORKS AND DOCTRINE

There are apocryphal alchemical and kabbalistic works under his name. His authorship of a "translation" of some hieroglyphs from Egyptian temples seems to be imaginary as well. Ibn al-Nadīm says that as a disciple of Jābir Dhū'l-Nūn wrote two treatises on alchemy, *Rukn akbar* and *Thiqa*, but these are lost.[421] I have not examined his *Kitāb al-^cajā^ɔib* in Cairo.[422]

The only authentic extant mystical fragments of Miṣrī are sayings, parables, and anecdotes. Some were written down by his disciples in Egypt, like Muhājir ibn Mūsā and Aḥmad ibn Ṣabīḥ Fayyūmī, others by his admirers in Baghdād. Already in his lifetime, Muḥāsibī was citing him as an authority. ^cAlī ibn Muwaffaq and especially Yūsuf ibn Ḥusayn Rāzī (d. 301)[423] propagated his fragments. Tirmidhī, in a gloss, treats one of his sayings as a *ḥadīth qudsī*.

Dhū'l-Nūn's rather complex doctrine attenuates the theses of ^cAbd al-Wāḥid ibn Zayd's school; nevertheless, the doctrine is more developed than Dārānī's attempt at conciliation. Miṣrī clarifies *tafwīḍ*,[424] he uses the term *ḥubb*[425] without hesitation, and he was the first to isolate the idea of *ma^crifa* clearly [*ṣifāti'l-waḥdāniyya*].[426] But his fervent, detailed introspection

417. Ibn al-Jawzī, *Ṣafwa*; Yāfi^cī, *Nashr*. II, 83.
418. Dhahabī, ms. Leiden 1721, f. 28a.
419. Mālinī, 32; Tagrib., I, 753.
420. The map of his tomb, his stela (Kufic inscription of the third century), the monument of his *khādim*, Ḥāmid (d. 634/1236), and the *marsūma* of the sultan Barsbay (838/1434) concerning his *waqf* were published by myself in 1911 (*Bull. Inst. Fr. Archéol. Caire*). A mosque at Giza is dedicated to him; there is a cenotaph bearing his name in the Shūnīz cemetery in Baghdād.
421. *Fihrist*, 358; 355.
422. Brockelmann, *G.A.L.*, I, 199, 521.
423. Ibn ^cArabī, *Muḥāḍ.*, II, 313, 315–16, 363.
424. *Passion*, Fr 3:120/Eng 3:108–9.
425. See above, text at n 346.
426. *Passion*, Fr 3:66/Eng 3:57; ^cAṭṭār, I, 126–27, 133; Ibn Qayyim, *Madārij*, III, 220.

is not supported by the philosophical method and dialectical force of, say, Muḥāsibī.[427] Miṣrī's defining characteristics are the sumptuousness of his poetic allegory and the slightly overdone luxury of his metaphors; he excels at using these devices to mask bold propositions. As we have seen,[428] one of his parables, on the "pilgrimage of the spirit" to Mecca, outlines a Ḥallajian thesis. Another parable, of which there are two extant versions,[429] attempts to give a glimpse of the delights that the divine love offers to the soul, under the thin veil of declarations of love sung by a houri. The parable contains lines by Rābiᶜa, as well as the passage, "(Drink) the wine of His love for you, as long as He is making you drunk on your love for Him," on which Tirmidhī comments.[430] In Dhū'l-Nūn's obviously allegorical tales, he shows adolescents at the end of the pilgrimage who suspend themselves, mad with adoration, from the veils of the Kaᶜba, or who strain to hear the murmurs of love emanating from it.[431] These two examples reveal a perilous sentimental transgression by Miṣrī, a love of mystical joy for its own sake.[432]

In rare moments, Dhū'l-Nūn abandons his intricate, precious style and makes brief, straightforward statements, such as this: "I desired to glimpse You, and when I saw You, I was overcome by a fit of joy and could not hold back my tears."[433] "He alone comes back, who has not been to the end of the road. None who has achieved union has returned."[434] But like the much later Kīlānī, whom he resembles, he would rather paint grand allegorical pictures full of artistic nuance. E.g.:

The joys of the samāᶜ (spiritual concert) in Paradise:[435]

I have read in the Torah of the pious, who believe, who walk in the way of their Creator and encourage obedience — I have read that these men will see the face of the Lord, for it is the highest hope of all sincere lovers to see the face of God. God will give them no greater grace in their assembly than the sight of His face. And I have learned that after the vision He will give them the grace of hearing the voices of the angelic spirits (*rūḥāniyūn*) and David's

427. Miṣrī is clearly anti–Muᶜtazilite (Baqlī, I, 390); he acquits himself of the accusation of *ḥulūl* (*Passion*, Fr 3:181/Eng 3:169).

428. See ch. 2, sec, 2.B., "Convergence of Guiding Intention," "The replacement of the *ḥajj* . . ."

429. Sarrāj, *Maṣāriᶜ*, 180–81; Ibn ᶜArabī, *Muḥāḍ.*, II, 69.

430. *Khātam*, (*Khatm*), quest. 118.

431. Cf. the tales of Ṣāliḥ Murrī and Ibn ᶜUyayna (Ibn ᶜArabī, *Muḥāḍ*, II, 304, 279).

432. Ḥallāj criticized both of them specifically (*Passion*, Fr 3:128–29, 1:589–90/Eng 3:116–17, 1:543).

433. [*Recueil*, p. 16.] ᶜAbd al-Raḥmān ibn Aḥmad, *Risāla fī'l-taṣawwuf*, ms. Naᶜsān, Ḥamāh, acephalous. Cf. his comment on divine union, without going through the Prophet (Sarrāj, *Lumaᶜ*, 104).

434. Suhrawardī, *ᶜAwārif*, IV, 291.

435. [*Recueil*, p. 16.] Published during his lifetime by Muḥāsibī (*Maḥabba*), whose source was Ḥusayn ibn Aḥmad Shāmī.

chanting of the Psalter. If you could see David! A special seat will be raised from among the seats of Paradise, and he will be permitted to sit upon it and make known the praise and glory of God, while all those around him in Paradise listen attentively: prophets, saints, *rūḥāniyūn,* and *muqarrabūn.* Then David, with a tranquil heart, will begin to recite the Psalms, raising and lowering his voice and pausing, with every beautiful nuance of vocal inflection. In his chanting he will take the right measure of the phrases, maintaining what must be constant, varying what must change. And then the ecstasy will begin for those who are smiling in excess of joy. The Royal "I"[436] will answer David, and the beautiful recluses of the castles (of Paradise) will acclaim the divinity. Then David will raise his voice to bring the joy to its height. When he has made his loudest voice heard, the elect of *ᶜIlliyūn* will raise themselves from their dwelling places (*ghuraf*) in Paradise, while the houris respond to David with songs of happiness from behind the veils of their apartments. Then the base of the chair will rise, the winds resound, the trees shake, and songs be exchanged. The King will expand the understanding (of the elect) to make their joy perfect. And if God had not decided in advance that their joy would last forever, they would die of happiness.

Miṣrī is one of the first propagators of *samāᶜ* sessions or "spiritual concerts,"[437] and I have quoted the entire passage above to show that he deliberately weakens the idea of direct dialogue between the saints and God on the day of the *ziyāda,* a thesis *Muḥāsibī* clearly affirms.

As Sulamī remarks, Miṣrī was the first to define and teach "the classification of the mystical states (*tartīb al-aḥwāl*) and the stages on the way of the masters of sanctity (*maqāmāt ahl al-wilāya*)."[438] Dārānī had outlined the path of the mystics, but in Miṣrī it took the definitive form that would appear in Sufism's classical manuals. Other authors would add or suppress particular stages, but he established the idea of fixed steps for the sanctifying graces. Compared to *Muḥāsibī's* method of analytical introspection, with which the mystic can find *ab intra* a principle for subordinating one state of consciousness to the next according to his preliminary intentions, Miṣrī's theory relies upon a rather insufficient formal esthetic. Compared to the very rough, bare, ascetic push of a Bisṭāmī (the best example before Ḥallāj), who would search our acts for Him alone for Whom we accomplish them, Miṣrī's veneration of virtues for their own sake, and cultivation of ecstasy for its own sake, at least suggest that he was guilty of formalist idolatry. But his theory, clearer and at first more accessible to av-

436. *Huwa al-Malakūt* (= the upper angelic world), implying a thesis that Muḥāsibī later makes explicit. Perhaps this is the "*huwa!*" of initiation ceremonies.

437. He pointed out the perils of it (*Passion,* Fr 1:431/Eng 1:384).

438. *Sunan,* ap. Ibn al-Jawzī, *Nāmūs,* XI. Cf. Suhrawardī, *ᶜAwārif,* IV, 252, 276.

erage mystics than the other two, had a broader influence. From the end of the third century, Tustarī and various Sufis of Baghdād were adopting Miṣrī's process of formal classification.[439] It would be amended and perfected by Wāsiṭī, Sarrāj,[440] Qushayrī, and Ghazālī.

Here is one of Miṣrī's characteristic passages:[441]

> There were some men who, being faithful to God, planted the trees of their sins where they could see them and showered them with the water of their penitence; the trees bore the fruit of sorrow and regret; and they, the eloquent, the gracious in speech, the wise in God and His Prophet — they became madmen without madness, idiots without stuttering or dumb silence. They drank from the cup of purity, and the length of their suffering gave them patience.
>
> Then their hearts began to burn for the Kingdom; their thoughts, to wander among the palaces and under the veils of the Majesty. They hid in the shadows under the portico of regret, and there they read the book of their sins. They made anxiety their own legacy to themselves, until, through complete abstinence (*wara*ᶜ), they attained the summit of denial (*zuhd*). That is how the bitterness of renouncing the world became so sweet to them, and the hard couch so soft, that they won love of salvation and the way to peace.
>
> Then their spirits were cast into the heights of Heaven, fell adoring into the gardens of Paradise, and plunged into the river of life. They closed the locks of anguish and crossed the bridges of desire; they stopped for the annihilation of knowledge (discursive knowledge) and drank from the *ghadīr*[442] of wisdom (the wisdom of union); they embarked in the ship of grace and opened their sails to the wind of salvation on the sea of peace, until they reached the gardens of Rest and the mine of Glory and Mercy.[443]

And this prayer:[444]

> O God, give us a place among those whose spirits have flown to the Kingdom; for whom the Majesty's veils have been lifted; who have plunged into the river of certainty; who have walked among the flowers in the garden of the pious; who have embarked in the boat of resignation (*tawakkul*) and unfurled the sail of the plea for intercession; whom the wind of love has blown to each port, nearer and nearer to the Glory, until they reached the coast of right intention

439. ᶜ*Awārif*, IV, 253, 198. Miṣrī is considered a saint by the Sālimiyya (Makkī, *Qūt*, II, 76).

440. *Luma*ᶜ, 42.

441. Yāfiᶜī, *Nashr*, II, 334–35 [*Recueil*, p. 17].

442. Allusion to the *ghadīr Khumm* (*Passion*, Fr 3:42/Eng 3:34).

443. The excessive esthetic care lavished on the comeliness of the images so reduces this *itinerarium mentis ad Deum* that it almost resembles the "Map of the Land of Tender" drawn by a disciple of Honoré d'Urfé.

444. Yāfiᶜī, *Nashr*, II, 335.

(*ikhlāṣ*) and left their sins behind, carrying with them only their acts of obedience; and all this is through Your mercy, O You Who are most merciful!

5. The End of the Ascetic School of Baṣra

A. ᶜAbd al-Wāḥid ibn Zayd, Rabāḥ, and Rābiᶜa

At the beginning of the second century A.H., Muslim circles in Baṣra[445] were characterized by intense religious fervor in exceedingly diverse forms, with no unity among disciplines or theological doctrines. Ḥasan's disciples would introduce these unities little by little. Even if they did not transmit precise oral "constitutions" (let alone a habit, a special garment, as it was later believed), the master's method was passed down. In the first generation, Mālik ibn Dīnār (d. 127)[446] instigated an attempt to regularize the tradition. Anṭākī allows us to understand that Ibn Dīnār was reacting against certain ascetic excesses, especially inconsistency and exaggeration of dress: Abān's sometimes luxurious, sometimes repulsive clothing,[447] and the *ṣūf* and chains of Ibn Wāsiᶜ, Farqad, and ᶜUtba. Ibn Dīnār also reproached Abān for adding to the number of reassuring stories already in Ḥasan's tradition, on the acts of devotion that would obtain indulgences, just as he reproached Ibn Wāsiᶜ and Farqad for giving all their possessions to the community without a care for the future.

In the second generation, thanks to the powerful organizational mind of Abū ᶜUbayda ᶜAbd al-Wāḥid ibn Zayd (d. 177),[448] a unification of the school

445. See Ḥarīrī, *Maqāmāt*, L.

446. Monograph on him by Ibn abī'l-Dunyā (d. 281); extracts in Thaᶜlabī, *Qatlä*.

447. Dhahabī, *Iᶜtidāl*; *Ḥuffāẓ*, IV, 39.

448. Not to be confused with the Zaydī traditionist ᶜAbd al-Wāḥid ibn Ziyād (d. 179). Ibn Zayd transmitted from Ḥasan Baṣrī, whose true successor he is, two *ḥadīth* of fundamental importance to Sufism: (a) the *ḥadīth al-ᶜishq* (*Ḥilya*, VI, 165), "*ᶜashiqanī wa ᶜashiqtuhu*," transmitted by Muḥammad ibn Faḍl ibn ᶜAṭiyya Marwazī (d. 180) to Ibrahim ibn Ashᶜath, the *khādim* of Fuḍayl ibn ᶜIyāḍ; (b) the *ḥadīth al-ikhlāṣ* (Qush., 113), transmitted by Ḥudhayfa to Ḥasan Baṣrī, ᶜAW ibn Zayd, Aḥmad ibn ᶜAṭā Hujaymī, Aḥmad ibn Ghassān Hujaymī Tamīmī (d. 240), Aḥmad Yaᶜqūb Sharīṭī, Aḥmad ibn Bashshār, to Nasawī and Qushayrī (cf. Kāzarūnī, *Musalsalāt*, 9a-b). Note that Ibn Zayd's disciple Abū ᶜUmar Aḥmad ibn ᶜAṭā Hujaymī (d. 200; see *Lisān*, I, 221), who compared Abū Bakr to Abraham, was rejected by Zak. Sājī (student of Dāwūd Ẓāhirī, *Lisān*, I, 422) and by Ashᶜarī (*Maq.*). One of Hujaymī's disciples was Muḥammad ibn Zak. Ghilābī (d. 281), a friend of Ibn abī'l-Dunyā, the teacher of the historian of Sufism, Ibn al-Aᶜrābī (d. 341). Ibn Zayd trained Abū Saᶜīd Muḍar al-Qārī (*Ḥilya*, VI, 156, 157, 160, 163, 164), who is quoted by Muḥāsibī and who transmitted Ibn Zayd's doctrine of the *ruʾya* to Kalābādhī and Ibn Manda through Ṣaliḥ ibn Muḥammad Tirmidhī, Khalaf Bukhārī (d. 350; *Lisān*, II, 404; cf. Kalābādhī, *Akhbār*, 155b), Dāwūd ibn Muḥabbir (author of the *Kitāb al-ᶜaql*), and ᶜUthmān ibn ᶜUmāra (*Iᶜtidāl*, II, 187). Ibn Zayd himself, admitted as a *rāwī*, by Wakīᶜ, Muslim, Ibn abī'l-Dunyā, Fuḍayl ibn ᶜIyāḍ, and Dārānī, is "weak" for Z. Sājī and Nasaʾī, and rejected (*matrūk*) by Bukhārī. Abū Bishr Ḥawshab ibn Muslim, who was older than Ibn Zayd, seems to have taught him about Ḥasan Baṣrī (*Ḥilya*,

was almost accomplished. Ibn Zayd organized the community of cenobites at ᶜAbbādān. He was a theologian and preacher, a leader renowned for effective holiness (*mujāb al-daᶜwa*).[449] In theology, he powerfully expressed the state of loneliness caused by a sincere mystical vocation:[450] "Many are the ways; the way of Truth is solitary/And those who enter the way of Truth are alone (*afrād*)."

He outlined the thesis that recitation of the *shahāda* had value only by a special divine favor: "Just as it is not permitted to alter the face of a coin, it is not permitted to recite the *shahāda* without the light of purification of intent (*nūr al-ikhlāṣ*)";[451] he even outlined the doctrine of deification (*ittiṣāf* of Ḥallāj, *takhalluq* of Wāsiṭī),[452] in this *ḥadīth*: "God has 117 moral virtues (*khulq*); a man who has one of them may enter Paradise."[453] Deferring to the theologians, he used only the words *ᶜishq* and *shawq* (indicating desire) for divine love, not *maḥabba* (indicating consummation).[454]

Here is a fragment from one of his sermons:[455]

> O brothers! Will you not weep from desire (*shawq*) for God? How could one who weeps from desire for his Lord be deprived of the sight of Him (one day)? O brothers! Will you not weep from fear of hell? How could one who weeps from fear of hell not be preserved from hell by God? O brothers! Will you not weep from fear of the bitter thirst that will seize you on the Day of Judgment? You do not weep? Ah, but you do! Weep then over the cool water of this world (which you seek too much), and perhaps your thirst will be quenched in the Dwellings of Holiness, with the best fellows, the Companions of the Prophet, the *ṣiddīqūn*,[456] the martyrs, and the pious, for is there a better company than theirs?

He puts Jerusalem (and the fountain of Siloah) in the same rank as Mecca (and the well of Zamzam) and affirms that Khiḍr lives at *al-Aqṣā*.[457]

VI, 199). One purported chain of congregational affiliation, in order to reach Ḥasan Baṣrī (and even Kumayl ibn Ziyād, *sic*), includes ᶜAbd al-Wāḥid ibn Zayd via Abū Yaᶜqūb Sūsī (Qushāshī, *Simṭ*, 99), over a chronological hiatus. The chain ends at Najm Kubrā and the Chishtiyya (cf. Beaurecueil, *Firkāwī*, Cairo, 1953, 13).

449. Imitating Sulaymān Taymī, he observed a vow of chastity for forty years.

450. Makkī, *Qūt*, I, 153.

451. Ibn ᶜArabī, *Muḥāḍ.*, II, 354. His nephew Bakr would retract the proposition (*"maᵓmūn fī'l-ikhlāṣ maᶜ al-ṭabᶜ"*: Ashᶜarī, *Maqālāt*, f. 96a). *Passion*, Fr 3:246/Eng 3:232.

452. *Passion*, Fr 3:142/Eng 3:130.

453. Dhahabī, *Iᶜtidāl*, s.n.

454. *Passion*, Fr 3:117–18/Eng 3:105–7.

455. *Ḥilya*, s.n (following Ibn al-Jawzī's *Ṣafwa*) [*Recueil*, p. 5].

456. This is one of the oldest mentions of this term; Ḥasan Baṣrī used to say *"ahl al-inqiṭāᶜ."*

457. Maqdīsī, *Muthīr*, ms. Paris 1669, f. 99, 121b. Zamzam visits Siloah on the night of ᶜArafāt (Yq. III, 762 [s.n., *ᶜayn Sulwān*]; Goldziher, *M. St.*, II, 136) or 15 Shaᶜban (Gaudefroy Demombines, *Pèlerinage*, 84).

Besides Ibn Zayd there were two of his contemporaries and friends. First, Rābiᶜa, a simple freedwomen, a former flutist, then a convert,[458] whose brief extant fragments are filled with a love of touching vehemence.[459] She spent her whole life in Baṣra almost as a recluse, and died there[460] at the age of at least eighty, in 185/801.[461] The fragrance of sanctity she left in Islam has still not been dissipated. Relying upon Qurʾān 5:59, she did not hesitate to use the word *ḥubb* for divine love. She makes this commentary:[462]

> I love You with two loves, (self-serving) love, for my own pleasure
> And (perfect) Love, (desire to make a gift to You) of that to which
> You are suited!
> In the love of my own happiness,
> I am concerned only to think of You, to the exclusion of all others.
> In the other Love, which is Your due,
> (It is my desire that) Your veils should fall, and that I should see
> You!
> There is no glory for me in one love or the other,
> No! But praise be to You, for one and the other!

This quatrain very concisely sets forth the duality of the soul's "two loves" for God: imperfect love (for personal enjoyment) and perfect Love (for the good of God, for His Glory for His sake alone);[463] she did not dare decide absolutely between the two. Ḥallāj would later make that decision in magnificent lines,[464] placing the *ḥubb al-Madhkūr* before the *ḥubb al-dhikr*, while the secular theoreticians of *ᶜudhrī* love, like Ḥallāj's adversary Ibn Dāwūd, would choose precisely the opposite solution.[465]

Another of Rābiᶜa's sayings offers an answer to the question of the two

458. I had thought she was of Qays (ᶜAdaw.), but she is of Azd, of the clan ᶜAtīk ibn Naṣr ibn Shunūw. One of the leaders of the Azd at the Battle of the Camel was an ᶜAtakī. Consult Margaret Smith, *Rābiᶜa*, Cambridge, 1928, and the texts collected for the first time by ᶜAR Badawī, in *Rābiᶜa shahīdat al-ḥubb al-ilāhī*, Cairo, 1950. According to Brockelmann, as cited by Goldziher (in *DI*, 1918, 208), Ibn al-Jawzī wrote a *Manāqib Rābiᶜa al-muᶜtazila.* Her apologue of the torch and the jug of water is well known (Aflākī, 310 [*Recueil*, p. 8], mentioned, oddly enough, by Joinville).

459. Jāḥiẓ, *Bayān*, II, 85, III, 66; Sarrāj, *Maṣāriᶜ*, 136, 181; ᶜAṭṭār, I, 60.

460. Her tomb was visited by Muḥammad ibn Aslam Ṭūsī.

461. Not in 135/752, as it has been said in order to make her a student of Ḥasan. Proof: her well-known friendship with Rabāḥ; her meeting with Thawrī, who came to Baṣra after 155; the anecdote of the marriage proposal from the ᶜAbbasid *walī* of Baṣra, Muḥammad ibn Sulaymān (*walī* from 145, d. 172; *Qūt*, II, 57). Some say she was born in the year Ḥasan began his preaching. (Perhaps they mean "began again," which would indicate the year 95 or 99.)

462. *Qūt*, II, 56 [*Recueil*, p. 6]. Margoliouth's translation (*Early Development*, 175), while philologically precise, does not bring out the dogmatic range of these lines.

463. Which Wensinck considers an esoteric doctrine (*Dove*, XXVII, LVII), though it has figured, since the Sermon on the Mount, in the humblest Christian teachings.

464. *Passion*, Fr 3:129/Eng 3:117.

465. *Ibid.*, Fr 1:404–16/Eng 1:356–68; and *Ṭawāsīn*, 129, translated passage.

recompenses in Paradise; when she heard boasts about the created joys prepared there for the elect, she cried, "First the Neighbor! Then the house (*al-jār! thumma'l-dār*)."[466]

When she was convalescing from a grave illness, she ceased to wake herself in the middle of the night for prayers; warned by the angels, she understood what she was missing, and recommenced. This anecdote recalls the one about ᶜImrān Khuzāᶜī.[467]

The principal theses taught by her compatriot and friend Abū'l-Muhājir Rabāḥ ibn ᶜAmr Qaysī (d. c. 180) are defined in a more studied, dogmatic form, which gave the theologians easier access. He introduced into dogma the following notions:[468] *tajallī* (*lumen gloriae,* to explain the vision of God, *ruᵓya*) at the Last Judgment (of which ᶜAbd al-Wāḥid ibn Zayd had given powerful reminders); *tafḍīl al-walī,* the superiority of the saint (to the prophet, in a discussion of Qur. 18:76); *khulla,* or "divine friendship" (in memory of Abraham). In morals, Rabāḥ firmly condoned vows of chastity,[469] acts of contrition,[470] and pious visits to cemeteries. The traditionist Khashīsh Nasaᵓī (d. 253) put him (with Kulayb) on a list of *zanādiqa,* for quietism. Nasaᵓī tendentiously made the following claims about the two of them:[471]

i.

They say that when the love of God has overcome their hearts, desires, and wills to such an extent that it has supplanted all other things, then God is, before them, what they are before God. In such a state, they receive the divine *khulla* (= grace of permanent divine love). And God permits them to drink, to commit theft and adultery, and to indulge every other vice. Before God they are like someone who has the right to use his friend's property without permission. [*Recueil,* p. 7]

ii.

They say that the act of renouncing the world is a preoccupation for the heart; that the world, when an interest in it is aroused, seems greater and more attractive; that the heart is bound to consider good meals, pleasant drinks, soft clothes, and sweet perfumes, by the very act of renouncing these things. Such

466. Ghazālī, *Iḥyā,* IV, 224. Allusion to the proverb, "Test the neighbor before the house, and the companion before the voyage.

467. See above, paragraph at n 130. Sarrāj, *Maṣāriᶜ,* 136.

468. Shaᶜrāwī, *Ṭab.,* I, 45; *Ḥilya* [*Recueil,* p. 8].

469. Not content to practice it himself, he recommends it to others: "I heard Mālik ibn Dīnār say, 'A man becomes a *ṣiddīq* only if he leaves his wife in a state of widowhood and goes to live in the ruins among the dogs'" [*Recueil,* p. 6].

470. *Istighfār*: "I have committed close to 40 sins, and for each one I have asked forgiveness of God 100,000 times" (*Ḥilya*).

471. *Istiqāma,* extract, ap. Malaṭī, f. 165.

men succumb to their desires as they occur, in order to develop contempt for them, so that the unworried heart may assign no importance to renunciation. [*Recueil*, p. 7]

These two propositions perfidiously deform[472] the thesis of saintly impeccability (i), and that of the superiority of the "converted sinner who no longer needs to *struggle* against temptation, over the converted sinner who must continue to struggle"[473] (ii).

Here is an anecdote that underscores the nuance separating Rabāḥ from Rābiᶜa:[474]

Abrad ibn Ḍirār of the Banū Saᶜd, a friend of Rābiᶜa, asked Rabāḥ, "Do you find the days and nights long? — Why? — From desire to meet God?" Rabāḥ was silent.[475] Uncertain of the cause of his silence, Abrad asked Rābiᶜa, "Would he have said 'yes' or 'no'?" She answered, "*I* say Yes."

And another:

One day Rābiᶜa was looking at Rabāḥ, who was holding a child of his family and kissing it. "Do you love him?" she asked.

— "Yes."

— "I did not think there was any space in your heart for the love of anyone but God, any place empty of thoughts of Him!"

Rabāḥ cried aloud and fainted. When he had come to his senses and wiped the sweat from his face, he said (to excuse himself), "Ah! It is a mercy that comes from Him, the love for small children that God has sown in the hearts of His servants . . ."

The posthumous condemnation of Rabāḥ and Rābiᶜa by the traditionists coincided with the spread of the disciples of ᶜAbd al-Wāḥid ibn Zayd. Bakr, Ibn Zayd's nephew, using a slightly attenuated version of his uncle's teaching,[476] tried to construct a school of neo-Sunni *mutakallimūn* (*nābitat al-ḥashwiyya*), in order to free Baṣra from Muᶜtazilite theological supremacy. He did not succeed. The interest of this ephemeral school, the Bakriyya, is that, like the later Karrāmiyya and Sālimiyya, it made a defense of orthodoxy based upon the experimental method of the mystics. Ibn Qutayba[477] and Baghdādī[478] enumerated the Bakriyyan theses condemned

472. Cf. herein, ch. 3, sec. 3.
473. *Passion*, Fr 1:132–33/Eng 1:92 [*Recueil*, p. 9].
474. *Ḥilya*, s.v.; Sarrāj, *Maṣāriᶜ*, 181 [*Recueil*, p. 6, also the following anecdote].
475. Like Muḍar Qārī on an analogous occasion (Muḥāsibī, *Maḥabba*): out of modesty.
476. *Passion*, s.v. index; v.s., text at n. 373.
477. *Taʾwīl*, 57.
478. *Farq*, 200–201.

by the heresiographers, some of which had already been made explicit in Ḥasan Baṣrī's teaching.[479]

B. Dārānī, Ibn abī'l-Ḥawwārī, and Anṭākī

The movement begun in Baṣra regained strength in Syria through Dārānī, ᶜAbd al-Wāḥid ibn Zayd's principal disciple. Abū Sulaymān ᶜAbd al-Raḥmān ibn ᶜAṭiyya Dārānī, born in 140 at Wāsiṭ, seems to have left Baṣra c. 180. He went to live at Dārāyā on the Damascus plain and died there in 215.[480] Dārānī developed his teacher's conciliatory tendencies, explicitly stating that he had made the results of his own mystical experiments fit into the frames constructed by the theologians. He refused to announce his other results, even though some inner illuminations (*nukat al-ḥaqīqa*) had suggested that they were real.[481] He was probably just being cautious when he declared a renunciation of personal exposure to public sanctions (against insistently drawing attention to his personal revelations) "from fear of taking pride in them";[482] perhaps he did not feel called to martyrdom.

Opportunism led him to make many concessions. On the subject of abstinence, he concedes that, "eating fine meals is an incitation to contentment in God" (*sic*);[483] he propagated a *ḥadīth* that veils Rabāḥ's doctrine of the superiority of saints to prophets by concluding that John is to be preferred to Jesus.[484] Dārānī liked to paint seductive apparitions of celestial brides, desirable *ḥouris* whose physical beauty is the materialization in Paradise of perfect virtues acquired in this life through tears and prayer; his formula describes an almost commercial transaction, and it pleased neither mystics[485] nor *fuqahā*; the latter expelled him from Damascus for describing visions (seen in a waking state) of angels and prophets.[486] Speaking for

479. *Fāsiq = munāfiq = mukhallad fī'l-nār.*

480. Dhahabī, ms. Leiden 1721, f. 180; Rifāᶜī, *Rawḍa*, printed in Damascus, 1330, p. 95.

481. *Passion*, Fr 3:196/Eng 3:184; Ālūsī, *Jalā*, 62.

482. Makkī *Qūt*, II, 137.

483. Ibid., II, 177.

484. Asin, *Logia D. Jesu*, no. 31; Ibn al-Jawzī, *Narjis*; cf. the bizarre sermon of Aḥmad Ghazālī (d. 517) on the "imperfect" poverty of Jesus [*Recueil*, p. 97]: "The angels came together at the ascension of Jesus; he sat, and his *muraqqaᶜa* was torn into three hundred pieces; they said, 'Lord, will You not make a shirt without stitches for Jesus?' 'No. The world (into which he will go down again) does not deserve that he should have one.' Then they searched the undergarment of Jesus and found a needle. And God said, 'By My glory if that needle had not been there, I would have rapt Jesus into My innermost Holiness, and I would have been unsatisfied for him even with the seventh heaven; but you see, a needle has put a veil between him and Me'" (Ibn al-Jawzī, *Quṣṣāṣ*, f. 118). Must the hermit carry a needle? Ibrahim Khawwāṣ is praised by Ibn al-Jawzī (*Talbīs*, 339) for carrying one with him. Foucauld, in his rule of 1899, wanted not to have one (ch. 4, p. 78).

485. Muḥāsibī would dissociate himself from this (*Tawahhum*); Bisṭāmī would reprove it (*Passion*, Fr 3:177/Eng 3:164–65).

486. Ibn al-Jawzī, *Nāmūs*, XI.

himself, Dārānī told a story[487] maintaining that the elect would see God face to face; Ibn abī'l-Ḥawwārī[488] recounts:

> One day I entered Abū Sulaymān's [Dārānī's] house. He was weeping, and I said to him, "What is making you weep?"
>
> — "O Aḥmad, why shouldn't I weep? When the night deepens, when everyone's eyes are closed, and every friend is alone with the Friend, then lovers wrap their feet in their carpets (rolled prayer carpets) while their tears fall drop by drop. God takes pity on them and cries out, 'O Gabriel! By my Essence! Surely those who are contented by my word and comforted by thoughts of me — surely I shall follow them into their retreats, listen to their sobs, and take their tears into account! O Gabriel, announce to them, "Why those tears? Have you ever seen a Friend cause suffering in those who love Him?" How could I allow those who seek to please Me in the middle of the night to be punished? I swear by Myself, When they are summoned to the Last Judgment, I shall reveal to them My merciful face (*wajhī al-karīm*), so that they may contemplate Me, and I them.'"

The stages of the mystical path had been only vaguely defined by Ḥasan, Ibn Adham,[489] even Wakīᶜ.[490] In Dārānī they were formed into an invariable sequence of graces that adorn the soul.[491] He made the following outline (which Miṣrī would later establish) of the doctrine of the *aḥwāl* and *maqāmāt*:

> (a) the Lord made them drink as they sat on the fringe of the carpet of Love; He quenched their thirst for the company of creatures by showing them the vision of the Truth; (b) then He sat them on the chairs of Sanctity, gave them the rare treasures of superabundance, and rained down on them the water of supernatural assistance (*taʾyīd*); (c) then the streams of desire and vicinity flowed over them; (d) and after afflicting them with the tortures of separation, He revived them with the secrets of nearness.

In another parable, that of the damned ascetic Qārūn,[492] Dārānī explains that all apparent sanctity is precarious and may be revoked before death.[493]

487. Which Ibn Adham attributed to John the Baptist.

488. Qush. 18; diluted, without the author's name, ap. *Iḥyā*, IV. 232. Also quoted by Ibn Qutayba, *ᶜUyūn*, II, 297.

489. Herein, ch. 5, sec. 2.

490. "'Remembering the saints procures *raḥma*.' Let him who contemplates that saying know that there are servants of God from among his creation whom He has chosen for Himself; He has given His grace specially to them, He has rejoiced in His light in them; He has made war on them with His sword and killed them with His fear, giving them supreme martyrdom; it is their Lord Himself Who is their recompense and their light" (ap. Thaᶜlabī, *Qatlā*, f. 4a).

491. Baqlī, II, 355.

492. Shiblī, *Ākām*, 218.

493. *Passion*, Fr 3:220/Eng 3:208.

Dārānī's favorite student, the editor of his parables, was Aḥmad ibn abī'l-Ḥawwārī ᶜAbdallāh ibn Maymūn Thaᶜlabī Ghaṭafānī, who was born in Kūfa in 164 and died in Mecca in 246.[494] His wife, Rābiᶜa, is buried across from Jerusalem,[495] in the cave of St. Pelagia and the prophetess Hulda, which is attached to the Mosque of the Ascension. Ibn abī'l-Ḥawwārī was also a student of Ibn ᶜUyayna, Anṭākī (v.i.), and ᶜAbdallāh ibn Saᶜīd, whose doctrine of the *rūḥ* is analyzed elsewhere.[496] During a long stay in Damascus (Junayd called him "the redolent mint of Damascus"), he was summoned by the government's inquisition and faltered, signing the Muᶜtazilite statement on the "created Qurᵓān." Finally, he was accused of teaching that saints were superior to prophets,[497] and he took refuge in Mecca.

While Dārānī and Ibn abī'l-Ḥawwārī in Damascus were reviving the memory of Ibn Adham's apostolate on Mt. Lukkām, new ascetic vocations were appearing in the area around Antioch itself. Two ascetics established there are the source of the first works mentioned by Kalābādhī,[498] which concern the *ᶜulūm al-muᶜāmalāt* (i.e., the inner discipline of our actions, our rule for living). As in Muḥāsibī's later works, information from the tradition is compiled in these. About the elder of the two ascetics, Abū Muḥammad ᶜAbdallāh ibn Khubayq Anṭakī, we know only that he came from Kūfa, was a Thawrite in law, a disciple of Yūsuf ibn Asbāṭ (d. 196), and one of Fatḥ Mawṣilī's teachers.[499] There are extant works only of the younger of the two: he is Aḥmad ibn ᶜĀṣim Anṭākī, whom we shall call Anṭākī (d. c. 220). His friend Dārānī called him "the spy of hearts" (*jāsūs al-qulūb*)[500] for his penetrating analyses of conscience. His works, edited by two disciples, ᶜAbd al-ᶜAzīz ibn Muḥammad ibn Mukhtār Dimishqī and Ibn abī'l-Ḥawwārī, are of inestimable value because they give us a detailed early model, before Muḥāsibī's codification, of the Islamic asceticism that was taking form. First, I shall analyze the extracts reproduced by Abū Nuᶜaym in his *Ḥilya*.[501]

Anṭākī expresses his love of meditation and solitude, his desire for penitence, and, especially, his desire for a knowledge of God that would be no longer simply the affirmation of His reality by faith (*maᶜrifat al-taṣdīq, al-iqrār*) but the experimental wisdom of those who obtain a response from

494. Dhahabī, ms. Leiden 1721, f. 5b.

495. Rifāᶜī, *Rawḍa*, 84. She was soon confused with Rābiᶜa Qaysiyya (Ibn Khallikān, I, 201); and she is still confused with her.

496. *Passion*, Fr 3:157/Eng 3:144–45.

497. Sulamī, *Miḥan*, ap. Ibn al-Jawzī, *Nāmūs*, XI.

498. *Taᶜarruf.*

499. Jāmī, 73; Shaᶜrāwī, *Ṭab.*, I, 82. Also in Kalābādhī (*Taᶜarruf*).

500. Ibn ᶜArabī, *Muḥāḍ.*, II, 339.

501. Ms. Leiden 892, f. 172a–177b [*Recueil*, pp. 12–13]. Ibn al-Jawzī reproaches Abū Nuᶜaym for having published them (*Ṣafwa*, preface).

Him (*ma^c^rifat al-istijāba*). That knowledge alone, which Anṭākī also calls *ilhām min Allāh,* brings happiness (*ghibṭa*).[502] Purgation of secret sins is what brings one closest to God. There are useful sins, "those that you place before your eyes[503] in order to weep over them until you die, so that you sin no more. *That* is true penitence." There are hurtful acts of obedience, "those that make you forget your faults, that you place before your eyes for personal satisfaction, to shield yourself from the fear of what you have incurred for past sins. That is vainglory."[504] The true believers

> speak few words to created beings, and they take pleasure in invoking their creator; their hearts are attached to the Kingdom of Heaven, and their thoughts are present at the terrors (*ahwāl*) of the Day of Judgment. Their bodies are stripped with respect to created beings; they are blind and deaf to the world and its people and whatever is associated with the world for them. They seem already to see the next life: some have achieved this by effort (*ijtihād*), by denial of the flesh (*riyāḍat al-nafs*), by hunger . . . [505]

"I am in a time when Islam has returned to the exile in which it began;[506] a time when the description of the truth has been exiled. As at the beginning, the learned are attached to riches, and the pious are without instruction . . ." Anṭākī prefigures Muḥāsibī's reform; he deplores the ignorance of ascetics and tries to find a rule to guide them; he reasons, he contemplates a way to link the states of consciousness[507] by following the direction God Himself prepares for us, a direction that must be divined, not invented. "It is God alone who has created the means (*asbāb*) leading to goodness; without them, believers can achieve no goodness of action; the believers are separated from their sins when God has made these means reside in the hearts of those who love Him and act for His sake."[508]

In addition to these two highly developed psychological analyses of spiritual "carelessness" and "ignorance,"[509] Anṭākī wrote a strikingly original *qaṣīda,*[510] somewhat prosaic in form, in which he condensed the results

502. Ms. Leiden 892, f. 172b. Cf. *Passion,* Fr 3:218/Eng 3:206.
503. Taken up again by Miṣrī (herein, text at n. 441.
504. Ms. Leiden 892, f. 173a.
505. Ibid., f. 173b.
506. Ibid., f. 174a. Muḥāsibī would present this thought, which is perhaps Anṭākī's, as a *ḥadīth.*
507. Ms. Leiden 892, f. 175a.
508. Ibid., f. 174b. Anṭākī, who did not have Muḥāsibī's training in theology, was already dissociating himself from the Mu^c^tazilite theologians on this point. He must have been attacked early, because one of his statements is attributed by Ibn A^c^rābī (d. 341: in *Kitāb al-zuhd,* ms. Cairo majm. 125, rep. 29) to someone else. The statement is, *"liman lā yajib dhikruhu"* (*Ḥilya,* f. 175 [IX, 291]: *"uṭlub mā ya^c^nīk bitark mā lā ya^c^nīk"*).
509. Ms. Leiden 892, f. 176a–b.
510. Ibid., f. 177a–b.

of his ascetic experience, his science "at once traditional and inspired." In the poem, he describes the life and death of true Islam in men's souls, and the misfortune of present times:

> ... How Islam, at the outset, commenced;
> Its growth into the fullness of its perfection;
> And how it has faded[511] like a worn garment ...
> Aḥmad[512] himself sang Islam's mourning chant[513]
> Like a man who laments the dead in his affliction.
> Then praise be to God, who created me for Islam out of pure
> beneficence,
> Making me a son of Adam, not a demon from among the *jinn*.
> He led me to the Monastery of Aḥmad[514]
> And taught me what the perverse do not know,
> Making me discern a light, or knowledge, a wisdom;
> And, with all those who are grateful to Him, I thank Him.
> And that is why I hope in Him, that He may not look towards
> My weakness and my ignorance, my void, in His Fullness ...
> [*Recueil,* pp. 13–14]

And this letter, to a friend:

> God! Listen, as I speak to you on His behalf. God raises up the humble not by the measure of their humility but by that of His generosity and bounty. He consoles the afflicted not by the measure of their sorrow but by that of His kindness and mercy. And so, because the Clement and Merciful witnesses His love even to those who wrong Him — who can foresee what He will do for those who have been wronged in Him?![515] Because the Pardoner, Merciful and Generous, turns to those who make war against Him — who can foresee what He will do for those against whom war is made for His sake?! Because He lets those who irritate and wrong Him continue to act[516] — what will He not be in those who have been hated for pleasing Him, who have preferred to be hated by other men in His name?![517]

Two small works studied by Sprenger in 1856, the *Dawā dāʾ al-qulūb wa*

511. *Dhawiya.*
512. The Prophet.
513. *Nadba.*
514. *Dayr Aḥmad*: curious image: for "The Islamic monastic life" [Cf. ch. 3 n 30].
515. This statement was taken up with great bitterness by Ḥallāj as he was tortured (*Passion*, Fr 1:658/Eng 1:607).
516. "*Yatafaʿʿal ʿalā ...*": lit. "He prolongs the activity."
517. Ms. Leiden 892, f. 175b [*Recueil*, p. 14].

maᶜrifat himam al-nafs wa adābihi and the *Kitāb al-shubuhāt,* should be attributed to Anṭākī. He claims to have written the first as dictated by a certain "Abū ᶜAbdallāh," whom Sprenger identifies with Muḥāsibī (d. 243). But internal criticism of Anṭākī's *Dawā*[518] attests to a clearly embryonic state of doctrinal development compared to that of Muḥāsibī's *Riᶜāya.* Sprenger argues that the latest author cited in the *Dawā*'s *isnād* lived until 227; he does not take into account the practice, common to mystics of the time, of citing contemporaries who were still alive.[519] "Abū ᶜAbdallāh" must mean not Muḥāsibī but Nibājī, the teacher of both Anṭākī and Ibn abī'l-Ḥawwārī.

The *Dawā* begins with a theory of *ᶜaql,* reason, as a divine grace that allows us to distinguish between truth and error; the theory occupies an intermediate position between those of Dāwūd ibn Muḥabbir and Muḥāsibī.[520] In order to reason and reflect, one must create solitude in a cell (*ṣawmaᶜa*) or in the house, and learn to know oneself through the fear of God. True *rahbāniyya* entails not talk but action, in meditation. In the *Dawā*'s fifteen chapters, Anṭākī gives treatments of reason, fatuousness, covetouseness, abnegation, the profession of Islamic faith, and asceticism. In chapter 4 he asks himself whether the words *tawḥīd, ᵓīmān, islām,* and *yaqīn* are identical.[521] He answers, "*Tawḥīd* means *ḥanīfiyya,* simple monotheism; *islām* means *milla,* prophetic revelation; *ᵓīmān* means *taṣdīq,* inner consent and action really conforming to canonical duty; *yaqīn* means *maḥḍ al-ᵓīmān,* the essence of faith, which is verified by purification of intent at the moment of action."

In his definition, asceticism (*zuhd*) is not yet as clearly distinct from scrupulous abstinence (*waraᶜ*) as in Muḥāsibī's: "Be just before you are generous, perform canonical duties before unrequired acts, abstain from evil before doing pious works;[522] we must abstain from all evil, but we are not required to do *every* good; we must lay the foundation before building the superstructure."

His *shubuhāt* contain a study of a series of cases of conscience about canonical obligations. The principle is not to abstain negatively, *a priori,* from an action, but only by tutiorism, after a careful study of each case has failed to clarify the matter. For example: the cases of fields forbidden to be cultivated (Ṭarsūs),[523] and of mosques where you may not pray, because the

518. Ms. Syrian Society, Beirut (dated 486 A.H.). Cf. Sprenger, ap. *JRASB,* 1856.

519. By the word, *baᶜḍhum,* which was replaced by their names after their deaths; Muḥāsibī mentions Miṣrī; Ibn ᶜAṭā mentions Ḥallāj.

520. *Passion,* Fr 3:68/Eng 3:58.

521. *Passion,* Fr 3:162/Eng 3:150.

522. *Passion,* Fr 3:195–96/Eng 3:183–84.

523. *Passion,* Fr 3:241 n 12/Eng 3:227 n 59.

land has been occupied illegally ... Anṭākī's solutions attest to a less developed (and more severe) doctrine than Muḥāsibī's *makāsib*.

All of the sayings in these two works are based on *isnād* referring to authorities such as Ḥasan Baṣrī, Ibn Sīrīn, Awzaᶜī, Ṭawūs, Thawrī, Ibn ᶜIyāḍ, and Ibn Asbāṭ. The texts attest to the author's unusual powers of reflection and the exceptionally strict faithfulness of his mind. Anṭākī used to say, "The marks of love are little external ritual (*ᶜibāda*), much meditation (*tafakkur*), and a taste for solitude and silence."[524] "Act," he also said, "as if on earth there were only you, and, in heaven, only God."[525]

6. The Founding of the Baghdād School

No sooner had the new ᶜAbbāsid capital been founded than hermits in isolated huts were noticed in the surrounding area. One such man was Abū Jaᶜfar Muḥawwalī, who said to Ismāᶜīl Turjumānī,[526] "A heart that loves the world could never acquire inner modesty (*waraᶜ khafī*). What am I saying? Not even outer continence." The most famous hermit was Abū Shuᶜayb Qallāl (d. 160)[527] of Burāthā, later condemned by the *mutakallimūn* for his thesis of God's demonstrations of affection for His saints. He told stories about non-Muslim ascetics, and Jāḥiẓ, with strong documentation, reproduces[528] one, on the various types of Christian cells and the Manichaean ascetics' vows, as illustrated by a man who preferred being severely beaten to killing an ostrich that had swallowed a pearl.

The new center attracted the Arab colonists of Kūfa, and the ascetics of Baghdād soon found themselves dependent upon Kūfan teachers. Three schools were formed. Bakr ibn Khunays Kūfī[529] trained Maᶜrūf Karkhī (d. 200; full name: Abū Maḥfūẓ Maᶜrūf ibn Fīruzān of Karkh Bājiddā),[530] a simple illiterate[531] whose effective holiness[532] was recognized even by the strict Ibn Ḥanbal. All that remains of Maᶜrūf are brief sayings proving he accepted the terms *ṭumaᵓnīna* (= *maᶜrifa*) and *maḥabba*[533] (which are still dis-

524. Baqlī, I, 78 (cf. I, 9).

525. The Syrian school, after him, includes Ibn al-Jallā and Abū ᶜAmr Dimishqī, who perhaps should be identified with Abū Ḥulmān.

526. Ibn ᶜArabī, *Muḥāḍ.*, II, 328.

527. Ashᶜarī, *Maqālāt*, 97a; Ḥazm IV, 226–27; Samᶜānī, 70a; Sarrāj, *Lumaᶜ*, 200; Tagrib, I, 460.

528. *Ḥayawān*, IV, 146; cf. herein, ch. 2 n 182, text at ch. 3 n 56.

529. Makkī, *Qūt*, I, 9; Dhahabī, *Iᶜtidāl*, s.n.; Ibn ᶜArabī, *Muḥāḍ.*, II, 345.

530. According to Maqdisī, *Homonyma*, 128. Cf. ᶜAṭṭār, I, 269–74; Mālinī, 27; Samᶜānī, 478b; *Ḥilya*, vol. IX, ms. Paris 2029, f. 49b–54b.

531. He was also the student of Rabiᶜ ibn Ṣabīḥ. A verse is attributed to him (Sibṭ Ibn al-Jawzī, *Mirᵓāt*, ms. Paris, f. 35a).

532. *Mujāb al-daᶜwa; tiryāq mujarrab* (Sulamī, ap. Qush. s.v.). Ibn al-Farrā, *Ṭabaq. Ḥanābila*, s.n.

533. *Passion*, Fr 3:37/Eng 3:29. The anecdote of the ostrich with the pearl is supposed to have been the object of one of Shāfiᶜī's legal opinions (according to Muzanī, ap. Subkī, I, 241); and apparently figures in the Chinese story of Tripitaka (Casanova). Bakr ibn Khunays, the author of

puted). In addition to his students in *ḥadīth*, Khalaf ibn Hishām Bazzār, Zakaryā ibn Yaḥyā Marwazī, and Yaḥyā ibn abī Ṭālib, he had imitators in mysticism, including Sarī Saqaṭī (d. 253) and Ibrahīm ibn al-Junayd (d. c. 270). Later, the whole school of Baghdād would make claims to him. The mosque built on his tomb (its minaret was redone in 612/1215) is still a busy place of pilgrimage.[534]

It was the example of another Kūfan, Abū Hāshim Kūfī, that inspired the sermons of a contemporary *qāṣṣ*, Manṣūr ibn ᶜAmmār Dindāngānī[535] (d.225; born in Baṣra, the son of an Arab of Sulaym who had been a colonist in the area around Marv). According to Ibn al-Jawzī,[536] Ibn ᶜAmmār was the first to import the art of the popular sermon (*waᶜẓ*) to Baghdād.[537] He studied with Ibn Lahīᶜa, whom he is supposed to have met in Cairo. He was a vehement, uneducated preacher, and he had disciples including Abū Saᶜīd ibn Yūnus, Ibn abī'l-Ḥawwārī, and ᶜAlī ibn Muwaffaq. Ibn ᶜAdī rejected his *ḥadīth*; Ibn ᶜUyayna and Bishr Ḥāfī considered him an illiterate.[538] The most famous titles of his eschatological sermons are preserved in the *Fihrist*:[539] "The Cloud over the Damned," "The 'Yes'" (*mīthāq*), "Thinking Well of God," "The Summons to Come before God and Be Judged," "Wait for Us, That We May Borrow from Your Light" (Qur 57:13),[540] etc. One preserved fragment, oratorical and full of images, allows us to form our own Judgment of his style.[541]

A third, more strictly Sunni (anti-Shiite) school, with a more solid base in law, is that of Bishr ibn Ḥārith Ḥāfī (d. 227), a student of Yūsuf ibn Asbāṭ. The school professes the common mystical doctrine in attenuated form (as we have seen, on the subject of the *ḥajj*).[542] The hypocrisy of the *ahl al-ḥadīth* provoked particularly sharp words from Bishr: "Pay the tithe of your *ḥadīth*!" he said, i.e., "Practice one tenth of the precepts you try to

---

the *ḥadīth* on the evil *qurrā* (*Talbīs*, 121) and a student, through Ḍirār ibn ᶜAmr, of Yazīd Raqqāshī (Kalābādhī, *Akhbār*, 8b, 16b), is given a biography in the *Ḥilya* (VIII, 364, 365). The life of Maᶜrūf Karkhī (his *waqf* in Baghdād is managed by the Suwaydi family) was recorded by Ibn al-Jawzī (*Faḍāʾil M.*). His *maqām* in Egypt, at Minia, is mentioned by ᶜAli Pasha Mubārak (XII, 37).

534. *Mission en Mésopotamie*, II, 108. The legend, accepted by ᶜAṭṭār, of his conversion from Christianity to Islam when he was a child, and the contrary legend, also accepted by ᶜAṭṭār, of the claim to his body made by the Christians at the time of his burial, seem to me to cancel each other. His relations with the eighth Shiite Imām also seem to be no more than an assumption.

535. Samᶜānī, s.v.; Dhahabī, *Iᶜtidāl*.

536. *Quṣṣāṣ*, s.v.

537. Before him a Muᶜtazilite, Bishr ibn Muᶜtamir (student of Wāṣil, through Bishr ibn Saᶜīd and Zaᶜfarānī, and teacher of Murdār), while in prison in Baghdād, had composed verse and popular sermons (Jāḥiẓ, *Ḥayawān*, VI, 92–93 and 97 ff., 94–96 and 136 ff.; *Bayān*, I, 76–78; Malaṭī, f. 65–66); the style is not unlike that of Murrī, Abū'l-ᶜAtāhiya, or Anṭākī.

538. Makkī, *Qūt*, I, 153.

539. *Fihrist*, 184.

540. Herein, ch. 4 n 9.

541. Sarrāj, *Maṣāriᶜ*, 126–28.

542. Herein, pp. 44–45.

impose on others."[543] In spite of his biographers' discretion, we know that he, like Muḥāsibī, came into conflict with Ibn Ḥanbal.[544] One of his mystical works is in the library of Bankipore,[545] and Ibn al-Jawzī wrote a *Faḍā'il Bishr.*[546]

At this time, Baghdād was the meeting place of many traditionists and literary men sympathetic[547] to mysticism. In their meetings, Abū'l-ᶜAtāhiya, from Kūfa, who had been cured of a profane love for ᶜUtba,[548] his favorite, sang lines of unaffected poetry on his conversion to love for God. The first collections of Islamic mystical anecdotes intended for the general public were made in these *majālis.* The moralizing value of the collections has not yet been exhausted. They contain short pieces, not at all didactic, very slightly arranged according to the moral virtues they illustrate. Together they constitute true encyclopedias for the popularization of Sufism. The oldest are by Muḥammad ibn Ḥusayn Burjulānī (d. 238): his *Kitāb al-ruhbān*[549] was edited by Ibrāhīm ibn ᶜAbdallah ibn al-Junayd (d. c. 270);[550] his *Karam wa jūd wa sakhā' al-nufūs*[551] by Aḥmad ibn Masrūq (d. 298). Then Ibn abī'l-Dunyā (208–281), who rose to become preceptor to the crown prince, wrote numerous works,[552] all intended for the lay public.[553] The great later sufi monographs took all of their information on the early masters from these third-century compilations, as summarized by Khuldī in his *Ḥikāyat* and by Abū Nuᶜaym in the *Ḥilya.* The doctrinal unification of the Baghdād school would be achieved in practice only with Junayd (d. 298), but its seed was in the powerful synthesis that Muḥāsibī (d. 243) had dared to make during this earlier period.

543. Mālinī, *Arbaᶜīn,* 30; Tagrib., 413.
544. Mālinī, *Arbaᶜīn,* 13.
545. No. 103, of the year 483.
546. Ms. Brill-Houtsma.
547. Cf. the *zuhdiyāt* of Abū Nuwās.
548. Sibṭ Ibn al-Jawzī, ms. Paris 1505, f. 78b.
549. Herein, text at ch. 2 n 127; *Fihrist,* 185.
550. On him cf. Dhahabī, *Iᶜtidāl,* II, no 1032; III, no. 2079.
551. Ms. Damascus Ẓah. majm. 38; Khaṭīb had studied it (ms. Damascus Ẓah majm. 18).
552. Brockelmann's article in the *Encyclopeadia of Islam,* s.n.
553. Not a mystic by intention, Ibn abī'l-Dunyā had influence because of his authentic piety, which was at once spontaneous and traditional, with sources in Burjulānī and Manṣūr ibn ᶜAmmār (*Ḥilya,* IX, 328). He had a vast audience that extended as far as the court. Followers began to make new editions of his works with naive fervor. The *Kitāb al-riqqa wa'l-bukā* (ms. Damascus) and *Kitāb faḍā'il 10 dhī'l-ḥijja* (ms. Leiden) ought to be published now that we have a *majmūᶜa* (Cairo, 1354) in which there are five *risālāt,* including the *Kitāb al-awliyā.* Among Ḥanbalites, a line of authors linked to Ibn abī'l-Dunyā survives, including Muḥammad ibn Muḥammad Manbijī (c. 777 A.H.), author of the *Taṣliyat ahl al-maṣā'ib* (ed. Cairo, 1929).

5

THE SCHOOLS OF THE THIRD CENTURY A.H.

1. Muḥāsibī's Codification of the Early Tradition

A. His Life and Works

LIFE

Abū ᶜAbdallāh Ḥārith ibn Asad ᶜAnazī (perhaps a pure Arab of the ᶜAnaza Bedouin tribe), called "Muḥāsibī," "he who examines his conscience" (the word *muḥāsaba* already meant *gharīza* in Ibn al-Muqaffaᶜ's *Adab ṣaghīr,* 15, 16), was born (c. 165/781) in Baṣra. He came to Baghdād as a young man and died there in 243/847.[1] Unfortunately, nothing about his life is known except his teachings. They combine, for the first time and in rare strength, fervent respect for the most naive traditions, implacable searching for inner moral improvement, and great care for precise philosophical definitions.

In 232/846, he was obliged to stop teaching by blindly reactionary Sunnis who forbade any recourse to theological speculation (*kalām*), even in the case of those who, like Muḥāsibī, used the Muᶜtazilites' own logical and dialectical methods only to fight them. Ibn Ḥanbal himself spoke out against Muḥāsibī.[2]

HIS SOURCES

Muḥāsibī seems to have had several levels of training in the schools of various teachers, without becoming especially attached to any one of them; he was converted to mysticism later, under the influence of an inner crisis. He is said to have been the pupil in *ḥadīth* of Abū Khālid Yazīd ibn Harūn Sulamī (118–186) and of Muḥammad ibn Kathīr Kūfī, who was rejected by Ibn Ḥanbal and Bukhārī for reporting a tradition with mystical tendencies.[3] An examination of the *isnād* of Muḥāsibī's works (especially his *Riᶜāya, Risālat al-makāsib,* and *Faṣl fī'l-maḥabba*) provides a long list of important

1. Samᶜānī, f. 509b; Dhahabī, *Iᶜtidāl,* I, 71; Tagrib., I, 775.
2. A detail confessed by Naṣrabādhī and masked by the others.
3. *Firāsa bi nūr Allāh* (accepted by Junayd; ap. Mālinī, f. 7).

sources. The principal ones are: (a) (years 40–110) Wahb ibn Munabbih (whom he quotes directly, as if from written works), Mujāhid, Ḥasan Baṣrī, Bakr Muzanī; (b) (years 80–160) Ibn Jurayj Makkī, Thawrī, Ibn Adham, Wuhayb ibn Khālid (d. 165), Muḍar al-Qārī; (c) (years 140–215) Abū'l-Naẓar Kalbī, ʿAbd al-ʿAzīz Mājishūnī, Abū Dāwūd Sulaymān ibn Dāwūd Ṭayālisī (d. 203), Ḥajjāj ibn Muḥammad Maṣīṣī (d. 206), ʿUbaydallah ibn Mūsä ʿAbsī Kūfī (d. 213), Dārānī (d. 215); (d) unlike others, he did not hesitate to refer to his contemporaries Sanīd (var: Sunbadh) ibn Dāwūd Maṣīṣī (d. 226), a student of Ḥammād ibn Zayd; Abū ʿAbd al-Raḥmān Musabbib ibn Isḥāq ʿAbdī ʿAllaʾyī (d. 229), a student of Ibn ʿUyayna; Rajā Qaysī; Muḥammad ibn al-Ḥusayn, i.e., Burjulānī (d. 238); Abū'l-Ḥasan ʿUthmān ibn abī Shayba (d. 239); Abū Hamām Walīd ibn Shajaʿ Sakūnī (d. 243); and Dhū'l-Nūn Miṣrī (d. 245), via Ḥusayn ibn Aḥmad Shāmī. This list should be examined closely; Muḥāsibī tells us in the *Naṣāʾiḥ* that he chose the authors to whom he refers not for the formal legitimacy of their *isnād* but because of the moral value of their lives and teaching.

HIS WORKS

1. *Kitāb al-riʿāya liḥuqūq Allah wa'l-qiyām bihā* (= *Riʿāya*), ms. Oxford Hunt. 611, f. 1–151b (copied in 539 A.H.)[4]

Cairo ms. II, 87, entitled *Al-riʿāya fī taḥṣīl al-maqāmāt*, copied in 581, is not by Muḥāsibī. It contains quotations from Ḥallāj and especially from Harawī's (d. 481) *Manāzil al-sāʾirīn*.

2. *Kitāb al-naṣāʾiḥ*,* ms. London Or. 7900.
3. *Kitāb al-tawahhum*, ms. Ox Hunt. 611, f. 152a, 171a.[5]
4. *Risālat al-makāsib wa'l-waraʿ wa'l-shubuhāt*,[6] ms. Fayḍiyya 1101 (copied in 523 A.H.), sec. V.
5. *Risālat ādāb al-nufūs*, ms. Fayḍiyya 1101, sec. VII (containing four letters at the end).
6. *Risālat māʾiyyat al-ʿaql wa maʿnāhu*,[7] ms. Fayḍiyya 1101, sec. VIII.
7. *Risālat badʾ man anāb ilä'llah*, ms. Fayḍiyya 1101, sec. II.[8]
8. *Risālat al-ʿaẓama*, id., sec. III.
9. *Risālat al-tanbīh*, id., sec. IV.

* Corrected in the second French edition from *Kitāb al-waṣāyā*, but see bib. for published version.

4. Margaret Smith has published an excellent edition of the *Riʿāya* (London, 1940, reissue 1947, G.O.F.). [Smith gives, in the margins of her edition, the folio numbers of the manuscript to which Massignon refers throughout the *Essay*.]

5. *Passion*, Fr 3:178/Eng 3:166.

6. Ibid., Fr 3:241/Eng 3:227.

7. Ibid., Fr 3:68/Eng 3:59 [or *māhiyya*, as it is usually written. *Māʾiyya* may be closer to the etymological source of the word (see R. Arnaldez in *EI2*, s.v., *Māhiyya*); the sense is not in dispute].

8. Ed H. Ritter, Glückstadt, 1935.

10. *Risālat fahm al-ṣalat,* id., sec. VI.
11. *Masāʾil fī aʿmāl al-qulūb wa'l-jawāriḥ,* id., sec. IX.
12. *Faṣl fī'l-maḥabba,* reproduced by Abū Nuʿaym (*Ḥilya*), from a written source.[9]
13. *Risāla fī'l-zuhd,* ms. Fayḍiyya 1101, sec. I. Perhaps identical to the *Kitāb al-zuhd* quoted by Ghazālī (*Iḥyā*).
14. *Kitāb al-ṣabr,* ms. Bankipore 105 (last three folios; the copy is from the year 631).[10]
15. *Kitāb al-dimāʾ,* showing that the "blood" shed among the Ṣaḥāba did not damage the Islamic Community's doctrinal unity (Abū ʿAlī Faḍl ibn Shādhān, d. c. 350,[11] ap. Samʿānī, s.n.) = *Kitāb al-kaff ʿamma sukhira* (*sic*: properly *shujira*) *bayn al-Ṣaḥāba,* read by Dhahabī (s.n.). Perhaps the long extracts in Yāfiʿī on the "riches of Ibn ʿAwf" come from this book (Yāfiʿī, *Rawḍ,* ms. Paris 2040, f. 11 a-b; *Nashr,* Cairo edition, II, 382–83, abridged).
16. *Sharḥ al-maʿrifa wa badhl al-naṣīḥa,* ms. Berlin, 2815, f. 208–10.
16 *bis.* Fragment on *al-muḥāsaba,* ms. Berlin, 2814, f. 80b-81a.
17. *Kitāb al-baʿth wa'l-nushūr,* ms. Paris 1913, f. 196a-203a. Comparison with number 3 shows that number 17 has been altered.
18. *Tafakkur wa iʿtibār;* cited in *Fihrist,* 184.
19. Sprenger thought he could attribute to Muḥāsibī the *Kitāb dawā dāʾ al-nufūs,* which Aḥmad ibn ʿĀṣim Anṭākī edited, with a *Kitāb al-shubuhāt,* as a work of his teacher "Abū ʿAbdallāh." Anṭākī, a well-known writer and a teacher of Ibn abī'l-Ḥawwārī (d. 246), was older than Muḥāsibī.[12] The teacher "Abū ʿAbdallāh" is probably Nibājī, another of Ibn abī'l-Ḥawwārī's teachers. As we have seen, upon close examination the remarkable text of the *Dawā* reveals an archaic doctrine that clearly predates Muḥāsibī.
20. *Irshād* (*mustarshid*), ms. Cairo (cited by ʿAbdarī, *Mudkhal,* II, 226).
21. *Fahm al-Qurʾān* (cited by Ibn Taymiyya, *Naql,* II, 4, 24; Madārishī-Nadjī, *Majm.* Ibn Taymiyya, 1329, 367–68).
22. *Akhlāq* (ms. Köpr. 725).

The *Riʿāya's* influence on the best North-African Muslims, Abū Madyan, Ibn ʿAbbād, Zarrūq (*ʿumdat al-ṣādiq*), is well known. Naṣrābādhī defended Muḥāsibī. Ibn al-Jawzī attacked him (*Talbīs,* 178 [cf. 124], 187–90, where he claims that Muḥāsibī invented the dialogue between Abū Dharr

9. [*Ḥilya,* X, 73–110], for which Ibn al-Jawzī (in the preface to his *Ṣafwa*) reproaches Abū Nuʿaym, as he does for the details given on Anṭākī and Shiblī (anecdote cited herein, text related to ch. 3 n 9 and ch. 4 n 501).

10. A fragment of the *Kitāb al-ṣabr wa'l-riḍā* was published by O. Spies in *Islamica* [Leipzig], 1934.

11. Cited by Anbarī, *Nuzhat al-alibbā,* 345.

12. Kalābādhī; and all chronological lists.

and Ibn ᶜAwf [quoted in *Murūj*, IV, 270]; Ibn al-Jawzī therefore puts the date of Abū Dharr's death back from 32 to 25 A.H.). Abdalhalim Mahmud is the author of a dissertation in French on Muḥāsibī.

B. Summaries and Extracts

The *Riᶜāya* takes the form of advice dictated to a disciple, divided into sixty odd chapters: an introduction (f. 4a) on *istimāᶜ*, explaining how to listen in order to obtain the most benefit from what is said; (ch. 1) on *rahbāniyya* (f. 5b), the monastic life mentioned in the Qurʾān; (ch. 2) *mughtarr nafsahu* (f. 8a), how the examination of conscience dissipates illusions about your own devotion; (3) the first required knowledge (f. 8b), the knowledge that you are a servant subject to a master; (4) rules for the examination of conscience, the *muḥāsaba* (f. 9a), concerning the future, concerning the past; (5) the stages of conversion (*tawba*, f. 11);[13] (6) being prepared for death (*istiᶜdād li'l-mawt*, f. 34b); (7–12) the implicit hypocrisy (*riyā*, f. 39b) of those who practice religion in order to be seen practicing it—incitements to remedies against this hypocrisy; (13) (f. 49b) how to learn to despise the world; (14–15) how *ikhlāṣ* allows you to prevail, and psychological defenses against Satanic temptation; (16–19) categories of implicit hypocrisy; (20–23) how to make yourself act only for God and without self-interest; (24–27) how to form an intent (*niyya*) at the moment of action; (28) how to turn towards God during action; (29) how to take the measure of the consequences of your actions upon others: the risks of scandal, of vainglory, of the sadness when you feel despised, of divulgence of hurtful secrets; (37–44) to what extent must you desire the contempt of others, not their esteem; (45–53) how to retire into yourself and struggle against conceit (*ᶜujb*); (54–57) pride (*kibr*) and humility; (58) the forms of illusion (*ghirra*) that deceive the servants of God; (59) permitted hate and zeal; (60) how to lead a unified life, night and day, before God; (61) remaining full of fear of yourself after beginning to serve God.[14]

Beginning of the *Naṣāʾiḥ* (ms. London, Or. 7900, f. 2b-3b) [*Recueil*, pp. 18–20]: In this autobiography or philosophical confession, which was no doubt the inspiration for Ghazālī's *Munqidh*, Muḥāsibī, like many of his contemporaries, observes that the Islamic Community is split "into about seventy sects" and that no one knows which one is in the right. He continues:

13. In this section there is a phrase taken from Dārānī: "The friend does not abandon His friend."

14. The comparison with Makkī (*Qūt al-qulūb*) and Ghazālī (*Iḥyā*) is very instructive. Makkī gives but a pale reflection of ch. 4 (I, 75), 5 (I, 178), 14, and 24 (*II, 158*); and Ghazālī, in his *Muhlikāt*, merely summarizes ch. 59 (III, 113), 7 (III, 203), 54 (III, 237), 58 (III, 264); cf. 5 (IV, 1). Neither of them gives the linked states of consciousness, the method of experimental psychology, taught by Muḥāsibī.

I was seized by the desire for a directive in my studies; I exercised my thought; I observed longer than before. From the Book of God and the consensus (*ijmāᶜ*) of the Community it became clear to me that covetousness hides the right path and leads away from the truth. Then I discovered, by the consensus of the Community, in the Book of God revealed to the Prophet, that the way to salvation is to hold fast to piety towards God, to the accomplishment of canonical duties, to the scrupulous observance (*waraᶜ*) of prescription and proscription of acts, and to all the sanctions of religious law; and in all things to act purely for God and follow the Prophet's example (*taʾassī*).[15] Then I began to learn the canonical duties and sanctions, the ways of the Prophet and the strict observance of the rules as described by the learned and in the sources. But I noticed that there was agreement on some points and disagreement on others. The Prophet of God said, "Islam began in exile (*gharīban*), and it will be exiled again as in the beginning. Happy are the expatriates of the nation of Muḥammad, for they live in solitude, alone with their religion."[16] My misfortune grew because of the lack of guides able to conduct me (to the blessed solitude of true Islam),[17] and I feared that sudden death would overtake me in the troubled state in which I was held by the Community's discord. Concerning what I could not discover alone, I exhorted myself to make inquiries of people (*qawm*) in whom I had noticed signs of piety, abstinence, and scrupulous observance, people who preferred (*ʾīthār*) the next life to this one. I found that their guidance and maxims (*waṣāyā*) agreed with the advice of the imāms of the right path, that they gave the same good counsel (*naṣḥ*) to the Community,[18] giving no man license to sin but not despairing of God's forgiveness for any fault, recommending patience (*ṣabr*) during unhappiness and adversity, contentment (in God, *riḍā*) with the (divine) decrees, and gratitude (*shukr*) for the gifts of grace.[19] And they sought to make God's servants love (*taḥabbub*) Him[20] by reminding them of His

15. *Passion*, Fr 3:196/Eng 3:184.

16. The famous *ḥadīth al-ghurba* (cf. R 13) is perhaps a *ḥadīth qudsī*. Ibn Rajab wrote a monograph about it in the *Kashf al-kurba* (in *Majm.* of Ibn Rumayh, Cairo, 1340, 311–28). It is attributed to ᶜAbdallah Ibn ᶜUmar by Muslim (*Manar*, 29, 493); to Jaᶜfar Ṣādiq by Ibn Zaynab (*Ghayba*, 174; *Firaq*, 63; and Nawbakhtī); and to Aḥmad Anṭākī (herein, ch. 4 n 506 and related text; see also Shaᶜrāwī, *Ṭab.* I, 82). It is cited by Muḥāsibī, Ibn Qutayba (*Mukhtalif*, 139), Sahl (*Ḥilya*, X, 190), the Ikhwān al-Ṣafā (IV, 279), the Ismaili Ibn al-Walīd (*Dāmigh*, ms. Hamdani, II, 502), and the Khārijite Sālimī (*Majm.* 649). Cf. also Mursī (ap. Ibn ᶜAṭā Allah, *Laṭāʾif*, I, 201), Aflākī (I, 273), Shaᶜrawī (*Laṭāʾif*, margin, I, 201), Haytamī (*Fat. ḥad.* 121). The question of the *gharīb*, the "expatriate," linked to the Hijra (of Hagar, well before Arab prophecy), is related to the Abrahamic idea of sacred hospitality, the *Ikrām al-ḍayf* (*dakhāla, jiwār*); Ibrāhīm Ḥarbī (d. 285) wrote an *Ikrām al-ḍayf*, ed. *Manār*, 1349 A.H. Cf. *Revue internationale de la Croix Rouge*, 1952, pp. 449–68, "Le respect de la personne humaine en Islam, et la *priorité du droit d'asile* sur le devoir de juste guerre" ["Respect for the Person in Islam, and the *Priority of the right to Asylum* over the Duty of Waging a Just War"].

17. The *Dayr Aḥmad* of Anṭākī.

18. *Passion*, Fr 3:203/Eng 3:191; Malaṭī, f. 143.

19. *Passion*, Fr 3:44/Eng 3:36.

20. Ibid., Fr 3:218/Eng 3:206.

favors and excesses of favor. They assembled the penitent faithful, bringing together those learned in God's majesty (*ᶜaẓama*), in the fullness of his power, in His Book and His ways; those who knew His ritual and what must be done and avoided; those scrupulous against innovation and personal proclivities; those knowledgeable about the next life, the terrors (*ahāwīl*) of the resurrection, the abundance of the rewards and the harshness of the penalties. God gave them a share of external sadness[21] and overwhelming anxiety, dissuading them from being distracted by the joys of this world. Desirous of their rule of conduct and appreciating their special advantages (*fawāʾid*), I decided that no one who had understood their argument* could fail to accept it; I saw that adopting this rule of conduct and acting according to its sanctions had become obligatory for me; I bound myself to the rule in my conscience, and I concentrated my inner eye upon it; I made it the basis of my ritual practice and the support of my acts; I passed through all the states of consciousness under it, and I asked God to grant me the favor to thankfulness to Him for the gift He had made to me of the rule; I asked Him to give me the strength to see that its sanctions be maintained, and to confirm the knowledge He had given me of my own powerlessness (*taqṣīr*). Surely I am unable to perform the right acts of thankfulness to my Lord for what He has made me understand; I pray to Him that in His pure generosity (*faḍl*) He may guide me and keep me without sin . . .

The beginning of the *Faṣl fī'l-maḥabba* [*Recueil,* pp. 20–21]:

The origin of the love of the faithful for religious acts is in the love of the Lord, for it is He Who made them begin to practice. Indeed, He made Himself known to them, led them to obey Him, and made them love Him (*taḥabbub*) — they were responsible for nothing. He placed the germs of love for Him in the hearts of those who love Him. Then he arrayed them in the brilliant light that lent their hearts phrases indebted to the violence of His love for them. When that was done, he showed them angels rejoicing in them . . . Before creating them, He praised them. Before they had praised Him, He thanked them, knowing in advance that He would inspire in them what He had written and announced for them. Then, after ravishing their hearts, He introduced them into His creation. When He delivered the bodies of the learned into creation, He had placed in their hearts the mysterious treasures inherent in their union (*muwāṣala*) with the Beloved. Then, when He wanted to bring them closer to Him, and to bring the creation closer to Him through them, He gave them their intentions (designs = *himma*) and placed them on the chairs of Wisdom. When they had to depart from their own wisdom because of pains (and

* This translation, as if the text read "*ᶜalā man fahimahu,*" was corrected in the Arabic, without comment, in 1929, to "*ᶜalayya min fahmihi*" (*Recueil*, p. 20). Either way, the pronoun is vague.

21. Cf. the quote from Wakīᶜ, herein, ch. 4 n 490.

illnesses), it was in the light of His wisdom that they cast their eyes toward the lands where remedies grow.[22] To teach them how the remedy works, He began by healing their hearts. He commanded them to comfort those who suffer and counseled them to be compassionately involved in the sufferers' requests. He entrusted them with the fulfillment of the prayers of the needy. Then, by concentrating the attention of their intelligence, He called them to hear Him in their hearts as He addressed them, saying, "All My witnesses! He who comes to you sick because he cannot find Me, heal him; he who comes a fugitive fleeing my service, bring him back; he who comes forgetful of My comforts and favors, remind him of them, for 'Surely I shall be the best physician for you, for I am gentle'; and he who is gentle takes as his servants only those who are gentle also."

Polemical fragment concerning Ibn ᶜAwf's riches:[23]

The doctors of the Law (whom worldly life has seduced) pretend that the Companions of Muḥammad possessed wealth; these wayward unfortunates use the memory of the Companions to excuse themselves for amassing riches. The devil deceives them and they do not suspect it. Woe to you, wayward man! Your argument of ᶜAbd al-Raḥmān ibn ᶜAwf's riches is but a ruse of the demon, who pronounces it with your tongue, to your eternal loss. When you claim that the best of the Companions of the Prophet have desired wealth in order to amass it for ostentation and ornament, you slander those venerated men, and you accuse them of a terrible thing. And when you maintain that amassing permitted wealth is better than giving it up, you show that you understand nothing of Muḥammad or the other prophets. You also judge them incapable, since they did not succeed in becoming as wealthy as you. In this opinion, you propose that the Prophet was not advising the members of his Community when he told them not to amass riches.[24] O you wayward slanderer of the Prophet, who in this has shown himself a counselor, merciful and mild. Woe to you, wayward man! For even Ibn ᶜAwf, with his virtue, piety, and good works, his material sacrifices for God's sake, his companionship with the Prophet who promised him Paradise, even he will have to wait in the dock in anguish (the *ahwāl*) because of riches that he gained legitimately and used soberly for good works. He will not be able to run towards Paradise with the poor *Muhājirūn*,[25] he will arrive only slowly, putting his feet in their footsteps.

22. Compare to St. John Climacus, *The Heavenly Ladder* [or *The Ladder of Divine Ascent*] step 26, nos. 13, 25.

23. [Fragment of another recension, *Recueil*, p. 21.] Quoted here from Yāfiᶜī, *Nashr*, II, 382 [see the complete text in *Rawḍ al-riyāḥīn*, Cairo, 1374/1955, 24–25]; v.s., sec. 1. A. no. 15; comp. *Naṣāʾiḥ* f. 8a.

24. This is a *ḥadīth* explaining Qur. 9:34 (cf. herein p. 98 and text at ch. 4 n 116).

25. Who will go there first, according to the *ḥadīth*.

But then what do you suppose will happen to us, who are submerged under the temptations of this world?

What a scandal to see this wayward man, possessing the suspect gains of illicit commerce, who howls against the filthiest sinners while wallowing in worldly seductions, vanity, and temptations. And then he comes and cites the case of Ibn ᶜAwf to justify himself!

We must observe here that the long campaign against worldliness by the *quṣṣāṣ*, the preachers (of whom Muḥāsibī was the most illustrious one), at least succeeded in establishing in Islam the collective observance of certain restrictions that had been practiced only by some of the devout, such as the bans on wine, silken garments, and paintings of living creatures.

C. His Principal Theses, His Disciples, and His Influence

Muḥāsibī had perfectly mastered the technical language of the theologians of his time.[26] Sometimes he effortlessly achieved phrases of great literary beauty: "Endurance (*ṣabr*) is making oneself a target (*tahadduf*) for the arrows of pain";[27] "Death is the touchstone of the believers."[28] But the exactness of a definition or the fine choice of an epithet was of merely secondary interest to him. The dominant note of his work is the insinuation of an intent, a proposal to transform man from within by means of a rule for living, not rigid, but supple and constantly revised; a method, *riᶜāya*, subordinating the regulation of our individual acts and social relations, ritual or not, to the recognition of a primary duty, continually renewed deep in the heart, to serve one Master, God (*ḥuqūq Allāh*), before everything else. This rule for living involves (a) distinguishing reason (*ᶜaql*) from science (*ᶜilm*),[29] because not all (theoretical) knowledge of something makes it (practically) reasonable (parable of the *bādhir*, the "sower"),[30] and because a certain kind of listening (*istimāᶜ*) is required for understanding; and (b) distinguishing faith (*ʾīmān*) from real wisdom (*maᶜrifa*),[31] because not all professions of faith are accepted by God (parable of the *waylakum*, the "*Vae vobis!*"),[32] and because obedience must be more important than observance.

When practiced loyally, with the aid of education strengthened by re-

26. He uses Muᶜtazilī vocabulary but in order to turn it against the Muᶜtazilites (*ᶜadl, faḍl, luṭf; ṭāᶜa lā yurād Allah bihā*: *Riᶜāya*, f. 82b).

27. Baqlī, II, 144.

28. *Riᶜāya*, f. 31b.

29. *Passion*, Fr 3:68, 225 n 7/Eng 3:59, 213 n 285.

30. *Riᶜāya*, f. 5a.

31. *Passion*, Fr 3:370–71/Eng 3:60–61.

32. *Naṣāʾiḥ*, f. 15b; Asin, *Logia*, no. 51.

solve,[33] experiments with a rule for living engender (in the soul) a succession of inner states,[34] *aḥwāl*, which are virtues linked in a certain order (*tawallud*).[35]

This last point does not indicate a concession to Muᶜtazilism.[36] It is not necessary for reason, *ᶜaql*, on which Muḥāsibī wrote a perceptive short work,[37] to be appointed the impartial judge of good and evil, "putting in the balance one thought for Satan and another for God".[38] Reason must discern what God prefers (i.e., "the more difficult of two direct commands"),[39] so that the soul, more and more open to grace, to the loving preeternal providence that is trying to reach it, may be infused with the divine touches (*ḥulūl al-fawāʾid*), which transform the will and make it renounce not the usage of any means as such but the *choice* of what means will be used (*siḥḥat al-ḥaraka*).[40] With delicate nuances, Muḥāsibī reviews and corrects quietist tendencies in his predecessors, including Shaqīq (*tawakkul*),[41] Rabāḥ (preference for those who do not suffer for their sins),[42] and Dārānī (*tark al-nāfila, ishfāqan*).[43] Maintaining a precise balance, he condemns the excessive rigor of some anathemas (still recommended by Anṭākī) against the *shubuhāt*,[44] and warns against vain observance of ritual by those who wear distinctive clothing (*shuhra*).[45] He remains very firm, as we have seen, on the necessity of universal asceticism.

Muḥāsibī is unusual in being an analyst adept in all forms of casuistry who nevertheless takes the most naive forms of devotion as his point of departure. In his *Kitāb al-tawahhum*, he even begins with the Ḥashwiyya's eschatology, including the bodily pleasures provided by the *ḥouris*. Then he slowly and imperceptibly leads the reader to the saints' solemn procession towards the pure vision of the divine Essence Which Alone gives perfect joy. Here we seize the difference between Dārānī's imperfectly enlightened piety and Muḥāsibī's intense inner life, the translucence of his conscience.

33. *Riᶜāya*, f. 18a: "the six means of strengthening it."
34. List ap. *Adāb al-nufūs*, f. 134–35.
35. *Tawallud al-ṣidq min al-maᶜrifa* (*Maḥabba*, f. 25; *Riᶜāya*, f. 8b, 22b, 31b, 32b).
36. One of Muḥāsibī's propositions (*Adāb al-nufūs*, f. 130 ff.; cf. Makkī, *Qūt*, I, 268–69) differentiates *ᶜadl* and *faḍl* (cf. *Passion*, Fr 3:132–33/Eng 3:120–21), *ṣabr* and *waraᶜ*, *zuhd* and *riḍā*, *inṣāf* and *iḥsān*, human effort and divine grace, the latter being preeminent and having the initiative (*Maḥabba*, f. 1 ff.).
37. *Passion*, Fr 3:68/Eng 3:58.
38. *Riᶜāya*, f. 52b.
39. Ibid., f. 30b; cf. *Passion*, Fr 3:195–96/Eng 3:183–84.
40. *Maḥabba*, f. 7 [*Ḥilya*, X, 79]; and herein, ch. 4 n 15 and text at ch. 5 n 86.
41. *Makāsib*, f. 67, 74.
42. *Riᶜāya*, f. 16a; cf. *Passion*, Fr 1:118/Eng 1:77.
43. *Riᶜāya*, f. 69a.
44. Herein, text at ch. 4 n 523.
45. *Masāʾil*, f. 237.

HIS DISCIPLES AND HIS INFLUENCE

The only *rāwīs* of Muḥāsibī mentioned by Dhahabī are Aḥmad ibn Masrūq Ṭūsī (d. 298), Aḥmad al-Ṣūfī al-Kabīr (d. 306), Aḥmad ibn Qāsim ibn Naṣr Farāʾiḍī, Muḥammad ibn Aḥmad ibn abī Sunḥ, Junayd, Ismāᶜīl ibn Isḥāq Sarrāj, and the Shāfiᶜite *qāḍī* Ibn Khayrān (d. 316). The list is abridged, showing the influence of the condemnation by strict traditionalists, notably the Ḥanbalīs, on his dialectical methods;[46] it gives an incomplete demonstration of the intense, sustained influence Muḥāsibī exercised upon consciences. He inspired Junayd and Ibn ᶜAṭā. He is one of the five masters acknowledged by Ibn Khafīf;[47] the Ashᶜarīs, under the latter's influence, salute him as the first precursor of their reform. References to the "works of Muḥāsibī"[48] are found everywhere in Ghazālī's *Iḥyā*, and I have located some of the sources for the quotations, in the *Riᶜāya* and the *Naṣāʾiḥ*.

Muḥāsibī is one of the three masters recognized by the Kāzarūniyya order.[49] Among the Shādhiliyya, there is an anecdote about Mursī, who gave a precise summary of the *Riᶜāya* to one of his students, when the student was returning a copy of it: "Serve God with full understanding (of your ritual acts), and never be pleased with yourself."[50]

Under the persistent attacks of traditionists, this admirable manual of the inner life was slowly and systematically removed from circulation. Abū Zurᶜa Rāzī (200–264), a direct disciple of Ibn Ḥanbal, was among the first to put Muḥāsibī's works on the index:[51] "Abū Zurᶜa said, 'Such books are nothing but heresy and error; keep to the (strict) traditions, and you will find profit in them.' Some objected that reading these books breathes a warning (*ᶜibra*)[52] into the conscience. He answered, 'Anyone who is not warned by the Qurʾān will find no warning in these books.'"[53] Attempts were made to accept at least certain extracts of the *Riᶜāya*, in attenuated and amended form:[54] ᶜIzz Maqdisī (d. 660) made a *Ḥall maqāṣid "al-Riᶜāya,"* an insufficient abridgment of chapters 1–4, 7, 47, 54, 57, 58, 59,

46. Junayd as well (*Passion*, Fr 3:62 n 1/Eng 3:53 n 1).

47. *Passion*, 1st ed., 411. [Ibn Khafīf's five shaykhs who possessed the science of external law (*ẓāhir* = *sharīᶜa*): Muḥāsibī (d. 243/857; Shāfiᶜite), Junayd (d. 298/910; Thawrite); Ruwaym (d. 303/915; Ẓāhirite); Ibn ᶜAṭā (d. 309/922; traditionist; = Sufyānī); ᶜAmr al-Makkī (disciple of Junayd). *Vide* Qushayrī, ed. 1318, 2; Yāfiᶜī, *Nashr*, f. 41. On the Kāzarūnī list, v. ᶜAṭṭār, II, 292.] Cf. *Passion*, 2nd ed., Fr 2:196 ff./Eng 2:186 ff.

48. *Munqidh*, 28.

49. *Passion*, Fr 2:196/Eng 2:186.

50. Shaᶜrāwī, *Ṭab.*, II, 28.

51. Ap. ᶜIrāqī, *Bāʾith*, ms. London Or. 4275, f. 18b [*Recueil*, p. 23].

52. Herein, ch. 3, sec. 4, and p. 95; *Passion*, Fr 3:253/Eng 3:239.

53. Also quoted in Dhahabī, *Iᶜtidāl*, I, 200 [see note 51].

54. Ibn Khiḍrawayh [or Ibn Khiḍrūya] and Hujwīrī had perhaps already tried it (*Kashf*, 338, 280).

and 60 of the master-work;[55] and Yūsuf Ṣafadī composed an analogous abridgment, even more condensed.[56]

Muḥāsibī's strong personality maintained his prestige; it was against him that, in the fourteenth century, ᶜAbd al-Raḥīm ibn Ḥusayn ᶜIrāqī (d. 806) directed his *Bāᶜith ᶜalā'l-khalāṣ min ḥawādith al-quṣṣāṣ,*[57] a refutation of an anonymous apology.[58] Dhahabī, so violent against the mystics, never dared directly attack Muḥāsibī, and, in judging him,[59] only summarized the article in Ibn al-Aᶜrābī's (d. 341) *Ṭabaqāt al-nussāk*: "Muḥāsibī was learned in *ḥadīth, fiqh,* and the history — sects, sayings, and anecdotes — of the ascetics (*nussāk*); but he gave personal opinions on *lafẓ,*[60] *ᵓīmān,*[61] and *kalām Allāh biṣawt,*[62] God's direct conversation with the elect of Paradise."

2. The Khurāsānian School of Ibn Karrām

A. Origins: Ibn Adham, Shaqīq, and Ibn Ḥarb

As we have seen, the *quṣṣāṣ'* movement of moral teaching spread among the Arabs from Baṣra who had colonized Khurāsān, starting in the second half of the second century A.H.; first in the city of Balkh, when the disciples of Ibn Adham, who had died an expatriate in Syria,[63] went back to evangelize their teacher's native country.

The details of Ibn Adham's life are still far from clear.[64] He directly borrowed the Baṣran school's doctrine and deepened several elements of it: *murāqaba,* contemplation[65] (which is more than *fikr,* reflection); *kamad,* contrition[66] (more than *ḥuzn,* attrition); *khulla,* permanent "divine friendship";[67] and *maᶜrifa,* "wisdom" (new notion).[68] The failures of his attempts

55. Ms. Berlin 2812.

56. Ms. Berlin 2813.

57. Ms. London Or. 4275.

58. On his argumentation, cf. herein, text at ch. 3 n 88.

59. *Taᵓrīkh,* ms. Leiden 1721, f. 22b.

60. *Passion,* Fr 3:106 n 2/Eng 3:95 n 266.

61. *Passion,* Fr 3:162/Eng 3:150.

62. *Passion,* Fr 3:156/Eng 3:143; the accused text is in *Tawahhum,* f. 170a. An application of his general thesis on *ᶜadl* and *faḍl.*

63. Like Ibn Asbāṭ, seeking to make a living on *ḥalāl* ground.

64. Herein, text at ch. 4 n 198.

65. *"Al-murāqaba ḥajj al-ᶜaql"* (ap. *Ḥilya,* Goldziher's reading [*Vorles.,* Eng. trans., 144 n 88]; the Damascus text reads, *"al-murāqaba mukhkh al-ᶜamal"*).

66. "Nothing is harder to practice than *kamad*; it is keeping a wound open, a wound that death alone can close with scars." Ibn ᶜArabī, *Muḥādarāt* [*Muḥād*], I, 219). Cf. Muḥāsibī, *Maḥabba,* f. 25.

67. *Passion,* Fr 3:219/Eng 3:207: "For him who knows what he is seeking, sacrifice is easy" (= *"ittiṣāf bi'l-riḍā,"* says the gloss, Baqlī, I, 162). "If I could devote my heart's sight to Him, I would think I had given Him more than if I had conquered Constantinople!" (Baqlī, *Shaṭḥ,* f. 27; cf. *Passion,* Fr 1:617/Eng 1:569). "Rules of agreement and solecisms — in our sentences, or in our actions?" (Jāḥiẓ, *Bayān,* I, 143).

68. *Passion,* Fr 3:66 n 3/Eng 3:56 n 19.

at an apostolic mission induced him to lead a more and more retired life. Of his hundred and twenty visions of God (during which he had asked seventy questions), he tried to present only four; "Since all of these were misunderstood, I became silent."[69]

Here is one of the four, published by Muḥāsibī in his *Maḥabba*:[70]

> Ibrāhīm ibn Adham said to one of his brothers in God: If you wish that God should love you and that you should be the friend of God, then renounce this world and the next; do not desire them, empty yourself of the two worlds,[71] and turn your face to God; then God will turn His face to you and fill you with His grace. For I have learned that God revealed himself to John, son of Zacharias, saying "O John! I made an agreement with Myself that none of My servants should love Me — I having sounded his heart and knowing his intention — and I not then become his hearing,[72] with which he listens; his vision, with which he sees; his tongue, with which he speaks; and his heart, with which he understands. When I have become these things for him, I shall make him hate to be concerned with any but Me, I shall lengthen his meditation (*fikra*), I shall be present with him during the night, and I shall be the familiar of his days. O John! I shall be the guest [*jalīs*] of his heart, the end of his desire[73] and hope; every day and every hour are a gift to him from Me; he approaches Me and I approach him, that I may hear his voice, out of love for his humility. By my glory and grandeur! I shall invest him with a mission (*mabᶜath*)[74] that will be the *envy*[75] of the Prophets and Messengers. Then I shall command a crier to cry, 'Here is *X*, son of *Y*, a saint sanctified by God, His elect among His creatures, whom He calls to visit Him (*ziyāra*)[76] so that his heart may be healed by a look at His face.' And when he comes to Me, I shall raise the veils between him and Me,[77] and he will contemplate Me at his ease;[78] then I shall say, 'Receive the good work (*abshir*)![79] By My glory and grandeur! I shall satisfy your hearts's thirst (during our separation) for the sight of Me; I shall renew your supernatural investiture[80] every day, every night, every hour.'" And when the announcers of the good word have come back to

69. Makkī, *Qūt*, II, 67.
70. Muḥāsibī, *Maḥabba*, f. 12 [*Recueil*, pp. 22–23].
71. Ḥallāj, in *Passion*, Fr 2:57 n 4/Eng 2:50 n 87.
72. Here, the Damascus ms. has been corrected by the one in Leiden, thanks to R. Nicholson. This became a *ḥadīth qudsī*: *"Kuntu samᶜahu wa baṣarahu."*
73. Cf. Ḥallāj, in *Passion*, Fr 3:50–51, 184/Eng 3:42–43, 172.
74. Ḥallāj, in *Passion*, Fr 3:206 n 9/Eng 3:194 n 85.
75. *Ghibṭa*; *Passion*, Fr 3:218/Eng 3:206.
76. Ibid., Fr 3:178/Eng 3:166; herein, ch. 3 n 17 and related text.
77. *Rafᶜ al-ḥijāb*; cf. herein, text at ch. 4 n 342.
78. Inadequate term; cf. *Passion*, Fr 3:179 n 1/Eng 3:166 n 188.
79. Cf. above, n 74.
80. *Karāma*.

God, He will receive them and say, "O you who return to Me, what have you suffered in your experiences in the world because I am your Lot (*ḥaẓẓ*)?[81] What have your enemies made you suffer because I am your Peace?"[82]

The text is fundamental, and it presents an entire series of problems related to mystical union.

Ibn Adham's principal disciple was Abū ᶜAlī Shaqīq ibn Ibrāhīm Balkhī, killed on *jihād* at the taking of Kawlāb (194). Shaqīq is the first to have defined as a "mystical state" the ideal concept of *tawakkul*, "resignation," permanent abandonment to God, which was rejected by Thawrī.[83] To define the idea, Shaqīq says, "Just as you are incapable of adding anything to your nature (*khalqika*) or your life, so you are incapable of adding anything to your daily wage (*rizq*). Therefore, cease to tire yourself in pursuit of it."[84] "Negotiable goods (*makāsib*) are now worth no more than damaged goods; merchant capital and the professions are suspect (*shubuhāt*) today, in the Qurᵓān; increasing or preserving them is not allowed, because of the prominence of fraud and the shortage of proper opinions."[85] Muḥāsibī rightly identifies the quietist risk in these formulas, which he summarizes by the statement, "It is wrong to move (*ḥaraka*) towards a definite gain,"[86] instead of abandoning oneself completely to God. The thesis, a signature of the Khurāsānian school, is that of *inkār al-kasb*.[87] It means, theoretically, a denial that man may desire to obtain anything; and, practically, a vow of voluntary poverty and begging,[88] later attenuated by Shaqīq's disciples.

The doctrine was propagated in Balkh by Aḥmad ibn Khiḍrawayh (d. 240),[89] Muḥammad ibn Faḍl Balkhī (d. 243),[90] and Abū ᶜAbd al-Raḥmān Ḥātim ibn ᶜUnwān Aṣamm (d. 237), who publicly stigmatized the behavior of the *qāḍī* of Rayy, Ibn Muqātil; in Nishāpūr, by Abū Ḥafṣ Ḥaddād (d. 264), the Malāmatī, and, especially, by Ibn Ḥarb (d. 234).

81. Cf. *Passion*, Fr 3:210, 177–78/Eng 3:198, 165.
82. Cf. *Passion*, Fr 3:227 l. 11/Eng 3:214 l. 38 (*silm*).
83. Sibṭ Ibn al-Jawzī, ms. Paris 1505, f. 16a.
84. Baqlī, II, 143 [*Recueil*, p. 10].
85. Makkī, *Qūt*, II, 295.
86. *Makāsib*, f. 74 [*Recueil*, p. 10].
87. Goldziher, ap. *WZKM*, XIII, 43 [*Recueil*, p. 10].
88. Shaqīq combined it with *tafḍīl al-faqr*, which the disciples abandoned as untenable (cf. the parallel break with the "vow of chastity" suggested by the Baṣran school). Ibn Karrām gave the first clear exposition of the problem of *tafḍīl al-faqr* (*Passion*, Fr 3:239 n 6/Eng 3:225 n 31), showing that a gradual "impoverishment" through renunciation (*tawakkul*) had to be a correlative of a gradual "enrichment" through grace: so "impoverishment" was considered a means, not an end (cf. Qutayba).
89. Author of a *Riᶜāya*; it seems the date of his death must be moved forward, because he expresses admiration for Bisṭāmī [see above, n 54].
90. Author of the *Kitāb al-zuhd* and the *Ṣifat al-janna wa'l-nār* (Samᶜānī, f. 377a).

Aḥmad ibn Ḥarb (176–234) seems to have been a powerful figure; a detailed biography of him ought to be exhumed from Ḥākim Ḍabbī's history of Nīshāpūr.[91] A disciple of ibn ᶜUyayna, Ibn Ḥarb was accused of Murjiᵓism by Jumᶜa Balkhī and Ibn Ḥibbān. They also criticized, without understanding it, the doctrine of abandonment that was the basis for his life of intense mortification. Ibn Ḥarb left behind a saintly reputation. He trained two disciples, notably, who would become illustrious in Islam: the theologian Ibn Karrām and the mystic Yaḥyä Rāzī (d. 258). The latter had himself buried at his master's feet.

B. Ibn Karrām

LIFE[92]

Abū ᶜAbdallāh Muḥammad ibn Karrām[93] ibn ᶜArrāf ibn Khizāna ibn al-Barā Nizārī, was born c. 190 near Zaranj (Sijistān) and came to study in Khurāsān: first at Nīshāpūr, where he was trained by Ibn Ḥarb; then at Balkh, by Ibrāhīm ibn Yūsuf Mākyānī (d. 241); at Marv, by ᶜAlī ibn Ḥajar; and at Herat, by the *qāḍī* ᶜAbdallāh ibn Mālik ibn Sulaymān Harawī. About 230, he left to spend five years at Mecca as a *mujāwir*. He came back (by way of Jerusalem) to Nīshāpūr, and to Sijistān, where he sold his goods in a spirit of poverty.

Then he began a resonant apostolate, interrupted by a trial, the only account of which is by an adversary, ᶜUthmān Dārimī, who succeeded in having Ibn Karrām banished by the *walī* for pretensions to *ilhām* (personal inspiration).[94] Ibn Ḥibbān mocks his mistakes of pronunciation, confusions of *h* and *ḥ*, *t* and *ṭ*, *s* and *ṣ*, *hamza* and *ᶜayn*. Ibn Karrām and his disciples traveled as mendicant apostles, clothed in new sheepskin (removed from the animal and tanned, but not sewn);[95] on their heads they wore white *qalansuwa*. Wherever he went, they erected an outdoor brick platform, on which he would sit, preaching and telling *ḥadīth*.[96] Upon his return with these attendants to Nīshāpūr, he was briefly incarcerated by order of Ṭāhir II (230–

91. Dhahabī, *Iᶜtidāl*, I, 42; ᶜAṭṭār, I, 240–44. His *Kitāb al-duᶜā* is cited by Ḥājj Khalīfa.

92. Sources: Ibn al-Bayyiᶜ Ḍabbī, *Taᵓrīkh Nīshāpūr*, extract ap. Samᶜānī, f. 476b–477a; Dhahabī, *Iᶜtidāl* (s.n.); *Taᵓrīkh kabīr* (sub anno 255: a "detailed" piece that appears, abridged, in Leiden ms. 1721, f. 73b–75a). Ibn al-Athīr (*Kāmil*, s. a. 255) gives his genealogy, Mujīr al-Dīn ᶜUlaymī (*Uns jalīl*, ed. Cairo, 1283, I, 262) tells of his stay in Jerusalem.

93. And not "Kirām" (Ibn al-Hayṣam, in Dhahabī, *Iᶜtidāl*).

94. *"Ilhāmun yuhimunīhu Allāh"* (Dhahabī, *Taᵓrīkh*, ms. Leiden 1721, f. 73b–75a).

95. Whence the anecdote of the needle of Jesus (herein, ch. 4 n 484).

96. The principal one, a sort of rule for living, as it comes down to Ḥamdūn ibn Ḥusayn Ṣaffār, is as follows: "Five things give life to the heart: enduring hunger (*jawᶜ*), reading the Qurᵓān, rising at night (for prayer), humbling oneself before God at dawn, and frequenting the pious" (Dhahabī, *Taᵓrīkh*, ms. Leiden 1721, f. 73b. [*Recueil*, p. 24]).

248). Then he went to Syria's military frontier (*thughūr*). Returning to Nīshāpūr, he was imprisoned again, this time for eight years (243–251); each Friday, after the required *ghusl,* he would beg the jailor to let him go to the mosque-cathedral for canonical prayer.[97] When the jailor refused, he would cry, "O my God! Do you not see that I have done everything possible, and that I am prevented not by myself but by another!" Set free by the emir Muḥammad (248/862–259/872) in Shawwāl 251, Ibn Karrām left for Jerusalem. His moral authority was growing steadily. He preached in public on the central esplanade of the Ṣakhra, near the column adjoining the "cradle of Jesus,"[98] and large crowds gathered around him. "Then," says an opponent, "it became clear that he was teaching that faith was no more than a recommended formula,"[99] and they left him. He died in Jerusalem,[100] twenty years after he had first come, in Ṣafar 255; he was buried at the gate of Jericho, near the tombs of the prophets[101] (var. "near the tomb of John, son of Zacharias"). His disciples would make the *iᶜtikāf* (pious retreat) at his tomb, and in Jerusalem they built a home for ascetics, *mutaᶜabbad,* called *khānqāh;*[102] this hermitage became the parent-house of the order of the Karrāmiyya, whose members were engaged in teaching, as well as begging. Van Vloten[103] has shown that the founding of the first Muslim *madrasas* must be traced to them: the Ashᶜarite schools were modeled upon the Karrāmiyyan colleges they replaced, when, in the eleventh century, Ashᶜarism began to do battle against the Qarmathians in the field of education, by setting universities against universities.[104]

97. Critique of the eremetic custom described in *Passion,* Fr 3:238 n 6/Eng 3:224 n 22.

98. The place is well known. It is at the SE angle of the Ḥaram platform (*sūq al-maᶜrifa,* a curious mystical name). It is known that Ghazālī went to meditate on his *Iḥyā* (with his *Qisṭās* [*Qusṭās*] and *Miḥakk*) 100 meters from there, in the *zāwiya Naṣriyya* (installed between the modern "Golden Gate" and the middle hidden door — *Bāb al-Raḥma* and *Bāb al-tawba* of early toponymy, following Qur. 57:13), one or two years before the taking of the city by the Crusaders. N.B. ᶜAbd al-Wāḥid ibn Zayd affirms that Khiḍr resides in the Ḥaram, between the *Bāb al-Raḥma* and the *Bāb al-Asbāṭ,* and that on Friday he prays, alternately, in Jerusalem and Mecca (Maqdisī, *Muthīr,* ms. Paris 1669, f. 99b).

99. See below, n 123 and related text.

100. It is said, also, "on the outskirts of Zughar" (*sic*).

101. The "Gate of Jericho" disappeared from toponymy with the Frankish occupation. The "Tomb of the Prophets" suggests the Jewish cemetery of Kidron, between Gethsemane and Siloah. But the mention of "John son of Zacharias" certainly indicates the two chapels of John and Zacharias, to the left as one enters *al-Aqṣā* (where Ibn Adham loved to pray). The *khānqāh* should therefore be identified with the *zāwiya Khataniya* of today (attached to the south wall of the Ḥaram).

102. Yāqūt, *Buldān,* II, 393; *Marāṣid,* I, 336.

103. *Hachwia et nabita,* 1901.

104. Additional notes on Ibn Karrām: ᶜUmar ibn Ḥy. Naysabūrī Samarqandī (d. c. 501 A.H.) and his *Rawnaq al-qulūb* (mss. P. 4929 and 6674) must be consulted; his *isnād* goes back, through Abū Naṣr A. Samarqandī (d. 455 A.H., under Tughril), to the book of Abū'l-ᶜAbbās A. ibn Isḥāq ibn Mamshādh (*Manāqib al-imām Isḥāq*), to Isḥāq ibn Mamshādh. The *Rawnaq* shows Ibn Karrām spending two days with his friend Abū Yazīd Bisṭāmī (ms. P. 6674, f. 35b); offering a candle at the Holy

HIS METHOD OF EXPOSITION AND HIS WORKS[105]

Like two other contemporary moralists, Anṭākī and Muḥāsibī, Ibn Karrām presents his teachings in the form of *ḥadīth*; most (about a thousand) of these traditions, which call for reformed ways and ascetic mortification (*taqashshuf*), are given as coming from Ibn Ḥarb; others from Mākyānī.[106] Samᶜānī remarks that some others from among these *ḥadīth* are given as coming from Aḥmad ibn ᶜAbdallāh Jawbiyārī and Muḥammad ibn Tamīm Firyābī, two forgers of false *isnād* "whose unscrupulousness was not known to Ibn Karrām."[107] The dubious sources were later fully exploited against him and his disciples; critics could claim that the Karrāmiyya were teaching[108] "the permissibility (*tajwīz*) of fabricating *ḥadīth* designed to inculcate fear of God (*tarhīb*) and desire for Paradise (*targhīb*)."

None of these works seems to have survived the persecutions that destroyed the Karrāmiyyan colleges; there remain only quotations that opponents compiled for purposes of polemic. The Shāfiᶜite *qāḍī* Abū Jaᶜfar Muḥammad ibn Muḥammad ibn Isḥāq made a collection of them, (*Alf*) *faḍā*ᵓ*iḥ Ibn Karrām*.[109] In the same genre of source, there are three extracts of the *Adhāb al-qabr*[110] in Baghdādī (on *jawhar*, ᶜ*arsh*),[111] and two extracts from the *Kitāb al-sirr* in Ibn al-Dāᶜī[112] (the epigraph, taken from Qur. 56:78, and a proposition on how difficult it is for reason to explain that God should have permitted the lion [or man, for that matter] to kill other animals in order to feed himself).[113] Baghdādī mocked the technical terms that Ibn Karrām had forged (in the form *fa*ᶜ*lūliyya*) for new concepts and introduced into scholastic philosophy.[114]

Sepulchre (ms. P. 4929, f. 52a = ms. P 6674, f. 35b); with Ibn Ḥarb (6674, 59a); in prison (6674, 37a); in his *madrasas* in Herat (6674, 48a) and Samarqand (4929, 53a, 54a); and dying (4929, 48a). It shows his asceticism and contempt for the world (4929, 51b, 60b); and it prints his *waṣiyya* to Maᵓmūn Sulamī (4929, 35b), from which Bīrūnī (*Chron.* 287) reproduces the piece on the tomb of Joseph of Arimathea. Another work by the same author, the *Ṣawn al-akhbār* (ms. P. 5039), mentions the Mazyadite prince Ṣadaqa (d. 501). The two mosques built within view of Segor (Zughar) in 352 A.H. (cf. *Rev. Et. Isl.*, 1952, 81) by Abū Bakr Ṣabbāḥī seem to be Karrāmiyyan. Ibn Yazdānyār (ms. P. 1369, 163b) quotes a saying of Ibn Karrām.

105. Which were written down under his dictation by someone named Maᵓmūn ibn Aḥmad Sulamī Harawī, of whom it is known only that he passed through Damascus in 250.

106. Indirect disciple of Ḥammād ibn Zayd, through Ibn ᶜUyayna and Ibn al-Mubārak; briefly suspected of *irjā*ᵓ.

107. The remark is Samᶜānī's.

108. ᶜUlaymī, *Uns jalīl*, I, 262.

109. Ibn al-Dāᶜī, 387.

110. Cf. *Passion* Fr 3:169/Eng 3:157.

111. *Farq*, 203, 206, 207.

112. Ibn al-Dāᶜī 381, 383.

113. A Manichaean or Hindu ascetic argument, considered so that it may be refuted.

114. *Farq*, 207: *ḥaythūthiyya, kayfūfiyya* (on the model *rubūbiyya*; cf. *ghaybūba* of Bisṭāmī; and *kaynūniyya* of Makkī, *Qūt*, II, 88).

HIS DOCTRINE[115]

Despite the contemptuous accusations accumulated against him, Ibn Karrām stands out as one of the great thinkers of Muslim scholasticism. The Sunni school that he founded would last three centuries. Its members converted eastern Khurāsān and Afghanistan as far as India, and they conceived the first Sunni religious schools. On all the questions raised by Muᶜtazilite inquiry, they provided rich illumination and new, precise analysis,[116] not only supported by solid reflection but verified by extended mystical and moral experimentation. The great interest of the Karrāmiyya (and the Bakriyya and Sālimiyya) is that they revised contemporary scholastic vocabulary in the light of the constants observed through mystical introspection. Moreover, the Karrāmiyya supplied Māturīdī with Ḥanafite scholasticism's corpus of classical doctrine.

Ibn Karrām begins by accepting the preeminence of thought (*iᶜtibār*) in the hierarchy of beings, and the natural role of reason (*ᶜaql*).[117] However, like Anṭākī and Muḥāsibī, he limits reason's powers, which are exaggerated by the Muᶜtazilites (*taḥsīn* for Ibn Karrām, but not *riᶜāya*). Though he uses reason, he is a spiritualist; he distinguishes the responsibility of the agent from the imputability of the act.[118] His work is a very careful general revision of scholastic terminology, with regard to which he takes a critical position, balanced between the attitudes of the Muᶜtazilites and the *ahl al-ḥadīth* (Ḥashwiyya). Analyzing the conditions of canonical acts, he differentiates (a) faith (*ᵓīmān*), the formal acceptance of monotheism; (b) the state of grace of the heart that is devoting itself (*ṭumaᵓnīna = maᶜrifa*); and (c) the external performance that signifies the act of devotion (*islām = farḍ al-ᶜamal*).[119] He revises three well-known technical terms: *jabr, irjāᵓ, shakk* [*Recueil*, p. 24]. *Jabr*, determinism, is[120] the claim that "grace (*istiṭāᶜa*) intervenes only at the moment of the act,"[121] not "saying that God creates our acts and imbeds evil in the divine *qadar*" (Muᶜtazilites) or "the intervention of grace only before the act" (*ahl al-ḥadīth*). *Irjāᵓ*, latitudinarianism, means "not counting the external accomplishment of the act" (plurality of the *maᶜānī* in God), and does not mean either "refusing (*waqf*) to believe that sinners will be damned" (Muᶜtazilites) or "affirming the primacy[122] of

115. Baghdādī, *Farq*, 202–14; Shahrastānī, *Milal*, I, 143–54; Ibn al-Dāᶜī, 381–84.
116. Ghazālī, *Tahāfut*, I, 22.
117. *Passion*, Fr 3:112, 70/Eng 3:100, 59–60.
118. Ibid., Fr 3:87–88/Eng 3:76–77.
119. Ibid., Fr 3:116, 65, 117, 163/Eng 3:105, 55, 105, 150. Cf. ap. Ibn al-Farrā (*Muᶜtamad*): *ᵓīmān = "iqrār bi'l-shahādatayn dūn ṭumaᵓnīnat al-qalb."*
120. Muqaddasī, *Aḥsān al-taqāsim* (written in 375/985).
121. *Passion*, Fr 3:121 n 4/Eng 3:109 n 77.
122. Not anteriority (cf. *Passion*, Fr 3:162 l. 3–4/Eng 3:149 no. 6).

faith over works" (*ahl al-ḥadīth*). *Shakk*, skepticism, means "making *istithnā* as to one's own faith,"[123] not "refusing to judge whether the Qurʾān is created or uncreated" (Muᶜtazilites) or "freely comparing opposed theological theses"[124] (*ahl al-ḥadīth*). For Ibn Karrām, *jism* ("body") = *al-mustaghnī ᶜan al-maḥall* ("that which is its own place"), against the Muᶜtazila [*Rec.* 24].

In theodicy, Ibn Karrām does not succeed so fully in freeing himself from the influence of Muᶜtazilī language. Denouncing the bizarre divine attributes that are "imagined *outside* the essence and without a suppositum* (*lā fī maḥall*)" by the Muᶜtazilites,[125] Ibn Karrām conceives an unsound inverse term, i.e., the "production" of events "*inside* the divine essence (*iḥdāth fī'l-dhāt*)."[126] He means that God really intervenes with the special graces He grants to perishable beings (He is positively interested in men), in order to attest to the actuality of His fiat's (*Kun*) visitation in them. Ibn Karrām himself, foreseeing the objection to this theory, declares that he absolutely excludes any possibility of complication in the Essence (*aḥadī al-jawhar*), any intrusion (*ḥulūl*) by the contingent into the transcendent (*ᶜaẓama, istiwā*).[127]

C. Ibn Karrām's Commentators

For almost two centuries, and even after Māturīdī (d. 340), the majority of the Ḥanafites who were careful to maintain an orthodox, anti-Muᶜtazilite theological doctrine declared themselves to be of Ibn Karrām's school:

(third century): Ibrahīm ibn Muḥammad ibn Sufyān; Aḥmad ibn Muḥammad Dahbān;[128] the preacher ᶜAbdallah ibn Muḥammad Qayrāṭī (d. 309); Ibrahīm ibn Ḥajjāj, who converted a famous Shāfiᶜite, Muḥammad ibn Ghaylān, to Karrāmism; Abū'l-Faḍl Tamīmī, *qāḍī* of Isfahān (d. 282, friend of ᶜAlī b. Sahl); Ibrāhīm Khawwāṣ, H. Mīkālī, and Ibn Qutayba (according to Bayhaqī, ap. preface to Ibn Qutayba's *Maysir*, 12; and Kawtharī, preface to Ibn Qutayba's *Ikhtilāf fī'l-lafẓ*, 2).[129]

* *Maḥall* is now usually translated "substratum."

123. Ibn Karrām was the first to make a proper statement of this thorny problem (*Passion*, Fr 3:100 n 5/Eng 3:89 n 241; I was wrong to use the word "fideism" about him, because he defines the word "faith" more strictly than in common Islamic usage), that of the believer's right to say "I am a believer." For Ibn Karrām (as not for most doctors of the law), this enunciation does not mean, "I am sure of my salvation"; it is therefore licit.

124. *Passion*, Fr 3:66 n 8, 62 n 1, 69/Eng 3:57 n 24, 53 n 1, 59–60.

125. To safeguard divine simplicity.

126. *Passion*, Fr 3:120, 122, 147/Eng 3:108, 110, 134: *ʾījād* and *iᶜdām*.

127. Ibid., Fr 3:73, 98, 137, 151/Eng 3:63, 87, 124, 138 (*takhṣīṣ al-qudra*). On his theory of the prophets, cf. *Passion*, Fr 3:210–12/Eng 3:198–99.

128. Ibn Qutayba (d. 276) seems to have joined the school (his *Taʾwīl*, 208, on *tafḍīl al-ghanī*; and his polemic against the Ḥashwiyya).

129. I have had to strike Ibn Khuzayma (223–311) from this list because he condemned Ibn Karrām, according to Ibn Ḥajar (*Lisān*, V, 356).

(fourth century): Ibrāhīm ibn Muhājir; Aḥmad ibn ᶜAbdūs Ṭarāʾifī (d. 347), probable founder of a subsect; Abū Isḥāq ibn Mamshādh (d. 383)[130] and his son Abū Bakr (d. 410), who celebrated Ibn Karrām as a "model man of religion, a second prophet"; Abū ᶜAmr Bazzāz, who set Ibn Karrām,[131] as an apostle, before Muḥammad; the refined poet al-ᶜAmīd abū'l-Fatḥ ᶜAlī ibn Muḥammad Bustī (d. 401), whose *qaṣīda* on Sufism has remained famous; and the great Ḥanafite historian and critical traditionist of Nīshāpūr, al-Ḥākim ibn al-Bayyiᶜ Ḍabbī (d. 403). At the end of this period, a theological duel between Ashᶜarites and Karrāmīs began. The Ashᶜarite Ibn Fūrak was killed, but Maḥmūd II signed an edict, which was proclaimed everywhere, outlawing the Karrāmiyya and cursing them as "anthropomorphists."[132]

(fifth century): Under Qādir (d. 422), Muḥammad Ibn al-Hayṣam[133] presented a detailed justification of Karrāmism's technical terms; his views remained the dominant doctrine in Persia until 488/1095, when the Shāfiᶜīs and Ḥanafīs made a coalition and sacked the colleges of Nīshāpūr.

(sixth century): Abū'l-Qāsim ibn Ḥusayn of Nīshāpūr and his disciple Abū'l-Qāsim Muwaffaq ibn Muḥammad Bijistānī Maydānī (c. 520).[134]

The Ghūrid princes of the time were Karrāmiyya. But the Ashᶜarite Fakhr Rāzī, who had been expelled from Herat in 595/1198 as a "philosopher" by the *qāḍī* Majd al-Dīn ᶜAbd al-Majīd ibn ᶜUmar Quduwwa, chief of the Karrāmiyya Hayṣamiyya, took his revenge by converting the prince of Ghūr to Shāfiᶜism (and to Ashᶜarism).[135] Then Karrāmism disappeared, just as its apostolate had opened India to Islam.

Only one work of Ibn Karrām's school has yet been discovered: an anonymous untitled manuscript in the British Museum (ms. Or. 8049), dated 731. It is an extremely diverse collection of moral and philosophico-mystical traditions, the majority of which are without *isnād*. The *isnād* of the others is of the pattern,[136] "My father told me, Abū Yaᶜqūb Jurjānī told me: according to Maʾmūn ibn Aḥmad, according to ᶜAlī ibn Isḥāq, according to Muḥammad ibn Marwān (Suddī), according to al-Kalbī, ac-

130. Controversy with the Shiite Abū'l-Barakat ᶜAlawī (Ibn al-Dāᶜī, 383).

131. "He was more mortified; he spoke more; he neither made war nor killed." (Ibid., 381).

132. Harawī, *Dhamm*, f. 118a; cf. ᶜUtbī.

133. Died perhaps in 407 (compare Ibn al-Athīr, IX, 209); his grandson ᶜAlī ibn ᶜAbdallah ibn Muḥammad ibn al-Hayṣam Harawī was one of Abū'l-Ḥasan Bayhaqī's (d. 565/1169) teachers (Yāqūt, *Udabā*, V, 233). On Ibn al-Hayṣam, consult the large extracts from his *Kitāb al-maqālāt* preserved by his adversary Fakhr Rāzī (ap. *Asʾas* [sometimes *Asās*] *al-taqdīs*, 79, 88, etc., from Ibn Fūrak), and by sympathizers such as Ibn abī'l-Ḥadīd (*Sharḥ nahj al-balāgha*, I, 296–99; II, 129) and Ibn Taymiyya (*Naql*; *Minhāj*, II, 24–25). The *qāḍī* Zammouri of Casablanca wrote to me on the Karrāmiyyan propsitions.

134. On this list, see Subkī II, 53–54, 130; III, 53; Yāqūt, *Buldān*, I, 97; Ibn al-Athīr, X, 171; Ibn ᶜAjība, I, 6; E. G. Browne, *Chahār maqāla*, 59; Suyūṭī, *Khulafā*, s.v. "Qādir."

135. Ibn al-Athīr, *Kāmil* XII, 99–101, 148.

136. Ms. London Or. 8049, f. 29b.

cording to Abū Ṣāliḥ, according to Ibn ᶜAbbās ..." This is "Maᵓmūn" is Sulamī, Ibn Karrām's editor, and the last three links of the *isnād* form a chain identified as a fabrication by Dhahabī in his *Iᶜtidāl.*[137] Ibn Karrām is cited as an authority in this manuscript,[138] which I would like to attribute to Abū Bakr ibn Isḥāq ibn Mamshādh (d. 410). Furthermore, the classification of heresies adopted by the Ḥanafite heresiographers, for example Nasafī,[139] depends directly on Ibn Karrām.[140]

D. Ibn Karrām's Mystic Disciples: Yaḥyā ibn Muᶜādh, Makḥūl, the Banū Mamshādh

The most illustrious is Yaḥyā ibn Muᶜādh Rāzī (d. 258/871 at Nīshāpūr),[141] who must have followed Ibn Karrām's rule for living since he published it word for word, except for the following three adjustments and alterations:[142] "The *strength* of the heart is in five things: reading the Qurᵓān *with meditation* (*tafakkur*), *keeping the stomach empty,* waking at night (to pray), humbling oneself before God at dawn, frequenting the pious." He follows Ibn Karrām's doctrine of *tafḍīl al-ghanī.*[143] Yaḥyā is the first to have professed a "course" of mysticism in public in the mosques;[144] he is also the first to admit his love for God in verse of a direct style.[145] His prayers (*munājāt*) and sayings have a contrite, confident humility, a timid, budding freshness not to be found afterwards:[146]

> O my God! My argument (that I invoke) is my need; my provisions (to which I have recourse) are my nudity; my way of access to You is Your grace bestowed upon me; my intercessor with You is Your beneficence for my sake!
>
> Works that vanish like a mirage, a heart with crumbling piety, sins as numerous as grains of sand or dust; and, with these, to desire "heavenly maidens, companions of the same age as you[147]?" Stop! You are drunk, though you have not drunk any wine!

137. S.v. However, the chain cannot be treated lightly because it figures in the *Maᶜānī'l-Qurᵓān* of the great grammarian Farrā (d. 203), as follows: "Farrā-Ḥayyān-Kalbī-Abū Ṣāliḥ-Ibn ᶜAbbās." This might be the thread leading back to a reconstruction of Ibn ᶜAbbās's real doctrine, misrepresented through so many false *isnād.*

138. Ms. London Or. 8049, f. 27b.

139. Who, besides, is a direct descendent of Makḥūl Nasafī.

140. He gives the same definition of *shakk, irjāᵓ, jabr;* and makes the same condemnation of Marīsī.

141. ᶜAṭṭār, I, 298–312.

142. [*Recueil,* p. 26.] Cf. herein, ch. 5 n 96; *Ḥilya.*

143. *Passion,* Fr 3:239/Eng 3:225–26.

144. Herein, text at ch. 4 n 107.

145. Sarrāj, *Maṣāriᶜ,* 181. Miṣrī was still masking it with allegories.

146. Taken from the *Ḥilya* [*Recueil,* p. 26].

147. Qur. 78:33; cf. herein, ch. 4 n 485 and related text.

O my God! How should I rejoice, though I have offended You; but how should I not rejoice, knowing (henceforth) who You are? How should I invoke You, sinner that I am; but how should I not invoke You, the Merciful![148]

If you are not content with God, how can you ask Him to be content with you?

The night is long, and you will not shorten it by dreaming (instead of praying); the day is pure, do not stain it with your sins.[149]

Let those whom God hates say, "Pardon!" And let those who are pardoned remain silent. The former say, "Pardon!" but their hearts remain sinful; the latter are silent, but they remember God.

Two accidents happen to a man when he dies (said Yaḥyä to Makhūl). Everything is taken from him, and everything is asked of him.[150]

He who knows his soul knows his God.[151]

What a difference between going to a wedding for the sake of the feast, and going to a wedding to be with the Beloved![152]

Take solitude for a house, hunger for food, prayer for conversation; then you must either die of your illness or find the cure.[153]

O my God! do not forget, I have been a guide on the road that leads to You, and I have witnessed that supremacy is Yours! Here, see raised towards You my hands left to rust by sin and my eyes made up with the antimony (kuḥl) of hope![154] Receive me, for You are a generous King; and pardon me, weak servant that I am.

This last invocation, quite characteristic of Yaḥyä, is almost laxist. To bring absolution, the call from the intelligence to the divine glory needs to be accompanied in the will by a glimmer of attrition at least. Yaḥyä often shows an excessive sense of security in God's mercy: "If I had the authority to judge, I would not condemn lovers, for they are constrained to sin and do not consent."

During his lifetime, Yaḥyä was criticized for not remaining, as he preached, strictly in poverty, and for not enduring trials to the end. "Poor Yaḥyä," said Bisṭāmī, "he does not know how to suffer adversity (dūn)! How could he bear happiness (bakht)?"[155] The controversy between Yaḥyä

---

148. "Kayf adᶜūka wa anaᵓ khāṭī wakayf lā adᶜūka wa anta karīm?" (weakened in Suhaylī's version, ms. Paris 643, f. 81b).

149. "Al-layl ṭawīl, falā yaqṣur bimanāmika, wa'l-nahār naqī, falā tudannishu bi āthāmika."

150. Ibn ᶜArabī, Muḥāḍ., II, 270.

151. Cf. Passion, Fr 3:46 n 5/Eng 3:38 n 96; criticized by Ibn ᶜArabī (cf. Goldziher, Streitschrift, ed. of Ghazālī's Mustaẓhirī, 113).

152. Passion, Fr 3:48 n 5/Eng 3:40 n 106.

153. Ibn ᶜArabī, Muḥāḍ., II, 370 (cf. 287, 288, 316, 363, 364).

154. Taken up in a quatrain of Ibn abī'l-Khayr.

155. About his clothes; Sarrāj, Lumaᶜ, 188. Cf. Passion, Fr 3:239/Eng 3:225.

and Bisṭāmī is symbolized by a cup of "wine":[156] Yaḥyā, after one drop, says his thirst is quenched, but Bisṭāmī, drunk, with his tongue hanging out, demands, "Is there any more?" He says: "I have drunk Love, cup after cup; / There was no lack of wine, but I am still thirsty."

Among the disciples of Yaḥyā,[157] those we can claim with certainty as Karrāmīs are Ibrahīm Khawwāṣ[158] and especially his student Abū Muṭīᶜ Makḥūl ibn Faḍl Nasafī of Balkh (d. 319), whose curious manual for communal living[159] has survived; it is a marked attenuation of Anṭākī's and Muḥāsibī's rules, and it was followed among monastic "brotherhoods."

Mysticism is but one aspect of the Karrāmiyyan religious life; when faced with a case as pronounced as that of Ḥallāj, their theological school seems to have maintained a prudent, if not mistrustful, reserve, or so would indicate Abū Bakr ibn Mamshādh's discreet account of Ḥallāj's trial, which I have published[160] (with an erroneous note on the genealogy of the Banū Mamshādh family[161] that appears to have supplied two centuries of leaders to the Karrāmiyya school).

If we are to believe the hagiographers of Indo-Persian Sufism, who put Mamshādh Dīnawarī at the top of the list of saints venerated by the Suhrawardiyya, then that order is of Karrāmī origin. We know that ᶜUmar Suhrawardī (d. 632/1234) denounced the "misdeeds of Greek philosophy"[162] in the same tone in which the Karrāmiyyan *qāḍī* Majd al-Dīn denounced the

156. On mystical union (Qush. 173; Shaᶜrāwī, *Ṭab.*, I, 76; Zarrūq, *Rawḍ.*, II, 294b; Maqdisī, *Badᵓ*, II, 80).

157. Abū ᶜUthmān Ḥīrī (*Kashf*, 133), Yūsuf ibn Ḥusayn Rāzī.

158. Who also accepted Ibn Karrām's rule for living (ᶜĀmilī, *Kashkūl*, 197; cf. herein, index).

159. Ms. Aya Ṣūfiya 4801, in 29 chapters [*Recueil*, p. 25]: brotherhood in God; pious works; being open with one's brothers (two chapters); hospitality; discretion and reserve; gifts and alms; the *sālikūn*; choosing one's companions; solitude; unfriendliness and cordiality; letters exchanged among the pious; modesty (two chapters); sayings of the ascetics about death; virtues and wishes; penitence and asking forgiveness; reminding others to observe the law; renouncing vainglory and affectation; the agony of death; various brief maxims; sayings of the ascetics on illness; furnishings; holy war; leaving possessions to one's heirs; cemeteries and their inhabitants; the importance of being mindful of God; weep from fear of God; the resurrection (copied in 610 A.H.). Makḥūl is perhaps the first author of the manual of Ḥanafite heresiography said to be by Nasafī (ms. Ox. Poc. 271, studied by Thatcher).

160. *Passion*, Fr 1:575/Eng 1:528.

161. *Passion*, 1st ed., 259 n 3 [Fr 1:575/Eng 1:528, notes]. The true genealogical table is as follows: (a) Mamshādh Dīnawarī, a well-known ascetic, d. 299; (b) his son Abū Bakr I, *rāwī* of the story about Ḥallāj; (c) the grandson, Abū Yaᶜqūb Isḥāq ibn Mamshādh Karrāmī, who died at Nīshāpūr on the 25th of Rajab 383, after an ascetic life including a fertile apostolate (conversion of five thousand *kitābīs* and Mazdeans in the city), as recounted by Ibn al-Bayyiᶜ; (d) the great-grandson, Abū Bakr II Muḥammad ibn Isḥāq ibn Mamshādh, d. 410, who was, at first, the spiritual adviser to Maḥmūd of Ghazna, at whose court he was all-powerful [being more willing than Khurqānī to accommodate the prince's liaison with Ayāz] before being forced out by the Ashᶜarites; (e) a last descendent, Mamshādh II, who was mentioned in 488 as chief of the Karrāmiyya of Nīshāpūr. Cf. Subkī, III, 223, on another (possible) member of this family.

162. In his *Rashf naṣāᵓiḥ ᵓīmāniyya fī faḍāᵓih yawnāniyya*, which Masᶜūd Shīrāzī (d. 655) answered in three short works (Ibn Junayd, *Shadd*, 37).

"philosophy" of Fakhr Rāzī. And ᶜUmar Suhrawardī (of Baghdād) wrote the *Iᶜlām al-hudā* (= *ᶜaqīdat arbāb al-tuqā*), a sort of dogmatic profession of faith, very short and dense, which is still consulted today. Experimental mystical vocabulary (*ḥayāt, tashaᶜshuᶜnūr al-īqān fī'l-qalb, ᶜaẓama, iḥtirāq bi'l-tajallī*) gave him theological formulas, related to Ibn Karrām's, that suggest an intermediate position between Ḥanbalism and Ashᶜarism.

3. Two Isolated Cases: Bisṭāmī and Tirmidhī

A. Bisṭāmī

HIS LIFE

The biography of Abū Yazīd Ṭayfūr ibn ᶜIsā ibn Surushān[163] Bisṭāmī Akbar[164] (*vulgo* "Bāyazīd Bisṭāmī") is far from complete. Dāsitānī's tales, accepted by ᶜAṭṭār, on Bisṭāmī's beginnings in the service of Imām Jaᶜfar, are grossly unrealistic as to time and place. In fact, he must have remained throughout his life in his native city of Bisṭām, except when the hostility of the Ẓāhirī *faqīh* Ḥusayn ibn ᶜIsā Bisṭāmī forced him to leave. The date of his death, 15 Shaᶜbān 260 (= 25 May 874) seems certain; it is corroborated by what is known of his relations with Ibn Ḥarb, Yaḥyā Rāzī, and Abū Mūsā.[165]

The details of his psychological development and religious education are lacking; he first studied sacred law (Ḥanafite), which he claims to have explained to Abū ᶜAlī Sindī.[166] Sindī, in exchange, taught him the *fanā bi'l-tawḥīd*, a method of prayer to be studied below. Bisṭāmī was a rugged, solitary spirit who refused all signs of brotherly affiliation, even with Ibn Ḥarb or Miṣrī.[167] Nevertheless, he maintained an awareness of mystical literature, as Dubaylī proves in a curious anecdote.[168] In Bisṭām his tomb is still venerated; he has a *maqām* at Bahdaliyya near Damascus.[169]

163. Mazdean.

164. As opposed to Ṭayfūr Ṣaghīr (herein, p. 184).

165. *Iḥyā*, IV, 160, 187.

166. Sarrāj, *Lumaᶜ*, 177; Baqlī, *Shaṭḥ*, f. 27; Qush, IV, 169. His comment: "There is a state in which it seems I am 'I,' in myself, as in every being; there is another state in which I am 'He,' to Him, in Himself." I think this Sindī is ᶜAR Sindī, who was the teacher of Bisṭāmī, according to the only *ḥadīth* he transmitted (Sahlagī, *Nūr*, f. 25), and a student, through ᶜAmr ibn Qays Mulāʾī and Aṭiyya ᶜUrfī, of Abū Saᶜīd Khuḍarī (this chain of three names is that of the *ḥadīth* of Ibn Kathīr, cited herein, ch. 5 n 3).

167. ᶜAṭṭār, I, 144; Baqlī, *Shaṭḥ*, f. 46.

168. Makkī, *Qūt*, II, 63.

169. Rifāᶜī, *Rawḍa*, 97. Also, Dermenghem has made a photograph of a *maqām* of Bisṭāmī, at Bakti (O. Zousfana, around Oran). There is one in Egypt as well (at Girga: ᶜAlī Pasha Mubārak, XII, 5). [Photos in *Essai*.]

SOURCES

In the fourth century: the *ḥikāyāt* of Ibn Farrukhān Dūrī, who received them from Junayd;[170] and those of ᶜAlī ibn ᶜabd al-Raḥīm Qannād (d. c. 340),[171] who gathered the large collection of tales of Abū Mūsä Dubaylī, Bisṭāmī's direct disciple.[172] In the fifth century, Abū ᶜAbdallāh Muḥammad ibn ᶜAlī Dāsitānī (d. 417) renovated Bisṭāmī's doctrine and dictated to his favorite disciple (*talmīdh*), Abū'l-Faḍl Muḥammad ibn ᶜAlī Sahlagī (b. 389; d. Jum. II 476),[173] the elements of the *Kitāb al-nūr*, a collection[174] of Bisṭāmī's sentences, now preserved in manuscript in the Mevlevi *tekke* of Aleppo.[175] Dāsitānī's *isnāds*, when they do not come from previous collection, are suspect; he refers principally, by way of Ṭayfūr Bisṭāmī Ṣaghīr, to a man called ᶜUmayy,[176] an indirect disciple of Bisṭāmī; attenuated variants of Bisṭāmī's statements are intentionally introduced. Another work, the *Munājāt*, is a collection made by Khurqānī (d. 426) of Bisṭāmī's prayers.[177] ᶜAṭṭār's sixth-century biography[178] is stuffed with legend; Baqlī's commentary on the master's principal sayings, in the *Shaṭḥīyāt*,[179] have been the object of much study. I do not know when to date the Persian *manāqib* of a certain Yūsuf ibn Muḥammad,[180] or the "Conversations between Bisṭāmī and a Monk,"[181] a simple apocryphal pamphlet that says he has made forty-five pilgrimages and depicts him converting an entire monastery "in Rūm."

HIS WORKS

Bisṭāmī wrote nothing, and his disciples, who did not form a school until a century after his death, were able to collect only isolated fragments, stories, and sayings. The longest of these constitute two collections, *Shaṭaḥāt* and *Munājāt*. The former were probably collected by Ibn Farrukhān Dūrī;

170. On Dūrī, see Dhahabī, *Iᶜtidāl*; Qush. IV, 112, 173; and *Passion*, Fr 3:267/Eng 3:250. He is probably the editor of the *Shaṭaḥāt* examined by Sarrāj (*Lumaᶜ*, 380–94).

171. On him, consult *Passion*, Fr 3:267/Eng 3:250.

172. Extracts, ap. Sahlagī, *Nūr*.

173. Samᶜānī, f. 81a; Hujwīrī, *Kashf*, 164.

174. Very Ḥallājized in places (f. 32 [*Laylā ana'*], 93 [verse] 135–40).

175. The pagination is that of my copy. the *Kitāb al-nūr* has since been published by ᶜAR Badawī in the first volume of his *Shaṭaḥāt al-Ṣūfiyya* (devoted to Bisṭāmī), 37–148. Sahlagī also wrote a *Kitāb rūḥ al-rūḥ* (ms. Paris Supp. turc 983, pp. 144a–154a).

176. Sahlagī (*Nūr*, f. 108) explicitly identifies ᶜUmayy with Abū ᶜImrān Mūsä ᶜIsä ibn Adam, grand-nephew of Bisṭāmī (v.i., ch. 5 n 350).

177. Preserved in Turkish translation with preface (Schefer Turkish ms. 1019, Mihrshāh ms. 202); cf. ᶜĀshir ms. 452.

178. *Tadhkira*, I, 134–79.

179. Pp. 27–51.

180. Cited by Ḥājj Khalīfa (cf. Fātiḥ, 5334).

181. *Sūᵓlat al-ruhbān*, ms. Paris 1913, f. 195a–196a; Fātiḥ, 5381.

their author tells various ecstatic stories (Sarrāj reproduces three of these in his *Lumaᶜ*)[182] on Bisṭāmī's *miᶜrāj* or "spiritual ascension,"[183] with a commentary by Junayd (perhaps authentic).[184] The *munājāt,* prayers, of the second collection, edited by Khurqānī, seem to be in an altered, weakened state.

HIS LEADING PROPOSITIONS

A former Ḥanafite (*min ahl al-raᵓy*) with Muᶜtazilī tendencies, then a convert, Bisṭāmī is a figure without peer. Later the eponym of several Ottoman sultans,[185] he became the model of the perfect Muslim ascetic. Reacting violently against the Karrāmiyya's resigned renunciation and the slightly indolent confidence of Yaḥyā Rāzī, he devoted himself to an implacable,[186] forced program of ascetic training, thereby freeing his teeming intelligence for its magnificent flights; he did not ask enough of the humble wait for divine grace. "For twelve years[187] I was the smith forging my self, for five years I was the mirror of my heart; for one year I observed both my self and my heart; I discovered a belt of infidelity (*zunnār*) around me, and I took twelve years to cut it; then I discovered an inner belt, which I took five years to cut; finally I had an illumination; I considered the creation; I saw it had become a corpse to me, and I said four[188] *takbīr* for it (i.e., I buried it, and it did not exist for me any more)!"

Bisṭāmī was the first to make an open proclamation of the goal desired but barely perceived by his predecessors, Rabāḥ, Ibn Adham, Ibn Zayd, and Dārānī, i.e., isolation before the pure unity of God (*tajrīd al-tawḥīd*). We shall review the method of contemplation he used to reach this end. The method led to an attempted meeting of the soul and the divine Essence, in which Ibn ᶜArabī and his followers believed they saw their own monism. They were probably wrong.[189] "How did you achieve this?" "I was stripped of my self, as a serpent sheds its skin; then I considered my essence, and *I* was He!"[190] "God considered the consciences in the uni-

182. Pp. 382, 387, 384.

183. The diluted, nontechnical text that ᶜAṭṭār published under this name is posterior to these fragments. Nicholson published a late version of Bisṭāmī's *miᶜrāj.*

184. Though it is Ḥallājized.

185. Abū Yazīd-Bayezid-Bajazet.

186. [*Recueil,* pp. 28–29, for this note and the following notes containing quotations.] "I have so loved God that I hate myself, and so hated the world that I love obedience to God" (ap. Baqlī, I, 78).

187. Sahlagī, f. 40–41 [*Recueil,* p. 28]; Kilānī, *Ghunya,* II, 159.

188. In Sunni and Zaydī usage; the Shiites say five. Parallel texts: "Cast away your carnal self and come!" "I had a mirror; then I became a mirror." "One night among nights I was looking for my heart, and I could not find it; at dawn, I heard a voice saying, 'O Abū Yazīd! What are you doing, looking for something besides Us?'" (Sahlagī, *Nūr*).

189. Herein, p. 189.

190. Bīrūnī, *Hind,* I, 43. A saying taken up by Jākir Kurdī (Shaṭṭanawfī, *Bahja,* 168).

verse and saw that all were empty of Him except mine, in which He saw Himself in all His fullness.[191] Then He said, praising me, 'The entire world is in slavery to Me, *except* you'"; Nibājī, endorsed by Jurayrī, notes that Bisṭāmī might have added in conclusion, "because I am you."[192] The remark shows that Bisṭāmī was not consciously a monist, and that his God transcends him. Though he possessed acute intuition and an unprecedented firmness of will, Bisṭāmī's intelligence was greater than his love. He never paused in his abstract pursuit of an external, impassive perception of the divine Essence, laid bare to his infinite humility; but the overwhelming vision never ravished his heart in the transforming union of love, and consequently his invocations contain some strangely proud outbursts: "You obey me more than I obey You!";[193] on Qur. 85:12, "I seize you more firmly than You seize me!";[194] or, on the muezzin's cry ("Allāh Akbar!"), "I am greater still!";[195] and his saying to a disciple, "It is better for you to see me once than to see God a thousand times!"[196]

HIS RECONSTRUCTION OF MUḤAMMAD'S ECSTACY OF THE *Qāb qawsayn* (*Miᶜrāj*)[197]

Bisṭāmī was banished from the city of his birth several times for "claiming to have made a *miᶜrāj* (Nocturnal Ascension), like the Prophet's." Indeed, Bisṭāmī is the first Muslim mystic whose Qurʾānic meditation resulted in an inner reconstruction of Muḥammad's ecstasy. Here are the details of the experiment, recorded in his *Shaṭaḥāt*:[198]

i.

> He ravished me once and placed me before Him, saying, "O Abū Yazīd! My creatures desire to see you." And I said to Him, "Make me beautiful in your unicity, clothe me in your ipseity (*anāniyya*), seize me in Your oneness so that when Your creatures see me they will say, 'We have seen You'; and You will be where I am no more."

Here Junayd's commentary is pertinent: "This request proves that Bis-

191. Weakened version, in Baqlī, I, 141: "God contemplated the world, and in it He saw no one worthy to understand Him; then He busied men in His service (as slaves)."

192. Qannād, *Ḥikāyāt* (in Sahlagī, *Nūr*). "Abū Yazīd, Jurayrī says, was removed from the state of slavery (the normal one, that of all creatures), but he did not perceive the state to which God had raised Him."

193. Shaᶜrāwī, *Laṭā'if*, I, 125.

194. Ibid., I, 126.

195. Baqlī, *Shaṭḥ.*, f. 35; cf. Ḥallāj, in *Passion*, Fr 3:215/Eng 3:203.

196. Shaᶜrāwī, *Laṭā'if*, I, 126.

197. See the detailed account in *Passion*, Fr 3:311 ff/Eng 3:293 ff.

198. Ap. Sarrāj, *Lumaᶜ*, 382, 387, 384.

ṭāmī was very close, without being there. What follows shows that he saw how to get there."

ii.

Once, I reached the arena of nonbeing (*laysiyya*) and flew there continually for ten years, until I had passed from the "No" to the "No" by means of the "No." Then I attained Privation (*taḍyīᶜ*), which is the arena of *tawḥīd,* and I flew continually by means of the "No," in Want, until I wanted want in want, and was deprived of privation by the "No" in the "No," in the want of Privation. Then I attained *tawḥīd,* in the distancing (*ghaybūba*) of the creation from the *ᶜārif* (= himself) and in the distancing of the *ᶜārif* from the creation.[199]

iii.

As soon as I had come to His unicity, I became a bird whose body is oneness and whose two wings are eternity, and I flew continually for ten years in the air of similitude; and in those years I saw myself in the same skies a hundred million times. I did not stop flying until I came to the arena of Preeternity. There I perceived the tree of oneness. (He describes its earth, its trunk, its branches, leaves and fruits.) I contemplated it, and I knew that it was all a snare (*khadᶜa*).[200]

These texts are an experimental commentary on the *Qāb qawsayn* (Qur. 53:6–17), a setting of boundaries around the transcendence of God, isolated from all secondary causes and withheld from all that is created. Bisṭāmī bitterly observes that even this concept, though it self-evidently belongs to monotheism, is nothing but deception, *khadᶜa.* Maintaining the intellect in simple contemplation, as a mirror exposed to the flashing attributes of the divine Majesty, would result only in the destruction of the mystic's personality.[201]

THE DIVINE SAYINGS AND THE *"Subḥānī"*

Then, at the pinnacle of intellectual ecstasy, Bisṭāmī observed, and tried to overcome, his inability to effect union. Where Muḥammad had merely articulated the Qurᵓānic revelation indirectly, repeating it in the second person, Bisṭāmī attempted to become aware of it in the first person, identifying himself first with the various created subjects ("I am the seven sleepers! I am the Throne of God!"[202] "I am your Supreme Lord!" [as Pharaoh said]);[203] then with the supereminent "I" that is understood in every verse

199. Cf. Patañjali, herein, ch. 2 n 243.

200. [Usually, *khudᶜa.*] Ḥallāj directly criticized the content of these texts, in *Ṭawāsīn,* trans., ap. *Passion,* Fr 3:314, 318/Eng 3:297, 300.

201. *Passion,* Fr 3:57–58/Eng 3:48–49; as Patañjali never recognized.

202. Which he is said to explain as follows: "This heart can indeed contain the Throne thousands of times, because it apprehends the Uncreated" (Ibn ᶜArabī, *Fuṣūṣ,* 210). Cf. Sahlagī, f. 98.

203. In Qur. 79:24; Tustarī took up this saying (cf. *Passion,* Fr 3:375/Eng 3:357). Bisṭāmī used it among mystics in Samarqand (Baqlī, *Shaṭḥ.,* f. 34).

of the Qurʾān: "Praise be to Me (*subḥānī*)! Praise be to Me! How great is My glory!" Then he said, "That is enough of Me alone! That is enough!"[204] Some commentators explain that he spoke in this way because he was in ecstasy, and that when he had come to his senses and learned what he had said, he was visibly terrified at the involuntary impiety. His contemporaries hesitated: Ibn Sālim considered the phrase as impious as Pharaoh's, and condemned it;[205] Sarrāj[206] attempted to justify Bisṭāmī by saying that he had pronounced it as a *qirāʾa ʿalā'l-ḥikāya*[207] (as a quotation from someone else, not a claim about himself).[208] According to Khuldī,[209] Junayd justified the saying as follows: "He who is consumed in the manifestations of glory speaks for what is annihilating him; when God distracts him from self-perception and he perceives in himself only God, he describes Him!" This gloss, better suited to some of Ḥallāj's ecstatic utterances, which are more explicit,[210] did not prevent Junayd from concluding that, "Bisṭāmī remained at the beginning; he did not reach the full and final state (*kamāl wa nihāya*)."[211] Shiblī, in his own style, drew the same conclusion,[212] which Ḥallāj would deepen, adding details, in his critical commentary on the *"subḥānī!"*:[213]

> Poor Abū Yazīd! He was at the threshold of divine speech (*nuṭq*), and it was from God that the words came (to his lips). But he did not know it, blinded as he (still) was by his (persistent) preoccupation with the one named "Abū Yazīd" (i.e., himself, whom he believed he saw raised up, an imaginary obstacle), there between the two (= between God and himself). If he had been a (consummate) wise man, who listens (immediately) when God forms words (deep within him), he would not have contemplated the one named "Abū Yazīd" (= his self); he would not have worried about retracting his words, or feared that they were outrageous.[214]

204. Text of Ibn al-Jawzī, *Nāmūs*, XI, after Sahlagī, f. 96, 148.

205. In appearances (Sarrāj, *Lumaʿ*, 390); but his disciple Makkī accepts it (*Qūt*, II, 75).

206. *Lumaʿ*, 391.

207. Cf. *Passion*, Fr 3:47, 93 n 5/Eng 3:39, 83 n 197.

208. Ibn al-Jawzī (*Nāmūs*, XI) exchanges the theses between Ibn Sālim and Sarrāj.

209. Probably after Dūrī (in Ibn al-Jawzī, *Nāmūs*) [*Recueil*, p. 30].

210. *Passion*, Fr 3:53, 226/Eng 3:45, 213–14.

211. Sarrāj, *Lumaʿ*, 397. Elsewhere he says Bisṭāmī is in the state of *ʿayn al-jamʿ* (ibid., 372), which is therefore not *nihāya*.

212. "If Abū Yazīd were still alive, he would profess Islam again under the direction of our novices!" (Baqlī *Shaṭḥ.*, ms. QA, f. 80) [*Recueil*, p. 30].

213. Text, ap. *Ṭaw.*, 177 (of Baqlī, *Shaṭḥ.*, f. 131).

214. From which comes the verse attributed to him, criticizing the *subḥānī*: "I am Yourself, there can be no doubt. The 'Praise be to Thee' (of the Qurʾān) is 'Praise be to me'; your *tawḥīd* is what unifies me; your disobedience is my disobedience; to irritate you is to irritate me; your pardon is my pardon" (ms. London, 888, f. 342b); to which Maʿarrī (*Ghufrān*, 152) adds, satirically, "Then it is not I who should be whipped, O my Lord, if they say of me, 'There is the adulterer.'"

Bisṭāmī himself seems not to have tried to justify the *"subḥānī."* He simply outlined the theory of union with certain divine attributes, but not with the Essence.[215] This kind of union, taken up by Wāsiṭī[216] and then by Gurgānī,[217] became established in the *"ṣifatī"* mysticism of the great later orders. But the abstract and discursive vision of the divine perfections did not satisfy Bisṭāmī. "He who is killed by His love (*maḥabba*) is ripped[218] from death by His vision (*ruʾya*); but he who is killed by His desire (*ʿishq*) is seized from death only by sharing His cup (*munādama*)":[219] desire, that is, for intimate amical union, which Bisṭāmī could merely glimpse before death. "All have died *ʿalā'l-tawahhum,"*[220] said Junayd, quoted by Wāsiṭī,[221] "even Bisṭāmī; he died having realized his design for union only in the imagination" (= by situating the problem to be solved and supposing it solved, as one who meditates is transported and enclosed by thought in the ideal frame he has composed for himself, without being ravished and taken to that place in reality).

THE PRAYERS FOR INTERCESSION

The same unusual tone, the same outrageous, insolent muttering of an intelligence inebriated by the sublime Goal that escapes it, the same haughty, cynical, disappointed nuance, are prominent in these astonishing prayers. Bisṭāmī, having acquired full awareness of the doctrine of the *ḥanīfiyya*[222] common to the whole human race, prays to God for all men: he asks that God extend to everyone the indulgence that Muḥammad requested only for the great sinners of his nation, and declares that the Paradise of the houris could not satisfy[223] the hearts of the elect: "My banner[224] is broader than Muḥammad's!"[225] Before a cemetery of Jews, Bisṭāmī asks, "What are these, that You should torture them! A handful of dry bones against which sanctions have been pronounced; pardon them!"[226] Or, according to another version, also before a cemetery of Jews, "They are excusable (because of their invincible ignorance)"; and, before a cemetery of

215. Shaʿrāwī, *Ṭab.*, I, 76. — However, Sahlagī, f. 49, 52.
216. Sarrāj, *Lumaʿ*, 89, 366.
217. *Passion*, Fr 2:41/Eng 2:35.
218. *Fidya.*
219. According to Suhrawardī, ap. Kürküt, *Ḥarīmī.*
220. On this word, see herein, p. 169.
221. Baqlī, *Shaṭḥ.*, f. 100; *tafsīr* of 53:18–23; Ibn ʿAṭā Allah, *Laṭāʾif*... Mursī, I, 192.
222. *Passion*, Fr 3:116–17/Eng 3:105. A word much discussed, which occurs in some versions of the Qurʾān.
223. Sahlagī, f. 66, 122.
224. I.e., my intercession, at the Last Judgment.
225. Baqlī, *Shaṭḥ.*, ms. QA, f. 132; ʿAṭṭār, I, 176.
226. Baqlī, *Shaṭḥ.*, ms. QA, f. 103 [*Recueil*, p. 31].

Muslims, "They are dupes (since the created Paradise will not satisfy them)."[227] "O my God! You have created these creatures without their knowing it; You have charged them with the burden of faith (*amāna*)[228] when they did not desire it; if You do not help them now, who will help them?"[229]

He prayed for Adam, "who sold the divine Presence for a mouthful (*luqma*)."[230] That prayer, according to Bisṭāmī, meant more[231] than praying for all mankind: "If God had pardoned me for all men, from the first to the last, I would not have been much impressed; but how astonishing that He should have bestowed upon me the pardon for a mouthful of clay!"[232] "O my God! If you in Your prescience have foreseen that You will torture one of Your creatures in Hell, stretch out my being to him, so that I alone may be in his place!"[233] "What is that Hell? Surely I shall go among the damned on the Day of Judgment and say to You, 'Take me as their ransom, or else I shall teach them that Your Paradise is but a child's plaything!'"[234] "If I had to be deprived of meeting Him in Paradise, if only for an instant, I would make life unbearable to the elect of Paradise!"[235] "The wise, in the next life,[236] will be of two classes in their visit with God: those who will visit Him whenever and however much they want, and those who will visit Him only once. — Why? — When the wise see God for the first time, He will show them a market in which effigies of men and women are for sale; he (from among the elect) who enters this market will never return to visit God. Ah! God has tricked you, in this life, at

227. Sarrāj, *Lumaᶜ*, 392–93.

228. Cf. *Passion*, Fr 3:20 n 7/Eng 3:13 n 14.

229. Shaᶜrāwī, *Ṭab.*, I, 75.

230. Shaᶜrāwī, *Laṭāᵓif*, I, 127; *Ṭab.*, I, 76.

231. [*Recueil*, p. 30.] A sort of "original sin" thus repaid; the *luqma* is a trace of the idea of original sin (cf. Ibn Adham and Sarī, apud Ibn ᶜAsakir, VI, 73).

232. Shaᶜrāwī, *Laṭāᵓif*, I, 127. Another, weakened version: "Would I ask," said Bisṭāmī to Ibrahim ibn Shayba Harawī, "for the pardon of all men?" "O Abū Yazīd, if God gave you the pardon of all creatures, it would not be much, for they are but a mouthful of clay" (Shaᶜrāwī, *Ṭab.*, I, 76; Sahlagī, f. 45).

233. Junayd, according to Dūrī, (Sahlagī, *Nūr*) [*Recueil*, p. 31].

234. [*Recueil*, p. 32.] Dhahabī, *Iᶜtidāl*. Compare the outrages of William Blake.

235. Baqlī, II, 14. There are two variants, following two different theses on the *ruᵓya*: (a) "God is intimate with some among the faithful, who, if they were deprived of the sight of Him for one hour in Paradise, would cry out (from thirst) to leave, as the damned cry out to leave hell" (Sahlagī, *Nūr*); (b) "If God did not take care to conceal His face from the elect in Paradise, they would cry out (from thirst) for help, like the damned in hell" (Kalābādhī, *Akhbār*, f. 155b; Suhrawardī, *ᶜAwārif*, IV, 279).

236. Ibn al-Jawzī, *Nāmūs*, XI [*Recueil*, p. 32]. A variant, according to Sahlagī (*Nūr*): "The elect in Paradise visit (God); when they come back from the visit, effigies are offered to them; he from among the elect who chooses one never comes again for the visit." This seems to be a veiled criticism of Muḥāsibī's *Kitāb al-tawahhum* (v. herein, p. 169). Cf. *Passion*, Fr 3:179/Eng 3:166–67.

the market, and, in the next, at the market; you are and ever shall be the market's slave!"

BISṬĀMĪ AND ḤALLĀJ

It became common among later mystics to compare these two.[237] The problems of the *qāb qawsayn* and the *subḥānī* have already allowed us to see how they differed. A comparative review of their language will perfectly clarify the distinction between the authors of the *subḥānī* and the *anā'l-Ḥaqq*.

Bisṭāmī teaches the superiority of *farḍ* to *sunna, dhikr* to *fikr,* and *ᶜilm* to *maᶜrifa;*[238] Ḥallāj takes the opposite position.[239] Bisṭāmī, outlining Wāsiṭī's theory (*takhalluq bi asmā Allāh*), makes mysticism's goal the *huẓūẓ al-awliyā,*[240] the "shares allotted" as each saint achieves union with one divine name (*"al-ẓāhir," "al-bāṭin,"* etc.). Ḥallāj goes further and envisages *ittiṣāf,* the transforming conformation of substance to substance.[241] On the problem of the divine conversations, Bisṭāmī raises himself, through a series of intellectual efforts (partial, momentary, mental identifications), to the *"anā huwa"* (= "I am the 'he'" of each phrase = "I have been invested with the right to preach logical identity").[242] He never considers Ḥallāj's *anā'l-Ḥaqq,*[243] which reaches the permanent source of all of these transitory identities; Bisṭāmī says only *"anta'l-Ḥaqq, wa bi'l-Ḥaqq narā . . . ,"*[244] which clarifies Ibn Adham's well-known theme.[245] Bisṭāmī's saying about the wise man who is "like the damned man in the fire, neither living nor dead," attests to his unconsummated desire for union, as in Ḥallāj's couplet *Urīduka;*[246] but Bisṭāmī's proposition *lā ḥāl li'l-ᶜarif* is corrected by Ḥallāj (*lā waqt . . .*).[247] Bisṭāmī's final mystical state, the *fanā bi'l-tawḥīd,* is a conceptual negative purgation, a suspension of the soul, which hovers immobile in the interval between the subject and object (both of these being equally annihilated). One is reminded of Patañjali.[248] For Ḥallāj, on the

237. Starting with Kīlānī.
238. Shaᶜrāwī, *Ṭab.*, I, 76.
239. *Passion*, Fr 3:238–39, 129/Eng 3:225–26, 117.
240. Shaᶜrāwī, *Ṭab.*, I, 76. But also, see Sahlagī, f. 49, 129.
241. *Passion*, Fr 3:18, 142/Eng 3:11, 130.
242. Ibid., Fr 3:193/Eng 3:181.
243. Ibid., index, s.v.
244. Sahlagī, *Nūr*, f. 137: "You are the Truth; through the Truth we see; through it we observe (*taḥaqquq*), the truth; You are the truth and what verifies the truth (*muḥaqqiq*) . . ." ". . . *I am the Truth,*" answers God, "and since, through Me, you are, now I am you and you are I . . ."
245. Herein, ch. 5 n 72.
246. Shaᶜrāwī, *Ṭab.*, I, 76. *Passion*, Fr 3:128/Eng 3:116.
247. *Passion*, Fr 3:79/Eng 3:69.
248. Analogy, not borrowing; Bisṭāmī achieves it by the alternating usage of two parts of the *shahāda*, negation and affirmation. Patañjali achieves the same thing by a completely different method (herein, p. 64).

other hand, the desired Object has transmuted the subject: the magic circle of the prohibitive statement of faith is broken.[249]

Several of the definitions and parables[250] that Ḥallāj developed had been outlined by Bisṭāmī. We must not judge his outrages of style, which were the result of an unprecedented intellectual inebriation, with those of the later monists, whose cold cultivation of the same phraseology was bitterly ironic. Bisṭāmī became drunk to the point of delirium with *tajrīd*,[251] with the previously unexplored *via remotionis*; but he remained a rigorous, fervent, and perhaps humble ascetic.[252]

To complete his portrait, here is an anecdote, obviously excessive,[253] but useful nevertheless, as much for amateurs who see in mysticism a pleasurable art as for the learned who think they can penetrate its language by consulting a library:

One day, an old, respectable, and zealous shaykh, who had been made to wonder by Bisṭāmī's pronouncements, gathered his courage and asked what he could do to obtain the same favors. Bisṭāmī, imperturbable, advised the stifled old apprentice mystic to follow this foolproof procedure: "Shave your head and beard, remove your clothes, wrap your *ᶜabā* around you, and hang a sack of nuts from your neck; then bring together some poor children and offer them a nut for each slap they give you; walk about with this group through all the markets, in full view of your friends and acquaintances."

B. The Works of Tirmidhī[254]

Abū ᶜAbdallah Muḥammad ibn ᶜAlī ibn Ḥusayn Tirmidhī (d. 285/898),[255] called al-Ḥakīm (the Philosopher), was above all a prolific and

249. *Passion*, Fr 3:110/Eng 3:99. Bisṭāmī has a glimpse of this liberation, when he refuses to pronounce the *shahāda* (Baqlī, I, 73; cf. *Passion*, Fr 3:246/Eng 3:232).

250. For example, "The reality of Sufism is a scintillating light (*nūr shaᶜshaᶜānī*), which our eyes come upon and discover, and by which our eyes are contemplated" (Sahlagī, *Nūr*; cf. *Passion*, Fr 1:520, 3:147/Eng 1:472, 3:134; this is the *lamḥat al-baṣar* of God — *Passion*, Fr 3:113/Eng 3:102); the spiritual *ṭawāf*, around the Throne (cf. *Passion*, Fr 1:588–89, 596–97/Eng 1:541–43, 550).

251. Cf. Ḥallāj, *infra*, ch. 5 n 410.

252. "I believe in Muḥammad the Messenger neither because he split the moon and broke stones nor because he made trees come together and plants and bricks speak, but because, with perfect wisdom, he forbade his Companions and his Community to drink *wine*, and made wine an illicit drink" (ap. Aflākī, trans. Huart, 121).

253. Makkī, *Qūt*, II, 75. Sahlagī, f. 59. This anecdote was for me, at Fez in May 1923, a significant test of *shirk khafī*, with the learned sherif Abdelhayy el-Kittani (see bib., Kittānī).

254. On his life, see (*Lisān al-mīzān*, V, 308) the attacks by Ibn al-ᶜAdīm (*Kitāb al-malḥa fī'l-radd ᶜalā Abī Ṭalḥa*) and his autobiography, discovered by H. Ritter (*Kitāb al-shaʾn*; cf. note in *Etudes carmélitaines*, 1951), in which his wife's piety serves as a spiritual electroscope for him.

255. Brockelmann made him into two different men with different dates for their deaths (*G.A.L.*, I, 164, 199).

original writer, on *ḥadīth* as well as mysticism. He is the first Muslim mystic in whom there are traces of the infiltration of Hellenistic philosophy;[256] in this he is a precursor of al-Fārābī. But in Tirmidhī, philosophy is only an accessory; he seeks to take the exposition of traditional dogma attempted by Ibn Karrām and recast it in the mold of a rational synthesis.[257] Less fervent and wise than Muḥāsibī, Tirmidhī was a Ḥanafite idealogue and a learned man, almost an esoterist, as diffuse in style as he was loquacious. He is a precious source because of his wealth of supporting documents.

LIST OF HIS WORKS

1. *Khātam al-wilāya* (also known as *sīrat al-awliyā,*[258] *ᶜilm al-awliyā*),[259] the "Seal of Sanctity." Cf. below, and *Passion*, Fr 3:173, 221/Eng 3:161, 209. Ibn ᶜArabī made a long meditation on this, Tirmidhī's fundamental work, which he used often; the work seems, except for a list of chapters, to have been lost entirely.*
2. *ᶜIlal al-ᶜubūdiyya* (alias *ᶜIlal al-sharīᶜa*).[260] "The Rational Grounds for Canonical Rites." Cf. below; and Cairo ms. VII, 177: f. 148–212b.
3. *Al-akyās*[261] *wa'l-mughtarrīn*, "The Wise and the Deluded," a book of examples of the different types of psychological illusions peculiar to believers, classified according to the canonical act and the trade of the believer. Damascus manuscript Ẓah. taṣ 104, sec. I.
4. *Riyāḍat al-nafs* (vulgo *Riyāḍa*), "Mortification of the Flesh." Important manual of asceticism. Damascus ms. Ẓah. taṣ 104, sec. V.

4 *bis*. *Al-riyāḍa fī taᶜalluq al-amr bi'l-khalq*, ms. ᶜĀshir 1479, sec. VIII, and Paris 5018, sec. VI (=*Al-ḥaqīqa al-adamiyya*), edited by ᶜAbdalmuḥsin Ḥusaynī, Alexandria, 1946 (60 pp.).

These are the fundamental ascetic/mystical works. The others works are:

5. *Jawāb kitāb* [ᶜUthmān ibn Saᶜīd] *min Rayy*, Damascus ms. 104, sec. II.
6. *Bayān al-kasb*, Damascus ms. 104, sec. III.
7. *Masāʾil*, Damascus ms. 104, sec. IV.
8. *Adāb al-murīdīn*, lost (cited in Hujwīrī, *Kashf*, 338).

* But now found. See below, "Table of the chapters of the *Khātam al-wilayā*."

256. See ᶜAṭṭār, II, 91–99.

257. Cf. the attempted reform by the Thawrite *malāmatī* Ḥamdūn Qaṣṣār (d. 271), who tried to reintroduce the notion of *kasb*.

258. His own reference, ap. *Masā'il*, f. 280 of my copy.

259. His own reference, ap. *ᶜIlāl al-ᶜubūdiyya*, f. 166b; on the esoteric meaning of *thanā* (consult quest. 100 and 139).

260. *Passion*, Fr 1:432; 3:11/Eng 1:384; 3:4.

261. On this unusual meaning of the term, cf. Jāḥiẓ, *Bayān*, III, 81.

On dogmatic theology:

9. *Kitāb al-tawḥīd*, lost (cited in Hujwīrī, *Kashf*, 141).
10. *ᶜAdhāb al-qabr*; lost (cited in Hujwīrī, *Kashf*, 141).
11. *Durr maknūn fī asᵓilat mā kān wa mā yakūn*, Leipzig ms. 212.

The *ḥadīth* he compiled are gathered in several books:

12. *Nawādir al-uṣūl*,[262] Köpr. ms. 464–65, Yeni Jāmiᶜ 302, Madrid 468 (v. I).
13. *Kitāb al-furūq*, ms. Aya Sūfiya 1975 [and two other mss., see *Recueil*, p. 37].
14. *Kitāb al-nahj*, lost (cited in Hujwīrī, *Kashf*, 141).
15. *Tafsīr* (unfinished Qurᵓānic commentary), lost (cited in Hujwīrī, *Kashf*, p. 141).

Finally, he is the author of the first collection of biographies of the Muslim saints:

16. *Taᵓrīkh al-mashāᵓikh* (var. *Ṭabaqāt al-ṣūfiyya*);[263] lost (cited Hujwīrī, *Kashf*, 46).

Add to this list the *Adab al-ᶜālim wa'l-mutaᶜallim*, ed. M. Z. Kawtharī, Cairo, 1358, and some other works preserved in manuscript, which are listed as nos. 17–30, in an addendum to the preceding list, in *Recueil*, p. 37.

Analysis of the ᶜIlal al-ᶜubūdiyya. It is a series of critical notes on the canonical rituals. Tirmidhī attempts to discern the rational motive for instituting each ritual, as much to respond to the Qarmathians' philosophical objections as to present a synthesis satisfactory to the mind. After the *dībāja*, there are twelve notes on the purifications preceding canonical prayer, *siwāk, khalā, wuḍūᶜ* (6–7, 9–12), *ghusl al-janāba*; then forty-four historico-liturgical notes on the *ṣalāt* itself,[264] an effort to find a plausible answer to the following questions: Why the *takbīr*? To teach humility. And the *taḥiyāt*? According to Ḥasan, it is the islamization of a pagan rite. Why is the number of *rakᶜas* not the same[265] in the last five prayers? What is the etymology of the word *ṣalāt*? (according to ᶜIkrima, it is "to tie" [man] to God); and of the Persian word *namāj* [= *namāz*]? (it comes from *Namīj*, the "Syriac" name of the first angel who obeyed and prostrated himself before Adam). In conclusion there are eight articles on ascetic psychology: the various dispositions (*manāzil*) of hearts during prayer, temptation, the three species of hearts, the heart as the house of God, the five defects to avoid

262. Extracts, ap. Ibn al-Dabbāgh, *Ibrīz*; and Nabhānī (*Muḥammad*: on his preexistence). The *Nawādir al-uṣūl* prove the authenticity of his *Khātam al-awliyā*, ed. Ibn ᶜArabī (*Futūḥāt*, II, 44–154; cf. p. 454).

263. A rather credulous work, as to legends, since it classifies Abū Ḥanīfa among the mystics.

264. Comp. *Fahm al-ṣalāt*, a short work by Muḥāsibī.

265. A typical Qarmathian objection (*Farq*, 293); cf. ᶜA. M. Kindī, *Risāla*, 10.

while praying, how the self-denial of the fast raises the four veils of the heart, the heart's three foods and four graces, and the internal directives that allow proper performance of prayers: *farḍ*, *sunna*, or *taṭawwuᶜ*.

Table of the chapters of the Khātam al-wilāya. This curious book explains, in 160 articles, the principal ecstatic statements (*shaṭḥiyāt*), be they derived from the Qurʾān or not, that were put into circulation during the first two centuries of the Hijra.[266] Thanks to Ibn ᶜArabī, we possess the table of contents:*

§§1. The number of stations (*manāzil*) of the saints.

— 2. Where are the stations of the *ahl al-qurba*. — 3. Their meetings, behind this veil. — 4. Their limitations. — 5. Where is the stage (*maqām*) of the *Ahl al-majālis wa'l-ḥadīth*. — 6. How numerous are they. — 7. What made their Master bestow that *maqām* upon them. — 8. What are their conversation (*ḥadīth*) and intimate encounter with God. — 9. How they begin their *munājāh*. — 10. How they end them. — 11. What are His response to them and their response to Him. — 12. How to describe their conduct. — 13. Who has the right to the "Seal of the Saints," as Muḥammad had the right to the Seal of Prophecy. — 14. What is the quality of having this right. — 15. What is the cause of this seal and what is its meaning. — 16. How many meetings are there for the Angel of the Realm (*malak al-mulk*). — 17. Where is the stage of the apostles in relation to that of the prophets. — 18. Where is the stage of the prophets in relation to that of the saints. — 19. What constitutes the special dowry of happiness (*ḥaẓẓ*) received by each apostle from his Master [20–23].

— 24. What is the origin of the names. — 25. [What is the origin] of the revelation (*waḥy*). — 26. Of the spirit (*rūḥ*). — 27. Of *sakīna*. — 28. What is justice. — 29. What is the superiority of certain prophets (and saints) to others. — 30. God made the creation in darkness (*ẓulma*). — 32. How to describe the *maqādīr*. — 33. What is the cause of this science of *qadar* that was revealed to the prophets. — 34. Why it was revealed. — 35. When it (the secret of *qadar*) was revealed. — 39. What is this Supreme Intellect (*al-ᶜAql al-Akbar*) from which were parceled out the intellects of all His creatures. — 40. How to describe Adam. — 51. Where are the treasures of grace [*minan*]. — 52. Where are the treasures of the energy of souls. — 53. How they reach the prophets. — 54. Where are the treasures of those among the saints who converse with God (*muḥaddithīn*). — 55. What is their *ḥadīth*.

* In fact, this list is not the table of contents but a simple list of questions constituting the fourth chapter of the *Khatm al-awliyāʾ*, which was discovered in 1954 (Bib., s.n. Tirmidhī). Osmān Yahia's ed. (pp. 142–236) reproduces Ibn ᶜArabī's responses from the *Fut* (see also Cairo ed. [reprint Beirut 1968] 2:39–139 [cf. ch. 5 n 262, v.s.]) and the *Jawāb mustaqīm*. Massignon also fills in the gaps in this list; see *Recueil*, p. 253.

266. Without mention of their authors.

— 56. What is revelation (*waḥy*). — 57. The difference between the *muḥaddithīn* and the prophets. — 59. Where are most of the saints. — 64. What is the "word" [*kalām*] addressed by God to the *muwaḥḥidīn*. — 65. What is His word to the apostles. — 66–71. What are the dowries of the prophets in the vision they have of God; what are the dowries of the *muḥaddithīn*; of the other saints; and of ordinary men. For among their dowries (*huẓūẓ*) on the Day of the Visit (*yawm al-ziyāra*) there is a distinction, and no good news can describe it. And just as in Paradise there are degrees, so for them, on the Day of the Visit, there are degrees. — 75. How much Muḥammad's dowry differs from those of the other prophets. — 82. How many parts of prophecy there are. — 84. How many parts of the *ṣiddīqiyya*. — 87. What the Truth demands of the *muwaḥḥidīn*. — 88. What is the Truth (*al-Ḥaqq*). — 89. Who made it appear. — 90. What is its action on creation. — 91. Who is its delegate. — 92. What is the fruit of it. — 93. Who is a "verifier" (*muḥiqq*). — 94. What is the place of him who is one. — 95. What is the *sakīna* of the saints. — 96. What is the dowry of the believers. — 97. What is their dowry, "All things perish, except His face." — 98. Why does one say "face," in particular. — 100. What is "Amen." — 101. What is the *sujūd*. — 102. How did it start. — 103–107. What is His statement, "The glory is My turban, the grandeur is My mantle." What are the turban, the mantle, pride. — 108. What is the "crown" of the Realm. — 109. What is "dignity" (*waqār*). — 110. How to describe the "assemblies (*majālis*) of veneration." — 111. And the "Realm of the graces." — 112. And the "Realm of Light." — 113. And the "Realm of divine Sanctity." — 114. What is divine Sanctity. — 115. What are the scintillations of the face (*subuḥāt al-wajh*). — 116. What is the drink of love. — 117. What is the chalice of love. — 118. Where is it. — 119. What is "Drinking His love for you so deeply that He inebriates you with love for Him." — 120. What is the embrace (*qabḍa*). — 123. How many looks God casts upon his saints every day; and what He looks at in them. — 124. What He looks at in the prophets, how many He receives in His intimacy every day. — 125. What is "to be with" (*ma^{c}iyya*) for God, for he "is with" His creation. — 126. What are his *aṣfīyā*. Prophets and intimates (*khāṣṣa*). — 127. How they differ. — 128. What is the *dhikr* of God; surely the *dhikr* of God is supreme. — 129. "*Udhkurūnī adhkurukum*." — 130. What the Name means. — 131. What is the Name, upon which the (created) names are conditional. — 132. What is the Name that is hidden from all creation, but not from His intimates. — 133–134. How Solomon's friend received it and revealed it to Solomon, the apostle of apostles; and why. — 135. Did he learn the letters of this Name or its meaning. — 136. Where is the door that gives access to this Name; where is it hidden from all creation. — 137. What is its vestment (*kiswa*). — 138. What are the consonants in the alphabet. — 139. The isolated consonants (of the Qur$^{\supset}$ān) are the key to every one of the (divine) names;

where are the names, where are their consonants. — 140. How *alif* became the first letter. — 141. And *lām-alif* the last. — 142. The count that stopped the number of letters at 28. — 143. What is the meaning of "God made Adam in His own image."— 144. And of "Add twelve prophets from my nation." — 145. What Moses' cry, "Lord, make me belong to the nation of Muḥammad!" signifies. — 146. And "God has worshipers other than the prophets, and whose bliss the prophets envy, for they are close to God alone." — 147. And the *basmala*. — 148. And "Peace be with you, O Prophet!" — 149. And "Peace be upon us and upon the pious worshipers of God." — 150. And "The people of my family are the safeguard (*amān*) of my nation." — 151. What is the "family of Muḥammad" (*āl Muḥammad*). — 152. Where are the treasures of the Proof, in the treasures of the Work, in the treasures of the knowledge of divine autonomy (*tadbīr*). — 153. Where are the treasures of the knowledge of God in the knowledge of creation (*bad*ʾ). — 154. What is the "mother of the Book" (*Umm al-kitāb*) that He reserved for our Prophet among all the prophets, and for our nation. — 155. What is the pardon (*maghfira*) bestowed upon our Prophet, and previously announced to all others.

Remarks: art. 13–15: cf. *Passion*, Fr 3:221/Eng 3:209. Ibn ʿArabī (*ʿAnqā mughrib*, Cairo ms., f. 4a) gives an extract of this section: "The seal of the saints is superior (*afḍal*) to Abū Bakr; he is Jesus; he is at once a prophet *ab intra*, and a saint *ad extra*! For his heart works in two ways: he receives *ab intra* the divine inspiration (*ilhām*), and he impresses upon his limbs (*ad extra*) the commandment (*amr*) of God." — 18. Therefore it is said, "starting point of the saints, end point of the prophets" (Simnānī, in Jāmī, 509; Mursī interprets the phrase falsely, according to Shaʿrāwī, *Ṭabaqāt*, II). — 19. *Passion*, Fr 3:210/3:198, and herein, text at ch. 5 n 81. — 20–23. Headings skipped in my copy. — 32. Cf. *Passion*, Fr 3:135/Eng 3:123. — 39. Cf. Tustarī, in *Passion*, Fr 3:301/Eng 3:283. — 40. Cf. *Passion* Fr 3:115–16/Eng 3:104. — 55. Cf. *Passion*, Fr 3:156/Eng 3:143. — 66–71. A theme treated by Ibn Adham, Muḥāsibī, and Bisṭāmī (*Passion*, Fr 3:178–79/Eng 3:166–67; herein, index, s.v.). According to the *Ḥilya*, Tirmidhī explains [*Recueil*, p. 36], "God has chosen the *muwaḥḥidīn* so that they may glorify Him on the day of the *Jamʿ Akbar*, in His court, before His Angels. In the nature of Adam and his descendants was manifest a seed of Love, while in the nature of the Angels was manifest the divine Omnipotence. Because of His love for the Adamites, God will rejoice in their conversation and say, in this *Jamʿ*, 'O troop of My angels, your splendors issue from yourselves, for you were created from light; but the splendors of men come from their covetous souls, while demons encircle them in the vilest dwelling-place. I made them from earth. That is why they now deserve My dwelling-place, and nearness to Me.'"

Which is an attenuation. — 75. Cf. *Passion,* Fr 3:210/Eng 3:198. — 88. Cf. *Passion,* Fr 3:88/Eng 3:77–78. — 93. On *muḥiqq,* see Ḥallāj (Akhb. 44 [50]) and Ibn ᶜAṭā (Baqlī, II, 587). — 119. The saying is Miṣrī's (Sarrāj, *Maṣāriᶜ,* 180). — 123. Cf. *Ḥallāj, Riw.,* 28. — 129. Cf. Ibn ᶜIyāḍ (herein, ch. 3, sec. 5. B.). — 131. The "Name" is the *ism aᶜẓam* (*Passion,* Fr. 3:110/Eng 3:99; and herein, ch. 2, sec. 2. B. — 138. ff. Cf. *Passion,* Fr. 3:109/Eng 3:98. — 145. Cf. Sahlagī, *Nūr,* f. 37. — 146. It is the *ḥadīth al-ghibṭa* (*Passion,* Fr 3:218/Eng 3:206). — 147. Cf. Ḥallāj (*Passion,* Fr 3:52/Eng 3:44). — 151. Cf. anti-Shiite exegesis of the *qurbä* (Qurᵓān) according to Ḥasan, herein, ch. 4, text at n 272.

HIS DOCTRINE

Tirmidhī is a theoretician. He proceeds methodically through the inventory of inner mystical experiences, "simply savoring" them in his innermost self, and then classifying them. With his balanced, logical mind, he succeeds in freeing the design of his principal works from servitude to *isnād.* But he attaches too much importance to the letter of definitions. He tends to confuse concepts with their verbal presentation; he is the first Sunni mystic to be inclined towards a kabbala of the letters of scripture.[267] Compared to Muḥāsibī, Tirmidhī is less humble and wise, more professorial, better arranged. He is a Ḥanafite deeply influenced by Ibn Karrām,[268] whose doctrine he tries to rework, taking objections into account; Tirmidhī makes great efforts to identify *maᶜrifa* with *ᵓīmān,*[269] and to reduce the notion of *rūḥ* to that of *ᶜaql.*[270] His doctrine that reason, *ᶜaql,* has been cut into pieces and divided among the believers alone,[271] prepares the way for Tustarī's philosophico-gnostic compromise.[272] Tirmidhī, reacting against Murjiᵓism, reintroduces the notion of *kasb.*[273]

In mystical psychology, he gives an excellent presentation of the "science of hearts";[274] he distinguishes *ṣadr* from *qalb,*[275] explicitly observing that *qalb* (heart) designates both the organ regulating thought and the piece

267. *Passion,* Fr 3:106/Eng 3:95–96. Here I cite the pagination of my copy of ms. Damascus 104. Cf. *ᶜIlal,* f. 166b.

268. *ᶜAdhāb al-qabr—muᵓmin ḥaqqan* (f. 398); Tirmidhī and Ibn Khuzayma were fellow disciples, with Rawwāsī, (f. 402). Discussion of a *ḥadīth* of al-Kalbī (f. 11; cf. herein, text at note 136). The role of *ᶜaql.* He is *ᶜumarī* (f. 317), like Abū Hāshim. He classifies Abū Ḥanīfa among the mystics.

269. *Passion,* Fr 3:65 n 3/Eng 3:55 n 12.

270. Ibid., Fr 3:24, 158/Eng 3:15, 145–46.

271. Ms. Damascus 104, f. 353.

272. *Passion,* Fr 3:302/Eng 3:283.

273. *Riyāḍa.* Cf. *Ḥilya.*

274. *Passion,* Fr 3:19–20, 25–26/Eng 3:12–13, 18–19.

275. Cf. Qur. 5:10–11; Ghazālī, *Munqidh,* 7. Ms. Damascus 104, f. 216, 291; The Angels cannot guess the secrets of men's hearts (cf. Ṣabīḥī, in Baqlī, II, 22). *Passion,* Fr 3:26–27/Eng 3:19.

of visceral flesh.[276] He also defines degrees of sanctity,[277] especially from the point of view of intellectual illumination,[278] without the intervention either of ecstasy (*tawājud*) to transfigure[279] the body, or of love to transform the will. Tirmidhī's angelology is highly developed and approaches spiritualism; he claims to be in constant contact with spirits both good (Khiḍr) and bad (Khannās).[280] According to him, the angels drink canonical prayer, with their lips to the lips of the one who is praying.[281]

Through his direct disciple Abū Bakr Muḥammad Warrāq, Tirmidhī influenced the Malāmatiyya mystical school. But it was his books that had the greater effect, first on Ibn ᶜArabī, whose precursor he was; then on Bahā al-Dīn Naqshband, the founder of the Naqshbandiyya order.[282]

4. Sahl Tustarī and the Sālimiyya School

I have examined Tustarī's life elsewhere. Here I shall summarize his doctrine[283] and that of his disciples, the Sālimiyya, and give the text of the sixteen Sālimiyyan propositions condemned by the Ḥanbalites.

Through his teacher Ibn Sawwār, Tustarī is the disciple of Thawrī, of the philologist Abū ᶜAmr ibn al-ᶜAlā, of strict Sunni traditionists; and of two mystics, Mālik ibn Dīnār and Maᶜrūf ibn ᶜAlī.[284] He is hostile to the *mutakallimūn*, and he uses a special type of dialectical argumentation (*radd al-farᶜ ilā'l-aṣl*).[285] He has a tendency to confuse what is evident to reason (*ᶜaql*) with the light of faith; "renunciation (*tawakkul*) is deduced from certainty (*yaqīn*)"; *maᶜrifa* is the *fikra* of the *mīthāq*; the role of reason is to recognize what is allowed under the sacred law. "The proof of *tawḥīd* is the very affirmation we make (*al-jazm dalīl*)."[286] I have pointed out his psychological theories of the three *laṭāʾif* and the three *tawaffī*;[287] his intense

276. Ms. Damascus 104, f. 300: *"badᶜat min laḥm fī jawfika"* = the *muḍgha jawfāniyya* of Ḥallāj (*Bustān*, sec. 15).

277. Letter to ᶜUthmān of Rayy.

278. The lights of (*anwār*) that are the antidote for poisoned hearts (ms. Damascus 104, f. 390).

279. His theory of the destructive *tajallī* (ms. Damascus 104, f. 402) is a forerunner of the Sālimiyyan theory (herein, ch. 4, sec. 4, thesis iv, and see longer text, *Recueil*, p. 40). This preterition of ecstasy is one of the distinctive traits of the Malāmatiyya.

280. On Khannās, cf. Chauvin, *Bibliographie*, VIII (*Syntipas*), sec. 131, 176. ᶜAṭṭār, II, 96–97.

281. *ᶜIlal*, f. 148b.

282. Jāmī, 132.

283. From the following sources: (a) his *Tafsīr*, printed Cairo, 1326, 204 pp. (ed. Naᶜsānī); (b) two apologetic works of Abū'l-Qāsim Ṣaqallī (about 390/999): *Sharḥ wa bayān limā ashkala min kalām Sahl* and *Muᶜāraḍa wa radd*, both preserved ap. ms. Köpr. 727. For Ṣaqallī's *ṣifat al-awliyā*, see Ibn ᶜAṭā Allah, *Ḥikam*, 78, 163.

284. *Passion*, Fr 1:110 ff./Eng 1:69 ff.

285. Cf. *Passion*, Fr 3:96/Eng 3:85.

286. [*Recueil*, p. 42 (and all fragments of the *Muᶜāraḍa* on pp. 41–42).] Ṣaqallī, *Muᶜāraḍa*; cf. *Passion*, Fr 1:366/37/Eng 1:290.

287. *Passion*, Fr 3:26–27/Eng 3:19.

spiritualism leads him to say that man positively "lives" on faith. Like Ibn Karrām, he affirms, against the common doctrine, the soul's personal survival after death,[288] though the Hellenistic theory of impersonal survival (*ᶜaql*) might have tempted him.[289] His theory of the four elements is the same as Tirmidhī's,[290] and he applies it to the soul.

In theodicy, Tustarī affirms the fullness of divine reality, against the Muᶜtazilī restrictions [*Recueil*, p. 42]:

> *Waḥdāniyya*,[291] fundamentally, means that God is, before everything can be. He is alone (*fard*) and knowing, He has willed, determined, balanced ... rewarded, and punished; acts are attributed to men, but He possesses their origin and end (*tamām*); the guilty do not defeat Him by sinning, and the just do not obey without recourse to Him. All things are, through His knowledge and power; they are not this knowledge and power, to be sure, but they exist by means of them both.

Tustarī tends to allow only for a virtual distinction between the various divine attributes, and to catch a glimpse[292] of them in every created thing, viewed at a certain angle. In cosmogony, he tries to stay at an equal distance from Qadarism and Murjiʾism; he admirably explains that God's grace intervenes not only at the moment of the act but also before and after (*istiṭāᶜa qabl, maᶜ, baᶜd al-fiᶜl*).[293] He links the two questions of *iktisāb* and *tafḍīl al-faqr*.[294] In eschatology, he affirms the necessity under sacred law of continuous contrition, *tawba*, but he understands this term to signify the mind's "return" to awareness of the divine presence, thanks to the act of faith, of which he makes a fine analysis.[295] For him faith, *ʾīmān*, includes the entire religious position of the believer. Faith's essence is divine; it is an uncreated, evident Certainty, *yaqīn*, which is God Himself.[296] Tustarī also accepts that at the Judgment all creatures will receive the vision of

288. Ibid., Fr 3:23–24/Eng 3:16.

289. Cf. Tirmidhī.

290. *ᶜIlal*, f. 209a; it is supposed to be Hellenistic. Also, according to Ibn ᶜArabī, Sahl calls God *"al-sabab al-awwal"* (*Rashḥ al-zulāl*, ms. P. 4802, 4) and calls the primary matter *"ḥaqīqa"* (*habā*) (*Fut.*, I, 132). Firyābī attributes to Sahl (*Khulāṣa*, ms. Arles 428, p. 391) a *Ghāyat ahl al-nihāya* (Qurashī, *Ṭab. ḥanaf.*, I, 153).

291. Ṣaqallī, *Muᶜārada.*

292. Whence the *tafᶜīl* of Ibn Sālim (*Passion*, Fr 3:47/Eng 3:39).

293. Ṣaqallī, *Muᶜāraḍa; Passion*, Fr 3:122/Eng 3:109–10.

294. Cf. *Passion*, Fr 3:239/Eng 3:225. Ibn Karrām, by an inverse process, links the *inkār al-kasb* to the *tafḍīl al-ghinā* (herein, ch. 5 n 87–8 and related text).

295. *Passion*, Fr 3:32/Eng 3:24–25 [see also *Passion* Fr 3:120/Eng 3:108].

296. Ibid., Fr 3:46/Eng 3:38.

God, the *ruʾya*; even Satan, who will be forgiven.[297] Tustarī's theory of *tajallī*[298] and the *anwār* (illuminations) is the work of an intellectualist. In politics, he admits that the prophetic mission is an emanation of the primordial "column of light," particles of which are found in the hearts of the believers. (He has made a compromise between the Hellenistic *ʿaql akbar* and Imāmī gnosticism.)[299] Tustarī hesitates, but he still seems to differentiate saints from prophets.[300] He is very firm for the obedience owed to the government of the caliphs[301] and for the unity of the Community.[302] His theory of the four senses of the Qurʾān is important.[303]

Various suggestions from Tustarī were developed by Ḥallāj;[304] notably on the *basmala* and the *ghayba bi'l-madhkūr.*[305] The Sālimiyya, however, were led towards monism by their own distortions of other suggestions he had made:[306] *sirr al-rubūbiyya, sirr al-"anaʾ".*

Ibn Sālim of Baṣra, the founder of this important mystical school and a Malikite in jurisprudence, wanted simply to be the editor of the "thousand questions" asked of Tustarī, his master.[307] But Ibn Sālim seems to have emphasized, and even to have exaggerated, some of the bolder features of Tustarī's doctrine. For two centuries, the school was engaged in copious theological and literary activity, and it can claim to have produced works as valuable as Abū Ṭālib Makkī's (d. 390) *Qūt al-qulūb* and Ibn Barrajān's (d. 536) *Tafsīr.* It finally disappeared, under the pressure of the condemnations incurred.

Here is a list, adapted from an account in the *Muʿtamad* of Abū Yaʿlä ibn al-Farrā (d. 458),[308] of the sixteen Sālimiyyan propositions condemned by the Ḥanbalites (Kīlānī reproduces ten of them in his *Ghunya*)[309] [*Recueil*, pp. 39–40]:

297. Ibid., Fr 3:325/Eng 3:307–8.

298. Ṣaqallī, *Sharḥ*, III.

299. *Passion*, Fr 3:301, 376/Eng 3:283, 358.

300. Ibid., Fr 3:175/Eng 3:163.

301. Ibid., 3:302–3/Eng 3:190–91.

302. *Ḥubb al-ṣaḥāba farḍ*; and not *tabarrī, ʿan al-fussāq* (Ṣaqallī, *Sharḥ*); *Passion*, Fr 1:110–11/Eng 1:69–70.

303. *Passion*, Fr 3:186–87/Eng 3:174–75.

304. Ibid., 3:16/Eng 3:9.

305. Ibid., Fr 3:46 n 7/Eng 3:39 n 95.

306. Attenuation by Ibn Sālim of his doctrine of *balā* (= *ghurba ilä al-Maḥbūb*, in *Qūt*, II, 67; cf. *Passion*, Fr 3:131/Eng 3:119); exaggeration about the *muʾmin ḥaqqan* (*Passion*, Fr 3:100 n 5/Eng 3:89 n 241). Tustarī, on the contrary, used to say, "I pray to God that He should give us back our true faith, *an yuḥaqqiqa ʾīmānanā*," and to profess the *tabarrī ʿamman yaddaʿī al-tawakkul wa'l-riḍā wa'l-shawq* (Ṣaqallī, *Sharḥ*; cf. Ghulām Khalīl and Ibn Baṭṭa ʿUkbarī).

307. *Passion*, Fr 3:112/Eng 3:71.

308. *Muʿtamad fī uṣūl al-dīn*, ms. Damascus Ẓah., *tawḥīd*, 45.

309. *Ghunya*, I, 83–84: in the following order: iii–iv, v, iii *bis*, vi, vii, xiii *bis*, x, xii, xiii, xiv, xvi.

i. God does not cease, in His essence, to contemplate[310] the universe, whether the universe exists or not.[311]

ii. God grasps by one attribute alone[312] what He grasps by all of His attributes.

iii. God will be seen, on the Day of Judgment, in the form of a Muḥammadiyyan man. (Even the infidels will see him in the next life, and He will summon them to be judged.)[313]

iv. God will irradiate[314] on that day on all His creatures: *jinn* and human beings, angels and animals; and each one, recognizing Him, will acquiesce to His signification.

v. The divine omnipotence[315] has a secret (*sirr*) — if it were discovered, prophecy would become worthless; prophecy has a secret — if it were discovered, knowledge of the Qurʾān would become worthless; and knowledge has a secret — if it were discovered, the judgments of the doctors of the law would become worthless.[316]

vi. Satan prostrated himself (before Adam) at the second divine command.

vii. Satan never entered Paradise.[317]

viii. God never ceases creating.[318]

ix. A work (*fiʿl*) is a created thing, but the act that creates it is uncreated.[319]

x. This was the punishment for the vainglory Moses had conceived after his conversation with God (*mukālama*): upon asking to see Him (*ruʾya*), he suddenly perceived a hundred identical Sinais, and a Moses on each one.[320]

xi. Divine decision (*irāda*) is a created thing.[321]

xii. Divine decision concerning the errors of creatures foresees those faults in them (*bihim*) (as involuntary defects), but not as coming from them (*lā minhum*)[322] (= voluntary).

310. *"Lam yazal raʾiyan . . . fī dhātihi."*

311. There is a surviving fragment of the *Radd ʿalā Ibn Sālim* of Ibn Khafīf, in which he condemns proposition (i) as professing the eternity of the world (*qidam al-dahr*); to which Harawī answers that it is perhaps nothing but the divine prescience (*ʿilm*: *Maʿṣūm ʿAlī Shāh, Ṭarāʾiq*, II, 222).

312. *"Yudrik biṣifa wāḥida."*

313. Added by Kīlānī (in an independent section). [In the *Recueil*, the section in brackets is added to (iv), not (iii).]

314. *Yatajallā*, Kīlānī abridges.

315. *Rubūbiyya*. Cf. *Passion*, Fr 1:111 n 5/Eng 1:70 n 21.

316. This secret is that of the preeternal investiture of each person's "I."

317. Cf. Shiblī, *Ākām*, 156.

318. *Passion*, Fr 3:47/Eng 3:39. This proposition is summarized as *"khalq fī kull nafas"* by Ibn ʿArabī (*Fut.*, I, 211; IV, 23).

319. Ibn al-Farrā notes that, nevertheless, *"tafʿīl, wāḥiduhu fiʿl . . ."* in grammar (*"tafʿīl*, a collective noun, has the singular, *fiʿl"*).

320. *Ṭaw.*, P. 164.

321. *Passion*, Fr 3:129/Eng 3:117.

322. *Passion*, Fr 3:130–31/Eng 3:118–19. Kīlānī exaggerates the characteristic: "From His creatures, God wants the acts of obedience, but not the faults, which He foresees in them, but not as coming from them."

xiii. The Prophet knew the whole Qurʾān by heart before Gabriel came to recite it to him.[323]

xiv. God speaks, and it is He that we hear speak through the tongue of each reader of the Qurʾān.[324]

xv. God has one will (*mashīʾa*), as He has but one (uncreated) knowledge (*ᶜilm*).[325] And, in conjunction with every decided thing (*murād*), He has a (created) decision (*irāda*).[326]

xvi. God is present in every place (*fī kull makān*);[327] there is no difference, from this point of view, between the Throne and other places.

The Sālimiyya suffered ridiculous invective of a very vulgar tone against their "anthropomorphism," but they inspired respect, as much for their high piety as for their intellectual activity, in many adversaries. Ibn al-Farrā, in a paragraph in which he condemns them, expresses his admiration for Abū Ṭālib Makkī; and we know of the latter's influence on the second stage of Ghazālī's life.

5. Kharrāz and Junayd

A. The Doctrine of Kharrāz

Kharrāz, like Junayd, updated the vast syntheses[328] of Tustarī and Tirmidhī in a spirit better conforming to the demands of Sunni orthodoxy, correcting an excessive resemblance, in some respects, to Imāmī gnosticism and Hellenistic philosophy.

Abū Saᶜīd Aḥmad ibn ᶜIsä Kharrāz Baghdādī[329] (d. 289/899 in Cairo)[330] was an independent author without any personal affiliation to Sufism but much influenced by the Sufis of Kūfa and Baghdād. He was also an admirer of Abū Hāshim and a disciple of Ibrahīm ibn al-Junayd, whose favorite *ḥadīth* he loved to recite: "He who macerates his flesh sees his sins

323. In an independent section, xiii *bis*, Kīlānī adds, "Gabriel did not move when he came to speak to the Prophet."

324. *Passion*, Fr 3:93 n 5/Eng 3:83 n 197. Monist degeneration from the rule of meditation (cited herein, ch. 2 n 1).

325. *Qadīma* (notes Ibn al-Farrā).

326. *Muḥdatha* (ibid.). Nevertheless, adds Ibn al-Farrā, "the word *irāda* designates one of the uncreated attributes of God."

327. "God is the food (*qūt*) of the universe," says Makkī (Shaᶜrāwī, *Laṭāʾif*, II, 28; Cf. Tustarī); and equivocal formula that does not distinguish grace and nature.

328. Kalābādhī cites him as the foremost among Sufi writers *"fī ᶜulūm al-ishārāt"* (as opposed to *muᶜāmalāt*), ap. *Taᶜarruf*.

329. Jāmī, 69, 81, 158. Shaᶜrāwī, *Yawāq*, 13; *Ṭab.*, I, 91, 81.

330. Date given by Abū'l-Qāsim ibn Mardān Nahāwandī, his student from 272 to 286 (Mālinī, 14).

fall away, as a tree sees its falling leaves."[331] He was a friend of Junayd and Ibn ᶜAṭā.

When his major work, the *Kitāb al-sirr*, was condemned in Baghdād, Kharrāz was exiled to Bukhārā. The book is lost, except for one quotation.[332] His *Kitāb al-ṣidq* and *Masāᵓil*, which are extant,[333] are simple collections of traditions (with *isnād*) on asceticism.[334] But numerous isolated fragments attest to a precise mystical doctrine, of which we can reconstitute an outline:

In theodicy, he limits himself to defining the divine Essence "as that alone which has two opposite attributes (*ḍiddayn*) simultaneously,"[335] a trait Ḥallāj preserves in his *ᶜaqīda* but criticizes as insufficient in his *Bustān*.[336]

In mystical psychology, Kharrāz affirms against Tirmidhī the distinction between *ᶜaql* and *rūḥ*,[337] and reacts strongly against the master's intellectualist idealism.[338] Even more than Tustarī, Kharrāz underscores the actual possibility for the soul of mystical union, realized *a parte post*. In the process, he introduces several characteristic terms, which will become classical models. The "science of annihilation (*fanā*) and perpetuation (*baqā*)" consists of "*annihilating* oneself in God, in order to *survive* in Him."[339] Ascetic mortification must end in a positive, personal transfiguration of the soul by grace.[340] Kharrāz defines this final state as *ᶜayn al-jamᶜ*, "essential union," of substance and substance.[341] His doctrine of sanctification is riper and fuller than Bisṭāmī's. "As for the believer who has penetrated the anagogic sense[342] of acts God gives him, and who persists in praising God above all

331. Mālinī, *loc. cit.*

332. Text (condemned proposition) given below (text at n 342). Another text, on *samāᶜ*, is also quoted: ". . . the faithful man who has come back to God, attached himself to Him and settled near Him, forgotten himself and all that is not God. And if he is asked, 'Where are you from?' or 'What do you want?' his only response is 'God!'" It is almost *dhikr*. (ᶜAṭṭār, II, 40; Shaᶜrāwī, *Ṭab.*, I, 60).

333. Ms. Shahīd ᶜAlī Pasha 1374, sec. V. The text of the *Kitāb al-ṣidq* was published, with an Eng. trans., by A.J. Arberry, Calcutta, 1937.

334. Sarrāj cites his *adab al-ṣalāt* (*Lumaᶜ*, 153).

335. Ibn ᶜArabī adds an ambiguous clause to this formula (*Fut.* IV, 42).

336. *Passion*, Fr 3:139/Eng 3:126–27.

337. Ibid., Fr 3:24/Eng 3:16. He opposes *rūḥānī* to *juthmānī*. His doctrine of understanding, *ilqā al-samᶜ*, then *istinbāṭ* (Sarrāj, *Lumaᶜ*, 79), was borrowed from Muḥāsibī and was later taken up by Suhrawardī of Aleppo (*hayākil*, on Qur. 75:19).

338. His use of the word *ᶜaẓama* is Karrāmiyyan.

339. Baqlī, *Tafsīr*, f. 215b; *ᶜAwārif*, IV, 302, 303. Junayd condemns this innovation (Jāmī, 82).

340. He explains that if souls are not "burned" by divine irradiation, it is because they were created with divine light (ap. Baqlī, on Qur. 24:35; cf. Tustarī); Ḥallāj, less emanationist, explains the phenomenon by *amāna* (*Passion*, Fr 3:20/Eng 3:12).

341. On Qur. 58:22: "As for those whose sign is glory and bliss, who have received grace and suffered no loss, they are permanently under His guard and protection, their defeats are light, the stage they have attained is beyond all stages, and their thoughts are beyond all thought; they are in essential union with God forever (*fī ᶜayn al-jamᶜ maᶜ al-Ḥaqq abadan*)" (Baqlī, II, 316; cf. I, 400).

342. *Passion*, Fr 3:130/Eng 3:118; notion outlined by Miṣrī (ᶜAṭṭār, I, 127).

else — God sanctifies his soul." As corollaries of this statement, Kharrāz sketches two Ḥallājian theses: the failure of Satan, for "having strained to please God" (*idlāl*),[343] and the *ṣalāt* ʿ*alā'l-Nabī's* inoperativeness for advancement along the mystical path: "Forgive me, but loving God makes me forget to love you,"[344] he said to Muḥammad, because mystical union bypasses the Prophet.[345]

Kharrāz is not without faults. Imitating Tirmidhī, he descends into *jafr*.[346] Following Miṣrī, he demonstrates some indulgence in the *samā*ʿ, mental inebriation, the cult of ecstasy for its own sake, which is the source of the sensual nuance that somewhat obscures the sentiment in this lovely fragment:[347]

> Happy the man who has drunk from the cup of His love, who has savored ecstatic conversation with the glorious Lord, who has approached Him through the joys found in loving Him. His heart is filled with delight, he flies to God with happiness, he aspires to Him with desire. Ah what a trance of regret the Lord makes him savor! What servitude! What languor for the man who has no fellow traveler but the Lord, no intimate but Him!

But Kharrāz explicitly rejects the dangerous deviations of the *samā*ʿ.[348]

B. The Works and Role of Junayd[349]

Junayd's doctrine is an even more severe and circumspect revision of the systems previously proposed than Kharrāz's. I give only a list of his works and a summary of his doctrine.

343. Text, ap. *Ṭawāsīn*, p. 171; cf. *Passion*, Fr 3:324/Eng 3:306–7.

344. Qush., 174; cf. *Passion*, Fr 3:215–16/Eng 3:203.

345. Miṣrī had hinted at this (Sarrāj, *Luma*ʿ, 104).

346. *Passion*, Fr 3:106/Eng 3:95.

347. Ap. Sarrāj, *Luma*ʿ, 59. The remark was made by "one of the Sālimiyya" (Makkī, *Qūt*, II, 61; Tustarī, *Tafsīr*, 9), about Kharrāz applying poems of profane love to God, as he sang of Laylā or Sawdā. Compare Ḥallāj on Qur. 30:45 to this fragment.

348. Qush., I, 168.

349. Junayd is to be carefully distinguished from his homonyms: Ibrāhīm ibn al-Junayd (d. c. 270), Junayd al-Khaṭīb (*Fihrist*, 186; Harawī, *Dhamm*, 117a), Abū ʿAbdallah Iskāf Junayd Isfahānī (Samʿānī, *Ansāb*, s.n.; a disciple), Abū Zurʿa Muḥammad ibn al-Junayd Kashshī and Abū'l-Khayr Junaydī (Maqdisī, *Homonyma*, supp., p. 184), Abū ʿAbdallah ibn Junayd, friend of Ibn ʿArabī (*Ḥilyat al-abdāl*), and the Shīrāzī family of the Banū Junayd (from our twelfth to fifteenth century). On Sarī Saqaṭī (d. 253), Junayd's teacher, see *Ḥilya*, X, 116–27; Ibn ʿAsākir, VI, 71–79. Sarī, at whose feet Junayd had himself buried in Shūnīz, appears to have been a profound mystic. In his youth he had known Maʿrūf, the solemn illiterate of Karkh in Baghdād, who loved God alone (according to ʿAlī ibn Muwaffaq [*Iḥyā*, IV, 221]), and who prayed ten times a day for God to pacify the Community of believers (*Passion*, Fr 3:224/Eng 3:212). Sarī, during his long voyages, notably to Syria (where he learned the story of the Three Men Walled-in Alive, which popular tradition combined with that of the Seven Sleepers; and where he also learned complex technical

1. *Dawā al-arwāḥ*, Cairo ms. (3 folios) = ms. Shahīd ᶜAlī Pāshā 1374, sec. IX. Compare with the title of his *Dawā al-tafrīṭ*, mentioned by Sulamī (*Tafsīr*, on Qur. 8:24).
2. *Risāla ilä Yūsuf ibn Ḥusayn Rāzī*, ms. S.A. 1374, sec. I.
3. *Risāla ilä baᶜḍ ikhwānihi*, id., sec. II.
4. *Risāla ilä Yaḥyä ibn Muᶜādh Rāzī* (d. 258), id., sec. III. This famous letter is mentioned by Sarrāj (*Lumaᶜ* 358) in the following century. Whether the purported recipient could in fact have received it is a matter of chronological dispute.
5. *Risāla ilä baᶜḍ ikhwānihi*, id., sec. IV.
6. *Risāla ilä ᶜAmr Makkī*, id., sec. V (9 double folios).
7. *Risāla (no. II) ilä Yūsuf Rāzī*, id., sec. VI.
8. *Risāla fī'l-sukr*, id., sec. VII.
9. *Faṣl fī'l-ifāqa*, id., sec. VIII.
10. *Kitāb al-fānā*, id., sec. X.
11. *Kitāb al-mīthāq*, id., sec. XI.
12. *Kitāb fī'l-ʾulūhiyya*, id., sec. XII.
13. *Kitāb al-farq bayn al-ikhlāṣ wa'l-ṣidq*, id., sec. XIII.
14. *Kitāb al-tawḥīd*, id., sec. XIV.
15. *VI masāʾil* (cf. his *Masāʾil al-shāmiyīn*, cited by Qush.), id., sec. XV.
16. *Adab al-muftaqir ilä Allāh*, id., XXVI.
17. *Sharḥ shaṭaḥāt Abī Yazīd* (Ibn Farrukhān Dūrī's recension), extracts in Sarrāj, *Lumaᶜ* 380–82, 385, 386, 387, 387–89 (cf. 347).[350]
18. *Taṣḥīḥ al-irāda*; lost; cited by Hujwīrī, *Kashf*, 338.

HIS DOCTRINE

I must make a fundamental correction of what was said on this subject in my preceding work.[351] Prolonged scrutiny has made me recognize that

---

terminology), maintained intact Maᶜrūf's double vocation: "to take on oneself all the sorrows of the world" (*Ḥilya*, X, 118), and to be one of the ten "true servants of God," after a triple decimation (of 10,000 called, 9,000 preferred the world; of 1000, 900 preferred Paradise; of 100, 90 retreated before Hell). Expiation of Adam's original sin of the *luqma*, by proposing that he himself should suffer this divine burden, which the strongest mountains could not bear. Here the exegesis of Qur. 33:72 that Ḥallāj would later employ is recognizable. In Egypt there have been descendants of Sarī (ᶜAli Pasha Mubārak, XII, 5) at Girga. On Sarī, cf. also Khaṭīb, IX, 187–92; and Ḥurayfish, *Rawḍ*, 196, 197, 206, 232. A *maqām* to Junayd exists at Gouraya (near Cherchell [Algeria]), beneath a *masjid* dedicated to Ibr. Khawwāṣ (photo in *Essai* supplied by Dermenghem).

350. According to Sahlagī (*Nūr*, f. 114), Junayd claimed to have made the Arabic translation of these texts, which had come down to him in Persian through Bisṭāmī's nephew, Abū Mūsä ᶜIsä ibn Adam.

351. *Passion*, 1st ed., pp. 37–38, 401 [and 2nd ed., Fr 2:108/Eng 2:101]. I had attributed too much importance to Khuldī's tales [cf. ch. 5 n 365].

Junayd's doctrine is much nearer to Ḥallāj's than I had thought. I hesitated for a long time because of Junayd's great reserve on decisive points; also, it was repugnant to me to see in that reserve any dissemblance, or to make Junayd the author of two simultaneous, contradictory teachings, the first exoteric and the second esoteric. In reality we must take the just measure first of the personal temperament of this cautious, shy savant, who was conscious of the dangers of heterodoxy peculiar to mysticism; and then of the proven wisdom of a spiritual director who would suspend judgment, leaving questions open, as long as he thought the experimental results were not decisive, crucial.

Junayd was orthodox, and found fault with Muḥāsibī for using *kalām*.[352] As for Ḥallāj, on the other hand, if he reasoned like the *mutakallimūn* in certain ways, he did so only in order to show that their dialectic was inconclusive.[353] Junayd criticized the mental attitude of those who attribute a permanent objective reality to the *aḥwāl* (states of mystical consciousness);[354] though Ḥallāj is in some respects vulnerable to this criticism, all of his works finally show that he adopted Junayd's doctrine.[355] Junayd affirmed the preeminence of *ᶜilm* over *maᶜrifa,* and of *taḥrīm* over *ibāḥa;*[356] he meant only the provisional precedence, acknowledged by Ḥallāj, of a precept (for the group) over advice (only for certain individuals).[357]

Junayd was the first author to embrace the problem of mystical union in all its fullness and to explain it correctly; he found the exact threshold of the operation of transcendence, the night of the will[358] whose anguish Bisṭāmī had foreseen and whose trial Ḥallāj would undergo. Junayd did not push the experiment as far as they: he presented its conditions and allowed his listeners to draw their own conclusions from personal experience. When the case of Ḥallāj came up, Junayd's school split between Jurayrī, a partisan of the obvious intellectual solution,[359] in which it is observed that God is the supereminent "I" of any sentence spoken by any

352. *Passion,* Fr 3:62/Eng 3:53.

353. *Passion,* Fr 3:141–42, 359/Eng 3:128–29, 341–42.

354. Ibid., Fr 1:167/Eng 1:125–26.

355. Ibid., Fr 3:48 n 5/Eng 3:40 n 106.

356. Ibid., Fr 3:239, 70/Eng 3:225, 61. Cf. the bitter quotation from Junayd, refuted by Ibn al-Qayyim in his *Iᶜtirāḍāt*: "If children are the punishment reserved for permitted desire, what will be the punishment for that which is forbidden?" This statement is attributed to Ibn Fūrak (Huart, *Lit. arabe,* 224).

357. *Passion,* Fr 3:201, 228/Eng 3:189, 216.

358. "Let the servant, with respect to God, be like a marionette (*shabaḥ*) ... let him come back, at the end, to his point of departure, and let him be as he was before he was given existence" (ap. Qush., 177; Shaᶜrāwī, *Ṭab.,* I, 84; taken up by Kīlānī, *Bahja,* 79).

359. Which satisfied the monists, and led them to esoterism; Jurayrī, who would have liked Bisṭāmī to confess, of God, "I am you," was the first to declare that Ḥallāj had to be executed (*Passion,* Fr 1:575–76/Eng 1:528–29; herein, text at n 192).

man;[360] and Ibn ᶜAṭā, who accepted the possibility of a transcendent intervention by grace, filtered through the chosen personality of a saint.[361]

Like Ḥallāj, Junayd meditated on the primordial Covenant and conceived it as a declaration, made in our name in advance, of love for God.[362] Therefore, he taught, in order to rediscover this pure word of acquiescence to God's will in ourselves, we must progressively and implacably cleanse our entire being, achieving abandonment of the memory, intelligence, and will. The purpose is to reach the *fanā bi'l-Madhkūr*,[363] "annihilation in Him of Whom we are thinking." Junayd rejected the second of Kharrāz's pair of terms, *fanā–baqā*, as inadequate; he was right to judge that there was no logical symmetry between the state of consumption that the creature can obtain and the state of transfiguration in which the Creator can immortalize him. Thirdly, Junayd tried to define what this final state might be. It is the "return to our origin (*bidāya*)," to the idea that God formed as a model for us in the Covenant.[364] Therefore, I came to think Junayd was teaching that the person of the mystic could be reduced to a divine idea, a mere, irrealizable virtuality. I was mistaken. He explains that the phrase, "return to our origin," indicates access to the Creator's life itself:[365] "The living being is he who bases his life so completely on the life of his Creator, not on the survival of his corporeal form (*haykal*), that the reality of his life is his death, which is the way to the level of primordial Life (*ḥayāt aṣliyya*)."[366] How can we characterize this new life? Junayd, after studying Bisṭāmī, observes that his experiment is incomplete;[367] instead love must achieve, "through a permutation with the qualities of the lover, a penetration of the qualities of the Beloved."[368] That is the final hypothesis.

It is now apparent that Junayd made a complete theoretical outline of Ḥallāj's doctrine. The *Dawā al-arwāḥ*[369] shows that some men, through the grace of loving preference of divine providence, are invested with the very

360. The question of the *huwa huwa* (*Passion*, Fr 3:193/Eng 3:181).

361. Ibid., Fr 1:339–40/Eng 1:293.

362. Ibid., Fr 1:117; 3:117/Eng 1:76; 3:105–6.

363. Ap. Baqlī, I, 584 (cf. *ghayba*, ibid. I, 185) [v. herein, ch. 5 n 305].

364. *Passion*, Fr 1:117; 3:53/Eng 1:76; 3:45.

365. Or, in his first formulation, "extraction of the Absolute from the contingent" (*ifrād al-qidam*, which prefigures the Ḥallājian *ifrād al-Wāḥid*; *Passion*, Fr 1:117, 664/Eng 1:76, 614). The formula is inadequate, but its anti-monism irritated Ibn ᶜArabī so much (*Tajalliyāt*) that he declared, "You can only distinguish the absolute from the contingent if you are neither one nor the other" (Salāmī, *Radd*, I, 363). Therefore we must correct the assimilation of Junayd and Ibn ᶜArabī, suggested in *Passion*, 1st ed., 37–38. [For the corrected version of the same passage, on Junayd's doctrine, see *Passion* Fr 1:117–18/Eng 1:76–77. Cf. herein, ch. 5 n 351.]

366. Baqlī, II, 173.

367. Herein, text at n 211.

368. *Passion*, Fr 3:18/Eng 3:11.

369. *Dawā al-arwāḥ*, ff. 1–5 of my copy: preeternal *iṣṭināᶜ*, then *iṣṭifā* (Moses), then *ruʾya* (Muḥammad), then *munājāh* given only to the *ahl al-muwālāh*.

secret of revelation itself and are allowed an experimental taste of the prophetic vocation's successive stages. In this short work, Junayd constructed the first "dynamic synthesis of the Qurʾān" conceived as a "manual of ascension towards God," which is precisely the theme of the *Najm idhā hawā* of Ḥallāj.

Junayd, correcting Tustarī, also presents the Ḥallājian theme of the *Ṭā Sīn al-Azal*,[370] describing a vision of Satan that he has obtained after fifteen years of prayers to God. He claims to have asked, "Why did you not bow down before Adam?" "Zeal in love stopped me from bowing down before anyone but God." (Horrified, Junayd heard an inner voice say, "Tell him 'You lie! If you had been a true servant, you would not have transgressed against His command.'")[371]

Ibn ʿAṭā's critiques. Another cause of my hesitation to affirm the kinship of Junayd's and Ḥallāj's formulas, in spite of their relationship as teacher and student, was the existence of critiques made by Ibn ʿAṭā, Ḥallāj's friend, against several points of Junayd's teachings. A reexamination has shown that these critiques are rectifications rather than true divergences: a reduction (from eight to four) of the number of major prophets to be imitated;[372] and the soul's fuller and more loving embrace of all of God's will,[373] no matter how awful it may seem. Ibn ʿAṭā clarifies Junayd's idea of "the primordial life":[374] "According to the divine science, God revives him who is 'living' and communicates with him through (direct) vision, understanding, hearing and *salām*."[375] Ibn ʿAṭā also makes formulations more explicit than Junayd's of Ḥallāj's theses on replacing the *ḥajj*[376] and on the Real that is "beyond reality."[377]

6. Ḥallāj's Synthesis and Later Interpretations

The preceding monographs show how much the presentation of doctrine in Ḥallāj's work depends upon the terminology gradually established by his predecessors. Almost all of his vocabularly,[378] his principal allego-

370. Hujwīrī, *Kashf*, 129–30; Ibn al-Najjār, ap. Ṣafadī, *Sharḥ risālat Ibn Zaydūn*, 83–84.

371. The section in parentheses is added in Hujwīrī's, version.

372. *Passion*, Fr 3:31 n 7, 212–13/Eng 3:24 n 27, 200.

373. Sacrifice and suffering (*Passion*, Fr 1:131; 3:125–27, 130/Eng 1:91; 3:114–15, 118); *wajd* (Ibid., Fr 3:78/Eng 3:68); *khāṭirān* (Ibid., Fr 3:30–31/Eng 3:23).

374. Baqlī, II, 174.

375. *Passion*, Fr 1:133; 3:179/Eng 1:93; 3:167.

376. Ibid., Fr 3:244/Eng 3:230; herein, text at ch. 2 n 63.

377. *Al-ḥaqq asbaq min ḥaqīqat al-muḥiqq* (Baqlī, I, 587); *Passion*, Fr 3:89/Eng 3:78. Ibn ʿAṭā, like Kharrāz, yields to the charms of parables of profane love (on Zulaykha: Baqlī, I, 422).

378. *Passion*, Fr 3:14–15/Eng 3:7–8.

ries,[379] even his rule for living,[380] can be found in those who preceded him. His originality is in the superior cohesion of the definitions he brings together; and in the firmness of the guiding intention that led him to affirm in public, at the cost of his own life, a doctrine his teachers had not dared make accessible to all. Just as the rationalist movement in Greece ended in Socrates with the affirmation of a religious philosophy valid for all, so the ascetic movement in Islam ended with the proclamation of an experimental mysticism, providing aid to all. Ḥallāj, far from being an aberration within the Islamic Community of his time, represents the final completion of the mystical vocations that had sprung up throughout the first centuries of Islam through meditated reading of the Qurʾān and the "interiorization" of a fervent, humble ritual life.

Here is the translation *in extenso* of the eighteen sentences of Ḥallāj chosen by Sulamī to place their author in the gallery of psychological portraits in chronological order that constitutes his *Ṭabaqāt al-Ṣūfiyya*:*

1. He has clothed them (by creating them) in the veil of their name,[381] and they exist; but if He made the knowledge of His Power manifest to them, they would faint away; and if He unveiled His reality to them, they would die.[382]

2. The names of God?[383] From the point of view of our perception, they are synonymous (lit.: there is one name [alone]);[384] from God's point of view, they are reality.[385]

3. The inspiration that comes from God[386] is that about which no doubt[387] arises.

4. When the faithful servant[388] is freed and reaches the stage of wisdom, God sends him a permanent inspiration, which then preserves his conscience so that only (true) suggestions coming from God may be conceived in it. And the mark of the sage is that he is emptied of (concern for) this world and the next.[389]

* See Pedersen's edition, p. 308–13, and *Akhbār* *1, where the numbering is different.

379. Herein, ch. 3, sec. 1. B.

380. Comp. Ḥallāj (ap. Sulamī) on Qur. 49:3; with the *risāla* supposedly by Ḥasan (*Passion*, Fr 3:242 n 7/Eng 3:228 n 71), and the rules of Ibn Karrām and Tustarī (*Tafsīr*, 61).

381. *Akhb.* *1 *alif-zāl* (4) [see ch. 1 n 1 for the form of this and several of the following citations] = nos. 1–5. *Passion*, Fr 3:183/Eng 3:171.

382. A variant (*Akhb.*) reads, "they would be annihilated."

383. *Passion*, Fr 3:184/Eng 3:171.

384. Var. (*Akhb.*): "there is one description (alone)." [Pedersen, going against most of the manuscripts, including the one from which Massignon quotes, reads not *ism* but *rasm*.]

385. *"Wa min ḥayth al-Ḥaqq, ḥaqīqa"* (Sulamī). A variant (*Akhb.*), probably Ḥanbalite: "from the point of view of divine reality, they are God Himself."

386. *Passion*, Fr 3:31/Eng 3:24.

387. Var.: nothing. [LM later decided (A * 1 *jīm*), with Pedersen, against *shakk*, which is translated here, for this variant, *shayʾ*, giving the sense, "that which nothing opposes."]

388. *Passion*, Fr 3:31; 2:54–56/Eng 3:24; 2:47–50.

389. This clause is missing in the London ms. Ibn ʿAqīla adds the gloss, "and to be concerned

5. (Ḥallāj, when asked[390] why Moses had coveted the vision [of the divine Essence] and asked God for it [Qur. 7:139], answered), Since Moses had gone into solitude (away from every created thing) for God, God was alone in Moses, for whom He became the one Object of all thought. God became[391] what prevented him from seeing all perceived objects, what came face to face with him and erased all other perceptible presences, by an unveiling (*kashf*),[392] not a concealment (*taghayyub*). That is what pushed Moses to ask for the vision, not anything else.[393]

5 *bis*. (Here Sulamī gives the quatrain *Anta bayn al-shaghāf*..., translated in *Passion* Fr. 3:50/Eng 3:41–42.)

6. The novice[394] who desires (*murīd*) God must fire (straight) at Him,[395] on target with the first shot, and not shift[396] (his bow), having failed to hit Him.

7. The novice who desires God is outside secondary causes and both worlds, and that is what gives him mastery[397] over the inhabitants (of the worlds).[398]

8. The prophets have received power[399] over the divine graces [*al-aḥwāl*]; they have them in their possession; they have them at their disposal (to distribute them), the graces do not have the prophets at theirs (to transform them). As for the others (the saints),[400] the graces have received power over them; it is the graces that have them at their disposal.

9. O my God! You know I am powerless[401] to offer You the appointed thanks that must be given to You. Come into me then, and thank Yourself; that is true thankfulness! There is no other.

10. Whoever considers his (own) works[402] loses sight of Him for Whom he

---

with God alone." Cf. *Passion*, Fr 3:226/Eng 3:213–14; and Ibn Samᶜūn, ap. Ibn ᶜArabī, *Muḥāḍarāt*, II, 184.

390. *Akhb.* *1 *wāw* (4), a continuation of Kaᶜbī 1.

391. Sulamī's text, which is corrected by *Akhbār* as follows: "God became what cut off his vision from all sides, erasing all sides, in every perceived object; what confronted him, taking the place of everything and every presence in front of him. The mark (of supremacy) of the invisible which appeared on the visible, by an unveiling of the mystery of disguise (the diacritics of the C. ms. make this read *ghayb al-taghayyub*, not *ᶜayn al-yaqīn*), is what led him to request the vision. In this, the tongue of the visible (form) only translated the invisible reality; not anything else."

392. A word weakened by the Ḥanbalite tradition, through attempts to explain it. *Taghayyub* is the disguise of creative action, what hides it from our senses.

393. Refutation of the Sālimiyyan thesis.

394. *Akhb.* *1 *ḥaʾ-yaʾ* (6) = nos. 6–9.

395. Var.: rise towards Him.

396. Var.: interrupt (his shooting).

397. Miracles.

398. Here Kaᶜbī interpolates the sentence translated in *Passion*, 1st ed., 314, l. 5. ["What is mysticism?" "It is what you see" (= the cross), cf. *Passion* Fr 1:659 ff./Eng 1:609 ff.]

399. *Passion*, Fr 3:211–12/Eng 3:199.

400. Added rightly by Ibn al-Dāᶜī and Ibn al-Ṣabbāgh.

401. *Passion*, Fr 1:319/Eng 1:273.

402. *Akhb.* *1 *yab-yaw* (7) = nos. 10–14.

does them; whoever considers Him for Whom he does his own works loses sight of those works.[403]

11. God is He towards Whom ritual gestures are directed, and He upon Whom acts of obedience are founded.[404] One bears witness only before Him, and nothing is perceived without Him. It is thanks to the (guiding) effluvia of His counsels that the qualities (= virtues of mysticism) cohere. It is by concentrating your efforts on Him that you will advance in the degrees (of the mystical path).

12. It is not fitting that someone who (still) considers or mentions a created thing should declare, "Certainly I understand Who the One is, from Whom the monads[405] have come."

13. Our tongues[406] serve to speak words, and they die from this spoken language; our carnal selves (*anfus*) are employed in our actions, and they die from this employment.

14. (Maintaining) a fearful reserve in the presence of the Lord deprives His friends' hearts of the joy (to be had) in receiving His favors; what am I saying? Keeping a fearful reserve during the ritual act suffices to deprive His friends' hearts of the joy of obedience (to Him).

14 *bis.* (Here Sulamī gives the *Mawājīdu Ḥaqq* ..., translated ap. *Passion,* Fr 3:58 n 4/Eng 3:50 n 174.)

15. He who is inebriated[407] by the cups[408] of divine union can no longer use the language[409] of divine inaccessibility;[410] and there is more: he who is inebriated by the (first) gleams of divine inaccessibility already speaks of the realities of divine union; for the inebriate is he who speaks of every secret that is (still) hidden (before it is unveiled to him).

16.[411] He who seeks (to discover)[412] God by the light of faith[413] is like someone seeking (to discover) the sun by starlight.

17. (Ḥallāj said to one of the disciples[414] of [Abū ᶜAlī] Jubbāʾī), Exactly as God came to create the bodies (= substances) without (being incited to it by a

403. Cf. herein, ch. 3, sec. 4; *Passion,* Fr 3:86/Eng 3:75.

404. *Al-Maṣmūd ilayhi.*

405. *Āḥād.*

406. *Passion,* Fr 3:365/Eng 3:347.

407. *Akhb.,* *1 *yaḥ-kā* (8) = nos. 15–18.

408. Var. Sulamī's text has "lights."

409. *ᶜIbāra.* Var.: *ᶜibāda,* ritual.

410. *Tajrīd,* divine transcendence.

411. *Passion,* Fr 3:67/Eng 3:57.

412. The technical word *iltimās* means "the search to determine (the new moon)," the calculation (of the first of the month) either by direct observation of the sky (to which Ḥallāj alludes) or by reference to tables.

413. "Without personal revelation," added gloss.

414. *Passion,* Fr 3:123/Eng 3:111.

mediate)★ cause, so He came to create (in them) their attributes (= accidents) without (being incited to it by a) cause. Just as the servant (= the man) does not strictly possess the root of his act, so he does not strictly possess the act itself.

18. He has not separated Himself from carnal nature,[415] nor has He attached Himself to it.[416]

The gradual distortion of the doctrine and legend of Ḥallāj has allowed me to follow the stages of decomposition of the great mystical movement in Islam. The correct solution of the central problem, mystical union, was insinuated by Ḥasan and Ibn Adham, sensed by Bisṭāmī, glimpsed by Tustarī and Junayd, and finally presented by Ḥallāj through a complex method defining it as an *intermittent identification*[417] of subject and Object. The identification is renewed only by a continual, amorous exchanging of roles between the two, a vital alternation (like oscillation, pulsation, sensation, consciousness) that is imposed in superhuman, transcendent fashion on the heart of a given human subject, without ever achieving permanence or a stable regularity during the subject's mortal life.[418]

This solution avoided both the ideological intellectualism of the *mutakallimūn* and the Hellenists' championing of individual freedom, both the antagonistic dualism of the Ḥashwiyya and Qarmathian monism.[419] It was promptly distorted. Wāsiṭī, the first theoretician of Sufism after Ḥallāj, bent and slid towards the monist libertarianism of the Sālimiyya; Fāris tried to react against this tendency, without success. It is to Wāsiṭī that we should give the role assigned to Ḥallāj by Kremer, that of precursor, in the fourth century A.H., to Ibn ᶜArabī's monism. Beside Wāsiṭī, ᶜAbdallāh Qurashī[420] and Abū Bakr Qaḥṭabī[421] attempted analogous systematizations.

Some mystics saw the danger of the Sālimiyyan doctrine; it was denounced with clairvoyance by Ibn al-Hayṣam of the Karrāmiyya and by the Ḥanbalites Ḥuṣrī, Ibn Samᶜūn, Harawī, and Kīlānī. Ibn Khafīf thought he had found a decisive weapon against it in the scholastic ideology of the

★ "Cause" here is not *wasīṭa* (cf. ch. 1, sec. 2, translator's note under the root *LBS*) but *ᶜilla*. There are two possibilities for Massignon's interpretation of the Arabic: (1) an intermediary is seen as a cause relative to God's originating the act of creation, in which case "mediate" is used as in ch. one; (2) in Ḥallāj's straw-man sentence, something would more effectively "cause" God to create the bodies (if God's being "caused" to do anything were not impossible), in which case "mediate" would be used in the true sense.

415. *Bashariyya.*

416. *Passion*, Fr 3:58/Eng 3:49. Compare the formula of the *falāsifa* criticized by Ghazālī (*Tahāfut*, I, 45): "The First could not be associated with another by genus, nor could it be differentiated by difference." And Jīlī's monist formula, "You are not weaned (from us), and You do not wean us (from You)" (*ᶜayniyya*; condemned ap. Shaᶜrāwī, *Minan*, II, 29).

417. *Passion*, Fr 3:360/Eng 3:342.

418. Ibid., Fr 3:341–42/Eng 3:324.

419. Ibid., Fr 3:299/Eng 3:281–82.

420. *Sharḥ al-tawḥīd*, extract ap. *Ḥilya*.

421. Baqlī, II, 226; *Farq*, 259.

Ashᶜarites, and the last Ḥallājians imitated him: Abū ᶜUthmān Kirkintī Maghribī and Daqqāq rallied to Ibn Fūrak; Naṣrābādhī, to Isfarāʾinī (both were Ashᶜarites).[422]

But Qushayrī's attempted synthesis of Ashᶜarite dogma and mystical elements was insufficient. Ghazālī's synthesis, upon which he meditated for so long, made such grave concessions to the Sālimiyya (because of the necessities of the struggle against the Qarmathians) that theologians who adopted it were led backwards to monist solutions; this danger, already visible in Suhrawardī of Aleppo, triumphed in Ibn ᶜArabī.

Smitten with formal logic, Ibn ᶜArabī effectively eliminated all transcendent intervention of the divinity from the mystical domain. Such is the foundation of his critique of the old mystics, Yaḥyā, Rāzī, Junayd, and Ḥallāj, and of his sympathy for the Sālimiyya. And Ibn ᶜArabī accepted the extreme consequences of his thesis: he retracted the primacy once accorded to introspection, to the humble inner struggle to examine the conscience; he conceded preeminence to a subtle, theoretical culture, in which purely speculative souls without moral control over themselves experienced the nuances of intellectual ecstasy. Socially, a divorce was consummated between the monastic vocation's reserves of spiritual energy and the Islamic Community, which should have been revived by the daily intercession, prayers, example, and sacrifice of the ascetics.

All of these internal symptoms of social decadence appeared in the fourth century. Their aggravation in secular society is the true cause, deeper than economic and military developments, of the current disintegration of the Islamic Community, for whose salvation the first Muslim believers struggled and suffered so much, with ascetics and mystics in the first line of attack, making holy war in the name of the one God not only on the frontiers but in the capital, not only among idolaters but deep in their own hearts: Ḥasan, Ibn Wāsiᶜ, ᶜUtba and Shaqīq, Ibn Ḥanbal and Ḥallāj.

422. Subkī, III, 52; *Passion*, Fr 2:215–18/Eng 2:205–8.

APPENDIX: ON MASSIGNON'S "SUPPLEMENT OF ḤALLĀJIAN TEXTS"

In the French editions of the *Essai*, the "Supplement of Ḥallājian Texts," in Massignon's handwriting, most of the texts in Arabic, some in Persian (on pages *1–*104 in the 1922 ed. and, slightly expanded, pages 336–449 in the 1954 ed.; cf. *Passion*, Fr 3:294, 367/Eng 3:276, 349), contains most of the referents for the inventory of Ḥallāj's technical vocabulary in chapter 1, above. The supplement has not been reproduced here. In 1922, only 21 of the 386 fragments had already appeared elsewhere in print, but many of the sources have been edited since then. What follows here is a brief identification of the texts and, where possible, a concordance between the numbering system to which Massignon refers in chapter 1 (see ch. 1 n 1) and the page or paragraph numbers in printed editions.

A) 27 *Riwāyāt* of al-Ḥallāj, in Persian. See bib., s.n., Ḥallāj, for the Arabic original and the French and English versions. The text given in the supplement of the *Essai* corresponds to Corbin's ed. of Baqlī's *Sharḥ al-shaṭḥiyāt,* as follows:

LM's number	Corbin's paragraph number
introductory statement	1192 (p. 601)
1	1193
2	1201
3	1211
4	1215
5	1217
6	607 (p. 335)
7	610
8	612
9	617
10	620
11	623
12	626
13	627
14	631
15	633

LM's number	Corbin's paragraph number
16	635
17	637
18	639
19	641
20	644
21	646
22	648
23	652
24	656
25	658
26	660
27	663
faṣl fī adilla . . .	667–72

B) Isolated fragments, remarked upon in *Passion*, Fr 3:294/Eng 3:276, taken from the following works:

1. Kalābādhī, *Taᶜarruf.* P *143a*, mss. QA, Oxford, Vienna, Fayḍiyya, Br. The three Cairene eds. — Arberry (1933), ᶜAbd al-Ḥalīm Maḥmūd (1960), and Nawāwī (1969) — seem to be based (although Arberry's is the only ed. to state it) principally on two mss. in the Dār al-kutub, which are not the ones Massignon used. Several of his quotations are absent from the printed eds., and, as a result, the concordance below is incomplete. The extracts are numbered consecutively through 61. The name of Ḥallāj is intentionally omitted from most of the quotations. (On Kalābādhī's intentions regarding Ḥallājianism, see Jacqueline Chabbi, "Réflexions sur le soufisme iranien primitif," *JAP* 266 [1978], 37–55). And, already in 1922, Massignon noted that 36 of the extracts were certainly to be attributed to Ḥallāj (marked below with an exclamation point) and 7 of them certainly to other authors (marked below with an asterisk). Massignon's numbering in the *Essai* corresponds to Arberry's and subsequent eds. (col. 2) and Nawāwī's ed. (col. 3) as shown below; attributions to authors other than Ḥallāj are noted in parentheses:

LM's number	Ch. number in Arberry and Cairo eds.	Nawāwī's page number
1	20 (Sahl Tustarī)	78 (text differs)
2		
3		
4		
5!		
6!		
7!	5	48–49

LM's number	Ch. number in Arberry and Cairo eds.	Nawāwī's page number
8!	10	55
9* (Sahl)	14	64
10		
11!		
12!	21	79
13!	21	79
14		
15!	21	80
16!	21	81
17!	21	81
18!		
19		
20*		
21!		
22!		
23!	28, 27	100, 99
24! (cf. Baqlī on Qur. 39:57)	28	100 (partial)
25	38	114
26!	38	115
26 bis!	38	115
27*		
28* (Probably Muḥ. b. ᶜAlī al-Tirmidhī)	43	119
29!	43	120
30!	44	121
31!	44	121
32!	47	123
33!	47	124
34!	47	125
35!	48 (Junayd)	126
36	50	130
37		
38!	51	131
39	53	135
40!	55	139
41	55	140
42!	57	143
43	57	143
44!	58	145
45	58	146
46	58	147
47*	59	147
48!	60	158
49!	60	159
50	60	160
51!	61	161
52!	62	164
53	64	168
54*	65	172–173
55*	65	173
56	65	174
57!	66	175–176

LM's number	Ch. number in Arberry and Cairo eds.	Nawāwī's page number
58!	66	177
59!	69	181
60!	74	189
61	64	168 (partial)

2. Sulami, *Tafsīr*. P *170d*, mss. YJ, QA, Azh, et al. This work, a collection of commentary by various authors, is not yet published complete (though some excerpts have been, as the *Tafsīrs* of Ibn ᶜAṭā and Imām Jaᶜfar: see bib., s.n. Nwyia). The extracts, numbered 1–208, are comments on the verses of the Qurʾān given below, in Flügel's numbering system; LM's numbers are given in italics, once every ten, so that, for example, number *10* from the system of the *Essay*, ch. 1 and the supplement, corresponds to the first of three Ḥallājian comments on sura 3, verse 16, in Flügel's ed.:

   1 1:1 (2x), 2:14, 51 (2x), 109, 256 (2x), 3:16, *10* 3:16 (3x), 3:25 (2x), 29, 77, 89, 138, 188, *20* 3:188, 4:103, 124, 138, 5:3, 23, 39, 101, 116, 119, *30* 6:2, 18, 19, 53, 66, 69, 73, 76, 91 (2x), *40* 6:103, 7:1 (2x), 22, 28, 97 (2x), 139, 140, 158, *50* 7:171 (3x), 204, 9:43, *54bis* 9:112, *55* 9:112, 129, 10:1, 33 (2x), *60* 10:35 (2x), 43, 82, 11:1, 3, 47, 12:67, 76, 106, *70* 13:9, 28, 42, 14:15, 15:75, 15:99 (cf. Baqlī's *Tafsīr*, 14), 16:21, 17:72, 76, 110, *80* 18:8, 17, 48, 64, 78–81, 107, 109, 19:13, 55, 57, *90* 19:57, 20:18 (2x), 26, 106, 21:38, 43, 83, 110, 23:12, *100* 23:12 (2x), 14, 15, 93, 24:26, 31, 35 (3x), *110* 24:37 (2x), 24:53, 25:2, 4, 22 (2x), 60, 27:29, 60, *120* 28:24, 46, 73, 85, 30:39 (2x), 45, 32:16, 33:23, 35, *130* 33:72 (2x), 35:16, 29, 36:10, 21, 55, 82, 37:106, 39:23, *140* 39:23 (3x), 55, 63, 67, 40:15, 67, 42:17, 44:51, *150* 46:25, (2x), 47:21 (2x), 48:10, 29, 49:3, 17, 50:1, 36, *160* 50:36 (2x), 50:37, 51:21, 52:47 (2x), 53:3, 24, 43, 55:1, *170* 56:23, 57:3 (4x), 5, 58:8, 22 (2x), 59:8, *180* 62:4, 64:3, 65:2, 68:4 (5x), 69:38, 72:7, *190* 74:3–4, 52, 82:8, 85:3, 88:8, 13, 19, 90:17, 96:19, 98:4, *200* 98:5, 102:5, 7 (2x), 109:1, 112:1 (3x), 113:1.

   One additional extract (1954), on 19:73.

3. Baqlī, *Tafsīr* (*ᶜArā'is al-bayān*). P *380a*, Cawnpore lithograph, see bib. Extracts numbered 1–32. LM's numbers correspond to the Ḥallājian commentary on different verses of the Qurʾān in this way:

LM's number	Sura and verse
1	1:5
2	1:5
3	2:32
4	3:4
5	4:62, 85
6	6:148
7	7:140
8	10:36
9	12:83
10	12:83
11	14:7
12	14:37

LM's number	Sura and verse
13	14:41
14	15:99
15	15:99 (cf. Stf 75)
16	22:2
17	24:14
18	27:63
19	37:7
20	37:7
21	37:164
22	38:44
23	39:11
24	48:10
25	50:1–2
26	52:1
27	54:50
28	55:56
29	58:22
30	74:31
31	81:1
32	99:2–4

There are two additional extracts in the 1954 ed. of the *Essay* from the Cawnpore lithograph, the first from vol. 2, p. 310, on Qur'ān 57:21; the second from vol. 2, p. 319, on Qur'ān 59:9.

4. Baqlī, *Shaṭḥiyāt*. P *1091b*. Numbered (with interruptions) 163–214, corresponding to Corbin's ed. as follows (an asterisk shows where the original Arabic of the *Manṭiq*, from Qazan ms., ff. 36–38, is also printed in the 1954 ed. of the *Essai*):

LM's number	Corbin's paragraph number
163*–64	686 (p. 381)
169*	698
172*	706
173*	708
174*	710
174 *bis*	712 (p. 393, ll. 10–11 only)
175*	713
176	715
177*	717
178*	720 (p. 398, ll. 4–6 only)
179*	724 (p. 402, ll. 9–12 only)
181*	726
182*	728
183	730
184	732
185	735
187	739

LM's number	Corbin's paragraph number
188	741
190	746
191	748
192	751
193	753
195	758
209	781
211	784
213	791–93
214	794

C) A few fragments from other collections:

I. Sulamī, *Jawāmiᶜ*. P *170c*, ms. L J. Extracts numbered 1–8. Ed. Kohlberg, see bib. Correspondence as follows:

LM's number	Kohlberg's paragraph number
1	
2	83
3	84
4	86
5	86
6	87
7	155 (correct by means of Stf 122, on Qur. 28:73; trans. P Fr 3:18–19/ Eng 3:11–12)
8	156

II. Sulamī, *Ghalaṭāt* (= *Uṣūl* . . .). P *170f*, ms. Cairo. See bib. The extract corresponds to the Cairo, 1985, ed. *in fine*, in the *faṣl fīhi al-radd ᶜalä al-qāᵓilīna bi'l-ḥulūl*, p. 199. LM remarks that *"wa ṣifātuhu . . . maᶜbūdan"* seems to be Sulamī's commentary.

III. Kharkūshī, *Tahdhīb*. P *180a*, ms. Berlin. Cf. Arberry's article, "Khargūshī's Manual of Ṣūfism," *BSOAS* 1937–39, 345–49.

IV. Ibn Yazdānyār, *Rawḍa*. P *228a*, ms. Cairo.

V. Qushayrī, *Risāla*. P *231a*. Ed. Cairo, 1290, see bib. Massignon went through the *Risāla* and numbered the quotations from Ḥallāj, 1–16. In the Arabic supplement he reproduces only numbers 2–5 and 7–9, but in ch. 1 he refers to some of the others. The table below includes, for the extracts written out by him, the vol. and p. numbers of the 1290 ed. from which he was quoting, and, for all of the quotations, the pages in the Cairo edition (1385/1966) of Maḥmūd and Sharīf.

LM's number	Ch. and, for the ones LM writes out, vol. and p. in the 1290 ed.	P. in 1966 ed.
1	*faṣl* 1	28–31
2	*faṣl* 1; I, 62	43
3	*bāb al-khawf*; II, 198	312
4	*bāb al-jaw*ᶜ; III, 6	333
5	*bāb al-tawakkul*; III, 15	370
6	*bāb al-tawakkul*	372
7	*bāb al-ḥurriyya* (2x); III, 152	462 (2x)
8	*bāb al-firāsa*; III, 177	483
9	*bāb al-firāsa*; III, 179	484
10	*bāb al-firāsa*	487
11	*bāb al-khulq*	494
12	*bāb al-taṣawwuf*	551
13	*bāb al-tawḥīd*	586
14	*bāb al-ma*ᶜ*rifa billāh*	604–5
15	*bāb al-maḥabba*	617
16	*bāb ḥafẓ qulūb al-mashā*ʾ*ikh wa tark al-khilāf* ᶜ*alayhim*	636

VI. Hujwīrī, *Kashf al-maḥjūb.* P *1055a,* ms. Paris. Eng. trans., p. 281. Ed. Zhukovshy, Tehran reprint, p. 361

VII. Kirmānī, *Ḥikāya.* P *330a.* 9 extracts.

VIII. Harawī, *Ṭabaqāt.* P *1059a,* ms. NᶜU. Extracts numbered 1–3, corresponding to ᶜAbd al-Ḥayy Ḥabībī's ed. (see bib.) as follows:

LM's number	ᶜAbd al-Ḥayy Ḥabībī
1	sec. 334, p. 395 ll. 5–6
2	sec. 186, p. 208 l. 2
2 bis	Cf. sec. 278, p. 323, l. 10: Arabic version (= Stb 16) of part of this handwritten extract
3	sec. 278, p. 324 ll. 3 ff.

IX. Kaᶜbī, *Manāqib.* P *330a,* mss. Cairo, London. 2 Extracts.

X. ᶜAṭṭār, *Tadhkira.* In the 1922 ed. of the *Essai,* LM reproduced thirteen selected quotations from the ch. on Ḥallāj (in Nicholson's ed., vol. 2, 139–40, for the first twelve, 144 for the last one; in the Tehran ed., vol. 2, 118–19, 122). The code letter "W" with its following number from ch. 1 indicates one of these quotations. For the 1954 ed. of the *Essai* Massignon more systematically numbered the quotations from Ḥallāj (1 = Nicholson's vol. 2, 138, l. 3). Between no. 7 (*"yā dalīl al-mutaḥayyirīn . . ."*) and no. 26 (vol. 2, 140, l. 16, *". . . zohd-e jān"*), he indicated his own additions, which he either wrote out by hand or mentioned as appearing in a published source. He then added nos. 27 to 35. The siglum "ᶜAṭṭār" in ch. 1 corresponds to this system.

LM's no. (1922) "W"	LM's no. (1954) "ᶜAṭṭār"	Location, either (N) in vol. 2 of Nicholson's ed. (p. and l. are given), in the supplement (handwritten), or elsewhere
34	7	N 139 l. 5 ff.
	8	N 139 l. 10 ff.
	8 *bis*	T V:8–10
	8 *tr*	T VI:13
	8 *qtr*	A 26
36	9	"*va az Abū'l-Sawdā berasīdand . . .*" + N 139 l. 14 ff.
	10	A 73
38	11	N 139 ll. 19–20
	11 *bis, tr*	handwritten
39	12	N 139 ll. 20–21
	13	Stb 4
	13 *bis*	Stb 9
	13 *tr, qtr, qnt*	handwritten
	14	N 139 l. 22 ff.
	15	N 139 l. 24 ff.
	16	N 140 l. 1
44	17	N 140 ll. 1–2
	18	N 140 ll. 2–4
	19	Stf 161
46	20	N 140 ll. 7–9
	20 *bis*	handwritten
47	21	N 140 ll. 9–10
	21 *bis*	handwritten
	22	Stb 3
49	23	N 140 l. 11
	24	N 140 ll. 12–13
51	25	N 140 ll. 13–14 + "*tā cheh chīz az ṣadaf bīrūn āyad*"
52	26	N 140 ll. 15–16
53		N 140 ll. 16–17
54		N 140 l. 18 ff.
	27	handwritten
	28	Stb 21
	29	end of A 41
	30	Stb 14
	31	Stb 2
	33	var. of Stb 1
	34	Stb 12
	35	Stb 10
92		N 144 ll. 2–3

XI. Sibṭ ibn al-Jawzī, *Mirʾāt al-zamzān.* P *440a,* ms. London. 1 extract.
XII. Munāwī, *Kawākib.* P *795a, 840a.*
XIII. Fānī, *Sharḥ khuṭba.* P *1174a,* ms. India Office. 1 extract.

Additional extracts from the 1954 ed. of the *Essai* that have not been incorporated above (as have nos. XIV, XV, XVI, XVIII, and XXII):

XVII. Aḥmad Ghazālī, *Sawāniḥ al-ᶜushshāq.* P *281c, 1082a.* 1 extract.
XIX. Nāgūrī, ms. Calcutta 1 extract.
XX. ᶜAyn al-Quḍāt al-Hamadhānī, *Tamhīdāt.* P *1082a,* ms. India Office. New ed.: ᶜAfif ᶜUsayrān (Afif Osseiran). Tehran: Manoochehri Press (3rd printing, 1370 h.s.). 6 extracts.

LM's number	P. and l. in text of Tehran ed.
1	22 l. 4
2	129 ll. 13–14
3	247 ll. 3–7
4	257 l. 7
5	260 l. 7
6	295 l. 8

XXI. Firyābī, ms. Arles. 1 extract.
XXIII. Ḥallāj, *Kitāb al-ṣayhūr* (preface). Ms. Leningrad.
XXIV. Daylamī, *ᶜAṭf.* P *175b* and *c* (redundant), ms. Tübingen 81. 5 extracts corresponding to Vadet's edition (see bib.) as follows:

LM's numbers	Vadet's section numbers (in both the Arabic ed. and the French trans.)
I = 27b–28b	87–92 (not in the same order)*
II = 47b–48b	163–65
III = 73b–74a	246
IV = 92b	309
V = 122b	404

*LM notes that his 28b–31a (which he does not reproduce) is a trans. with variants of his number 213 of Baqlī's *Shaṭḥiyāt* = Corbin's paragraphs 791–93 = Vadet's sections 92–97.

BIBLIOGRAPHY

The French *Essai* has no bibliography. The *Passion's* last chapter, a thorough guide to mentions of Ḥallāj in both Islamic and western orientalist literature, is meant to suffice. Massignon invites the reader, when this "Ḥallājian bibliography" cites a work incompletely or not at all, to consult the first edition of Brockelmann's *Geschichte der arabischen Litteratur.* Unfortunately, the desired information is not always there. Certain old editions were unavailable to me and could not be verified, and the following list of works is not complete. It fills a few holes and should be useful not only as a guide to the footnotes of this translation of the *Essay,* but for readers of the *Passion* as well.

Manuscripts have not been pursued. If further information is needed beyond what is given in citations in the footnotes or text, consult the *Passion.*

An indication of the form "P *316a,*" refers to the numbering system of the *Passion's* bibliography, vol. 4. "P (Eng) *316a*" would mean that the entry in the English translation (1982) corrects the second French edition of 1975, or contains an error not in the French. Otherwise either the original or the translation will do.

The absence of brackets or braces around an entry indicates that the book or article is listed in the edition that Massignon was using, or one indistinguishable from it. Square brackets, [ ], mean that he refers, directly or indirectly, in either 1922 or 1954, to the work in question, but that the listed edition appeared too late for his use or was not used. Braces, { }, mean that he does not refer to the work in question. The date will make it obvious which of these books he probably consulted and which are relevant only to the translation. This system of classification leaves some room for ambiguity: Ritter's article on Ḥasan Baṣrī, for example, though mentioned in a note of 1954, is enclosed in braces because there is no reference to a page, and Massignon's main discussion of Ḥasan does not benefit from Ritter's work. Consult the Abbreviations if a reference is cryptic, especially if only a fragment of the title is given, without the author's name.

Transliterations that do not belong to the system used throughout the book either are taken from the Roman title pages of the works in the bibliography or are obviously for Persian titles. It is hoped that the resulting ease in locating the books in catalogues will make up for any confusing inconsistencies (e.g., different spellings of the names Ḥallāj and Flügel). *Kitāb* and *al* do not affect the order of alphabetization, but *risāla* does.

Writings and Editions by Massignon

This list of studies and editions by Massignon should be supplemented in general by Moubarac's *Oeuvre,* v.i. See also the main portion of this bibliography, s.n. Ḥallāj, for other of Massignon's edition.

(ed.) *Akhbār al-Ḥallāj.* In *Quatre Textes,* v.i. 2d ed. (with Paul Kraus): *Akhbār al-Ḥallāj: Texte ancien relatif à la prédication et au supplice du mystique musulman al-Ḥosayn b. Manṣour al-Ḥallāj.* Paris: Editions Larose, 1936. With French translation. 3rd ed. (with Paul Kraus): *Akhbār al-Ḥallāj: Recueil d'oraisons et d'exhortations du martyr mystique de l'Islam, Husayn ibn Mansur Hallaj.* Etudes musulmanes, 4. Paris: Vrin, 1957. With French Translation.

"'Ana al Haqq.' Etude historique critique sur une formule de théologie mystique, d'après les sources islamiques." *Der Islam* 3 (1912): 248–57. Collected in *OM,* vol. 2.

"Le Dīwān d'al-Hallāj, Essai de reconstitution, édition et traduction." *Journal Asiatique* (Jan.–March 1931): 1–158. See also, s.n. Ḥallāj.

with Clément Huart. "Les Entretiens de Lahore [entre le prince impérial Dara Shikūh et l'ascète hindou Baba La'l Das]." *Journal Asiatique* 209 (1926): 285–334. Persian text and Fr. trans.

Essai sur les origines du lexique technique de la mystique musulmane. Paris: P. Geuthner, 1922. 2nd ed.: Etudes musulmanes, eds. Gilson and Gardet, no. 2. Paris: J. Vrin, 1954. A reissue of the 1954 ed. in 1968 has caused confusion in some bibliographies; there is no third edition.

"Interférences philosophiques et percées métaphysiques dans la mystique hallagienne: Notion de 'l'essential Désir.'" In *Mélanges Joseph Maréchal,* 2: 263–96. Brussels and Paris, 1950. Corrects earlier thinking on *ᶜshq* and *ḥbb.*

"Ḳarmaṭians," *EI*1.

"Les méthodes de réalisation artistique des peuples de l'Islam." *Syria* 1 (Apr. 1921).

Muḥāḍarāt fī tārīkh al iṣṭilāḥāt al-falsafiyya al-ᶜarabiyya; Cours d'histoire des termes philosophiques arabes du 25 Novembre 1912 au 24 Avril 1913. Ed. Zeinab Mahmoud el-Khodeiry. Textes Arabes et Etudes Islamiques, 22. Cairo: Institut français d'archéologie orientale du Caire, 1983.

"Nouvelle bibliographie hallagienne." In *The Ignace Goldziher Memorial Volume,* ed. S. Löwinger and J. Somogyi, vol 1. Budapest, 1948. (Vol. 2 was published in Jerusalem in 1958.)

Opera Minora. Ed. Moubarac. 3 vols. Beirut: Dar al-Maaref, 1963. Collected essays. A planned fourth volume has not appeared.

Parole Donnée, précédée d'entretiens avec Vincent-Mansour Monteil. Paris: Julliard, 1962. Selected Essays.

La Passion d'al-Ḥosayn-ibn-Manṣour Al-Ḥallaj, Martyr mystique de l'Islam, exécuté à Bagdad le 26 mars 922. Paris: Geuthner, 1922. 2nd ed.: *La Passion de Husayn Ibn Mansūr Hallāj.* Paris Gallimard, 1975. English: *The Passion of al-Hallāj, Mystic and Martyr of Islam.* Trans. Herbert Mason. Bollingen Series, 98. Princeton: Princeton University Press, 1982. The same, abridged (translated and edited by Herbert Mason). Princeton: Princeton University Press, 1994.

(ed.) *Quatre textes inédits relatifs à la biographie d'al Ḥosayn ibn Manṣour al Ḥallāj.* Paris, 1914.

(ed.) *Recueil de textes inédits concernant l'histoire de la mystique en pays d'Islam.* Collection de textes inédits relatifs à la mystique musulmane, 1. Paris: Geuthner, 1929. See corrections, s.n. Wahitaki. Note errors in P *1695u*, corrected herein, s.n. Schacht and ^{c}Abd al-Rāziq. The latter gives the Arabic title as *Majmū^{c} nuṣūṣ lam yasbiq nashruhā muta^{c}alliqa bitaʾrīkh al-taṣawwuf fī bilād al-islām.*

"Recherches nouvelles sur le 'Diwan d'al-Hallaj' et sur ses sources." In *Mélanges Fuad Köprülü* [v.i., under title], 352–68. 1953. Reproduced as an appendix to the 1955 reprint of the *Dīwān* of 1931.

"Shaṭḥ." In *EI*1 and *Shorter EI.*

Testimonies and Reflections: Essays of Louis Massignon. Ed. Herbert Mason. Notre Dame, Ind.: University of Notre Dame Press, 1989. Selected essays in translation.

Writings by Others

^{c}Abd al-Rāziq, Muṣṭafā (Moustaphe Abderraziq). *"Nashʾat kalimat ṣūfiyya wa mutaṣawwif wa aṣluhumā." Ma^{c}rifa* of Cairo 2 (1931): 149–52. Note error in P *1695u* (this article contains a mention, not a translation, of the *Recueil*). Cf. *supra,* Massignon, ed., *Recueil.*

^{c}Abdarī, Muḥammad ibn al-Ḥājj al-Fāsī. *Madkhal al-shar^{c} al-sharīf.* Alexandria, 1293. P *524* (Eng).

Abū'l-^{c}Atāhiya, Ibrāhīm b. al-Qāsim. *Al-Anwār al-zāhiya fī Dīwān.* Beirut: Maṭba^{c}a Kāthulīkiyya, 1888.

[Abū'l-Faḍl (Faẓl) ibn Mubārak, Akbar's minister. *Áín-i Akbarī* Ed. H. Blochmann. Calcutta, 1867–77. Persian text. Trans., vol. 1, Blochmann, 1868] then continued, as cited in text here, by H. S. Jarrett, s.n.

[Aflākī (Eflaki), Shams al-Dīn Aḥmad. *Manāqib al-^{c}ārifīn* (*Kāshif al-asrār*). Ankara, 1959–61.] See also trans., s.n. Huart, the ed. referred to in the text.

Ālūsī, Nu^{c}mān Khayr al-Dīn ibn Maḥmūd. *Jalā al-^{c}aynayn fī muḥākamat al-Aḥmadayn.* Cairo, 1298/1880. [New ed., Cairo: Maṭba^{c}at al-Madanī, 1980.]

Ālūsī, Shihāb al-Dīn Maḥmūd. *Rūḥ al-maᶜānī fī tafsīr al-Qurʾān al-ᶜazīm* Būlāq, 1301–10.

ᶜĀmilī, Bahā al-Dīn Muḥammad. *Al-Kashkūl.* Cairo, 1316.

Père Anastase (al-Ab Anastās al-Karmalī). "*Al-Abdāl.*" *Al-Machriq* 12 (1909): 194–204.

Anbārī (Anbarī), Abū'l-Barakāt ᶜAR b. M. *Nuzhat al-alibbā fī ṭabaqāt al-udabā.* Cairo, 1294/1877. P (Eng) *2017.*

Andrae, Tor. *I myrtenträdgården: Studier sufisk mystik.* Stockholm: Albert Bonniers, 1947. [Reprint 1981. Trans. Birgitta Sharpe as *In the Garden of Myrtles,* SUNY Series in Muslim Spirituality in South Asia, Albany: SUNY Press, 1987.]

Arberry, A. J., ed. *Pages from the Kitāb al-Lumaᶜ of Abū Naṣr al-Sarrāj.* London, 1947.

Arnold, Sir Thomas Walker. *The Preaching of Islam.* 2nd ed. London: Constable, 1913.

[Ashᶜarī, Abū'l-Ḥasan ibn Ismāᶜīl. *Al-Maqālāt al-Islāmiyyīn, Die dogmatischen Lehren der Anhänger des Islam.* Ed. Ritter. Biblioteca Islamica, 1. Istanbul, 1929–30. Reprint Wiesbaden: Franz Steiner, 1963.]

Asín Palacios, Miguel. *Algazel, dogmática, moral, ascética.* Estudios filosófico-teológicos, 1. Zaragoza, 1901.

———. *Bosquejo de un diccionario técnico de filosofía y teología musulmanas.* Zaragoza: M. Escar, 1903.

———. *La espiritualidad de Algazel y su sentido christiano.* Madrid and Granada: E. Maestre, 1934–41.

———. *Logia et agrapha Domini Jésu apud muslemicos scriptores, asceticos praesertim.* Paris: Firmin-Didot, 1916–29. [Reprint Turnhout: Brepols, 1974.]

———. *Los Precedentes musulmanes del pari de Pascal.* Santander: Menendez y Pelayo, 1920.

ᶜAṭṭār, Farīd al-dīn. *Tadhkirat al-awliyā.* Ed. R. A. Nicholson. London, 1905–7. See P *1101c.*

ᶜAyn al-Quḍāt al-Hamadhānī, also known al-Miyānijī al-Hamadhānī. *Shakwä al-gharīb.* In Mohammad ben Abd el-Jalil, "*Šakwä-l-Ġarīb ᶜani l-awṭān ʾilā ᶜulamāʾ-l-buldān de ᶜayn al-quḍāt al-hamaḏānī.*" *Journal Asiatique* 216 (1930): 1–76 (text) and 193–297 (French trans.). [Subsequent ed.: *Risālat shakwä al-gharīb (La Plainte d'un exilé)*, Tehran, 1962. Trans. A. J. Arberry as *A Sufi Martyr,* London, 1969.]

[Badawī, ᶜAbd al-Raḥmān. *Shaṭaḥāt al-Ṣūfiyya* (vol. 1: *Abū Yazīd al-Bisṭāmī*). Darāsāt Islāmiyya. Cairo: Maktabat al-Nahḍat al-Miṣriyya, 1949.]

Baghdādī, Abū Manṣūr ᶜAbd al-Qāhir Ibn Ṭāhir (Ibn Ṭāhir Baghdādī). *Al-Farq bayn al-firaq.* Ed. Badr. Cairo, 1328/1910. [Trans. Kate C. Seelye and A. S. Halkin, 2 vols.]

———. *Uṣūl al-dīn.* Istanbul: Maṭbaᶜat al-Dawla, 1346/1928.

[Baqlī, Ṣadr al-Dīn Abū Muḥammad Rūzbihān. *Manṭiq al-asrār bi bayān al-anwār.* See P *380b.* N.B. a confusing error: LM stated in 1922 that this work was lost. In the 1930s, he discovered 2 mss. at Mashhad. These are noted in the new *Passion,* but the old note, "lost," is erroneously maintained. See herein, ch. 3 n 69.]

[———. *Sharh-e shathiyāt.* Ed. Henry Corbin. Bibliothèque Iranienne, 12. Tehran-Paris, 1966. See P *1091b.* Persian text (trans. with alterations of the Arabic *Manṭiq,* above).]

———. *Tafsīr ᶜArāᵓis al-Bayān.* 2 vols. Cawnpore, 1883. P *380a*; and herein, ch. 1 n 1.

Bar-Hebraeus. *Bar Hebraeus's Book of the Dove.* Trans. A. J. Wensinck. Leiden: E. J. Brill, 1919. With an introduction.

{Basetti-Sani, Giulio, O.F.M. *Louis Massignon: Christian Ecumenist, Prophet of Inter-Religious Reconciliation.* Ed. and trans. Allan Harris Cutler. Chicago: Franciscan Herald Press, 1974.}

Bīrūnī, Abū'l-Rayḥān M. b. A. *Al-Āthār al-bāqiya ᶜan al-qurūn al-khāliya (Chronologie orientalistischer Völker).* Ed. Edward Sachau. Leipzig, 1878. Trans. Sachau as *Chronology of Ancient Nations,* London, 1879.

[———. *Kitāb bātanjal al-hindī fi'l-Khalāṣ min al-amthāl.* S.n. Ritter.]

———. *Ta'rīkh al-Hind.* Ed. Edward Sachau. London: Trübner, 1887. Arabic text. Trans Sachau as *Alberuni's India.* London.: Trübner, 1888 (Reprint 1900, 1914).

Blochet, Edgar. *Etudes sur l'ésoterisme musulman.* Louvain: J. B. Istas, 1910. (See JAP, 1902; *Le Muséon,* 1906–9.)

———. *Catalogue des manuscrits persans de la Bibliothèque Nationale.* 4 vols. Paris: Imprimerie Nationale, 1905–34.

Brockelmann, Carl. *Geschichte der Arabischen Litteratur.* 2 vols. Wiemar: Felber, 1898–1902. Supplement. 3 vols. Leiden, 1937–42.

Brockelmann, Carl. *Geschichte der Arabischen Litteratur.* 2 vols. 2nd ed. Leiden: E. J. Brill, 1943–49.

Browne, E. G. *Arabian Medicine.* Cambridge: Cambridge University Press, 1921.

Browne, E. G., trans. *Chahár Maqála.* S.n. Niẓāmī ᶜArūḍī.

Brünnow, Rudolf Ernst. *Die Charidschiten unter den ersten Omayyaden.* Leiden: E. J. Brill, 1884.

Carra de Vaux, Baron Bernard. "La Philosophie illuminative ('hikmet el-ichraq') d'après Suhrawerdi Meqtul." *Journal Asiatique* series 9, 19 (1902): 63–94.

Chauvin, Victor. *Bibliographie des ouvrages arabes ou relatifs aux arabes publiés dans l'Europe chrétienne de 1810 à 1885.* 12 vols. Liège, 1892–1922.

{Chittick, William C. *The Sufi Path of Knowledge.* Albany: State University of New York Press, 1989.}

Daylamī, Abū'l-Ḥasan ^{c}Alī ibn Muḥammad. *Kitab ^{c}Aṭf al-alif al-ma$^{\supset}$lūf ^{c}alā'l-lām al-ma^{c}ṭūf.* Ms. Tübingen 81. P *175* [Ḥallājian fragments, trans. LM, in "Interférences," 269–79. Ed. J.-C. Vadet. Arabic text. Cairo: IFAO, 1962. Trans. J. K. Fadih. Geneva: Droz, 1980.]

———. Sīrat al-shaykh Ibn Khafīf. Trans. (Persian) Ibn Jurayd Shīrāzī. P *144*. [Ed. A. M. Schimmel. Ankara: Türk Tarih Kurumu Basimevi. 1955.]

De Goeje, M. J. *Mémoire sur la conquête de la Syrie.* Leiden, 1900.

Delitzsch, Friedrich. *Die Grosse Taüschung.* Stuttgart: Deutsche Verlags-Anstalt, 1920.

Dhahabī, Shams al-dīn Muḥammad ibn Aḥmad. *Kitāb mīzān al-i^{c}tidāl.* Cairo: Maṭba^{c}at al-Sa^{c}āda, 1325/1907.

Dozy, Reinhart. *Supplément aux dictionaires arabes.* Leiden: E. J. Brill, 1881 (reissued Leiden and Paris, 1927, 1967).

Dussaud, René. *Histoire et religion des Noseiris.* Paris, 1900.

{Ernst, Carl W. *Words of Ecstasy in Sufism.* Albany: SUNY Press, 1985.}

Fānī, Muḥsin (ascribed author). *Dabistān-i Maẕāhib (Madhāhib): An Account of Eastern Religions and Philosophies.* Ed. Nāẕir Ashraf and W. B. Bayley. Calcutta, 1809. Trans. Shea and Troyer. London, 1843.

Festugière, A. J. *La Révélation d'Hermès Trismégiste.* Paris: Lecoffre, 1944–54. Appendix by Massignon *in fine* vol. 1, on "L'hermétisme arabe."

Firuz Bin Kaus, Mulla, ed. and trans. *The Desātīr: or Sacred Writings of the Ancient Persian Prophets.* Bombay: Courier Press, 1818. Reprints of the trans., Bombay, 1888 and Minneapolis: Wizards Bookshelf, 1975.

Fīrūzābādī, Muḥammad b. Ya^{c}qūb. *Al-Qāmūs al-muḥīṭ.* Cairo: Būlāq, 1301/1883.

Fluegel, Gustav, ed. *Corani Textus Arabicus.* 3rd ed. Leipzig: Ernest Bredt, 1869. Numbering system used herein for references. {See table of conversion in *Bell's Introduction,* s.n. Watt.}

———, ed. *Definitiones viri ... Ali ben Mohammed Dschordschani* (followed by) *Definitiones Theosophi ... Ibn Arabi* (= *Kitāb al-ta^{c}rīfāt* of Jurjānī followed by *Iṣṭilāḥāt* of Ibn al-^{c}Arabī). Leipzig: Vogel, 1845. Arabic text with introduction and critical apparatues in Latin. [Reprint Beirut: Librairie du Liban, 1978, entitled simply *Kitāb al-Ta^{c}rīfāt* (*A Book of Definitions*) by Ali Al-Gurgānī but including Ibn ^{c}Arabī's work as well.]

Friedländer, Israel. *The Heterodoxies of the Shiites in the Presentation of Ibn Ḥazm.* 2 vols. New Haven: 1907–9. Originally published in *JAOS* 28, 29.

Galtier, Emile, *Mémoires et fragments inédits.* Cairo: IFAO, 1912.

Gandhi, Mahatma M. K. "La Doctrine du 'Satyagraha'." *Revue du Monde Musulman* 44–45 (Apr.-June 1921): 55–63. Text in English. In a larger article: "Documents sur la situation sociale dans l'Inde et les projets de réforme".

{Gardet and Anawati. *Introduction à la théologie musulmane: Essai de théologie comparée*. Paris: Vrin, 1948. 2nd ed., 1970.}

{———. *Mystique musulmane, aspects et tendances*. 2nd ed., Etudes Musulmanes, 8. Paris: Vrin, 1968.}

Gaudefroy-Demombynes, Maurice. *Le Pèlerinage à la Mekke*. Annales du Musée Guimet, Bibliothèque d'Etudes, 33. Paris: Geuthner, 1923.

Ghazālī, Abū Ḥāmid. *Iḥyā ᶜulūm al-dīn*. Cairo: 1312/1894. See P *280a*.

———. *al-Munqidh min al-Ḍalāl*. Cairo: Maṭbaᶜa Iᶜlāmiyya, 1303/1885. [Trans. R. J. McCarthy as *Freedom and Fulfillment: Al-Ghazālī's Al-Munqidh min al-Ḍalāl*, Library of Classical Arabic Literature, 4, Boston: G. K. Hall, 1980.]

———. *Mustaẓhirī = Streitschrift*, s.n. Goldziher.

Goldziher, I. *Muhammedanische Studien*. Halle, 1889–90. [Reprint Hildesheim: G. Olms, 1971. Trans. C. R. Barber and S. M. Stern as *Muslim Studies*, London and Chicago, 1967–71.]

———. *Die Richtungen der islamischen Koranauslegung*. Leiden: Brill, 1920. [Reprint 1970.]

———. *Streitschrift des Ġazālī gegen die Bāṭinijja-Sekte* (= *al-Mustaẓhirī = Kitāb al-faḍāᵓiḥ wa faḍāᵓil Mustaẓhiriyya*). Leiden: Brill, 1916.

[———. *Vorlesungen über den Islam*. Heidelberg, 1910.] Trans. Arin into French as *Le dogme et la loi de l'Islam*. Paris: Paul Geuthner, 1920. [Footnotes herein refer to the Eng. trans. by Andras and Ruth Hamori, *Introduction to Islamic Theology and Law*, Modern Classics in Near Eastern Studies, eds. Charles Issawi and Bernard Lewis, Princeton: Princeton University Press, 1981.]

Graf, Georg. *Die christliche-arabische Literatur bis zur frankischen Zeit*. Strassburger Theologische Studien. Freiburg im Breisgau: Herder, 1905.

———. *Geschichte der christlichen arabischen literatur*. Rome: Biblioteca Apostolica Vaticana, 1947–53.

{Graham, William A. *Divine Word and Prophetic Word in Early Islam*. Religion and Society, 7. The Hague: Mouton, 1977.}

Ḥājjī Khalīfa Muṣṭafā b. ᶜAA (Kātib Chelebī). *Kashf al-ẓunūn ᶜan asāmī al-kutub wa'l-funūn, Lexicon Bibliographicum et encyclopaedicum ... a Katib Jelebi ... Haji khalfa ... compositum*. Ed. G. Flügel. Leipzig, 1835–58. Arabic text and Latin trans. [*Keşf-el-zunun*, Istanbul: Maarif Matbaasi, 1941–43.]

Ḥalabī, ᶜAlī ibn Burhān al-dīn. *Insān al-ᶜuyūn fī sīrat al-Amīn al-Maᵓmūn* (= *Sīra Ḥalabiyya*). Cairo, 1320/1902.

Ḥallāj, Abū'l-Mughīth al-Ḥusayn ibn Manṣūr. *Bustān al-maᶜrifa*. = last section of *Kitāb al-Ṭawāsīn*, ed. 1913 only (v. i.). Nwyia (his ed., p. 4, v.i., under editor's name) presents evidence that the *Bustān* is not part of the *Ṭawāsīn*.

Ḥallāj, al-Ḥusain ibn Manṣūr. *Dīwān*, 1931, s.n. Massignon, v.s. Also: *Le Dīwān d'al-Ḥallāj*, ed. LM, Paris: Paul Geuthner, 1955, an exact reprint with an appendix reproducing Massignon's article "Recherches nouvelles," which makes this edition the handiest one of the *Dīwān*. There is another edition of 1955, in French only (Paris: Cahiers du Sud), with amended translations only of those poems Massignon was certain were by Ḥallāj. [New ed., Kāmil Muṣṭafā al-Shaibī, Baghdād: Maṭbaʿat al-Maʿārif, 1394/1974.]

———. Ḥallāj. *Riwāyāt*. Arabic in *Akhbār*, 3rd ed., p. 147–49; Persian in *Essai*, appendix, now printed in Baqlī, *Sharh* (v.s.), 335–69, 601–11; French or English in *Passion*, Fr 3:344–352/Eng 3:327–34.

———. Ḥallāj, Aboû al Moghîth al Ḥosayn ibn Manṣoûr. *Kitâb al-Ṭawâsîn*. Ed. Louis Massignon. Paris: Geuthner, 1913. [New ed., s.n., Nwyia.] Trans. in *Passion*, vol. 3.

Hamadhānī. See ʿAyn al-Quḍāt.

Hammer-Purgstall, Josef von. *Geschichte des Osmanischen Reiches*. Pest, 1827. Reprint Graz, 1963.

Ḥaqqī, Ismāʿīl. *Tafsīr rūḥ al-bayān*. Cairo, 1255. See P *844*.

Harawī, ʿAbdallah al-Anṣārī. *Manāzil al-sāʾirīn ilā rabb al-ʿālamīn*. Contained in Ibn Qayyim al-Jawziyya's *Madārij al-sālikīn*, v.i.

———. *Ṭabaqāt al-ṣūfiyya*. See P *1059a*. [Ed. ʿAbd al-Ḥayy Ḥabībī. Kabul: Historical Society of Afghanistan, 1341 h.s./1962.]

Hartmann, Richard. *Darstellung des Sūfitums*. Berlin: Meyer and Müller, 1914.

Haytamī, Shihāb al-Dīn Aḥmad b.M.b. Ḥajar. *Al-Fatāwā al-ḥadīthiyya*. Cairo, 1325.

Horovitz, Saul. *Über den Einfluss der greichischen Philosophie auf die Entwicklung des Kalām*. Breslau, 1909.

Horten, Max. *Die philosophischen Systeme der spekulativen Theologen im Islam nach original quellen Dargestellt*. Bonn, 1912.

Huart, Clément. *Littérature arabe*. Paris, 1902.

———. *Les Saints des derviches tourneurs*. Vol. 1. Paris: E. Leroux, 1918 [1922 (v. 2)]. Trans. of Aflaki's *manāqib*, v.s.

———, and Rizá Tevfiq. *Textes persans relatifs à la secte des Horoufîs (Majmūʿeh-ye rasāʾel-e Ḥorūfiyeh)*. E. J. W. Gibb Memorial, old series, 9. London, 1909. In French and Persian.

Hujwīrī, ʿAlī b. ʿUthmān Al-Jullābī. *Kashf al-Maḥjūb of Al Hujwiri: The Oldest Persian Treatise on Sufism*. Trans. Reynold A. Nicholson. E. J. W. Gibb Memorial, old series, 17. London: Luzac, 1911. See P *1055a*, *1692f*. [Subsequent ed. of the original, Valentin Zhukovsky, 1927, reissued Tehran: Amir Kabir, 1336 h.s., with introductory material translated into Persian.]

Ḥurayfish Makkī, Abū Madyan Shu^{c}ayb b. ^{c}AA. *Kitāb al-rawḍ al-fā$^{\supset}$iq fi'l-mawā^{c}iẓ wa'l-raqā$^{\supset}$iq.* Cairo, 1310. Note misprints in P *579.*

Huysmans, Joris-Karl. *Sainte Lydwine de Schiedam.* Paris, 1901.

Ibn ^{c}Abd Rabbihi, Shihāb al-Dīn Aḥmad. *Al-^{c}Iqd al-Farīd.* Cairo, 1316/1898.

Ibn abī Uṣaybi^{c}a, Aḥmad b. Qāsim. *Kitāb ^{c}uyūn al-anbā fī ṭabaqāt al-aṭibbā.* Ed. A. Müller. Königsberg and Cairo: 1882–84.

Ibn ^{c}Ajība, A. b. M. *Futūḥāt ilāhiyya.* P *888.*

———. *Iqāẓ al-himam fī sharḥ al-ḥikam.*

Ibn al-^{c}Arabī, Muḥyī al-Dīn. *Fuṣūṣ al-Ḥikam.* Istanbul, 1309.

———. *Al-futūḥāt al-makkiyya.* Cairo: Būlāq, 1329/1911. Reprint Beirut: Dar Sader, 1968. See P *421.*

———. *Iṣṭilāḥāt (Definitiones).* S.n., Fluegel.

———. *Kitāb muḥāḍarat al-abrār wa musāmarat al-akhyār.* Cairo, 1282/1865.

Ibn ^{c}Asākir, Abū'l-Qāsim ^{c}Alī b. al-Ḥasan. *Tahdhīb ta$^{\supset}$rīkh ibn ^{c}Asākir* (on some title pages, *al-Ta$^{\supset}$rīkh al-Kabīr;* also *Ta$^{\supset}$rīkh Dimashq*). Damascus: 1329–31 (vols. 1–5), 1349–51 (vols. 6–7).

Ibn Aṭā Allah, Tāj al-Dīn Abū'l-Faḍl. *Laṭā$^{\supset}$if al-minan.* In margins of Sha^{c}rānī's *Laṭā$^{\supset}$if al-minan,* v.i.

Ibn al-Athīr, ^{c}Izz al-Dīn Abū'l-Ḥasan ^{c}Alī b. M. *Al-Kāmil fi'l-tārīkh.* Ed. C. J. Tornberg. Leiden: Brill, 1867.

———. *Al-Nihāya fī gharīb al-ḥadīth.*

———. *Usd al-ghāba fī ma^{c}rifat al-ṣaḥāba.*

Ibn Baṭṭa ^{c}Ukbarī, S.n. ^{c}Ukbarī.

Ibn Bābūya, Abū Ja^{c}far M. b. ^{c}Alī *Kitāb ikmāl ad-dīn.* Heidelberg, 1901. See P *160c.*

Ibn Bākūya, Abū ^{c}AA M. b. ^{c}AA. *Bidāyat ḥāl al-Ḥallāj wa nihāyatuhu.* In *Quatres Textes,* s.n. Massignon. Errors in P *191.*

Ibn al-Dā^{c}ī Rāzī, Abū Turāb Murtaḍä. *Tabṣirat al-^{c}awāmm fī ma^{c}rifat maqālāt al-anām.* Tehran lith., 1312/1895. P *1081.*

Ibn Dāwūd Iṣfahānī, Abū Bakr Muḥammad. *Kitāb al-Zahrah (The Book of the Flower).* Ed. A. R. Nykl and Ibrahim Tuqan. Chicago: University of Chicago Press, 1351/1932.

Ibn Diḥya, ^{c}Umar. *Nibrās.* Ed. Azzawī. Baghdād, 1946.

Ibn Durayd, Abū Bakr Muḥammad. *Kitāb Jamharat al-Lugha* [*Al-Jamhara fi'l-lugha* in the ed. of Ramzi Baalbaki, Beirut, 1987–88].

Ibn Farḥūn, Ibrahīm ibn ^{c}Alī. *Al-Dībaj al-mudhahhab fī ma^{c}rifat a^{c}yān ^{c}ulamā al-madhhab.* Fez, n.d.

Ibn al-Fāriḍ. *Al-Tā$^{\supset}$iyyat al-kubrä (Naẓm al-sulūk).* Many eds., e.g., Hammer-Purgstall, *Das arabische hohe Liede der Liebe,* Vienna, 1854.

[Ibn al-Farrā, Al-Qāḍī Abū Ya^{c}lä. *Kitāb al-mu^{c}tamad fī uṣūl al-dīn.* Ed. Haddad. Beirut: Dar el-Machreq, 1974.]

Ibn Ḥajar ʿAsqalānī, Aḥmad b. ʿAlī. *Lisān al-mīzān.* Hyderabad, 1329–31/1911–13. See P *632b.*

Ibn Ḥanbal, Aḥmad, *Musnad.* Cairo: Al-Maṭbaʿat al-Saʿāda, 1313/1895.

Ibn Ḥazm, Abū Muḥammad ʿAlī b. Aḥmad. *Al-Fiṣal fī'l-milal wa'l-ahwā wa'l-niḥal.* 5 vols. Cairo: Maṭbaʿa adabiyya, 1317.

Ibn Jahḍam, Abū'l-Ḥusayn ʿAlī. *Bahjat al-asrār wa lawāmiʿ al-anwār.* See P *182a.*

Ibn al-Jawzī, Abū'l-Faraj. *Akhbār al-ḥumaqä wa'l-mughaffalīn.* Damascus: Maṭbaʿat al-Tawfīq, 1345.

[———. *Al-Ḥasan al-Baṣrī, ādābuhu, ḥikamuhu.* Ed. Ḥasan al-Sandūbī. Al-rasāʾil al-nādira, 6. Cairo: Maṭbaʿa raḥmāniyya, 1350/1931. See H. Ritter in *DI* 21, pp. 7–10, dismissing this ed. as being of no verifiable authenticity. See also M. Swartz's ed. of Ibn al-Jawzī's *Quṣṣāṣ,* 151 n 2.]

———. *Al-Muntaẓam fī taʾrīkh al-mulūk wa'l-umam.* Ḥaydarābād, 1359.

———. *Kitāb al-nāmūs fī talbīs Iblīs (Talbīs Iblīs).* See P *370b.* Notes reading *"Nāmūs"* are of 1922 and refer to a chapter in the manuscript; they are therefore generally usable, if somewhat vague. Notes added later read *"Talbīs"* and refer to the Cairo ed. of 1923.

[———. *Kitāb al-quṣṣāṣ wa'l-mudhakkirīn.* Ed. and trans. Merlin Swartz. Recherches: Pensée arabe et musulmane, 47. Beirut: Dar el-Machreq, 1971.]

———. *Ṣifat al-Ṣafwa.* Ms. P. 2030.

Ibn Junayd, Muʿīn al-Dīn Abū'l-Qāsim (Junayd Shīrāzī). *Shadd al-izār fī ḥaṭṭ al-awzār ʿan zawwār al-mizār.* Ed. E. Denison Ross. 1919. [Tehran, 1328 h.s./1950.]

Ibn-Khaldūn. *Muqaddima.* Trans. de Slane. Algiers, 1852.

Ibn al-Murtaḍä, Aḥmad ibn Yaḥyä (*Bāb Dhikr al-Muʿtazila min) al-Munya wa'l-amal fī sharḥ kitāb al-milal wa'l-niḥal.* Ed. Thomas Arnold. Leipzig, 1902. See P *2109.*

Ibn al-Nadīm, Abū'l-Faraj Muḥammad b. Isḥāq. *Kitāb al-fihrist.* Ed. Gustav Flügel. Leipzig: F. C. W. Vogel, 1871–72. Reissued Beirut: Khayyāṭ.

Ibn Manẓūr, Muḥammad b. Mukarram. *Lisān al-ʿarab.* Cairo, 1300–1307/1883–89.

Ibn Mukarram = Ibn Manẓūr, v.s.

Ibn Qayyim (Qayīm) al-Jawziyya, Shams al-Dīn Muḥammad. *Iʿlām al-muwaqqiʿīn ʿan rabb al-ʿālamīn.*

———. *Madārij al-sālikīn fī manāzil al-sāʾirīn.* 3 vols. Cairo: Maṭbaʿat al-Manār, 1331–34/1912–14.

Ibn Qutayba, Abū M. ʿAA b. Muslim. *Kitāb al-Maʿārif, Ibn Coteiba's Handbuch der Geschichte.* Ed. Wüstenfeld. Göttingen: Vandenhoeck and Ruprecht, 1850. P (Eng) *2112c* cites other editions, but Massignon's notes refer to this one.

———. *Kitāb taʾwīl mukhtalif al-ḥadīth* [= *Mushkil al-ḥadīth, Ikhtilāf fī'l-lafẓ*]. Cairo: Maṭbaʿat Kurdistān, 1326/1908.

———. *ʿUyūn al-akhbār* (on title page: *ʿUjun al-aḫbār*). Ed. Brockelmann. Berlin: E. Felber, 1900–1908.

Ibn Saʿd, Abū ʿAA M. *Kitāb al-ṭabaqāt al-kabīr*. Ed. Sachau et al. 9 vols. Leiden: 1904–40. [New ed. Iḥsān ʿAbbās, Beirut, 1957.]

Ibn Sīda, Abū'l Ḥasan ʿAlī b. Ismāʿīl. *Al-Mukhaṣṣaṣ fī'l-lugha*. Cairo: Būlāq, 1316–21. [Amended ed. A. S. M. Hārūn, Beirut, 1386.]

Ibn Sīnā, Abū ʿAlī, *Tisʿ rasāʾil*. Constantinople: Maṭbaʿat al-Jawāʾib, 1298.

Ibn Taghrībirdī (Ibn Tagri Bardiy), Abū'l-Maḥāsin. *Al-Nujūm al-zāhira fī mulūk miṣr wa'l-qāhira* (*Annales*). Ed. T. G. J. Juynboll. Leiden: Brill, 1855–61 [first two volumes of an edition continued by Popper, at Berkeley, Cal., 1909–30]. P (Eng.) *660a* cites an edition (Cairo: Dār al-kutub al-miṣriyya, 1929) to which Massignon does not refer.

Ibn Ṭāhir Maqdisī. S.n. Maqdisī.

Ibn Taymiyya, Aḥmad. *Majmūʿ al-rasāʾil al-kubrä*. Cairo: 1323.

———. *Majmūʿat fatāwī . . . Ibn Taymiyya*, Cairo: Maṭbaʿat Kurdistān, 1326–29/1908–11.

———. *Minhāj al-sunna*. 4 vols. Cairo: 1321–22. See P *512*.

———. *Naql al-Manṭiq*.

Ikhwān al-Ṣafā. *Rasāʾil*. Bombay, 1305–6/1887–89.

Inostrantzev, Konstantin Aleksandrovich. *Iranian Influence on Moslem Literature*. Trans. G.K. Nariman. Bombay: Taraporevala, 1918. With appendices from Arabic sources.

Iṣbahānī, Abū'l-Faraj ʿAlī b. Ḥusayn. *Kitāb al-Aghānī*. Ed. Aḥmad al-Shanqīṭī. 21 vols. in 7. Cairo: Maṭbaʿat al-taqaddum, 1905. See P *2122*. ("1st ed." in the notes refer to Būlāq, 1868, 21 vols.).

Iṣfahānī, Abū Nuʿaym. *Ḥilyat al-awliyā*. Cairo, 1932–38.

Ivanow, Vladimir. *A Guide to Ismaili Literature*. London: Royal Asiatic Society, 1933. Esp. pp. 1–2, on LM on "Qarmathians."

ʿIyāḍ Sibtī. *Kitāb al-shifā*. Istanbul, 1312.

Jaʿfar al-Ṣādiq. *Tafsīr*. S.n., Nwyia.

Jāḥiẓ. *Kitāb al-bayān wa'l-tabyīn*. Cairo, 1332.

Jāmī, Nūr al-Dīn ʿAbd al-Raḥmān b. Aḥmad. *Nafaḥāt al-uns*. Ed. Nassau-Lees. Calcutta, 1859.

Jarrett, Henry Sullivan, trans. *The Áín-i Akbari by Abul Fazl Allámi*. Bibliotheca Indica, 3. Calcutta: Asiatic Society, 1873–. [See text, s.n., Abū'l-Faḍl.]

Jawharī, Ismāʿīl b. Ḥammād. *Tāj al-lugha wa siḥāḥ al-ʿarabiyya*. Cairo: Būlāq, 1282.

Jīlānī, ʿAbd al-Qādir. See Kīlānī.

[Junayd. *Rasāʾil*. In *The Life, Personality, and Writings of Al-Junayd*. Ed.

A. H. Abdel-Kader. E. J. W. Gibb Memorial, new series, 22. London: Luzac, 1962.]

Jurjānī, ᶜAlī b. Muḥammad al-Sharīf. *Kitāb al-taᶜrīfāt (Definitiones)*. S.n. Fluegel.

{Juynboll, G. H. A. *Muslim Tradition*. Cambridge Studies in Islamic Civilization. Cambridge: Cambridge University Press, 1983.}

[Kalābādhī, Tāj al-Islām Abū Bakr Muḥammad. *Kitāb al-Taᶜarruf li-madhhab ahl al-taṣawwuf*. Ed. Muḥammad al-Nawāwī. Cairo: Maktabat al-kulliyāt al-azhariyya, 1388/1969.]

Kāshānī (Kāshī), ᶜAbd al-Razzāq. *Iṣṭilāḥāt al-ṣūfiyya*. S.n., Sprenger. [New ed. ᶜAbd al-Khāliq Maḥmūd, Cairo: Dar al-Maᶜārif, second printing 1404/1984.]

Kattānī (Kittani), ᶜAbd al-Ḥayy ibn ᶜabd al-Kabīr. *Fihris al-fahāris wa ithbāt wa muᶜjam al-maᶜājim wa'l-mashyakhāt wa'l-musalsalāt*. Fez, 1346.

[Khalīl b. Ahmad. *Kitāb al-ᶜayn*. Vol. 1. Ed. A. Darwīsh. Baghdād: 1967. Vol. 2. Ed. M. al-Makhzūmī. Baghdād: 1981.]

Kharrāz, Abū Saᶜīd Aḥmad b. ᶜIsä. *Kitāb al-Ṣidq, The Book of Truthfulness*. Ed. and trans. A. J. Arberry. Oxford and Calcutta: Oxford University Press, 1937. With Arabic text.

Khaṭīb Baghdādī, Abū Bakr ibn Thābit. *Taʾrīkh Baghdād*. Cairo, 1831.

Khūnsārī (Khwānsārī or Khawānsārī), Muḥammad Bāqir. *Rawḍāt al-jannāt*. Iranian lithograph, 1307.

Kīlānī, ᶜAbd al-Qādir (usually Jīlānī). *Al-Ghunya li ṭālibī ṭarīq al-ḥaqq*. Cairo, 1288. P *341h*.

Kindī, ᶜAbd al-Masīḥ. *Risala ilä al-Ḥāshimī*. Portions trans. William Muir as *The Apology of al-Kindy*, London: Smith, Elder, 1882. See P (Eng) *2139*.

Kindī, Abū ᶜUmar Muhammad b. Yūsuf. *The Governors and Judges of Egypt or Kitāb el 'umarā' (el Wulāh) wa kitāb el Quḍāt of el Kindi*. Ed. Rhuvon Guest. E. J. W. Gibb Memorial, old series, 19. Leiden: Brill, 1912. See P (Eng) *2139a*.

Kraus, Paul. *Jābir ibn Ḥayyān*. Paris: Maisonneuve, 1936. [Reprint Paris: Editions les Belles Lettres, 1986].

Kremer, Alfred von. *Culturgeschichtliche Streifzüge auf dem gebiete des Islams*. Leipzig, 1873. [Trans. in vol. 1 of S. Khuda Bukhsh, *Contributions to the History of Islamic Civilization*, Calcutta, 1929–30.]

Kürküt, Shāhzādeh. *Ḥarīmī*. Ms. Fayḍiyya 1764. The author is called Qorqut in P (Eng).

{Lalande, André, ed. *Vocabulaire technique et critique de la philosophie*. Paris: Félix Alcan, 1926. 10th ed. Paris: Presses Universitaires de France, 1968.}

Lammens, Henri. "Etudes sur le règne du calife omaiyade Mo'āwia Ier." *Mélanges de l'Université Saint-Joseph* (1908): 145–312. {The first parts of this series of articles are in *MUSJ* 1 (1906): 1–108, and 2 H (1907): 1–172.}

{Landolt, Hermann. "Simnānī on *waḥdat al-wujūd*." In Mohaghegh and Landolt, eds., *Collected Papers* (v.i.), 91–111.}

Lane, E. W. *An Arabic-English Lexicon*. London: 1863–77.

{Lieu, Samuel N. C. *Manichaeism in the Later Roman Empire and Medieval China: A Historical Survey*. Manchester: Manchester University Press, 1985.}

Lioni Africano, Giovan. *Descrittione dell'Africa*. In Ramusio, *Navigatione e viaggi*. Venice, 1550.

Ma^{c}arrī, Abū'l-^{c}Alā. *The Letters of Abū 'l-'Alā*. Arabic ed. and Eng. trans., D. S. Margoliouth. Anecdota Oxoniensa. Oxford: Clarendon, 1898.

———. *Risālat al-ghufrān*. Cairo, 1907.

Makkī, Abū Ṭālib. *Qūt al-qulūb*. Cairo, 1310/1892.

Malaṭī, Abū'l-Ḥusayn. *Al-Tanbīh wa'l-radd ^{c}alä ahl al-ahwā wa'l-bida^{c}*. Reed. of Khashīsh Nasā^{ͻ}ī's *Istiqāma*. [Ed. Sven Dedering, with add. title, *Die Wiederlegung der Irrgläubigen und Neuerer*, Biblioteca Islamica, 9. Leipzig and Istanbul, 1936.]

Maqdisī, Ibn Ṭāhir (Ibn al-Qaysarānī). *Kitāb al-bad^{ͻ} wa'l-ta^{ͻ}rīkh* (*Le livre de la création et de l'histoire*). Ed., trans. Clément Huart. Paris, 1899–1919.

———. *Homonyma inter nomina relative, auctore Abu'l-Fadhl Mohammed ibn Tahir al-Makdisi vulgo dicto Ibno'l-Kaisarani*. Ed. P. de Jong. Leiden: Brill, 1865.

Maqrīzī, Taqī al-Dīn Ahmad b. ^{c}Alī. *Kitāb itti^{c}āẓ al-ḥunafā bi akhbār al-a^{ͻ}imma al-fāṭimiyyīn al-khulafā*.

{Maréchal, Joseph. "Le problème de la grâce mystique en Islam." In *Rech. Sc. Rel.* (1923): 244–92 (P Eng *1755*). Reed. and trans. in *Studies in the Psychology of the Mystics*, London, 1927. Early summary and appreciation of the *Essay* and *Passion*, on ramifications for Catholic theology.}

Margoliouth, D. S. *The Early Development of Mohammedanism*. Hibbert Lectures. London: Williams and Norgate, 1914.

———, ed. *Letters*. S.n. Ma^{c}arrī.

{Maritain, Jacques. See P *1784*.}

{Massignon, Daniel, ed. *Présence de Louis Massignon*. Paris: Maisonneuve, 1987. Tributes, several in English.}

Mas^{c}ūdī (Maçoudi), ^{c}Alī b. Al-Ḥusayn. *Murūj al-dhahab* (*Les prairies d'or*). Collection d'ouvrages orientaux publiée par la société asiatique, ed. Barbier de Meynard and Pavet de Courteille. 9 vols. Paris: 1861–77. Arabic text and French trans., [Rev. Charles Pellat, Paris (French 1962–, Arabic 1966–)].

———. *al-Tanbīh wa'l-ishrāf* (*Kitāb at-Tanbīh wa'l-ischrāf auctore al-Masūdī*).

Ed. de Goeje. Bibliotheca geographicorum arabicorum, 8. Leiden: Brill, 1894. P *134c*.

Ma^{c}ṣūm ^{c}Alī Shāh Ni^{c}matallāhī Shīrāzī. *Ṭarā$^{\supset}$iq al-ḥaqā$^{\supset}$iq*. Tehran, 1316–19/1898–1901.

Mélanges dédiés à la mémoire de Félix Grat. Paris: Mme. Pecqueur-Grat, 1946.

Mélanges Fuad Köprülü. Istanbul, 1953.

Mélanges Joseph Maréchal. Paris: Desclée de Brouwer, 1950.

{*Mélanges Louis Massignon*. Damascus: Institut Français de Damas, 1956.}

Mehren, August F., ed. *Traités mystiques d'Avicenne*. Leiden: 1889–99. Arabic text and French explanations. Four fascicules. [Reprint in 1 vol. Amsterdam: APA-Philo Press, 1979.]

{Mohaghegh, M., and H. Landolt, ed. *Collected Papers on Islamic Philosophy and Mysticism, Majmū^{c}eh-ye sokhanrānī-hā va maqāleh-hā darbāreh-ye falsafeh va ^{c}erfān-e eslāmī*. Wisdom of Persia, 4. Tehran, 1971.}

{Molé, Marijan. "Les Kubrawiya entre sunnisme et shiisme aux huitième et neuvième siècles de l'Hégire." *Revue des Etudes Islamiques* 29 (1961): cah. 1, 63–142.}

Moubarac, Youakim. *L'Islam et le dialogue islamo-chrétien*. Pentalogie, 3. Beirut: Editions du Cénacle Libanais, 1972.

———. *L'Oeuvre de Louis Massignon*. Pentalogie Islamo-Chretiénne, 1. Beirut: Editions du Cénacle Libanais, 1972. Chronological bibliography.}

Mubarrad, Muḥammad ibn Yazīd. *Al-Kitāb al-Kāmil*. Ed. William Wright, with add. title *The Kāmil of el-Mubarrad*. Leipzig: Kreising, 1864–82.

Muḥāsibī, al-Ḥārith b. Asad. See list herein, ch. 5, sec. 1. A., and P *2166*.

[———. *Kitāb al-Ri'āya liḥuqūq Allāh*. Ed. Margaret Smith. E. J. W. Gibb Memorial, new series, 15, London: Luzac, 1940.]

[———. *Kitāb al-tawahhum*. Ed. A. J. Arberry. Cairo, 1937.]

[———. *Al-Masā$^{\supset}$il fī a^{c}māl al-qulūb wa'l-jawāriḥ*. Cairo: ^{c}Alam al-kutub, 1969 (also includes the *Makāsib* and a *Kitāb al-^{c}aql* containing no. 6 from the list in the text). Error, *"Ma'iyya,"* in P (Eng) *2166c*.]

[———. *Risālat al-Mustarshidīn*. Aleppo, 1384/1964.]

[———. *Al-Waṣāyā aw al-Naṣā$^{\supset}$iḥ al-dīniyya wa'l-nafaḥāt al-qudsiyya li naf^{c} jāmi^{c} al-bariya*. Ed. ^{c}Aṭā. Cairo, 1384/1964.]

Muir, Sir William. *The Life of Mahomet*. London: Smith and Elder, 1858.

Muqaddasī, Abū ^{c}AA M. b. A. *Asān al-taqāsīm fī ma^{c}rifat al-aqālīm* (*Descriptio Imperii Moslemici*). Ed. M. J. de Goeje. Leiden, 1877. See P (Eng) *2167*.

Murtaḍä. See Ibn al-Murtaḍä.

Muttaqī, ^{c}Alā$^{\supset}$ al-Dīn ^{c}Alī b. Ḥusām al-Dīn. *Kanz al-^{c}ummāl fī sunan al-aqwāl wa'l-af^{c}āl*. On the margins of Ibn Ḥanbal's *Musnad*, v.s. See P *2168*.

Nabhānī, Yūsuf b. Ismā^{c}īl. *Al-Majmū^{c}at al-Nabhāniyya fī'l-madā$^{\supset}$iḥ al-Nabawiyya*. Beirut, 1320/1903.

———. *Jāmi^c karāmāt al-awliyā*. 2 vols. Cairo, 1329. Reprint Beirut: Dar Sader, n.d.

Nasā$^\supset$ī, Khashīsh. *Istiqāma*. See Malaṭī.

Nawbakhtī, Abū Muḥammad al-Ḥasan b. Mūsä. *Kitāb firaq al-shī^{c}a (Die Sekten des Schi'a)*. Ed. Ritter. Istanbul, 1931.

Nicholson, Reynold A. "An Early Arabic Version of the *Mi'rāj* of Abū Yazīd al-Bisṭāmī." *Islamica* 2 (1926): 402–15. Arabic text and English trans.

Niẓāmī-i-^{c}Arūḍī-i-Samarqandī, Aḥmad ibn ^{c}Umar ibn ^{c}Alī. *Chahār Maqāla*. Ed. Mīrzā Muḥammad. E. J. W. Gibb Memorial, old series, II, no. 1. Leiden and London, 1327/1910. Trans. E. G. Browne in II, no. 2, 1921.

Niyāzī Miṣrī, Muḥammad. *Dīwān*. Istanbul, n.d. Lithograph. P *1353*.

Nöldeke, Theodor. "Die aramaïsche Literatur." In *Die orientalischer Literatur*, 103–23. Berlin, 1906.

———. *Geschichte des Qurāns*. Göttingen: 1860. P (Eng) *2172*. [Augmented ed., F. Schwally et al., 3 vols. Leipzig 1909, 1919, 1936].

{Nūrī, Abū'l-Hasan. *Maqāmāt al-qulūb*. S.n. Nwyia, "Textes".}

{Nwyia, Paul. *Exégèse coranique et langage mystique: Nouvel essai sur le lexique technique des mystiques musulmans*. Pensée arabe et musulmane, 49. Beirut: Dar el-Machreq, 1971. Nwyia, correcting LM (pp. 14–15 and *passim*), shows that newly discovered texts and further analysis of Tirmidhī, Nūrī, and Kharrāz demonstrate a doctrine as bold as Ḥallāj's, before his time. The *Essay's* thesis that Ḥallāj grew out of the early mystical movement is thereby strengthened.}

[———. "Hallāǧ: Kitāb al-Tawāsīn." *Mélanges de l'Université Saint-Joseph* 47 (1972): 183–238. Full Arabic text except for the *Bustān al-ma^{c}rifa*; partial French trans., where different readings change the sense.]

[———. "Le Tafsīr mystique attribué à Ǧa'far Sādiq, édition critique." *Mélanges de l'Université Saint-Joseph* 43 (1968): 181–230.]

———. "Textes mystiques inédits d'Abū-l-Ḥasan al-Nūrī." *Mélanges de l'Université Saint-Joseph* 44 (1968): 115–54.}

{———, ed. *Trois oeuvres inédits de mystiques musulmans: Šaqīq al-Balḫī, Ibn ^{c}Aṭā, Niffarī*. Beirut: Dar el-Machreq, 1973.}

Pantañjali. *Yoga-Sutra*. Trans. M. N. Dvivedi. Bombay: Tattva Vivechaka Press, 1899. [See Bīrūnī's trans. s.n., Ritter.]

Patrologiae Cursus Completus. Series Latina. 221 vols. Ed. J.-P. Migne. Paris, 1841–64.

Qushāshī, A. Dajjānī, *Simṭ Majīd*. Hyderabad, 1327.

Qāsimī, Jamāl al-Dīn. *Majmū^c rasā$^\supset$il fī uṣūl al-fiqh (= majmū^c mutūn uṣūliyya)*. Damascus, 1912. See P (Eng) *2188*.

Qushayrī, ^{c}Abd al-Karīm ibn Hawāzin. *Al-Risāla*. See P *213a*. Citations with vol. and p. nos. refer to Anṣārī's ed., Cairo, 1290/1892 (4 vols.); with p. nos. alone, to the Cairo ed. of 1318/1900 (1 vol.).

Rāghib Pāshā, Muḥammad Beg. *Safīnat al-Rāghib*. Cairo, 1282.

Rāzī, Fakhr al-dīn. *Tafsīr Kabīr (Mafātīḥ al-ghayb)*. P *385c*.

Rāzī, Najm al-Dīn Dāya. *Mirṣād al-ʿibād*. P *1107a*.

Renan, Ernest. "Fragments du livre gnostique intitulé Apocalypse d'Adam, ou Pénitence d'Adam ou Testament d'adam, publiés d'après deux versions syriaques." *Journal Asiatique*, 5th series, 2 (1853): 427–71.

Rinn, Louis. *Marabouts et Khouan, étude sur l'Islam en Algérie*, Algiers, 1884.

[Ritter, Hellmut. "Al-Bīrūnī's Übersetzung des Yoga-Sūtra des Patañjali." *Oriens* 9 (1956): 165–200. Arabic text.]

———. "Studien zur Geschichte der islamischen Frömmigkeit: I. Ḥasan al-Baṣrī." *Der Islam* 21 (1933): 1–83. Contains Arabic text of ḤB's letter to ʿAbd al-Malik b. Marwān.}

Sabziwārī, Mullā Hādī. *Jawshan kabīr*. Tehran, 1267.

Sacy. See Silvestre de Sacy.

Samʿānī, Abū Saʿd ʿAbd al-Karīm b. Muḥammad. *Kitābu'l-Ansāb of as-Samʿānī*. E. J. W. Gibb Memorial, old series, 20. Leiden and London, 1913. Facsimile of Hyderabad ed. See P *350a*.

Sarrāj, Abū Naṣr (b. A. b. al-Ḥusayn). *Kitāb al-lumaʿ fī'l-taṣawwuf*. E. J. W. Gibb Memorial, old series, 22. Leiden, 1914. [Supplement, s.n. Arberry.]

———. *Maṣāriʿ al-ʿushshāq*. Constantinople: Maṭbaʿat al-Jawāʾib, 1301 / 1884.

Schacht, Joseph. *Der Islam, mit Ausschluss des Qur'āns*. Tübingen: J.C.B. Mohr, 1931.

{Schaeder, Hans Heinrich. "Al-Ḥasan al-Baṣrī: Studien zur Frühgeschichte des Islam." *Der Islam* 14 (1925): 1–75.}

{Schimmel, Annemarie. *Mystical Dimensions of Islam*. Chapel Hill: University of North Carolina Press, 1975.}

Shahrastānī, Abū'l-Fatḥ M. b. ʿA. Karīm. *Al-Milal wa'l-niḥal*. In margins of Ibn Ḥazm's *Fiṣal*, v.s.

{Shaibī, Kāmil Muṣṭafä. "*Dhayl Dīwān al-Ḥallāj*." *Zānkā* 3:2 (1997): 1–31.}

{———. *Al-Ḥallāj Mawḍūʿan*. Baghdād: Maṭbaʿat al- maʿārif, 1976.}

{———. *Sharḥ Dīwān al-Ḥallāj*. Baghdād/Beirut, 1394 / 1973.}

Shammākhī, Abū Zakariyā. *Chronique*. Trans. Masqueray. Algiers, 1878.

Shaʿrānī, ʿAbd al-Wahhāb b. Aḥmad. *Al-Kibrīt al-aḥmar*. Cairo, 1306.

———. *Laṭāʾif al-minan*. Cairo: Maṭbaʿa Maymaniyya, 1321 / 1903.

———. *Kitāb Lawāqiḥ al-anwār al-qudsiyya fī bayān al-ʿuhūd al-Muḥammadiyya*. Cairo: Maṭbaʿa Maymaniyya, 1308 / 1891.

———. *al-Mīzān al-Khiḍriyya*. Cairo: Maṭbaʿa Maymaniyya, 1276 / 1858.

———. *Al-Ṭabaqāt al-kubrä*. Cairo, 1305.

———. *Kitāb al-yawāqīt al-jawāhir fī bayān ʿaqāʾid al-akābir*. Printed in the margins of his *Mīzān Khiḍriyya*, v.s.

Shaʿrāwī. See Shaʿrānī.

Shaṭṭanawfī, Nūr al-Dīn Abū'l-Ḥasan ʿAlī. *Bahjat al-asrār wa maʿdan al-anwār.*
Cairo, 1330. Error in P, 2nd ed., *502a.*

Shiblī, Badr al-dīn Muḥammad ibn ʿAA. *Ākām al-marjān fī aḥkām al-jānn.*
Cairo: Maṭbaʿat al-saʿāda, 1326/1908.

Sībawayh, ʿAmr b. ʿUthmān. *Le Livre de Sibawaihi.* Ed. Hartwig Derenbourg.
Paris, 1881. Reprint Hildesheim: G. Olms, 1970.

Sijistānī, Abū Ḥātim. *Kitāb al-muʿammarīn.* Ed., with intro., I. Goldziher as
Das kitāb al-Muʿammarīn des Abū Ḥātim al-Siǧistānī. Leiden: Brill, 1899.

Silvestre de Sacy, Baron Antoine Isaac. *Exposé de la religion des Druzes.*
Paris, 1838.

————. *Notices et extraits des manuscrits de la Bibliothèque Nationale et autres
bibliothèques.* Paris, 1787–1819.

{Smith, Margaret. *Rabi'a the Mystic and Her Fellow-Saints of Islam.* Cambridge: Cambridge University Press, 1928. Reissue, intro. by A. Schimmel, 1984.}

Snouck Hurgronje, Christian. *Mekka.* The Hague: M. Nijhoff, 1888–89.

————. "Politique musulmane de la Hollande." *Revue du Monde Musulman* 14, no. 6 (June 1911): 381–509, esp. 446–49.

Sprenger, Aloys. *Mohammed und der Koran.* Hamburg: J. F. Richter, 1889.

————, ed. *'Abd-r-Razzāq's Dictionary of the Technical Terms of the Sufies.*
Calcutta: Asiatic Society, 1845. Arabic text. Cf. Kāshānī.

————, ed. *Dictionary of Technical Terms.* S.n. Tahānawī.

Steiner, Heinrich. *Die Muʿtaziliten.* Leipzig: Breitkopf and Härtel, 1865.

Steinschneider, Moritz. *Polemische und apologetische Literatur in arabischer
Sprache zwischen Muslimen, Christen une Juden.* Leipzig: F. A. Brockhaus,
1877.

Subkī, Tāj al-Dīn Abū Naṣr ʿAbd al-Wahhāb b. Taqī al-Dīn. *Ṭabaqāt al-
shāfiʿiyya al-kubrä.* 6 vols. Cairo: Maṭbaʿa Ḥusayniyya, 1324/1906.

Suhrawardī, Abū Ḥafṣ Shihāb al-Dīn ʿUmar. *ʿAwārif al-Maʿārif.* Cairo: In
margins of *Iḥyā,* s. n., Ghazālī. Cf. P *401a.*

Sulamī, Abū ʿAbd al-Raḥmān. *Ḥaqāʾiq al-Tafsīr.* P *170d.* There is also a ms.
in the British Library (Oriental 9433).

————. *Jawāmiʿ ādāb al-ṣūfiyya.* P *170c.* [Ed. Etan Kohlberg. Jerusalem: Jerusalem Academic Press, 1976.]

[————. *Kitāb ṭabaqāt al-Ṣūfiyya.* Ed. Johannes Pedersen. Leiden: E. J. Brill,
1960. Numbering system corresponds to references here.]

[————. *Uṣūl al-malāmatiyya wa ghalaṭāt al-ṣūfiyya.* Cairo, 1405/1985.]

Suyūṭī, ʿAbd al-Raḥmān. *Kitāb al-Laʾālī al-maṣnūʿa fī'l-aḥādīth al-mawḍūʿa.* 2
vols. Cairo: 1317/1899.

Ṭabarī, Abū Jaʿfar Muḥammad b. Jarīr. *Ta'rīkh al-rusul wa'l-mulūk, Annales.*
Ed. de Goeje et al. Leiden, 1879–1901.

Ṭabarsī, Abū ʿAlī Faḍl b. Ḥasan. *Kitāb al-iḥtijāj.* Lithograph Tehran, 1302.

Ṭabāṭabā'ī, Muḥammad Kāẓim. ᶜ*Urwa wuthqä*. Baghdad, 1328/1910.

Tahānawī (Tahānuwī), Muḥammad ᶜAlī b. ᶜAlī, A. Ed. Sprenger, *Kashshāf iṣṭilāḥāt al-funūn, Dictionary of Technical Terms*. Calcutta, 1854–62. [Later eds.: Istanbul, 1317; Cairo, 1382/1963].

[Thawrī, Abū ᶜAA Sufyān b. Saᶜīd b. Masrūq. *Tafsīr al-Qur'ān al-ᶜaẓīm* ("Ṣawrī *Tafsīru'l-Qur'ān*"). Ed. ᶜArshī. Rampūr: 1385/1965.]

Tholuck, F. A. G. *Ssufismus, sive Theologia Persarum Pantheistica*. Berlin: F. Duemmler, 1821.

Tirmidhī, al-Ḥakīm. *Khatm al-awliyā*. S.n. Yahia.

{Trimingham, J. Spencer. *The Sufi Orders in Islam*. Oxford: Clarendon, 1971.}

Tustarī, Sahl. *Tafsīr al-Qur'ān al-ᶜaẓīm*. Ed. Naᶜsānī. Cairo, 1326/1908. Misprints in P *2237*.

Ṭūsī, Abū Jaᶜfar Muḥammad b. Ḥasan. [*Fihrist kutub* (*Kitāb*) *al-Shīᶜa*] (*Tūsy's List of Shy'ah Books*). [Ed. Sprenger and ᶜAbd al-Ḥaqq.] Trans. Sprenger. Calcutta, [1853–] 55. See P *242c*.

[ᶜUkbarī, ᶜUbaydallāh ibn Baṭṭa. *Sharḥ wa ibāna ᶜalä uṣūl al-sunna wa'l-diyāna*. Ed. and French trans. Henri Laoust. Add. title: *La Profession de foi d'Ibn Baṭṭa ᶜUkbarī*. Damascus: Institut Français de Damas, 1958.]

ᶜUlaymī, Mujīr al-Dīn. *Uns Jalīl*. Cairo, 1283.

{Underhill, Evelyn. *Mysticism*. London: Methuen, 1977. (First pub. 1911.)}

Van Arendonk, Cornelis. *De opkomst van het Zaidietische Imamaat in Yemen*. DeGoeje Series, 5. Leiden: Brill, 1919.

Van Vloten, Gerolf. "Les Hachwia et Nabita." In *XIe Congrès International des Orientalistes*. Paris, 1897. Off-print 1901.

Vaux. *See* Carra de Vaux.

{Waardenburg, Jean-Jacques. *L'Islam dans le miroir de l'occident*. The Hague: Mouton, 1962.}

Wahitaki, Hussein. "Verbesserungen und Bemerkungen zu Massignon's 'Recueil de textes inédits concernant l'histoire de la mystique en pays d'Islam'." *Islamica* 5 (1932): 475–92.

Wahrānī, A. *Firdaws al-murshidiyya*. P *2243*.

{Watt, W. Montgomery, ed. *Bell's Introduction to the Quran*. Rev. Islamic Surveys, 8. Edinburgh: Edinburgh University Press, 1970.}

Wensinck. *The Book of the Dove*. S.n. Bar Hebraeus.

{Wright, W. *A Grammar of the Arabic Language*. 3rd ed. Cambridge: 1896–98.}

Wüstenfeld, H. F. *Register zu den arabischen Stämmen und Familien*. Göttingen, 1853.

Yāfiᶜī, Abū M ᶜAA ibn Asᶜad. *Marham al-ᶜilal al-muᶜḍila* [*fī dafᶜ al-shabh wa'l-radd ᶜalä'l-muᶜtazila*] (*Marhamu 'l-'Ilali 'l-Mu'ḍila*). Ed. E. Denison Ross. Bibliotheca Indica. Calcutta: Asiatic Society, 1910–.

———. *Nashr al-maḥāsin al-ghāliya.* 1329. Printed in the margin of Nabhānī's *Jāmi*ᶜ, v.s.

———. *Rawḍ al-Riyāḥīn.* Cairo: Būlāq, 1297. [Cairo: 1374/1955].

[Yahia, Osman, ed. *Kitāb ḫatm al-awliyā' d'al-Tirmiḏī.* Pensée arabe et musulmane, 19, Beirut: Dar el-Machreq, 1965.]

al-Yaman, Jaᶜfar b. Manṣūr. *Kitābu'l Kashf of Ja'far b. Mansūr'l Yaman.* Ed. R. Strothman. Islamic Research Assocation Series, 13. London: Oxford University Press, 1952. Arabic text.

———. *Taʾwīl al-zakāt.* Ms. Leiden.

Yāqūt. *The irshad al-arīb ilä ma'rifat al-adīb, or Dictionary of learned men of Yāqūt (Muᶜjam al-udabā).* Ed. D. S. Margoliouth. E. J. W. Gibb Memorial Series, London: Luzac, 1907–. See P *410.*

———. *Marāṣid al-iṭṭilāᶜ ᶜalä asmā al-amkina wa'l-biqāᶜ, Lexicon Geographicum.* Ed. T. G. J. Juynboll. 6 vols. Leiden: Brill, 1852–64.

———. *Mu'jam al-buldân: Jacuts geographisches Wörterbuch.* Ed. F. Wüstenfeld. Leipzig: Deutsche Morgenländische Gesellschaft, 1866–73. Arabic text. Reprints Leipzig, 1924; Tehran, 1965. Error in P *410b.*

{Young, M.J. L., J.D.Latham, and R.B.Serjeant, ed. *The Cambridge History of Arabic Literature: Religion, Learning, and Science in the ᶜAbbasid Period.* Cambridge: Cambridge University Press, 1990.}

Zamakhsharī, *Fāʾiq fī gharīb al-ḥadīth.* Hyderabad, 1324.

Zwemer, Samuel. "The So-called Hadith Qudsi." *Moslem World* 12 (1922): 263–75.

INDEX

This is essentially a combination of Massignon's separate indexes of names and technical terms. The definite article is suppressed in some of the names. The technical terms are italicized, here and in the text; when, that is, they appear in the text at all: sometimes the presence of a French equivalent was enough for Massignon to put the Arabic word in the index. Chapter one, insofar as words may be sought there by their triliteral Arabic roots, is not indexed here.